O9-ABG-920

JUN 3 2008

WAYNE PUBLIC LIBRARY

INTRODUCING

BERT WILLIAMS

INTRODUCING

BERT WILLIAMS

BURNT CORK,
BROADWAY,
AND THE STORY OF
AMERICA'S FIRST
BLACK STAR

CAMILLE F. FORBES

BASIC
CIVITAS
BOOKS

A Member of the Perseus Books Group
New York

Copyright © 2008 by Camille F. Forbes

Published by Basic Civitas,
A Member of the Perseus Books Group

All rights reserved. Printed in the United States of America. No part of this book may be reproduced in any manner whatsoever without written permission except in the case of brief quotations embodied in critical articles and reviews. For information, address Basic Civitas, 387 Park Avenue South, New York, NY 10016-8810.

Books published by Basic Civitas are available at special discounts for bulk purchases in the United States by corporations, institutions, and other organizations. For more information, please contact the Special Markets Department at the Perseus Books Group, 11 Cambridge Center, Cambridge, MA 02142, or call (617) 252–5298 or (800) 255–1514, or e-mail special.markets@perseusbooks.com.

Designed by Pauline Brown.
Set in 10 point Century Old Style by the Perseus Books Group.

Library of Congress Cataloging-in-Publication Data

Forbes, Camille F.
   Introducing Bert Williams : burnt cork, Broadway, and the story of America's first Black star / Camille F. Forbes.
       p. cm.
   Includes bibliographical references and index.
   ISBN-13: 978-0-465-02479-7 (alk. paper)
   ISBN-10: 0-465-02479-3 (alk. paper)
 1. Williams, Bert, 1874–1922. 2. Entertainers—United States—Biography. 3. African American entertainers—Biography. I. Title.

   PN2287.W46F67 2008
   792.702'8092—dc22
   [B]

                                                        2007031620

10 9 8 7 6 5 4 3 2 1

In memory of
Jackie Forbes and Liz Maguire,
two wonderfully dynamic women

In truth, I have never been able to discover that there was anything disgraceful in being a colored man. But I have often found it inconvenient—in America.

—BERT A. WILLIAMS (1874–1922)

And behind that mask, he could say anything he wanted to.

—BEN VEREEN ON BERT WILLIAMS

Contents

A Note on Usage

In this work, I use the terms "black" and "African American" interchangeably. I refrain from naming Williams as "African American," however, because he always spoke of his ethnicity as West Indian. Instead I refer to him as black, or Negro, a term that he used to refer to himself. While the term "African American" is used to speak of black Americans, "Negro" was often utilized during the period to describe black people of various nationalities. With regard to the capitalization of the letter "n" in "Negro," although it is always written in commentary and analysis with an uppercase letter, the original is retained in quotations. I do this with a desire to acknowledge the effort that the NAACP and others undertook to convince Americans of the need to capitalize the "n," out of respect.

Preface

B lack Bahamian comedian Bert A. Williams (1874–1922) captivated American audiences for more than a quarter century in a career that spanned from ca. 1890 to the end of his life. His dynamic stage presence and skill as a storyteller, pantomime, and songster astounded black and white audiences alike, who pronounced him "The Greatest Comedian on the American Stage." During his career, Williams moved from the formulaic structure of late nineteenth-century minstrelsy to the independence of solo vaudeville performance and beyond. He became one of the most important black performers in American history. A trailblazer whose extraordinary achievements created opportunities for later generations of black entertainers, he also raised the bar for comic performance among both blacks and whites.

Striving to shed considerable light on the cipher that is Egbert Austin Williams, I explore the complexity of Williams's experience, illuminating the milieus in which he appeared throughout an illustrious career. The worlds of the medicine show, minstrelsy, Tin Pan Alley, the recording industry, black musical theater, vaudeville, motion pictures, and legitimate theater all contributed to Williams's work. He experimented, headlined, and matured as a performer as he worked in these various entertainment forms, which constituted much of the universe of nineteenth- and early-twentieth-century American popular entertainment. Williams's diversity in his abilities, which allowed him to travel through all these spaces, testifies to his unique strength as a performer. These entertainment forms deserve as much attention as the remarkable comedian who graced them with his effervescent theatrical presence. They receive as much attention here as do the challenges Williams faced during a career that began just as the embryonic institution of Jim Crow segregation concretized the divide between blacks and whites.

As I delve into vast entertainment worlds, I aim to reveal Williams. It is at times excruciatingly difficult to trace a life, however, particularly that of one who cherished his privacy as deeply as Williams did. Materials found primarily address his performances. Although a renowned entertainer, Williams remained reticent about his private life, protecting his interior world from the public eye. Seeking to unearth the details of his life in the face of archival challenges, I access Williams through various means: joke books, songs, interviews, letters, reviews, films, and tributes. I search for Williams both within and behind the mask of blackface, digging deeply despite archives that provide access mostly to his public face only. I remain loyal to those facts of Williams's life that rise to the surface, knowing that even all these efforts do not result in uncovering the "whole truth" of Williams.

Through that excavation, I find a compelling cryptic figure who demands our attention. Moving from black musical theater, in which he worked with his African American partner George William Walker, to Ziegfeld's *Follies*, in which he often performed solo, Williams shifted from one location to another. He went from working with blacks to working with whites; from performing for both whites and blacks, to performing for whites often exclusively. After sixteen years of working with George, a bold partner who spoke on the duo's behalf, Bert stepped out on his own. Creating his own terms of engagement, often at his peril, he broke new ground.

Previous eras have witnessed the manipulation of this man, the willful forgetting of this problematic figure in burnt cork. His representations of blackness onstage troubled those in the audience who desired radical resistance. His persistent use of blackface alienated those members of the public who demanded the rejection of convention. Yet during his life, Williams did endeavor to take control of his career and his image. He struggled to be seen as more than a comedian or a stereotype. He recognized his representative role among blacks, yet refused leadership. Honing his craft while maintaining his dignity, he reached out to his audience, but only so far. The rest of himself he withheld, remaining a mystery that baffled and titillated his audiences. How did a black Bahamian boy become "The Greatest Comedian on the American Stage"? He stood up and "barked," on the streets of California.

1
The Early Years

1

Growing Up

*L*adies and gentlemen! Do you have an ache of the body? A pain of the heart? No matter: step right up! Here's where you'll find the cures to all of your suffering, now and forever!"

In the clearing, the deep voice of a lanky, fair-skinned Negro boy boomed over the crowd hovering outside the circus tent. He thrilled to the sound of his own voice as well as the steady gaze of the enraptured throng, who stood gathered around him. This was power—as close to it as he had ever come. Merely sixteen years old, Egbert Austin Williams had quit high school to follow his dream of becoming an entertainer.[1] He had been snatched up by the world of the medicine show.

A carnivalesque atmosphere of overwhelming displays, magnificent claims, and stentorian voices, the medicine show was more show than medicine. Under makeshift tents filled with booths, famous and infamous self-proclaimed doctors hocked elixirs and promised magic and miracles to their ecstatic audiences. Engaging the audiences with dramatic testimonials and tales of new worlds plumbed to discover exotic ingredients, the "doctors" took their public on flights of fantasy that amused, shocked, and thrilled. Crowds of awed frontiersfolk swarmed, vying for the merest glimpse, the slightest touch, the most meager taste. And charlatans eagerly catered to the public's craving, producing purported customers to illustrate their products' effectiveness, and exhibiting circus-like "freaks" as the wretched unfortunates who went without treatment.

At the portal to this overwhelmingly white, nineteenth-century world stood Bert, the barker. An unlikely guide for the mostly white audience, not only because he was a Negro—though light-skinned enough to appear white—but also because he was Bahamian. Bert and his family had left their native home of Nassau in 1884 when he was ten, fleeing the depression that plagued the Bahamian economy during the last quarter of the nineteenth century.[2] They eventually settled in Riverside, California, whose economy boasted not only an impressive citrus industry—and the seedless orange—but also the railroads, which serviced Southern California from San Diego to San Bernardino, later extending to transcontinental lines.[3] Bert's father, having gained knowledge of citrus farming from his father, Frederick Williams, Sr., could seek work in the industry, or as a porter on the railroad.[4] Committed to life in a new country, the family pursued its fortunes in America, never to return to Nassau.

Although excitingly new to Bert and disturbingly unfamiliar to his immigrant parents, the medicine show had had a long history of capturing the imagination of audiences the world over. It could be traced back to Europe, to the mountebank, prevalent during the Renaissance and before.[5] Mountebanks had been performers, often quacks, who traveled the European countryside selling their cures. Desperate to attract the attention of a crowd, they used numerous gimmicks and tricks designed to entertain, as well as to help them market their wares. Without such amusements, they could hardly hope to have buyers.[6] Despite that distant history, right there, in the hinterland of rural Riverside, Bert had gained exposure to the fascinating world. Its tales and wonders had descended upon the town, eclipsing all else.

The medicine show tradition continued in America with a trajectory and evolution of its own. In the early nineteenth century, pitchmen traveled, selling their drugs on fairgrounds or busy street corners. By the middle of the century, the work had become so strictly legislated and controlled that the majority of these "street workers" no longer worked the streets at all.[7] Regardless of where they worked, however, pitchmen, who sold their wares singly or with the aid of a partner, kept themselves moving lest they risk being exposed. The performers often had to stay a step ahead of local authorities. To avoid being run out by enraged crowds who realized they had been duped, the performers moved through towns quickly.

In time, a pecking order developed in the medicine show world. The seeming unfortunates who worked doorways or sidewalks with a suitcase mounted on a tripod, a contraption known as a "tripes and keister," became the low pitch operators who were held, accordingly, in lowest regard.[8] Those who performed on a platform, "the high pitchmen," stood literally above them.[9] Medicine show owners reigned at the top of the heap, higher even than the so-called high pitchmen. They traveled as a company, combining their pitches with other entertainments. Regardless of status, though, medicine men and pitchmen all faced the same challenge: to draw a crowd, also known as a "tip," to their pitches. First, they drummed up attention, then sales of goods.[10]

Similar to theatrical producers, medicine showmen packaged shows, managed sales pitches and even sales themselves, and traveled with a considerable amount of equipment.[11] Medicine show companies of significant size took their performances to larger towns, carrying their gear and mounting their shows in fairgrounds or vacant lots within the area. Smaller troupes relied on villagers' willingness to travel far and wide in order to see a medicine show, counting on their eagerness to receive a possible cure for long-suffered infirmities.[12] In time, as performers followed the harvests, the Midwest and South became regions of choice for touring. Medicine showmen took advantage of access to Midwestern audiences during the summer wheat harvest, and then headed to the Deep South to entertain during the fall cotton harvest.[13]

Like the mountebanks of days gone by, medicine show performers and pitchmen faced some resistance. But, whereas the public generally regarded street workers or pitchmen with disdain, they viewed medicine men and their cures with less suspicion if not with respect.[14] In the Americas, resistance stemmed in part from the belief that the medicine show, with its idle self-indulgence, endangered "republican virtue." As a result, states passed acts aimed to control the influence and even presence of these entertainments. In Connecticut, a 1773 act forbade "any games, tricks, plays, juggling or feats of uncommon dexterity and agility of body," indicating the threat represented by amusements that drew "great numbers of people, to the corruption of manners, promoting of idleness, and the detriment of good order and religion."[15] Despite such legislation, the undeniable appeal of medicine shows could not be ignored. They were the leading—and often the only—source of entertainment available to people living in remote or rural areas.

Enthusiastic audiences generally gave medicine show performers a chance to present their shows and sell their wares. Nonetheless, all performers—whether working alone, in troupes, or sponsored by large medicine patent companies—had to compete for their attention.[16] Even patent companies had no further legitimacy than the small troupes. The bigger firms, although able to advertise widely and mass produce their elixirs, had no connection to the U.S. Patent Office. The term "patent" itself had merely been a holdover from the British monarchy, referring to proprietary medicines provided for the royal family, later given as a "patent of royal favor."[17] In the competitive atmosphere, entertainers needed a high degree of adaptability with a wide range of skills. They had to work hard to appeal to the various audiences they would encounter on the road.

Competition and escalating amusement offerings like the medicine show made up "[t]he show business." Although the expression was of relatively recent use, dating back to around 1850, the industry itself had a long history. Over the years, permutations of and variations on the term would attest to the increasing visibility of all things pertaining to entertainment.[18] By the time young Bert Williams became a part of the medicine show's wonders, he would declare "the show business" to be his ultimate goal.

It might seem impossibly incongruous: the generally subdued black boy being drawn to a largely white world of quackery, cures, and dramatic claims. Yet, in another light, it made sense. The touring medicine show companies provided great entertainment in the 1890s, especially in places like Bert's home of Riverside. Rural audiences—both black and white—in particular had their only exposure to popular entertainment through the traveling shows, which introduced them to miraculous worlds limited only by their imaginations. In addition, with the competitive scene of the medicine show world, the antics of a lively young Negro could be the difference between a large audience and no audience. A Negro placed in the midst of this frenetic scene of entertainers-turned-pseudodoctors was a curiosity. And curiosities certainly drew a tip.

Bert found a place in that world, albeit low, as a barker. He stood on a platform similar to those used for circus side shows, stationing himself outside the tent, where he strove to draw a tip.[19] He piqued his audience's curiosity by weaving tales about feats yet to be performed inside, the "doctor" whose secret remedies brought new life to weakened bodies. Although no grand position, the barker's job was nonetheless essential. It required poise, creativity, and charisma, for the barker charmed the crowd into seeing what they often did not plan—or care—to see.[20] The barker whetted the audiences' appetites by giving them a show before the show.

Whereas the medicine show intrigued Bert, it did not so easily beguile his father. An imposing, tall, yet elegant mixed-race red-haired man with a handlebar moustache, Frederick Williams held great ambitions for his son.[21] The stern, practical father remained always demanding, and his plans for Bert evidently did not include work in entertainment.

Frederick Williams's first full appreciation of his son's great gifts in performance likely came when he followed Bert to his post, hiding himself behind a tree in order to watch and hear his son's spiel. Watching the boy, Williams père approached to interrupt and demand that his son come home with him. No sooner did he think to do so, however, than he discovered that his son had already found a home of his own. A "mesmerizing" talker, Bert dramatically described the medicine show inside.

Magical transformations—an ailing body treated on the spot with "Warner's Safe Cure," purifying the blood and restoring vitality.[22] Miracle treatments—a weary, sickly body recovered with "Nature's True Remedy," which cured anything from cancer to curvature of the spine.[23] Dancers, singers, comedians, and hypnotists all played a part in the show, taking the audience to a place far removed from the drudgery of their small-town daily lives.

Frederick Williams, enthralled by the tales and his own son's persuasive pitch, stepped into that world, spellbound.[24] He gave Bert his blessing. Years later, he avowed, "I am mighty glad now that that spark was there and developed in spite of us older folk who were so slow to understand and appreciate it."[25] By the end of his life, Frederick Williams would become one of his son's greatest supporters.

The barker served as the last stop before the interested audience entered the medicine show tent. Advertising efforts would have begun long before the crowd stood in front of his station, however. Medicine peddlers and outright quacks depended on the nation's top newspapers to hawk their wares and gain visibility. Small-town papers as well as big-city ones like the *New York Tribune* ran ads pronouncing claims—some legitimate, others perfectly counterfeit; advertisers flooded them with their products. By the 1870s, patent medicine laid claim to a quarter of all advertising.[26] Even the larger firms, like Chicago's famous Hamlin Company, producers of Wizard Oil, seemed to support the philosophy of P. T. Barnum, who declared that only after the seventh advertisement insertion did readers actually make purchases.[27]

The plethora of ads often helped small newspapers stay afloat, an unintended effect of the medicine sellers' well-publicized claims. One such advertiser was Dr. Williams Medicine Company of Schenectady, New York, which told of one formerly paralyzed patient who allegedly regained sensation after six weeks of use and achieved full recovery by the end of four months.[28] The magical cure? Dr. Williams Pink Pills for Pale People, of course.

The advertising for medicine shows such as Bert's didn't stop with newspaper insertions. It took countless forms—from flyers to almanacs—all creating greater notoriety for the newly patented products. Local advertisements, in addition to the barker himself, played a significant role in the world of the medicine show. The key to this advertising was the large color poster, the omnipresent standard for 1890s advertising. Advertisers literally plastered it everywhere in town, from walls to fences to store windows. Multiplying the basic "one-sheet" four, eight, or even as much as twenty-four times, advertisers graced the sides of barns with spectacularly large posters.[29]

*A*dvertisements so hyperbolically heralded the arrival of the medicine show company that by the time the crowds gathered at Bert's post, they already would have been inundated by images of and tales about the products yet to be displayed inside. Nonetheless, they came as much for the show as for the products. In order to compel them to walk into the tent, the aggressive and dynamic barker had to have astounding skills in stimulating the cravings of the crowd.

Bert surely met the challenge. Somehow this inexperienced young man, a West Indian immigrant barely exposed to the entertainment world, learned to engage the imaginations of listeners. Before going to California, Bert's family had moved to Florida from their home in the Bahamas. Most likely, they lived in Key West, to which substantial numbers of Bahamians had immigrated from the 1870s to the early

years of the twentieth century.[30] Living among the black community
there, Bert recalled:

> [A]long the street where we lived there were outdoor booths, where old
> colored mammies sold sweet potato pie. It used to be a favorite haunt of
> mine, for I loved the pie they made, but I never had money to buy any, so
> I would begin at the first booth in the row and go up and gaze at the
> counter of pies.
>
> My mouth would begin to water, and my eyes would get big, and sad
> looking, and I'd try to mesmerize a pie—why, I guess I almost cried with
> internal longing and mental hunger, but after I had begged with my eyes
> long enough the owner of the pieces would say: "Bless you' heaht, honey,
> ain't yo' hed no suppah?"
>
> "No'm," I'd say, still looking starved and pathetic. Then I'd get a big
> piece of good old sweet potato pie.[31]

A compelling entertainer even at a young age, Bert was also simply
a boy, one who wanted to play with much older boys. Whenever
he got a piece of pie, "I'd have to give each of the fellows a bite," he admitted, "or I wouldn't get to play with them."[32] Indeed, if he were to be
allowed to play with them, he had "to pay for the privilege by being the
'goat,' so to speak."[33]

"I repeated the performance at each booth, never getting enough pie
until I had gone the length of the row," he explained.[34] Bert enchanted
the pie sellers so much that they could hardly resist him. Each time
he'd feed himself and a handful of friends, while he also developed his
act through repeat performances.

Such performances continued in school. These explained in part why
Bert never did better than average, despite his niece's later claim that she
saw his seventh-grade report card on which everything was marked
"Excellent."[35] Bert himself averred, "I was always doing something
funny, and my teachers didn't know what to do with me. They couldn't
spank me for being funny, and I wasn't a mischievous boy."[36] He deftly
walked a tightrope between being a cut-up and being a mischief-maker;
with this skill, he could get away with his tangential observations and
musings.

Church confirmed the restlessness of Bert's youth, however. Although his father recalled his good singing in the choir of their Episcopalian church, Bert himself reflected more often on his childish antics, and the power of his imagination. He struggled to resist sleep during sermons, even as he sat between his strict grandmother and grandfather:

> The monotony of the preacher's tone soothed me and to avoid its soporific effect I would glance about until I found something unimportant like some old gentleman's bald spot or a fly buzzing around some old sister's ear, upon which to fasten my attention. If then I could hold my imagination in check, I was all right[,] but most of the time even such simple subjects would suggest whole slapstick comedies to me and I would find myself shaking the pew with uncontrollable mirth, while dotted lines from the eyes of my relatives on both sides were aimed at me.[37]

Always active, the young Bert never seemed to tire of allowing his imagination to take flight. Perhaps this was, in part, an effect of being an only child. Wiling away solitary hours, the awkward youth took solace in both his observations and his mind's eye.

Although not mischievous in the classroom, Bert generally used books as ways of finding material for performance and honing his skills. He recalled, "Once when I was in the sixth grade I got tired having lessons, so I got out my almanac from my desk and buried myself in it. I was always reading every joke I could find, and I remember on this particular day I had read some good ones. The class was reciting in geography, and pretty soon I was called on.

"'Bert, you may recite,' the teacher said.

"Well, I hadn't the least idea what to say, but I got up and told the class a joke I had just read."[38]

Despite his irrepressible humor, Bert never became a hopelessly disruptive class clown. His father—years later—would admit:

> Bert never stood out as a shining light at school. He studied just enough so that he passed and his reports were good, but I am inclined to think that all the joy he ever got out of studying came from his own observations. Indeed he seemed delighted with each new achievement in mimicry as he developed this gift to a degree while only a child. He brought to light and emphasized the idiosyncrasies of every native man, bird, and beast including the barnyard gentry.[39]

Through study and quiet contemplation, Bert developed his talents as an entertainer. Bert's parents, immigrants who believed in the primary importance of education, "punished him for this [academic mediocrity] at first, but soon discovered that punishment was of no use."[40] Even at a young age, Bert persistently honed his extraordinary talents.

A tall, gangly boy, Bert never quite seemed to fit in among his peers. Noticing this, he instinctively fell into a practice of observation, rather than being in the middle of things: "I had that conspicuous feeling of being overgrown, in comparison to my playmates[,] that a Shepherd dog puppy might feel in a neighborhood of 'pekes.'"[41] In later years, he would say that his awkward size contributed to his tendency to step outside of his circle and be an observer rather than a participant. While the other children played, Bert served as a referee. Rather than playing games and leading teams, he instead applauded and supported the participants.

As a natural performer and an observer, throughout his youth Bert increased his skills in mimicry and characterization. Years later, he playfully explained his habit of being a passive observer: "As a young child, I never seemed to have the surplus energy to expend; certainly none to squander and I always got a great deal of fun out of observing the game, whatever it happened to be and the various and varying human reactions upon the individuals who were active in it."[42]

Watching others, Bert tucked away his observations, and over time the practice became unconscious:

> I suppose it was analysis, but in those times, I didn't think anything about it. If I had, I should probably have accused myself of idle curiosity. But in retrospect, I can go back very, very far in my life and as I live over those old childhood scenes now, I realize that I was storing away little character sketches that were always to serve me. . . . Truly, it seemed that I was and am still, constantly storing away dialects and little bits of mimicry, together with mental pictures.[43]

For Williams, these observations all became material; he cut his young teeth on the challenge of speaking in the voices of others, capturing not only their sound but also their actions, deepening the characterizations.

Bert's early studies in comedy were both thorough and informal. They went far beyond the reading of books and the observation of playmates. "*[O]ld mother nature* had me for her own," he once explained. "I would watch birds and bugs and butterflies for hours, until I really became well acquainted with their habits. Then my imagination would start to work and I would weave little stories about their lives as if their hopes and wishes were human ones: and who is there to say that they are so very different?"[44] Bert cherished these notions. At the end of his life, he would take this idea and develop it as part of his final stage play, *Under the Bamboo Tree*.

$\mathcal{I}$t was these storytelling skills that he honed as he stood at his post as a barker. Bert had only a few minutes to lure the crowd, and he needed to utilize all of his gifts to move the audience beyond the platform and toward the tent. Of course, at a medicine show the tent itself was an innovation worth visiting. When it came to traveling with their shows, many medicine show people had benefited from the canvas tent, first used in the 1820s, which afforded performers considerable flexibility. It could be set up and struck relatively easily, while it also provided a large seating area for almost one thousand spectators.[45] Still other medicine show performers used roofless or "airodome" tents, which were even less cumbersome as well as less expensive: ideal for a traveling show.[46]

The entrance fee for these tent shows varied rather widely; many were free, others as little as two cents, and still others as much as fifteen or twenty cents. Performers justified the expense by creating promotional "double shows" that incorporated more performance, less spiel, and, inevitably, fewer sales of products.[47] Many medicine show performers, however, simply focused on getting crowds to enter, so they kept their fees low. Some very confident medicine showmen insisted that they needed nothing more than time with the audience in order to move their product.

Through the entrance of the tent lay the medicine show itself. A well-balanced mix of entertainment, lecture, and sales pitch, the show grabbed audiences with dazzling performances, wore down their resistance to sales with absorbing lectures, and finally, went in for the kill with a sales pitch.[48] Medicine showmen made the entertainment segment of the show as important as the other elements so as to ensure that audiences stayed for the sales pitch to come. And when companies ran low on new material, they resorted to giveaways that nearly guaranteed to hold an audience.[49] The lectures that followed, the sales pitch precursors, closely resembled the pitch itself. The best of them flowed seamlessly into the pitch, so that the unwitting crowd hardly knew what hit them, and willingly opened their purses to buy.

From the medicine show's inception, entertainment incorporated comic bits, magic tricks, and music, but in the 1890s and later, the influence of vaudeville—i.e., variety shows—played a particularly meaningful role in the substance and structure of these shows. Using many entertainment forms as source material, including burlesque, dime museums, and minstrel shows, medicine shows created their own brand of variety.[50] As the entertainment developed, full performances could last as long as two hours, including eight to ten acts, with two or three lectures, in addition to pitches. The acts served as undiluted entertainment.

Often performances began with a solo banjo piece that warmed up the audience.[51] A comedy routine, using a comedian in blackface makeup and a straightman, came next. Medicine show performances frequently featured such comedy acts. Performers regularly improvised sketches based on versions of stories circulating in vaudeville, Wild West shows, and popular drama.[52] Regardless of their source, these acts tended to be scaled down and quick paced, their success depending on a small number of performers. They structured skits with a single joke and punch line that would be easily understood by people of all ages.[53]

The comedy acts sometimes led into another musical performance, or at other times, into a number incorporating magic, mind reading, or some other specialty. Medicine show performers' experience typically varied widely; many entertainers had been exposed to numerous other kinds of popular entertainment. Specialists who performed rare feats were often well skilled, such as Harry Houdini, who presented a fairly intricate magic act, and Frank Lexington, a "professional leaper" whose bounds over chairs, tables, and other performers awed audiences. Always, the medicine showmen strove to keep a crowd engaged, holding them in place long enough to present and sell as many products as possible.[54]

When the first lecture and pitch came, it began generally with the sale of an inexpensive item—such as soap—that was meant to loosen the purse strings of an audience that would later be offered the benefits of a more pricey tonic.[55] Some doctors first created an air of mystery around the product, even as they prepared to give a pitch. One Professor Ray Black would withdraw a rope, a Bible, and a human skull, arranging and rearranging the objects, to the increasing fascination and puzzlement of his audiences. When he finally initiated his lecture, he never returned to the curious items that had so intrigued the public.[56] Despite the seeming effectiveness of such ploys, a certain limit to such shenanigans existed. Although apparently gullible, the crowd was attuned to the moves of an over-rehearsed smooth talker, one who was a bit too unctuous to be trustworthy.

After sales closed on the first item, another act or two followed, either music or comedy. Music often featured nonsensical ditties, such as "Billy Goat," a song that spoke about a misbehaving goat. Comedy included speeches made humorous by characters who spoke in malapropisms.[57] These bits kept the show's flow steady with constant diversion.

"The secret of a successful sales pitch," medicine showman Thomas P. Kelley claimed, "is a smash opening, a crash finish—and keep them close together."[58] When the second lecture came, the doctor laid it on thick. When Kelley performed, he made sure he worked on the crowd's hypochondria, horrifying them with his persuasive lectures that played on their fears. By that point, he would have gained terrific momentum with the benefit of the entertainers.[59] He dug in, haunting the crowd with the specter of their imminent deaths—unless they bought elixirs quickly, before the supply ran out.

Some medicine show performers, attempting to justify their work, presented themselves as upstanding and respectable in the face of those who would regard them as amoral—or worse, immoral—confidence men. They strove to fashion themselves as decent.[60] One such troupe billed itself as the Quaker Doctors and took advantage of the pure and subdued image of Quakers in order to gain entrée into communities that would have otherwise held the members and their work in contempt.[61] Other troupes, however, actually had legitimate ties to religious groups. Dr. Lou Turner's Shaker Medicine Company had a relationship with Shaker communities in Ohio, creating and selling cures—as well as performing—in their name, with the benefit of their guidance.[62] This was all part of creating a stamp of approval for quack doctors who sold homemade concoctions often mixed on the road between towns, and consisting of all manner of ingredient: camphor, sassafras, cloves—even ammonia and turpentine.[63]

After the second lecture came another comedy bit or specialty number. The specialty of mind reading stood as a big crowd-pleaser. Violet McNeal, a performer who did an act with her partner, Will, utilized it to great effect. She entered blindfolded, and Will led her to the stage as he introduced her: "To an infinitesimal number of persons in a generation is granted the rare power of probing the thoughts of others. I will show you how this little lady, blinded and immobile can strip away bone and flesh, which separate her mind from yours. To her the innermost thought processes of each and every one of you are as clear as the pages of a book."[64] Prior to the act, the blindfolded Violet committed to memory a number of items, which she would call out as Will showed them to the crowd. They varied the performance each time, but the basic act remained.[65]

The cherished "prize candy" sale then followed, popular with both the performers and their audiences.[66] Troupes offered a piece of candy along with either a very small prize or a prize slip, which the customer could redeem to collect a larger gift from the stage. With a 100 percent profit margin, the candy sales guaranteed earnings for the medicine showmen. Indeed, for some troupes, sales of candy often outstripped sales of medicine.[67] For audiences, the prizes accompanying the candy were what proved appealing, rather than the candy itself. On the stage, medicine showmen generally displayed inexpensive prizes of quilts and blankets, but would also include a very few more substantial gifts of watches, dish sets, or French dolls, aimed at attracting buyers.[68]

The "afterpiece" then followed the show. It almost always incorporated a performer in blackface, a straightman, and a ghost in an act that entailed violence and haunting.[69] Such a scene in the late nineteenth-century medicine show harked back to medicine shows of yesteryear, which often concluded with a brutal autopsy conducted with outrageous instruments. Audience members, having already had an eyeful of the "doctor's" jars filled with purportedly disfigured body parts, were by then properly frightened and therefore motivated as buyers.[70] The jars, with their terrifying contents, served as warnings dramatized by the medicine show doctor, and shook the audience into action for the final chance to buy.[71]

The vast range of performance contained in the medicine show stimulated Bert's imagination. Although his post kept him on the show's periphery, he delighted in the heady experience of gripping audiences. Little by little, he gained knowledge of how to perform. And, between barking and observing the medicine show, he began to learn how to captivate an audience—first attracting them, and then holding their attention.

   ven as Bert developed his skills in California, young George William Walker, an up-and-coming performer, developed talents of his own in Lawrence, Kansas. A diminutive dark-skinned young man with confidence and charisma, George had been born in Lawrence in 1873, the youngest of three children.[72] He got his start working with twelve other young black boys in a company of minstrels, and although only amateurs, they reaped success with their annual performances. Walker remembered those performances fondly as "well patronized," their net receipts from the box "usually gratifying."[73]

A Negro company sent on the road by whites, the minstrel troupe typically played to type. In those annual performances—organized and supported by white men not long after the 1863 emancipation of slaves—they presented caricatures of happy, contented slaves, dancing and singing for their audiences. Yet even as a young boy in that environment, George hoped for more: "I started out with the idea that it was possible for the black performer to do better," he would later say.[74] Surrounded by fellow black performers who hoped that was true, but still doubted, George determined that "the longer I remained at home[,] the more impossible it seemed for me ever to realize my ambition."[75] Eventually he decided to leave Kansas; in 1893, at age twenty, he began his travel west to San Francisco, touring with Dr. Waite's medicine show.[76]

Known by the sobriquet of "Nash," George held great ambitions, and years later, he would reminisce about his early passion: "The stage has always fascinated me. To stand before the footlights and entertain large audiences has ever been the dream of my life."[77]

A dancer, singer, and comedian, the multitalented George learned increasingly about the nature of show business, while also keeping his spirits high with drive and passion. Eager for success, he did not merely limit himself to work with Dr. Waite, but rather, as he traveled from one town to another in wagons, he constantly sought his best opportunity:

> I was quite an entertainer. I could sing and dance, and was good at face-making, beating the tambourine, and rattling the bones [a rhythmic instrument, named as such because they were made of the ribs of a steer]. I was not lacking in courage, and I did not hesitate to ask quacks for a job. First one and then the other hired me.[78]

Similar to Bert, George advertised and served as the opener for a medicine show. When the traveling tour group arrived in town, George would set to work on a wooden platform, attempting to draw a crowd while doing anything from singing and dancing to making faces, telling stories, and rattling out rhythms with the bones. Like Bert, George also played a peripheral role at best in the medicine show. He did, however, quickly learn two important things that would substantially influence his career: "that white people are always interested in what they call 'darky' singing and dancing; and the fact that I could entertain in that way as no white boy could."[79] That education would prove invaluable as "Nash," the ambitious boy entertainer, became George Walker, the successful, deal-making businessman.

George learned these lessons and, against all odds, remained optimistic. He had to. In the traveling show world, the medicine show performer's position was low, and the barker's, even lower. For his job, George received only twenty-five cents in money—the rest he took in tonic. Not only did he earn low wages, he also shouldered the burden of labor that medicine showmen had to do for themselves, including pitching and striking their tents, preparing their products for sale—labeling bottles, for instance—and hawking innumerable goods. Nonetheless George gained what he could from medicine show work, knowing instinctively that, for him, it was merely a beginning.

As much as George's work in medicine shows marked a beginning for him, it also coincided with the shows' decline. By 1906, that decline would begin in earnest, with the Federal Food and Drugs Act placing controls on food, alcohol, and drugs, and thereby limiting the movement and sale of patent medicine across stages and the country. Inevitably, such regulation would forever alter the patent medicine industry—from packaging to advertisement to circulation of the products. With federal regulation, companies and even medicine show performers themselves faced severe consequences for noncompliance, which posed a much more considerable threat than had previous state or municipal policies.[80] Although the decline would mean the end of the medicine show and the patent medicine industry, by that time Bert Williams and George Walker would have been long removed from danger.

2

An Unlikely
Performer?

$\mathcal{A}$lthough Bert passionately pursued work as a barker, this auspicious start was no guarantor of future success in show business. While residing in his hometown, he at one point also worked as a singer-waiter, as part of a black quartet at the Mission Inn.[1] An oasis of cosmopolitanism in sleepy Riverside, the Mission Inn housed famous entertainers like actress Sarah Bernhardt, who stayed there while performing at the town's Loring Opera House.[2] The inn, however, provided scant chances for local performers. Although Bert's job of singing and serving kept him close to his new love, performance, an opportunity like his in such a small town would not lead him to stardom. Eventually, the big city called. In 1890s California, that city was San Francisco.

San Francisco had a rich theatrical community that compared well with its Eastern sister of New York. Originally an overwhelmingly male city, San Francisco in the 1890s still evidenced its gold miner roots of abundant pleasure-seeking single men with questionable mores. Prostitution continued along the Barbary Coast. Not far from there, gambling saloons admitted both common folk and criminals. The stage, however, offered more respectable amusements, although theater owners often tied their entertainment to a saloon that would provide refreshment either during or after performances.[3]

Theaters in San Francisco offered a diverse range of amusements. The Tivoli, which had opened in 1875 as a beer garden, by the 1890s had become an opera house. It produced popular shows like *Pinafore* and *She*, which was an adaptation of a novel. Although not always consistently dedicated to opera, it succeeded in attracting the patronage of middle-class families.[4] The Grand Opera House presented a range of acts, from opera to acrobats, on its stage. More concerned with filling seats than remaining true to its name, owners strove to make the theater accessible to the general public by keeping those seats cheap.[5] The Orpheum on O'Farrell, a popular-priced theater for the masses, hosted imported European sensations who took turns "making good" on the American stage. Consistently open, even while other theaters struggled to stay afloat, it maintained its status with a wide variety of entertainment.[6] San Francisco may have been a lesser city than New York, but compared to Bert's home of Riverside, it was a city of dreams.

Bert would later claim that his entertainment career in San Francisco began with his efforts to raise tuition for his education at Leland Stanford University. Regardless of statements to the contrary, and the obvious fact that he was well read and intellectual, there is no evidence to support that Bert was ever actually a Stanford student.[7] Nonetheless, a critical incident putatively dating from that period would forever define the trajectory of his career.

Although Bert fabricated his status as a student, he did team up with three white boys who were interested in raising money for school. Together, the group decided to tour, covering the Northern California towns of Felton, Santa Cruz, and Monterey. Rough-and-tumble places, these lumber and mining camps stood far removed from the city. When the boys took their makeshift show on the road, the rural audiences rejected their act. Ultimately, the tour failed.[8]

Before the tour ended, however, in one town the group faced an antagonistic and threatening audience. Although when Bert referred to it even years later, it was still shrouded in mystery, the encounter evidently gave the entertainer his first deep realization of the humiliation and degradation he would continuously face as a Negro. He returned to San Francisco, in his words, "without a stitch of clothing," having allegedly burned what little he had retained in order to protect himself from the hostility of the police—police who had been disinclined to protect him. Bert could only later explain that he had torched his meager rags "for reasons that everyone will understand who has read of the experiences of soldiers in the trenches."[9] This statement sufficed to describe the deep impact of his experience, coming as it did in an interview given soon after the unspeakable horrors seen and experienced during the Great War.

The trauma of that trip, significant and indelible, would always linger in Bert's memory. Even as he gained increasing success, he would refuse to perform in the Deep South, carefully selecting his tours' destinations. Knowing that Southerners not only supported but encouraged segregation, thereby ensuring substandard treatment of Negroes, Bert would deliberately avoid travel to the region throughout his career.

During his time in San Francisco, Bert pursued all chances to perform, including picking up a banjo and singing tunes in cafés in and around the city. He became a balladeer, much of the time singing simple, sometimes doleful, melodies, which he often revised. His life as a balladeer served him well: eventually, he landed a job performing with a group of Hawaiians. With his convincing coloring and wavy black hair, he easily *became* a Hawaiian, dressing in the group's costume: a white loose shirt with a yellow lei placed around the neck. For months, the group supplied him with regular work, but in time, he moved on.[10]

Around 1893, Bert landed an exceptional opportunity: a role in a troupe that performed minstrelsy, the nation's first popular entertainment form. Located in the heart of San Francisco, the job entailed working with Martin and Selig's Mastodon Minstrels, a company composed of five whites, a Mexican, and four Negroes.[11] It was a remarkable chance, and one with great import. Bert's work in minstrelsy would shape the reception of his performances by both black and white audiences throughout his career.

Minstrelsy had begun in the 1820s as the first truly original American popular entertainment. Developing in response to the needs of rural migrants who sought amusement in response to their removal from folk culture in growing Northern cities, minstrelsy provided a satisfying outlet. It gave non-elites a place of release and welcome, opening up the theatrical space for their enjoyment.[12] In minstrelsy's theaters, the people of the "middling classes," too poor to afford seats in the theater boxes, predominated the pit section, the seating area located directly behind the orchestra. The lower classes, a population who hadn't the means to afford even the pit, sat in the gallery, situated up in the rafters. A vociferous crowd that interacted with performers, minstrelsy's audience cheered when impressed, shouted when dissatisfied, and rebelled when angered.[13] The entertainment form had begun with the use of various regional white character types, such as the Yankee Peddler and Davy Crockett, who stood as American folk heroes.[14] By the 1830s, however, blackface performance became overwhelmingly popular.[15] And it was blackface minstrelsy that had the most lingering and damaging effects for blacks.

Historians typically mark the beginning of blackface minstrelsy's widespread fame with Thomas Dartmouth Rice's supposed 1828 appropriation and subsequent popularization of an old black man's idiosyncratic dance and song: "Weel about and turn about and do jus so;/Ebery time I weel about, I jump Jim Crow."[16] It was not only Rice's performance style and material that mimicked blacks, however; mixing burnt champagne corks with either water or a viscous material like petroleum jelly, Rice covered his face, marking himself as racially black in his portrayals of the Other.[17] He multiplied these effects by going even further, creating exaggerated full lips; playing a shuffling, slow-moving, dim-witted Negro; and speaking in an invented "darky" dialect. The character and stereotype took the name of the song: "Jim Crow."

Minstrelsy pronounced that blacks were a lesser people, subordinate to whites. It provided its Northern urban audiences a venue in which to release through laughter their uncomfortable feelings about blacks—who lived in the cities among them. Minstrelsy was a space in which whites could reject the notion that blacks needed to be incorporated into society, and they achieved this by demonstrating blacks' immanent inferiority.[18]

Although Thomas D. Rice started blackface minstrelsy's widespread—even international—popularity, not long after his Jim Crow character came "Zip Coon," or "Jim Dandy," created by George Washington Dixon. First performed in 1834, Zip Coon made a mockery of free blacks.[19] An urban man-about-town character, Zip Coon had a tendency to misspeak, using language full of malapropisms that offset his attempts to appear dignified. An arrogant, ostentatious figure, he dressed in high style, replete with "a long-tailed coat with padded shoulders, a high ruffled collar, white gloves, an eye-piece and a long watch chain."[20] The image became another compelling and lasting representation of the Negro.

Rice's dance and song enjoyed extraordinary success. Subsequently, in increasing numbers, white "Ethiopian Delineators" began to perform their notions of blackness on stage. The phrase underscored imitators' authenticity, and their putatively accurate depiction of blacks. It used a term over 300 years old to reference—and alienate—the black American population.[21]

Masking their faces with burnt cork, the performers seemed authentic to their audiences. Indeed, audiences often found the performances so believable that they even thought some white performers were, in fact, black. As a result, the entertainers began to distribute sheet music and bills with pictures of themselves both in and out of costume, attesting to the cogency of their representations. At the same time, they affirmed the importance of racial difference: they were *not* actually the Other.[22]

The black was the truly inassimilable individual in society. As performers blacked up, expressively pointing to what they were *not*, nothing could seem or be more opposite than the African American. By gesturing to the ultimate outsider, the performer himself found inclusion and acceptance in his ironic embodiment of blacks.

By the mid-1840s, as opposed to the individual "Ethiopian Delineators" of years before, groups of minstrels toured. Those groups began utilizing Southern states in their troupe names in order to evoke authenticity.[23] The tales regarding this shift are many and various, but they often focus on the music. The most popular version recounts a banjo player named Billy Whitlock asking violinist Dan Emmett to join him as he practiced his music in his New York boarding house. No sooner had Emmet joined him than another man, Frank Brower, arrived, taking up the bones at Whitlock's request. Finally Dick Pelham came; he picked up the tambourine as they continued to play as an ensemble. Shortly after that, the group performed as the Virginia Minstrels, with their first theatrical performance in New York's Chatham Theatre in 1843.[24]

Over time, minstrelsy's format became conventionalized. It took a three-part structure, with which Edwin Christy is credited, incorporating skits and songs performed in an imitation of black dialect.[25] The minstrel show included a first section, during which the troupe performed in a semicircle with one member on each end playing the tambourine or the bones. The endmen, as they were called, named

Brudder Tambo and Brudder Bones, engaged in an exchange of jokes between the group's songs and dances. Eventually, it became customary that Tambo was slim, whereas Bones was fat.[26] Throughout the performance, a character called Mr. Interlocutor sat in the middle of the group, acting as the master of ceremonies. He conducted himself in a dignified manner that countered the behavior of the rowdy endmen. The variety or olio section followed, which was a collection of entertainment including singers, gymnasts, and other novelty acts. A preposterous stump speech served as the highlight of this second act, during which a performer spoke in outrageous malapropisms as he lectured. In many ways reminiscent of the hilarious pomposity of Zip Coon, the stump speech deliverer aspired to great wisdom and intelligence, but always ultimately appeared foolish and ignorant. A one-act play concluded the show, typically a vignette of carefree life on the plantation.[27]

Although the structure of minstrelsy altered, the form of performance—blackface—and the content—caricatures and stereotypical representations of blacks—continued. During the antebellum period, blackface minstrelsy used these enactments as a way of addressing the vexing issue of abolitionism. Performers defended the proslavery argument by presenting denigrating representations of black subjects who needed the civilizing influence of slavery to keep them in check. In the years following emancipation, through the use of makeup and dialect, whites inhabited the black body in enactments that sought to control, contain, and define the meanings of blackness.

Minstrelsy's characterizations evidenced the degree to which the larger society imagined blacks as ahistorical figures. The white society viewed blacks as lacking a history, considering them a "timeless" legacy of the mythological Old South.[28] Minstrel shows emphasized eccentricities and peculiarities of blacks—physical and otherwise—creating a sense of foreignness about the population and underscoring the necessity of blacks' subjugation to whites.[29] Images ranged from artificially nostalgic representations of the lazy, childlike slave of the plantation to virulently derogatory characterizations of the maladjusted free black, a menace to society.

When blacks began to work as minstrels in the mid-1850s, becoming established as performers by the 1860s, their contribution ironically did little to alter the tradition.[30] Indeed, it may well have deepened the truth-value of minstrelsy, an idea already ingrained both in the theater and in the society. Able to participate in the theatrical form only by virtue of their declarations of authenticity, black entertainers claimed expertise as the "real" thing. As a result, black minstrels performed the traditional caricatures and donned burnt cork to blacken their often already dark skin in a hyper-performance of blackness staged for both white and black audiences alike.

Although burnt cork was known to be a mask that covered or transformed white performers, for a black performer audiences interpreted the mask as genuine. Blackface stood in for a black body presumed to exist beneath—or even instead of—the performative mask. The mask thus became the means by which the character, through the songs the comedian sang or the darky dialect in which he sang them, could be thought realistic.

As black audiences read against the grain of such performances, undercutting prevailing stereotypes that rendered blacks a despised and alien population, white audiences accepted those representations. Performers' onstage representations often further reified the notion that their performances merely reproduced reality. Indeed, their performances helped to elide the space between the real and the representational. Although the conditional acceptance of black performance facilitated blacks' involvement in the premiere American art form, it also ossified stereotypical images, despite performers' attempts to resist them.[31] And as the black entertainers performed the stereotypes, the damage extended even further: they risked ossifying their own representations.

By taking on a role in Martin and Selig's Mastodon Minstrels, Bert thereby also took on the weighty history and meaning of minstrelsy. He celebrated the entrance of blacks into theatrical performance as he also shouldered a burden for proliferating those images. Powerless to define absolutely the presentation and substance of his onstage character, he worked within the parameters of the type. From that moment forward, he would spend his career rearticulating and refining the Jim Crow stereotype, resolutely imbuing it with humanity, dignity, and individuality. Over the years, his success in doing so would be evaluated continually and variously by audiences who would either come to respect him or despise him.

Regardless of the deep and troubling signification of minstrelsy, Bert leapt at his new opportunity. Not yet twenty years old, he had the extraordinary chance to make a living as an entertainer. He accepted the job of endman, despite having to don burnt cork for the first time.

Before his first performance, Bert spread the heavy, sticky substance over his fair skin. Applying it in multiple layers, he covered cheeks, forehead, and neck. Smearing the cork over his ears and eyes, he obscured not only his color but also the features themselves, flattening them with the mask.

As he put on a kinky wig to hide his wavy locks, he wordlessly agreed to become the mocking image. As he prepared to put on a false darky's voice, he willfully silenced his own. And as he covered the last bit of evidence of his real self, his hands, in white gloves, he sealed the transformation. When he stepped out onto the stage with the rest of the large troupe of minstrels, his surrender was complete.

No sooner had Bert appeared onstage to perform, however, than stage fright gripped him. Although the blackface mask hid him, being on the stage exposed him. Standing before the audience, he began to sweat, overwhelmed. Underneath the viscous substance, his skin burned, and soon his profuse sweating began to show. The burnt cork gave way and the makeup ran, creating absurd zebra-like streaks. To make matters worse, when the other endman delivered a line directed at Bert, Bert's addled mind went blank. Shocked, his eyes flew open in terror: he could not recover his lines. He stood immobile, his mouth gaping.[32]

Seconds passed. The endman waited. The agonizing silence stretched on. Still, Bert could think of nothing. Suddenly, believing the silence part of the joke, the audience began to howl with laughter at the sight of the immobilized entertainer. Finally, Bert spoke up: "If I says anything, those folks'll laugh at me," he commented in dialect, running for the wings.[33]

Despite the catastrophe and Bert's mortification, the show went over well: the audience loved it. Even on his worst day, Bert had been a hit. In spite of the audience's overwhelmingly positive response, however, he resolved not to perform in blackface again.

While Bert sought opportunities in and around San Francisco, trying to gain access to the stage, George Walker continued to perform with medicine shows, slowly working his way west. He continuously faced travel, low pay, and meager rewards, despite his apparently bottomless determination to succeed. Years later, George would admit that even a dynamic and optimistic man like him experienced low morale. It hap-

pened as he had drifted into Chicago: "There I tried to convince managers that I could act, but as the meals didn't come regularly, I quit the
profession and got a job as a bell boy at the Great Northern Hotel,
where I remained during the World's [F]air."[34] Never one to lose heart,
however, George eventually rallied. The show business bug and wan-
derlust hit him again. He continued his journey until he landed in San
Francisco, where he abandoned the quacks to find work in the local theaters and music halls.

Stories abound about the first meeting of Bert and George; even
the two performers differed as to how they met. After being crowned
with success, George would describe his encounter and teaming up with
Bert in simple—even pat—terms: "While hanging around one day I
saw a gaunt fellow over six feet, of orange hue and about 18 years of
age, leaning on a banjo, haggling with a manager—that was Bert A.
Williams. He was stage struck, too! We got a job together at seven dollars a week each."[35]

According to Bert, however, their collaboration came over time. He
had met Walker first as a gifted dancer who taught him steps. Only
when Bert's employer, Martin and Selig's Mastodon Minstrels, found
the troupe a man short did Bert approach George: "I asked him where
I could find a certain fellow that I wished to get for the opposite end to
me. We could not find him, and then I turned to George and said,
'What's the use of looking any longer? You're the right man anyhow!'"[36]

Regardless of their differing stories, Bert and George agreed that
first they worked with Martin and Selig's minstrel show. They began
their work in the troupe purportedly each earning seven dollars a week.
Over the five months they worked with Martin and Selig's, however,
they often went unpaid. Bert remembered that, during the period, only
on three occasions did George receive eight dollars and cakes, while
Bert received nine dollars for work as stage manager. Overall, the two
were overworked and underpaid. After touring, they returned to San
Francisco, playing Halahan Horman's Midway for two years, all the
while seeking better opportunities.[37]

Located on the Barbary Coast, the Midway Plaisance, as it was
named, was an absolute dive and a tough venue to play. It was associated with "hootchy-kootchy" dancers and the sordid side of San Francisco life, with its shady dance halls, saloons, and brothels.[38] Bert and
George worked long hours at the Midway, often thirteen-hour days,

beginning at 1:30 P.M. and not ending until the wee hours of the morning. But it gave them a place at which to sharpen their skills, so they continued their efforts there.

When they played the Midway, George performed as comedian: his energy was boundless, his confidence clear, and his mirth irrepressible. The duo then began to establish themselves as Walker and Williams. They took a break from the Midway only when they gained a chance to perform at the San Francisco Midwinter Exposition, the city's version of the famed Chicago World's Columbian Exposition of 1893, also known as the World's Fair.

Created to honor the 400th anniversary of Columbus's discovery of the New World, the World's Fair had proved the profitability of large-scale expositions, having more than broken even with its effort. It pulled in $4 million from the concession stands alone and returned a $1 million surplus for distribution among its 30,000 stockholders.[39] San Francisco's organizers, inspired by such success, devised the Midwinter Exposition as a manner of generating income during a period of economic panic. In early 1893, diverse factors had come together to deal a crippling blow to the national economy: deflation, underconsumption and overproduction, and excessive government spending. Unemployment had soared, rising above 10 percent, where it would linger for five years, a phenomenon that would recur only during the Great Depression of the 1930s.[40] Organizers hoped their fair would stimulate the sluggish economy and pull the city out of its rut.

The Midwinter Exposition opened on 1 January 1894, and on that day nearly 9,000 people pushed past turnstiles onto the fairgrounds at Golden Gate Park. Organizers, determined to open the gates on the first of the year, had pressed on with plans despite the fair's state of incompletion. Attendees, greeted by festooned buildings—many of them unfinished—and an ununiformed band standing at the Manufactures Building instead of the much-ballyhooed Grand Court, enthusiastically entered the park. Although the Fine Arts building stood alone as the only finished main structure, crowds marched on, undeterred.[41]

Spread across 160 acres, the Exposition grounds consisted of few walkways. On that rainy, muddy, nippy first of January day, very little of the crowd could depend on them to smooth their paths. Despite this regrettable fact, the attendees happily braved the elements to see the booths, patronize the restaurants, and make the most of the day.

In San Francisco, *The Examiner* reporters wrote about the crowd, waxing poetic about the beauties who graced the fair with their dizzying varieties of hair color and bonnets. Some ladies sported the latest fashions from New York as they ambled through the grounds, with their blue, gray, green, or brown eyes flashing brightly. They all but gurgled with glee. Rapturous, writers described in detail the "ocean of feminine loveliness" in which the men drowned, awed and overwhelmed.[42]

Blacks' attendance at the fair, however, was closely monitored by fair organizers. During the closing month of the Exposition, when attendance had dipped disappointingly low, organizers allowed a separate special daylong program to be set aside for blacks' participation and enjoyment. Their day's events included piano solos, recitations, and addresses by prominent blacks—from local church elder Rev. Obadiah Summers, to "silver-tongued orator" Rev. Tilghman Brown, of Portland, Oregon.[43] Grudgingly recognized as members of the San Francisco community, blacks came as an afterthought to the fair organizers.

In part a state fair, the Exposition promoted California industry, with each county represented in booths and exhibitions. They featured citrus and mining displays as well as photographs of beet sugar factories and vineyards, pipelines, and public buildings. Fruit comprised a large proportion of the products, and the exhibitions included more than 150 varieties packed in syrup, as well as 50 types of jelly and jam. The countless items would be shipped to San Francisco over the months of the fair, with the aim of creating a full representation of the best the state of California had to offer its own citizenry and the world.[44]

In addition to the concession stands and state fair products, a great attraction at the fair was the numerous "villages," usually organized around exotic or foreign cultures. Hawaiians, Chinese, Laplanders, Sioux Indians, and even the miners of '49 were represented. Like many of the era's entertainments, the Exposition depended on the assertive advertising of innumerable barkers to draw crowds. Outside the Turkish Village one could hear cries: "See Bella Baya and the writhing, twisting, sinuous, sensuous, muscle dancers! The only genuine dancers in all this foreign land!" Next to that stood another spieler, luring folks into the "Egyptian mystery" with compelling promises: "Pharoah's daughter! The wonder of the Nile! See the marble statue turn to the living woman!" Shoulder to shoulder the barkers stood in heated competition, led by experienced spielers who were the best in the nation. Many of them, like Thomas Bird and Charles Biltz, had gained their skills and raked in thirty-five to forty dollars a week at Chicago's World's Fair the year before.[45]

The villages themselves appeared like freak shows, as "natives"— whether real or counterfeit—were paraded for the inspection of curious fair attendees. Presenters took their cue from master entrepreneur and showman Phineas Taylor Barnum. P. T. Barnum's spectacularly successful American Museums housed such "curiosities" as dwarves, exotic animals, and outright scams, like the "Dog-Face Boy."[46] The Midwinter Exposition organizers strove to ensure their exhibits fascinated audiences as Barnum's did. One "oddity" was the South Seas cannibals; another, the "wild man" of San Diego, seen for the first time "in captivity."[47] Depending on their means—and their agents—the oddities either lived in cages, like the wild man, or in a building of their own, like Millie Christine, the "colored woman and a half" who was actually conjoined twins.[48] When finally bored with the human exhibits, the attendees could view animals, like the well-tutored lion in Boone's arena, or Signor Alain d' Lacombe's trained fleas.[49]

Bert and George attended the Exposition as members of the Dahomey Village, called upon to substitute for actual Dahomeans (from the part of Africa now known as Benin), who were late in arriving. The enthrallment with Dahomey stemmed from recent events: Dahomey had established itself as a military power, asserting itself strongly in its resistance to French conquest. In 1892, in a bold act of defiance, leader King Behanzin had captured a number of Europeans, threatening to hold them in the event of an attack on Dahomey. When the battle began, Dahomeans fearlessly strove to hold ground against the encroaching French. By 1894, the French had gained full control, but not without sustaining losses of their own troops.[50]

The reason Dahomey appeared in the American and European presses, however, was not only because of its battle against the French. It also became infamous for its putative rituals of human sacrifice and cannibalism.[51] While reporters spoke of unwilling Europeans made witness to King Behanzin's chilling rituals, later displays at expositions brought the "savages" home to intrigued Americans.[52] It made perfect sense to them to present the barbaric backward peoples to crowds gathered at fairs while also celebrating America's unstoppable progress as the shining light of the New World.

At the Midwinter Exposition, the false Dahomeans lived in wooden huts intended, no doubt, to give the village an air of authenticity. Within those huts they slept in bunks. When the forty or so real Africans arrived toward the end of May, the counterfeit Africans promptly left.[53]

A reporter for *The Examiner* pronounced the replacements the real thing, offering his observations as evidence. "They cannot speak English as could the [other purported Dahomeans]," he commented, "and they do not display the same familiarity with the . . . ways of American civilization."[54] Furthermore, the similar dress—or undress—of the men and women marked them as real Dahomeans. Their skin, covered in coconut oil, gave additional evidence: it glistened even more brightly than that of the South Sea Islanders in residence.

The Dahomeans' actions persuaded the reporter as well. Their unique singing and dancing established their authenticity. And that they amused themselves by "coiling and uncoiling a lot of dreamy-looking serpents" confirmed it beyond a shadow of a doubt.[55] Yes, here were authentic Africans supposedly in their own element, even as they sat in huts on the fairgrounds of San Francisco's Golden Gate Park.

Taking the "anthropological" study even further, another *Examiner* journalist interviewed the various village inhabitants in order to reveal the "Strange Sports of Strange People."[56] Through an interpreter named Abeyvi, who had purportedly bargained on behalf of King Behanzin with the slave traders, the reporter inquired if the real Dahomeans played sports. The Dahomeans responded contemptuously: "Sports! We of Dahomey have no sports. Play is for children."[57] When further prodded, Topa, Prince and Chieftain of the village, spoke up, recalling a game of strength that also happened to be practical. Two villagers would sit across from each other with a stick placed between them at their feet. They would then pull at it, attempting to drag the other over. Whoever succeeded was the winner: the classic game of tug-of-war.

Despite the numerous questions posed, and the headline of the piece, the article seemed more a chance for the reporter to write at length about the imposing Africans' physiques than a description of pastimes. Noting that "muscles beneath their ebony skin stand out like knotted rope when they so much as grasp a club or paddle," the journalist declared, "They are born strong."[58] The writer then turned to regard the women, no less mesmerized by their Amazonian height, erect carriage, and fierceness, which seemed to exceed that of their men.

Later, two of the Africans played the game described, termed stick-tilting, in the presence of the reporter and for the benefit of the prince. He sat watching from his royal chair, scepter in hand. On either side of him stood a princess, holding an impressively weighty knife; at his feet sat the three slaves they had carried along for the journey to America. In addition, one Dahomean who had the duty of holding Prince Topa's umbrella, and another, described as "court clown," stood near. After the game, a final telling moment came as they snapped a photograph, the princesses pulling the hair of the slaves while brandishing their knives overhead. The writer explained: "This was not with sinister purpose, but in Dahomey in all critical times it is esteemed a good thing to remind the slave that the master holds his life in his hand."[59]

Notwithstanding the "anthropological" investigations of inquisitive reporters and others, the presentations of the Africans (as well as others in the villages) appeared to have the ring of truth to their viewers. After Bert and George's dismissal, the two continued to have free access to the fairgrounds. They took advantage of the chance to visit with the Africans. They learned from them and observed them, having been given the opportunity to have close interaction.[60]

The impact was lasting. Years later, George would write of the experience's influence on Bert and himself: "We were not long in deciding that if we ever reach the point of having a show of our own, we would delineate and feature native African characters as far as we could, and still remain American, and make our acting interesting and entertaining to American audiences."[61] Ever and always dreamers, the fledglings Bert and George held on to their memories and insights.

After their stint at the Midwinter Exposition and more hard work at the Midway Plaisance, Bert and George finally left San Francisco. Their journey to fame would entail near misses, fleeting successes, and a seeming response to the call "Go East, young men," inverting Horace Greeley's well-known exhortation. Having been encouraged by black performers who spoke about the opportunities possible in the East, they decided to pursue their dreams. They possessed a driving ambition to make it to New York, the city known, even in the late nineteenth century, as the home of show business.

First, Bert and George headed to Los Angeles, appearing on the same bill as acting and singing duo Clifford and Huth. Billy Clifford and Maud Huth, headliners earning $300 in gold a week, inspired the lowly pair. They showed Bert and George their monies and "our eyes popped out of our heads," as Bert said.[62] It showed the determined young performers what was possible if they ever really made it in show business.

The two then left Los Angeles and headed to Denver, Colorado, where they worked with a medicine show. Subsequently, they hit a mining town called Cripple Creek.[63] Following the hardships of performing for the rowdy frontiersmen, they moved on again, landing in Chicago.

In Chicago, they had a wonderful opportunity: the chance to perform in their first large black production, *The Octoroons*.[64] Billed as a "musical farce," *The Octoroons* maintained the three-part structure of the minstrel show. It discarded the endmen, however, and included the unusual addition of a black chorus line. The cast featured a female chorus and six female leads, a lineup of lovely women who sang and performed a variety of sketches, ending the show with a chorus-march finale.[65] *The Octoroons* was a tremendous show with a company of almost fifty people "in a Gorgeous Spectacular Opera Comique," the 1895 *Dramatic Mirror* reported.[66]

The production appeared to be an excellent opening for Bert and George. They suffered a terrible disappointment, however, and fell flat. Despite their failure with the audience, they initiated lasting friendships with performers in the show, such as Stella Wiley, Bob Cole, and Jesse Shipp, and composers, such as Will Marion Cook and Will Accooe.[67] Following *The Octoroons*, Bert and George struggled to find other breaks, but they did not forget the unusual pleasure of socializing with other young blacks who had the show business bug as acutely as they did.

Not long after their effort in Chicago, Bert and George had a true brush with success. It was also one that would transform both them and their career together. Booked to perform in Detroit's Wonderland theater, they made a significant change to their act: Bert made the surprising decision to perform in blackface. Although he hadn't worn the makeup in years—not since the incident with Martin and Selig's—he decided "just for a lark" to blacken his face and try singing a song.[68] It was the first he'd written, with both words and music of his own creation.

On that legendary day, he appeared before the audience singing "Oh! I Don't Know, You're Not So Warm!" In his words, "[I]t went like a house on fire."[69] A song of love and loss, the piece contained lyrics both

funny and sad in its telling of a suitor rejected by his sweetheart in favor
of another, more desirable one:

> *I had a girl, and her name was Pearl,*
> *I thought her heart was mine;*
> *I gave a French dinner,*
> *For I thought I was a winner,*
> *I'd have bet my life 'gainst a dime.*
>
> *I told her how I lov'd her,*
> *but she said she'd not be mine;*
>
> *Then I told her I was sweller,*
> *Than any other feller,*
> *But this was her reply . . . .*

Bert belted out the sweetheart's words of rejection in a refrain that declared the suitor "not so swell." Furthermore, she cheekily proclaimed,
"There's other gents as fine as you!"[70]

As before, the audience loved Bert. But this time when he wore
blackface, something dramatically different happened. Rather than embarrassment or discomfort, Bert felt something else. "I began to find
myself," he would simply say.[71]

Although Bert tried blackface "on a lark" that day, he had found
something in and through it. Covering his fair skin with burnt cork before gracing the stage, he removed all traces of the dignified young man
he was, replacing himself with the woeful darky who would sing about
the coldness of his beloved. The action of donning the cork remained the
same, but Bert's mind-set differed entirely. Instead of being trapped
inside the mask, he viewed it as "a great protection. . . . I shuffle onto
the stage, not as myself, but as a lazy, slow-going negro."[72] The blackface covered and effectively hid the real Williams, now protected not
only from stage fright but also from having to be the persona he portrayed on the stage. Burnt cork became part of what enabled him to
step into that onstage self, the buffer between the audience and the
inner Williams.

As he stepped into the role, Bert tucked himself away. "A black face,
run-down shoes and elbow-out make-up give me a place to hide," he

would later reveal. "The real Bert Williams is crouched deep down inside the coon who sings the songs and tells the stories."[73] Bert created a dichotomy between Williams in performance and Williams in life. He further protected himself, literally hiding himself from the attention and assumptions of an audience that would believe he *was* the simple, slow-moving, pathetic character he played onstage.

As he played the role, he saw in it the possibility of depth. Rather than rely on grotesque, outlandish acts, he imagined the humor of the moment as being dependent on character. "For I do not believe there is such a thing as innate humor," he averred. "It has to be developed by hard work and study, just as every other human quality."[74] Here, Bert challenged the idea of innate humor in a statement that strove to debunk the myth of the so-called natural black performer, as well as the assumption that he was the same as his character.

The character could not have differed more from Bert. This was a man who slouched rather than stood, wailed rather than reasoned. Yet, through makeup, both the character and Bert were transformed. The formerly denigrating substance became Bert's "great protection," liberating rather than confining him. The character became a protection rather than a prison—a persona behind which the performer could hide. As Bert tucked away his sensitive, intellectual self, he *became* another—vastly different—self. That distance gave him the space that he sorely needed. "It was not until I was able to see myself as another person that my sense of humor developed," he would later say. In that moment on the Wonderland stage, though the words to describe the transformation might have failed him, Bert became a comedian.[75]

As the comedian came into the foreground, Bert possessed such an electric presence that George perhaps had no other choice but to acknowledge—and adapt—to the change. With time, the two changed their billing to Williams and Walker. Bert, the former balladeer, became the comedian while Walker, still as vivacious as ever, became the straightman.

This landmark moment of Bert's emergence would forever shape their career. Not long after that performance, while the two enjoyed the curative hot springs of a West Baden, Indiana, resort, they got a gig in town. There they got spotted. That manager, Thomas Canary, offered them the chance of a lifetime: to perform in a musical opening in the incomparable, illustrious New York City.

2
The Williams
and Walker Years

3

Big City, Bright Hopes

The New York City that greeted Bert and George was a frenetic, if not outright chaotic, place of enormous disparities and unfathomable contradictions. As thousands of people suffered in slums, toiled in sweatshops, and died from disease and deprivation, increasing numbers of America's most affluent citizens—like John D. Rockefeller and Andrew Carnegie—migrated to the city. Millionaires built and luxuriated in grand mansions lining opulent Fifth Avenue, while two-thirds of the city's 1.5 million residents stifled in overcrowded tenements.[1]

Only four years before the duo's arrival, Danish immigrant Jacob Riis had reported on the destitute immigrants of the city in his groundbreaking photo-text *How the Other Half Lives: Studies in the New York Tenements*.[2] A police reporter who had written exhaustively about the slums of Manhattan's Lower East Side, Riis published one of the earliest works of photojournalism in America. Venturing into the dark tenements of lower Manhattan, he visually documented the appalling squalor immigrants endured, accompanying the images with text.[3] Not merely displaying the reality of urban poverty in America, *How the Other Half Lives* drew attention to the interrelatedness of poverty and progress in the modern age.[4]

Even as recent immigrants—such as those from Italy, Greece, and Russia—struggled to survive on the harsh and competitive Manhattan Island, thousands more continued to flood the city. They abandoned their countries, escaping poverty and religious persecution.[5] Through those immigrants, Manhattan became a tangle of peoples who sought to recreate the Old World in the New, and were themselves transformed. And as the people transformed, so did the city. At the dawn of 1898, Manhattan would be renamed "Greater New York" in an expansion that would incorporate the boroughs of the Bronx, Staten Island, Queens, and Brooklyn, creating a mammoth metropolis of more than 3 million souls.[6]

When Bert and George arrived in Manhattan from Indiana in 1896, they had come only three years after what may be considered the landmark date for the area later known as the Times Square Theater District. On 25 January 1893, producer Charles Frohman had opened the Empire Theater on Broadway below Fortieth Street. Despite the comments of naysayers, he had been determined to draw crowds to his risky venture. At that time, the Empire's location had been considered too far from the more vital Union Square Theater District.[7]

The Union Square Theater District had been central not so much due to the number of theaters found there, but rather because of the overwhelming presence of all business relating to theater, from piano makers to costumers to photographers.[8] The district had stretched north all the way to Long Acre Square in the low forties, with the greatest concentration of theaters being at Madison and Herald Squares. It had not yet encompassed Long Acre, however, the square renamed Times Square in 1904, thereby honoring the illustrious headquarters of the *New York Times*, located on the corner of Forty-second and Broadway.[9]

Ultimately, the daring Frohman triumphed with his endeavor. Eventually others followed, contributing to the creation of the new theater District.[10] Frohman's influence alone, however, had not been enough to make the new area a success. Public transportation, including the elevated train and streetcars, aided in bridging the gaps between the relatively far-flung theaters. It played an invaluable role in getting theatergoers to their destinations. And with the aid of such transit, audiences for performances thereby spread beyond the immediate localities surrounding the theaters themselves.[11]

Another pivotal player in the development of the Times Square Theater District had been Oscar Hammerstein I, who in 1895 built the Olympia on an entire city block between Forty-forth and Forty-fifth Streets. His ambitious endeavor had included "three theatres, a roof garden, billiard rooms, Turkish baths, cafés and restaurants."[12] Unfortunately, Hammerstein ran out of resources to complete the project. He later built and maintained possession of the Victoria, however, which would reign for many years as the leading vaudeville house in New York City from its location at Forty-second Street and Seventh Avenue.[13]

Bert and George's Broadway had not yet become the district of dazzling electric lights that would be known as "The Great White Way." A year after their arrival, the first electric sign would be installed, beginning the process of transformation that would make New York resolutely the entertainment capital of the nation and, perhaps, the world.[14] Nonetheless, Broadway had already established itself as the main thoroughfare of theater; it was the street destined to linger in the imagination as the very home of New York theatrical entertainment.

Although the team had been lured to the city by manager Thomas Canary, they quickly discovered that they would have to audition for the chance to perform. *The Gold Bug*, an operetta by Victor Herbert, would play at the Casino Theater on Broadway and Thirty-ninth, a venue devoted to domestic and foreign musical theater that generally attracted enthusiastic audiences to its productions.[15] *The Gold Bug*, however, was off to a weak start. A story of racial intermixing (miscegenation) told in two acts, the production had been beset with difficulties, requiring the postponement—numerous times—of opening night.[16]

When Bert and George auditioned, they performed before producer George Lederer and others. To the team's undoubted surprise, they failed to impress. Years later, Lederer would recall, "We gave them a hearing a day or so before *The Gold Bug* was to open, but the consensus of opinion of the invited audience was that not only were they mediocre material, but also that their color would be found to mediate against their chance of success on the legitimate stage."[17] In obeisance to the demands of the "invited audience," Lederer declined to have them appear. Here the two had traveled all the way to New York from the Midwest, determined and full of hope, expectant of grand new opportunities, yet it seemed that their career was to stop far short of their dreams. Indeed, even before their first real appearance in the city. Apparently, they would not have the chance to grace that New York stage, as *The Gold Bug* carried on without the duo, opening on 21 September 1896.[18]

The two, however, did have their chance. When reviews of *The Gold Bug* returned on opening night, critics had panned the show. Suddenly, the very team that seemed to be a possible detriment to the production became the show's only potential asset. Spurred on by a dim hope that Bert and George could somehow save *The Gold Bug*, Lederer immediately returned to them, requesting their appearance for the second night. The show's resulting merit seemed entirely reliant on the comedy team, as Lederer later had to admit, "The second night's show of *The Gold Bug* proved as spiritless as the premiere, but the audience couldn't get enough of Williams and Walker. It was the first time I had ever seen a musical muke team stop a show, and they stopped *The Gold Bug* that night until they eventually gave out physically."[19]

Bert's "Oh! I Don't Know, You're Not So Warm!" won them their audience, the same piece he had sung on the fateful night that he found his feet as a comic. There were two ironies of Bert and George's success, however. First, despite their having stopped the show, *The Gold Bug* still closed after a week's run. Second, their popular song had been particularly challenging for Victor Herbert's orchestra to learn. Although the tune had been well received and was a great hit for the duo, it was of a musical style unfamiliar to the orchestra, that being the syncopated rhythms of ragtime.

Ragtime had made its official appearance on the national American scene at the 1893 World's Fair in Chicago.[20] "The Dream Rag," a piece performed by Jesse Pickett at the fair, had been the rage for the twenty-odd million Americans who descended on the event between 1 May and 30 October.[21]

Pickett's performance introduced ragtime music to the general public, but it would be some time before it became widely accepted by society. Its syncopated rhythms were first played in bordellos and seedy saloons. With such disreputable beginnings, ragtime's ultimate transition to a respectable—even revered—popular music, appropriate for the family parlor as well as the legitimate stage, would come slowly.[22]

Yet, with the influence of Scott Joplin, a fair attendee who would later become known as "The King of Ragtime Composers," ragtime would overcome these sordid associations.[23] His "Maple Leaf Rag" would be published in 1899 to tremendous acclaim. Ragtime, particularly the "classic" instrumental rags, as they were termed, would become identified with musical virtuosity and culture.[24] Its success became so great that many sheet music publishers would seek to benefit from its popularity, merely by including "rag" or "ragtime" in the title of their tunes, or incorporating references to black life.

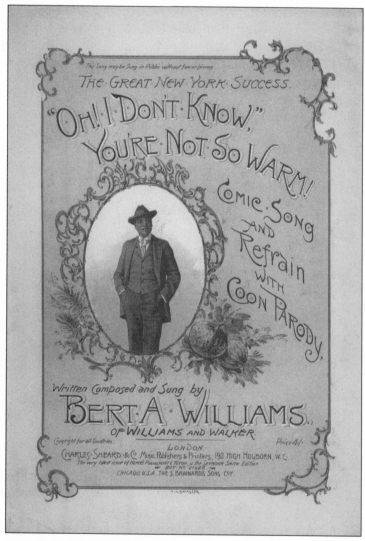

Sheet Music, "Oh! I Don't Know, You're Not So Warm!" COURTESY OF BROWN UNIVERSITY LIBRARY

As a result, the definition of ragtime was fluid, at times difficult to establish with any absolute certainty. The term itself was debated, said to refer to the syncopation of the music ("ragged time"), or blacks' use of handkerchiefs ("rags") to initiate a dance.[25] In part, the public had difficulty categorizing "ragtime" music because the term first described "a style of playing, rather than a genre of composition."[26] Musicians often "ragged" tunes, which essentially referred to adding and incorporating syncopated rhythms. Performers could thereby transform anything from waltzes to marches into a "rag."[27]

The musical form clearly had African origins, evident from its polyrhythmic qualities and its differing melodic and harmonic structures. It often utilized the pentatonic scale, which could be performed using only the black keys on the piano. It had not developed from African origins alone, however, and was surely influenced by the European system that composers used for notating the music.[28]

Williams's "Oh! I Don't Know, You're Not So Warm!" was a vocal rag, many of which were also known as "coon" songs, in the parlance of the day. Coon songs had preceded published ragtime. From the 1890s to 1910, such songs spread across the country, initiated in part by the success of African American blackface performer Ernest Hogan's "All Coons Look Alike to Me."[29] Inspired by a Chicago piano player who lamented the loss of his sweetheart in a tune with the words "all pimps look alike to me," Hogan wrote his own version of the song. He replaced the word "pimp" with "coon," and would later declare that he had interpreted the term as a positive reference to the smartness of the raccoon.[30]

Despite Hogan's explanation, the song had a grave effect on the perception of blacks. "All Coons Look Alike to Me" contained the leading features of the coon song: dialect, syncopation, and stereotypes of blacks.[31] It also had a catchy refrain:

All coons look alike to me,
I've got another beau, you see,
And he's just as good to me as you, nig!
Ever tried to be;

He spends his money free,
I know we can't agree,
So I don't like you no how,
All coons look alike to me.[32]

The song became extremely successful, playing a role in the popularization of the musical genre as well as the spread of the term "coon."

By the time of the song's popularization, the term had already come to have considerable power in the ridicule of blacks. Starting in the 1830s, "coon" had been used to refer to the Whig party, which had taken a raccoon as its emblem.[33] Active from the 1830s to 1850s, the Whigs had campaigned against Jacksonian Democrats, supporting a protective tariff and federally funded national development.[34] Although they had been deeply divided on the issue of slavery, their more tolerant attitude toward blacks may have been what rendered the coon party's name a derogatory term directed at that population.[35]

Coon songs' lyrics featured the antics of chicken-stealing, watermelon-eating blacks, old stereotypes that referenced the purported practices of indolent plantation slaves. Allegedly dishonest and lascivious characters, blacks were often also depicted as violent brutes who endangered society. Such images gained their power from the dominant representation of blacks toward the end of the nineteenth century, largely shaped by the political climate of the post-Reconstruction era. With Radical Republicans' relinquishment of the South to Democrats and the re-establishment of "home rule," blacks had watched their hopes of social equality quickly recede. The period historian Rayford Logan described as "the nadir" of American race relations had begun.[36]

American society aggressively maintained the denial of blacks' civil and social rights through the 1896 *Plessy v. Ferguson* verdict, upholding the constitutionality of the "separate but equal" doctrine. Through Homer A. Plessy's attempt to secure his right to take a seat on an intrastate coach set aside for white patrons, the nation's blacks would learn the devastating truth of how narrowly their Thirteenth and Fourteenth Amendment rights would be conceived. When *Plessy* argued that separate, race-based accommodations amounted to a "badge of inferiority" that re-established slavery, the Court dismissed that line of argument. Defining slavery specifically as "involuntary servitude," the Court separated distinctions based on race, class, and color from the definition.[37] When attorneys for Plessy attempted to defend his rights as a citizen, arguing for his justifiable access to the coach on the basis of his seven-eighths Caucasian blood, the Court disregarded his claim.[38] It then underscored that the Fourteenth Amendment, though establishing equality of the races before the law, did not do away with racial distinctions or enforce social equality. Distinguishing social equality from political equality, the Court "created a protected sphere that secured white enjoyment from black encroachments," thereby giving this limited interpretation of the Fourteenth Amendment legitimacy.[39]

Plessy v. Ferguson eventually touched all areas of interracial interaction and contact. The resultant institution of Jim Crow segregation solidified the *Plessy v. Ferguson* ruling, establishing racial separation under the law. It demanded the creation and maintenance of private and public institutions, ranging from schools to recreational facilities.[40] In addition to segregation, the escalating practice of disenfranchisement using poll taxes, literacy tests, and the ubiquitous threat of violence not only ensured differential treatment but also created a reign of terror for the South's blacks.[41] In this hostile environment, blacks desired empowerment and, even more fundamentally, survival: the number of lynchings of blacks between 1889 and 1902 averaged over 100 a year.[42]

Alongside this refusal of black rights, popular culture mass-produced debased images of the black population, like that described in the coon songs. Such representations had dated back to the beginning of minstrelsy, with caricatures disseminated in comic books, newspapers, and posters. In the post-Reconstruction era, however, even high-toned literary journals—such as *Harper's*, *Atlantic Monthly*, and *Scribner's Monthly*—further reified the notion of blacks' unfitness for American society. They pointed to blacks' quasi-savage behavior and degraded spoken English.[43] They harked back to a mythical image of idealized plantation society while they also denounced the Reconstruction and its aims.[44]

The force of pseudoscientific racial theory multiplied the twin influences of politics and popular culture. Combined with legislative controls and the stereotypical representations found in the media, scientific racialism served as a means to justify the creation of proscriptive policies, institutions, and practices that were meant to control the black population. Charles Darwin's 1859 work, *On the Origin of Species*, definitively established the discourse of scientific racialism. It introduced an evolutionary theory that connected the development of higher life forms to competition described as the "survival of the fittest," which resulted in the extinction of some varieties of organism and the continuance of others. Barely ten years later, Darwin linked these conclusions to the advancement of human civilization by applying "natural selection." Through conflict, races described as civilized would overpower those characterized as savage, leading to the latter's inevitable and natural extinction.[45]

With the weight of the presumed rationality of science undergirding their arguments, proponents of black racial inferiority began to write as social Darwinists. Some writers anticipated the race's natural extinction after emancipation. Although they abandoned this assumption—particularly following the 1880 census that showed the increased growth of the black population over that of whites in the South—by the time of the 1890 census, the discussion returned.[46] Moreover, new statistical data arose that seemed to support the application of Darwinian theory to blacks. These views gained increasing power, linking pseudoscientific research to conclusions regarding blacks' moral, intellectual, and physical inferiority.

Frederick Hoffman's 1896 book, *Race Traits and Tendencies of the American Negro*, the most influential work on race in the late nineteenth century, connected the social problems blacks suffered in society to their "race traits and tendencies," which led to the population's steady degeneration into a morally corrupt criminal element.[47] Hoffman's study would eventually develop into the movement of eugenics, with its focus on heredity as a social determinant.[48] As authorities, he and others like him moved from questions of black extinction to that of black degeneracy, making apocalyptic declarations regarding the importance of white domination of blacks.[49] In their avowed protection of whites from the uncivilized black masses, the system of Jim Crow, heinous acts of lynching, and disenfranchisement continued to gain support.

In this atmosphere, the appeal of coon songs for the American public was indisputable. The images of blacks presented in the lyrics matched blacks' representation throughout the society, and came in answer to racist whites' demands for such caricature. Fred Fisher's "If the Man in the Moon were a Coon" sold more than three million copies, and such success was not rare.[50] Incredibly, the coon song craze so overwhelmed the population during its time that white and black performers alike responded to it. The performers met the public's demand, compelled to give it what it wanted and expected.

Although "Oh! I Don't Know, You're Not So Warm!" parodied love songs, containing funny and ironic lines, it also included many elements characteristic of the genre:

Sheet Music, "The Coon's Trade-Mark." COURTESY OF BROWN
UNIVERSITY LIBRARY

*A coon went out to serenade
his girl in Thompson Street,
With a banjo in his hand,
I tell you he look'd grand,
From his head down to his feet.*

*But soon another feller who
was courting that same girl,
With his razor in his hand,
cut the serenading man,
And sang him this refrain:*

Well I guess not, you're not so gay,
There's other coons as gay as you,
Oh, I don't know, you may be warm,
I don't play music, and I'm not so cold![51]

The piece maintained the conventions of the coon song. It utilized black stereotype, particularly an alleged predilection for violence. It also re-cycled the term "coon" in its mention of blacks and in blacks' refer-ences to each other.

In the songs Bert and George performed together, they worked within the genre's conventions, seeing this as perhaps their only man-ner of gaining opportunities as entertainers. Their song "The Coon's Trade-Mark" included the following refrain:

As certain and sure as Holy Writ,
And not a coon's exempt from it,
Four things you'll always find together
Regardless of condition of sun and moon—
A watermelon, a razor, a chicken and a coon![52]

No longer did lyrics feature solely the image of the unthreatening though ignorant Southern black of minstrelsy, represented by Jim Crow. The lyrics now depicted a new, imposing and dangerous type: the vio-lent Northern urban black, whose preferred lethal weapon was the straight razor.[53]

Like the earlier white minstrels, however, perhaps in an effort to in-dicate that their roles and their songs were distinct from reality, Bert and George included pictures of themselves on their sheet music. Wearing the elegant tailored suits that they donned offstage, they un-derscored their roles as actors. What this seemed to express is that, although they played to type, their stereotypical roles did not equal re-ality. Despite such strategic self-presentation, however, the lyrics may well have spoken more loudly than Bert and George's offstage im-ages. Set to apparently inescapably infectious rhythms, the lyrics trav-eled the country, broadly disseminated as sheet music through Tin Pan Alley.

Tin Pan Alley had its home in New York City, having established it-self on West Twenty-eighth Street, where numerous companies based their headquarters. Reportedly, the sound of composers plucking out

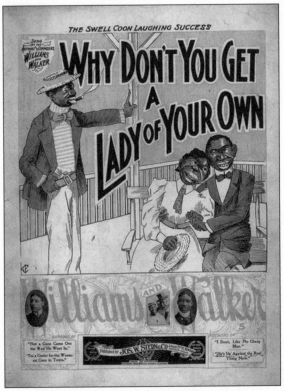

Sheet Music, "Why Don't You Get a Lady of Your Own."
COURTESY OF BROWN UNIVERSITY LIBRARY

tunes on tinny pianos could be heard up and down the street, thereby providing the moniker for the area. Rapidly, Tin Pan Alley expanded, and the term became synonymous not only with that part of the city, but also with the entire nation's music industry.[54] Twenty-eighth Street had been densely packed with businesses; over a dozen companies, their addresses west of Broadway, stood side-by-side. These included such publishers as M. Witmark, New-York Music, and Chas W. Ward, and over the years, it would come to include many others, such as Jerome H. Remick and Harry Von Tilzer.[55] Not all of the great companies were on Twenty-eighth Street, however; the rest had their headquarters throughout other parts of the city.

In time, the most important hallmark of Tin Pan Alley would not be the location of the music publishers' shops and studios, but rather the

Williams and Walker Offstage. COURTESY OF THE YALE
COLLECTION OF AMERICAN LITERATURE, BEINECKE RARE
BOOK AND MANUSCRIPT LIBRARY

characteristic drive of its publishers to sell. Tin Pan Alley's publishers treated music as a commodity exchanged on the market, engaging "pluggers" to publicize songs and promote them to performers. Publishers created incentives for entertainers to use the company's material in their performances.[56] The advertising mattered more than the quality of the music; publishers popularized a song through the use of famous entertainers, whose images often graced the sheet music along with the words "prominently featured by." This gave a song an instant audience, after having also been incorporated into stage performances.[57] These would be the songs played by the thousands of Americans who increasingly bought musical instruments for home entertainment—particularly the piano—which in 1897 cost $125 through Sears and Roebuck, and by 1905 would be as little as $85.[58]

Sheet Music, "Play That Barber Shop Chord." COURTESY OF
THE LESTER S. LEVY COLLECTION OF SHEET MUSIC, SPECIAL
COLLECTIONS, SHERIDAN LIBRARIES, THE JOHNS HOPKINS
UNIVERSITY

Williams and Walker benefited from the distribution of their music
through Tin Pan Alley. Yet, as the leading popular culture industry of
the period, Tin Pan Alley circulated not only derogatory *narratives*
about blacks through its lyrics but also derisive *images* of blacks on its
illustrated sheet music. Aiming to satisfy the desires of the public, the
industry remained conciliatory and generally unchallenging of the caricatures of blacks depicted in its sheet music. Coon songs had not been
the sole form of music disseminated through the industry. Still, Tin Pan
Alley's link to an emerging entertainment form that would ultimately replace minstrelsy would cause it to continue to play a leading role in the
use of blacks as "the butt of the national joke."[59]

*W*hen Bert and George's run at the Casino Theater quickly ended, they scrambled for other opportunities. They joined an out-of-town show playing in Boston, receiving credit in the roles of servant and waiter, respectively. Then, following the weeklong run, they returned to New York, and this time played a show featuring the muscle-bound strongman Eugen Sandow. That show also closed after barely a week.[60] After scraping by with these meager offerings, the two finally hit pay dirt. With the encouragement of George Lederer, who had been thoroughly impressed with their work in *The Gold Bug*, they got an incredible break, which Walker described best: "thirty-six consecutive weeks of what you may call 'velvet.'"[61] Their extraordinary chance was a run beginning at Koster and Bial's New Music Hall performing in America's new popular entertainment form: vaudeville.

In the city of New York, Tony Pastor, an Italian immigrant and entrepreneur born in 1834, would be credited with the development of vaudeville. "Vaudeville," thought to be derived from the French phrase *voix de ville*, or "voice of the city," had become the new name for variety theater.[62] Pastor became the first in bringing the change that would render the often bawdy, riotous variety theater acceptable to New York's middle class. After having worked as a performer for many years, establishing himself as singer and songwriter, he had begun an effort to create the new form of entertainment by removing the disreputable taint of the variety performance environment, that being the male-dominated saloon.[63] He began in 1865 with his own variety theater, located in the Bowery, south of Union Square. At that time, the Bowery mirrored San Francisco's Barbary Coast with its dives, saloons, and prostitutes serving a clientele of working-class males.[64] Following the success of his theater in the Bowery, Pastor moved onward—and northward—opening a theater in the area that would later be known as SoHo, attracting the middle and lower classes.[65]

Although at first Pastor's theaters offered alcoholic beverages, he eventually moved away from this practice, balancing the desires of Bowery audiences for "racy" entertainment with the need for suitable family fare. Yet, more important than the content of the shows and the material performed was the audience itself. Theater owners believed that, by attracting women specifically and securing their presence, their venues would acquire a stamp of respectability. Moving from the former audience of working-class men to the desired refined bourgeoisie that women represented, a theater manager or owner could ensure that his theater would be perceived as dignified. In sum, "[t]he primary distinguishing mark of the 'refined' vaudeville was not the show on stage but the women in the audience. A mixed audience was by definition a respectable one, a male-only one, indecent."[66] Pastor worked toward that goal by removing those aspects most apt to attract men only and aiming to attract women and families with giveaways of coal, flour, and dress patterns.

By 1881, when Pastor had settled in Union Square, he had established the custom of separating the saloon's services from the auditorium. He thereby discouraged the drunken revelry—as well as prostitution—with which variety theater had previously been associated. Later, he banned the serving of liquor altogether, further promoting vaudeville as a family entertainment.[67]

With time, vaudeville in America became a middle-class, urban entertainment; it developed further by incorporating the notion of providing "stage shows with something for everyone."[68] Or, rather, *almost* everyone. Usurping minstrelsy as the leading national amusement, vaudeville moved to prominence by the end of the nineteenth century. Similar to antebellum blackface minstrelsy, vaudeville's use of derogatory representations of blacks became a manner of controlling and defining the black image. With the decline of minstrelsy, vaudeville became the setting in which to provide this American entertainment.[69] Blacks were more likely fodder for vaudeville performances than a desired audience for its shows. Significantly, vaudeville became the leading means by which the coon songs and the music of Tin Pan Alley found their audiences and became nationally popularized.

Over time, vaudeville's leading entrepreneurs, B. F. Keith and Edward Albee, took Pastor's aim even further. Benjamin Franklin Keith had originally worked as an entertainer and promoter in the circus in the 1870s. He eventually moved on, opening a dime museum with a partner in 1883. Albee, who had also worked in the circus, began his work with Keith as an employee, overseeing construction of theaters in Providence and Philadelphia. He quickly moved up the ranks, however, and eventually became Keith's right-hand man. Working together, Keith served as the head of the Keith-Albee circuit and Albee ran the organization from behind the scenes.[70]

With the goal of attaining "the middle-class ideal of family-centered leisure," Keith and Albee stated that "catering to the best would cause the multitude to follow." They endeavored to draw the higher class of patron, whom the masses would emulate as a representative of culture and refinement.[71] The concept of "popular-priced" tickets aided them in their efforts, making the theater affordable for more than merely the upper class. In the mid-1880s, theater ticket prices averaged a dollar, an estimated two-thirds of a nonfarmworker's daily wage, which made theaters unaffordable for most of the city's inhabitants.[72] But with vaudeville's ten-cent seats, and years later "ten-twenty-thirty" theaters that sold the balcony for a dime and the best seats for thirty cents, middle- and working-class residents' access to amusements increased exponentially.[73]

Keith and Albee's 1893 opening of a Union Square theater in New York heralded the national development of vaudeville. Over the years the partners expanded their venture, and vaudeville became an industry unto itself. [74] Although Keith-Albee (later named the Keith Orpheum circuit following its expansion to the Midwest and the West Coast) was the dominant chain of theaters, numerous others also appeased New York City and the nation's craving for the new form of variety theater.[75]

As Keith and Albee's collection of theaters developed into a circuit, the partners established strict standards for their theaters, including rules of conduct for both performers and audience. An 1899 sign announced:

NOTICE TO PERFORMERS:

YOU ARE HEREBY WARNED THAT YOUR ACT MUST BE FREE FROM ALL VULGARITY AND SUGGESTIVENESS IN WORDS, ACTION AND COSTUME, WHILE PLAYING IN ANY OF MR. [KEITH'S] HOUSES, AND ALL VULGAR, DOUBLE-MEANING AND PROFANE WORDS AND SONGS MUST BE CUT OUT OF YOUR ACT BEFORE THE FIRST PERFORMANCE. IF YOU ARE IN DOUBT AS TO WHAT IS RIGHT OR WRONG, SUBMIT IT TO THE RESIDENT MANAGER AT REHEARSAL.

SUCH WORDS AS LIAR, SLOB, SON-OF-A-GUN, DEVIL, SUCKER, DAMN, AND ALL OTHER WORDS UNFIT FOR THE EARS OF LADIES AND CHILDREN, ALSO ANY REFERENCE TO QUESTIONABLE STREETS, RESORTS, LOCALITIES, AND BARROOMS, ARE PROHIBITED UNDER FINE OF INSTANT DISCHARGE.

GENERAL MANAGER[76]

Managers ensured that performers obeyed the rules by following through on their threats.

A contemporary writer testified, "Every word that is spoken or sung, gestures, pantomime, costumes, everything that goes to make up an act, undergoes a censorship infinitely more rigid than exercised in any high priced 'legitimate theater.'"[77] Performers had to toe the line, presenting material appropriate for the dignified audience of ladies that the theater owners envisioned. And such a demand was doubly enforced for black performers, as observed in other theatrical entertainment. In time, Keith-Albee theaters became known as the "Sunday School Circuit."[78]

Keith and Albee's endeavor may have been to provide "democratic entertainment for the masses," but their quest had obvious limits.[79] Although their popular-priced shows may have welcomed the working class as well as the middle class, they focused on whites and women in particular. They largely disregarded the black audience, strictly enforcing segregation in their theaters. Once admitted, regardless of their means, black theatergoers would be relegated to the worst part of the house: seating in the upper balcony or gallery.[80] Their placement in those sections, among poorly behaved white masses, often "accessible only from a back entrance off a dark and dangerous alleyway," reflected theater managers' thoughts about blacks in general.[81] Indeed, one manager would state his view simply yet cruelly, that it was not the "conduct of the Negroes [that] was objectionable, but their mere presence."[82]

Ultimately, blacks' greatest presence in vaudeville would be on the stage, rather than in the audience. By the 1880s and 1890s, blacks would become "the principal comic character," despite the previous prevalence of a variety of ethnic types, particularly the Irishman and the German greenhorn.[83] Not only would they serve as the butt of jokes for those white performers who would continue to make their names—and their careers—in blackface, but as entertainers they would be compelled to mock themselves as they played stereotypical representations of "blackness." Whereas white comics had a range of ethnicities available to them in their acts, from the "Irish" to "Hebrews" to "Dutch," blacks could only lampoon the "darky," or at other times, portray the Chinese.[84] That license to play Chinese characters most likely stemmed from the deeper sense of foreignness that society attached to them, despite the thousands who lived in New York and who had worked to build the transcontinental railroad.

In spite of blacks' role as leading entertainment, in the greatest of "big-time" vaudeville palaces, only one black act would be placed on a bill so as to limit their influence on the show and audience demographics. Blacks' participation in this theatrical world was clearly circumscribed and controlled by white performers' mocking characterizations as well as the preference of the white audiences.[85] Though black audiences often did attempt to register their dissatisfaction with their treatment in the theater both on and off the stage by boycotting venues, managers were not compelled to accommodate them. They comprised too small a portion of vaudeville's audience to persuade those in power to change their course.[86]

D espite the numerous constraints black performers faced, vaudeville also opened up new possibilities for entertainers. For Bert and George, vaudeville started their trajectory as stars. Koster and Bial's Music Hall, where they would perform, had been the venture of a team who had developed a lucrative business of numerous establishments, all offering alcohol and musical entertainment. Koster and Bial had taken over a former minstrel theater located on Twenty-third Street, utilizing a vaudeville format and selling liquor at the venue.[87] After many years of success, they later shifted to a theater located on the north side of Thirty-fourth Street between Broadway and Seventh Avenue. Oscar Hammerstein I, who had opened the Manhattan Opera House in 1892 with the futile hope of drawing an audience to operatic performance, approached the entrepreneurs, who took over his theater and opened Koster and Bial's New Music Hall in 1893 at the new location.[88] The three eventually broke their partnership over a disagreement regarding entertainers booked, however, with Hammerstein declaring his intention to create an even better quality vaudeville establishment that would drive Koster and Bial out of business. In the end, he would succeed.[89]

It was not long after Koster and Bial's move to the New Music Hall that Williams and Walker played the theater for their vaudeville turn, billing themselves as "Two Real Coons." The lean, dark-skinned diminutive George went without makeup, whereas the tall, fair-skinned Bert continued to don burnt cork and wear white gloves. They performed a comic singing and dancing act in vaudeville and variety houses, endeavoring to outdo whites in their claims of authenticity in the performance

Williams and Walker in Costume. COURTESY OF THE YALE COLLECTION OF
AMERICAN LITERATURE, BEINECKE RARE BOOK AND MANUSCRIPT LIBRARY

of blackness. In 1908, George would smartly express that choice: "We
thought that as there seemed to be a great demand for black faces on
the stage, we would do all we could to get what we felt belonged to us
by the law of nature."[90] Such decisions, encouraged by Walker as an
emerging business manager, helped Bert and George secure their singular place in entertainment.

Black entertainers' success depended on their ability to satisfy white
audiences' desire for "authentic" performances of blackness. Bert and

George's self-description as "Two Real Coons" was a recognizable response to that demand. The two refused the degenerate stereotype,
however, reshaping the caricature of white minstrels by replacing those
inauthentic portrayals with their "authentic" presentation. Utilizing the
exact language invoked by white performers, the two carved out a
space for themselves by reference to the genuine blackness evidenced
by their pigmentation.

Bert and George's choice to dub themselves "Two Real Coons" may
have actually aided them in their resistance of racial stereotyping. They
attempted to claim the despised term, using it consciously. Rather than
accept its assumption of inferiority, they took it on so as to assert their
"realness" in contrast to the counterfeit of white blackface performance. In that struggle, they gained some territory for the "natural
black" performer.[91] Furthermore, they called into question the possible
realness of blackface performers who only *emphasized* their artificiality
by recourse to burnt cork; after all, Williams did not really need the
burnt cork to be black.

Against this attempt at reinscription, however, convention demanded
that a fair-skinned man like Bert wear the minstrel mask to perform the
dominant society's idea of blackness. Lest he be misread as something
other than what he was—giving evidence of his traces of Caucasian
blood—he became the "darky" in blackface. Despite their desire to redefine blackness, Bert and George acted in accordance with the endur-
ing influences of minstrelsy. Bert donned burnt cork, and the two took
on the dreaded epithet of "coon." Because the demands made on the
black entertainer disallowed complete rejection of the stereotype, Bert
and George could not entirely refute the images of minstrelsy.

As performers, the two knew what their audience wanted. When
Williams and Walker took the stage, first at Koster and Bial's and later
moving to other vaudeville theaters both in and out of the city, critics
and audiences received them with increasing warmth. A 31 October 1896
review identified the two as "colored performers, who are coming
rapidly to the front," even as the bill listed and included numerous other
performers, both new and established, like Clifford and Huth, with
whom they shared a bill in San Francisco, and Maud Raymond, "serio-
comic."[92] Developing their "Two Real Coons" act, by December they had
moved to Proctor's at Twenty-third Street. The weeks passed, and by
the following January the *New York Dramatic Mirror* critic could say
that Williams and Walker, holding their own on a bill with the extremely

popular French singer, Yvette Guilbert, "continued to make their big hit with real 'coon' business."[93]

Onstage, Bert and George maintained minstrelsy's legacy through the very characters they played in their vaudeville turn. Indeed, they embodied two familiar classic types, Jim Crow and Zip Coon. Bert's stage character was the historical Jim Crow, or "darky," inspired by Thomas Dartmouth Rice's creation. A slow, dim-witted country-bumpkin, Jim Crow spoke in Southern black dialect and performed in blackface. He dressed in oversized, ill-fitting clothing as the indolent, ignorant character. George, on the other hand, played the Zip Coon or Jim Dandy, the urban man-about-town character George Washington Dixon developed. He dressed in high style, and acted the part of the smooth talker.

Although the two played stereotypical characters, they suppressed the more odious elements of those stereotypes. Like many other duo acts, including black comics Miller and Lyles, the famous white (non-blackface) ethnic comedy performers Joe Weber and Lew Fields, and later husband and wife team George Burns and Gracie Allen, they focused on the strength of their performance as opposites.[94] In rapid-fire dialogues, Williams and Walker utilized the Jim Crow and Zip Coon characters but chose to underplay dialect, instead focusing on the exchange between Williams as the innocent and Walker as the wily schemer:

WALKER: I tell you I'm letting you in on this because you're a friend of mine. I could do this alone and let no one in on it. But I want you to share in it just because we're good friends. Now after you get into the bank you fill the satchel with money.
WILLIAMS: Whose money?
WALKER: That ain't the point. We don't know who put the money there, and we don't know why they got it. And they won't know how we got it. All you have to do is fill the satchel; I'll get the satchel—you won't have nothing to bother about—that's 'cause you're a friend of mine, see?
WILLIAMS: And what do I do with this satchel?
WALKER: All you got to do is bring it to me at a place where I tell you.
WILLIAMS: When they come to count up the cash and find it short, then what?
WALKER: By that time we'll be far, far away—where the birds are singing sweetly and the flowers are in bloom.

Williams and Walker's Onstage Antics. COURTESY OF THE YALE
COLLECTION OF AMERICAN LITERATURE, BEINECKE RARE BOOK AND
MANUSCRIPT LIBRARY

WILLIAMS (*with doleful reflection*): And if they catch us they'll put
us so far, far away we never will hear no birds singin'. And everybody knows you can't smell no flowers through a stone wall.[95]

In a performance that moved toward a theme in ethnic comedy, the
country or Old World immigrant encountering the city or New World in-
habitant, Bert and George resisted the typical rendering of the stereotypes. Ending their repartee with the classic triumph—though here
understated—of the "stupid" country character through his use of "verbal trickery," Bert and George underscored elements of the exchange
that referenced the ethnic joke.[96] Bert's character engaged in rare but
incisive verbal manipulation, revealing his surprising awareness of the

social order, despite his recognized identity as simpleton. Thus, rather than drawing attention to stereotypes through dialect and raucous clowning, Bert and George settled their performance in the relationship between two characters whose divergent natures and manners of doing things resulted in comical situations.

The persistence of minstrelsy countered Bert and George's subtle resistances to the straight portrayal of stereotypes, however, carrying over and into the vaudeville scene. This resistance became increasingly manifest in society. It remained so, even though minstrelsy's demise putatively dated from 1895 with Nate Salsbury's *Black America*, a large-scale representation of plantation life staged in Brooklyn, complete with blacks in log cabins, which aimed to expose whites to the "real" Negro.[97] With payment of a twenty-five-cent admission, spectators could view *Black America*'s reproduction of a cotton field and observe interactions among blacks supposedly transported from the South, noting their vast range of dialects.[98] As a theatrical, *Black America* introduced a wide array of black entertainers, from dancers to singers, comedians to musicians. Yet, it also depended heavily on the representations of "old negro melodies . . . sung by large choruses of natural voices in the same manner that they have always been sung below Mason and Dixon's line." It emphasized this seeming authenticity, presenting it as an ethnological exploration, as the "peculiarities of Southern blacks [were] exemplified, and their treats [were] all shown."[99] Making the minstrel show a literal reality, the images it displayed continued to carry weight even after the minstrel show lost its particular and peculiar power.

Although *Black America* may have been the harbinger of blackface minstrelsy's end, its images extended into cartoons, the popular music of Tin Pan Alley, postcards, advertisements, vaudeville, musical theater, movies, and even after that, radio.[100] Meanwhile, Williams and Walker aimed to distinguish themselves in an act that rose above mere stereotype and offered the audience something extraordinary. Ultimately, their means would be the incorporation of a new spectacle, but only after they made a great discovery: Ada Reed Overton.

Even as Williams and Walker did their run in vaudeville toward the end of 1896, the American Tobacco Company invited them to be featured in advertising for its product, Old Virginia Sheroots. The company, however, wanted two women to appear in the ads with Bert and George. Having taken up residence in New York, the two quickly found

Aida Overton Walker. COURTESY OF THE YALE COLLECTION OF
AMERICAN LITERATURE, BEINECKE RARE BOOK AND MANUSCRIPT
LIBRARY

one woman to participate, named Stella Wiley. A performer whom
they'd met during their short-lived run with *The Octoroons* in Chicago,
Stella had found her way to New York. And the smooth and confident
George had found a way to get her to date him. When the American Tobacco Company job came along, Stella eagerly sought another girl to
complete the foursome. She found Ada.[101]

A strong, principled, and independent thinker, Ada had had a recent
disagreeable brush with stage life. When touring with the Black Patti
Troubadours, a company headed by black soprano Sissieretta Jones
(nicknamed Black Patti after Italian opera star, Adelina Patti), there

arose a disagreement between performers and managers. Ada had quickly removed herself from the fray, retiring from the stage. Viewing the American Tobacco Company opportunity as a short-term job, however, she posed with the others for the photos. She then took her pay and left, thinking that would be the end of their interaction.[102]

In fact, it was merely the beginning. Williams and Walker's manager, seeing the advertisement, decided to create a production based on the publicity photos. The photos had displayed the two couples dancing, pairing off in a series of gestures that suggested the elegance of the ladies and the grace of the men. Their manager had every intention of utilizing the same women, as well as the same costumes, in the production. When George sent for Ada seeking her participation, however, she stoutly refused. Undeterred, and perhaps further motivated by the challenge, George made it his personal mission to secure Ada's participation. It took several personal visits and requests for him to succeed in convincing her to perform. Eventually he did, but with the agreement that the performances would play only in New York.[103]

Bert and George's manager wanted them to perform as they did in the photos, featuring the dance, called the "cakewalk," in their show. Their choice to perform the dance and to add the two "dusky maidens" to their act would distinguish their performance on vaudeville bills. Ada in particular, who would become the leading choreographer of the future Williams and Walker Company, made a difference that not only equaled great success for Williams and Walker but also created a national craze for the dance. Although Williams and Walker were not the cakewalk's innovators, by the time they were done popularizing it, their names would be forever linked with the dance. And by the time they finished touring, Ada would have begun her transformation. With fame, she would change her name to Aida, and in less than three years she would marry George, becoming Aida Overton Walker.[104]

A dance tied to African tribal rituals, the cakewalk had links to cultural traditions predating blacks' arrival to the Americas. In the New World, however, the dance dated back to slavery as the plantation slaves' satire of the Southern aristocracy's dances and manners.[105] In many ways, it was a study as well as an integration of differing European and African aesthetics. African dance featured "gliding, dragging, shuffling steps, [a] flexed, fluid bodily position as opposed to the stiffly erect position of European dancers," and the cakewalk worked with and against these tensions, although slave masters did not likely recognize the dance for the partial satire that it was.[106] Slaves, dressed in their finest clothes, would perform before their masters and mistresses, attempting to outdo each other in their displays. At the end of the dance, the mistress of the big house might give the winner a prize cake.[107]

As the dance gained more visibility, it was exported to minstrelsy; in minstrel shows that included a "walkabout" or "strut," it became a featured part of the show.[108] The dance thereby became the performance of white entertainers in blackface who imitated a black dance created to lampoon whites. By the time Williams and Walker performed it, the irony was even further heightened—or deepened—as these blacks now performed a dance imitating whites who mocked blacks who satirized whites' pretentious and fussy mannerisms.[109]

The dance itself was "originally a kind of shuffling movement which evolved into a smooth walking step with the body held erect. The backward sway was added, and as the dance became more of a satire on the dance of the plantation owners, the movement became a prancing strut."[110] Through Williams and Walker, it reached the height of popularity and fashion as evidenced by the insatiable demand of elite society. The city and the nation's upper class eagerly sought Ada's instruction as they desired to learn and master the cakewalk.[111] In later years, Williams and Walker would present the dance in their musical comedy productions to great acclaim.

As for Williams and Walker's rendition of the cakewalk, years later white Harlem Renaissance patron Carl Van Vechten would excitedlly recall Walker's version: "How the fellow did prance in the cakewalk, throwing his chest and his buttocks out in opposite directions, until he resembled a pouter pigeon more than a human being!"[112] Williams, too, had much to do with the popularization of the dance. His distinctive moves so puzzled some reviewers that they could hardly describe them. One Boston critic attempted to explain: "He just wiggles his legs, crooks his knees, falls over his feet, bends his back."[113]

Despite the eager response of audiences to the cakewalk, there was also a risk: for reviewers, such dancing folded neatly into minstrelsy-inflected ideas of what constituted characteristic movement of the black body. The flamboyant Zip Coon and the dim-witted Jim Crow's bodies were viewed as "eccentric, strange, physically dynamic, hysterically out of control, and naïve," matching the perceptions of the characters themselves.[114] Mystifying bodily gyrations exemplified the hilarity of blackness and the barely contained energy of black subjects. There seemed to be no adequate description for what those out-of-control bodies did onstage. Yet, while white reviewers seemed baffled, other dancers, like James Barton, would recognize Williams's dance as the "Mooche" or "Grind," his loose-jointedness clearly stylized and specific, while dancer Walter Crumbley would see in Walker's prancing promenade a perfected strut.[115]

As the cakewalk caught momentum with Williams and Walker's performances, their production became larger and grander. On 16 January 1897, the "dusky maidens" were their only companions for the cakewalk, which they performed in addition to Williams's now hit song, "Oh! I Don't Know, You're Not So Warm!" But by February, the group had expanded to "a score of celebrated high-steppers," becoming a "big feature" on the bill.[116] At the month's end, much of the Koster and Bial review was dedicated first and foremost to discussing Williams and Walker's "big cake walk . . . which made an instantaneous hit." With considerable elaboration, the critic described the appearance of a drum major, "juggling a baton," and a master of ceremonies, "full of life and action . . . who led on the seven couples who took part in the walk." During the unfolding performance, each couple featured individually "as they stalked or pranced around the stage, [and] the audience was kept in constant laughter." Williams and Walker served as the highlight of the show, of course. After that point, they appeared with Stella and Ada: "Their actions were more eccentric than any of the others, and it is to be presumed that they won the cake."[117]

Clearly, with each passing performance, Williams and Walker mastered and added drama to their presentation of the cakewalk. The *New York Dramatic Mirror* critic affirmed this in March of 1897 when he wrote that the team "captured the house as they always do. They have made a hit which has placed them in the front rank of the top liners."[118] Their cakewalk performances eventually took them out of the city with the now more-than-willing Ada, as they traveled to Philadelphia creating "a genuine sensation," to San Francisco providing an "excellent" show, and to Chicago delivering "lots of fun."[119] Amidst this time of increasing success and travel, Bert and George also enjoyed the invitation to perform abroad in London. Unfortunately, the team did not go over well there. Looking back, Williams would archly remark: "I was at the Empire in London and went on immediately after the ballet, and promptly died. They taught me to know better than to try to follow a ballet."[120]

Even as Williams and Walker were "applauded to the echo" for their performances, they still faced the disdain and disrespect of those who would not accept them because of their race.[121] While performing their run in New York, they featured second on the bill with Maurice Barrymore, an actor of the legitimate stage, and a member of the great Barrymore acting family. While Williams performed, Barrymore stood in the wings, watching his technique, a regular custom for the actor. A stagehand nearby asked, "Like him, huh?" Barrymore replied, "Yes. He's terrific." It was then that the stagehand said, just as Williams left the stage and passed by, "Yeah, he's a good nigger, knows his place." To this, Williams reportedly muttered, "Yes, a good nigger knows his place. Going there now. Dressing Room One!"[122]

Even if a possibly apocryphal tale, there was no question that Williams and Walker encountered resistance in the face of their ensuing and extraordinary success. Once one among many offerings on a vaudeville bill, they increasingly became a highlight, drawing attention away from other acts and toward their distinctive performance. They more than held their own against leading white comedians in blackface like McIntyre and Heath.[123]

With their unique style, the cakewalk craze and its proliferation of contests and prizes, and, eventually, the attention of New York's elite, Williams and Walker rose to the top of the vaudeville scene. Years later, author James Weldon Johnson would write that the duo drove their publicity machine even further, approaching William Vanderbilt in 1898 to propose a cakewalk contest to determine who "shall deserve the title of champion cake-walker of the world."[124] Even more would come of their efforts as Ada continued to teach the dance to elites, particularly after Williams and Walker's reprisal of the cakewalk in their biggest production, yet to come.

Despite their astounding success with the cakewalk and their performances, however, Williams and Walker faced the denouncement of some black critics for their use of the dance. They were up against a certain segment of the black community who rejected it. In an 1898 editorial in the black periodical the *Indianapolis Freeman*, a writer stated his case:

> As a representative of the colored race I desire to enter my protest against the "cake walk" which is now becoming a fad among some colored people,

encouraged by the whites. . . . The whites go to these exhibitions of buffoonery to laugh at and ridicule the monkefied contortions of the principal actors. . . . I insist that the cake walk is beneath the dignity of the
better class of "the race," and that it brings them into ridicule and contempt . . . and so should be frowned down by the better class of colored
people.[125]

One critic believed that the cakewalk had had a previously more dignified past. By its inclusion in the minstrel show and presentation on the
stage, however, it had become a degraded spectacle, "humiliating because of the monkey shines and the further fact that whites who use it
as a means of making money engage the lowest strata of society."[126]
Even as they launched themselves with the extraordinary success of
the cakewalk, Williams and Walker would have to answer increasingly
to a black public that wanted to promote "racial uplift." That black public would militate against the constraints of a racist white audience fascinated by and seemingly obsessed with black stereotypes. They would
insist that Williams and Walker take their place in the fight. And as
Bert, George, and the talented Ada moved onward with future projects,
they would be compelled to demonstrate again and again their commitment to a community that saw their success as a means to represent the
best and brightest that black America had to offer.

4

Rolling into
Black Musical Theater

When Bert and George touched down in New York, despite its magnitude they quickly found a home that put them in contact with the finest young black artists in the city. They arrived at the perfect time—the cultural scene of black New York was about to explode. Long before the duo had finished their run at Koster and Bial's, as George would say, "[W]e discovered an important fact . . . the one hope of the colored performer must be in making a radical departure from the old 'darky' style of singing and dancing. So we set ourselves the task of thinking along new lines."[1] Even as Bert and George made the most of their "Two Real Coons" act, knowing that they had to strive for more, they moved on. The artists they discovered in New York not only shared their dreams but would help make those dreams a reality.

Years later, the duo would claim to have had a plan. "The first move was to hire a flat in Fifty-third Street, furnish it, and throw our doors open to all colored men who possessed theatrical and musical ability and ambition," George would explain. "The Williams and Walker flat soon become [sic] the headquarters of all the artistic young men of our race who were stage-struck."[2] For George in particular, this would be a mission, as he and Bert "decided to make the break [from the ragtime limitations of the "darky"] so as to save ourselves and others."[3]

Through the duo's association with some of the most established
artists, including poet and novelist Paul Laurence Dunbar, "America's
first professional black literary man,"[4] and internationally known violinist and composer Will Marion Cook, Williams and Walker would become the premier black act in New York as well as the nation. They
would strive to break free from stereotypes and achieve unparalleled
success in the theater. And they would take their places among such
ambitious and successful performers as vaudevillians Bob Cole and
Billy Johnson, and comedian Ernest Hogan, of "All Coons Look Alike to
Me" fame.

At the time of Bert and George's arrival in New York, the black population in the city was miniscule; in fact, through the first decade
of the twentieth century, it would never exceed 1.9 percent of the city's
total population.[5] By the turn of the century, the entire black population
in New York City would number a mere 60,666 souls. That sum would
include residents in all five boroughs, although most blacks lived in
Manhattan. Less than 10 percent of that 60,666 would be foreign-born,
many of them having fled poverty in the Caribbean. And increasingly,
Southern migrants, who sought economic freedom from the crop-lien
system and an escape from the injustice of the post-Reconstruction
South, would contribute to the population's growing numbers. Despite
the black population's small size, it grew continuously, with a 79 percent
increase between 1890 and 1900.[6]

Over the years, as New York's population had grown, the city had
also expanded, spreading northward. Blacks had moved northward just
as others of the population did. And although the city had no official
policy of segregation in housing, as blacks moved into new neighborhoods, white landlords restricted their access to certain areas. In time,
those sections of the city quickly became segregated. With each northward push into a new area, the population found itself pressed into living in a newly established "Negro" section with little or no freedom of
choice regarding where they might take up residence. While it was true
that some blacks preferred living among other members of their race,
the fact that those individuals did not have the option of integration evidenced the reality of *de facto* segregation.[7]

Furthermore, blacks generally resided in the poorest working-class
areas. The neighborhoods in which they lived, often located near wa-

terfronts neglected by the city, seemed fated to become slums.[8] Blacks were "allowed to occupy the houses of unsavory reputation which the police had cleared and for which decent white tenants could not be found," Jacob Riis wrote in *How the Other Half Lives*.[9] And regardless of the area in which blacks resided, they consistently paid the highest rents of all the neighborhood's residents.[10] Riis explained: "The reason advanced for this systematic robbery is that white people will not live in the same house with colored tenants, or even in a house recently occupied by negroes, and that consequently, its selling price is injured."[11] Landlords recouped their purportedly lost investments by demanding higher rents from blacks whom they admitted.

From the middle to the end of the nineteenth century, the black population moved from the south end of the city, in Greenwich Village, toward midtown, having been displaced by Italian immigrants. In the 1870s, the majority of blacks eked out an existence in the Tenderloin district, which stretched roughly between Fifth and Seventh Avenues, from Twenty-third to Forty-second Streets on the west side.[12] Named as such by Police Captain Alexander Williams, who upon transferring to the precinct archly declared that while previously he had had chuck steak, from then on he would have tenderloin, the area was one with nefarious nighttime activity, infamous for corruption and scandal.[13] By the 1890s, the black population had been pushed still further northward, as the Tenderloin area expanded into "Old" and "New," the new neighborhood ending at the upper fifties.[14] Past that was San Juan Hill. The neighborhood's name, with its reference to the battle during the Spanish-American War, satirically acknowledged the battles waged between blacks and white immigrants in the contested area.[15] Located roughly between Sixtieth and Sixty-fourth Streets and Tenth and Eleventh Avenues on the city's west side, San Juan Hill was a densely populated area. By the time of Bert and George's arrival to the city, the vast majority of blacks lived in the New Tenderloin and San Juan Hill.

In the 1890s, most blacks labored at unskilled jobs for low wages. More than 90 percent earned their living doing menial work. Although white immigrants also suffered the degradations of low-paying, backbreaking labor, the difference for blacks was their limited upward mobility—the inability to get ahead, beyond subsistence. The black middle class, a tiny portion of the population, worked as clerks, in entertainment as actors and musicians, as music instructors, and in small business for themselves. Many blacks in both the working and middle classes lost their foothold in their métiers, however, as the greater acceptance of white immigrant workers resulted in their further displacement.[16]

Even as the black residents of San Juan Hill and the New Tenderloin struggled to survive in congested tenements, prominent blacks and the black theatrical community enjoyed a rare oasis: "Black Bohemia." As Reverdy C. Ransom, pastor of Bethel African Methodist Episcopal Church, would recall, it was "the principal place of resort for *our* group." A vital area that flourished in the midst of poverty, disease, graft, and vice, it evidenced the continued endurance and hope of the community. By around 1900, Black Bohemia would boast churches, headquarters of black fraternal orders, and the Negro YMCA.[17]

Located on Fifty-third Street west of Eighth Avenue, the blessed Black Bohemia was regrettably far afield from the lights of Broadway and the center of vaudeville. This resulted in black performers having considerably less exposure to opportunities for work, compared to the convenience white performers enjoyed. Many white entertainers lived in the areas surrounding Union and Madison squares, the center of it all.[18] Nonetheless, for whatever drawbacks there were to living in the more distant area, there were equally—or perhaps more—significant benefits. The community of black artists thrived, fueled by drive and commitment.

In 1898, Bert and George lived at 127 and 129 West Fifty-third Street: the illustrious black-owned Marshall Hotel, in the midst of Black Bohemia. More like a boardinghouse than a proper hotel, the establishment, housed in two four-story brownstones, was elegant and sophisticated with a classy restaurant that provided patrons with sumptuous food in plush surroundings.[19] Owned by Jimmie Marshall, it was well known as a center for black intellectuals and artists, and hosted several of the entertainers with whom Williams and Walker would make their name.

Furthermore, it was a black-and-tan establishment, at which black entertainers performed before audiences of both blacks and whites. That alone made the place seem scandalous rather than upscale to city reformers, who claimed that it had a largely white female and black male clientele who indulged in "questionable orgies and revels . . . nightly."[20] Actually, artists converged at the Marshall, participating actively in creating and maintaining a community. In one of its two public spaces, musicians and singers entertained as couples either danced or listened. In the other, guests gathered for conversation and "discrete rendezvous," at times between black men and white women.[21]

Opportunities for interracial interaction allowed some, like black musician James Reese Europe, to more freely enjoy the company of white female friends or mixed gatherings.[22] For others, it was a means to nurture dalliances. The suave George Walker would gain a reputation for appealing to both black and white women during his time spent at the Marshall. And his attractiveness to interracial female audiences would continue, despite his relationship with and later marriage to Ada.

In time, prominent black artists joined the Marshall Hotel's community, like the Johnson brothers, James Weldon and J. Rosamond. James Weldon would establish himself as a composer, writer, and later, activist, whereas J. Rosamond would make his name as a musician and composer, working with Bob Cole. Cole would marry actress Stella Wiley, George's former girlfriend. Performers whom George and Bert encountered in Chicago playing *The Octoroons* would also turn up, like Jesse Shipp and Will Accooe.

When the Johnson Brothers arrived in New York and at the Marshall Hotel in 1899, James Weldon was overwhelmed. The location was the height of fashion for the city's blacks, as he noted "crowds of well-dressed colored men and women lounging and chatting in the parlors, loitering over their coffee and cigarettes while they talked or listened to the music."[23] Yet at the Marshall, these crowds did more than loiter. Many of them debated about the future of the Negro artists and organized. They recognized the importance of their contributions, and together, they sought to further dignify the image of the black entertainer. By 1910, James Reese Europe would create and head the Clef Club for musicians, which was part union and part benevolent association and booking agency.[24]

Although in New York black artists engaged in developing and honing their skills among a critical mass of emergent talent, in many cases they continued work that had been most encouraged by exposure to world's fairs in Chicago and other cities, like Atlanta. The fairs had introduced the nation—and indeed, the world—to technological, artistic, and commercial advances suggesting the "beginning of a new age."[25] Although they did not generally consider the contributions of

African Americans to American civilization, the fact of ragtime's reception heartened some hopeful blacks.[26]

The fairs, which had been impressive and inspiring for people like ragtime composer Scott Joplin, had been a significant way for black artists and intellectuals to meet each other. Two of the most important artists with whom Bert and George would work in New York encountered each other first at the Chicago World's Fair: Paul Laurence Dunbar and Will Marion Cook.

Dunbar, an aspiring poet, had traveled to Chicago in 1893. There he met Joseph Douglass, the grandson of Frederick Douglass, the nineteenth-century black leader.[27] Frederick Douglass, who had written *Narrative of the Life of Frederick Douglass, an American Slave* in 1849, had established himself as an eloquent, passionate abolitionist and orator. He continued to reign as singularly influential among blacks in the nation. At the time of the fair, he served as the U.S. minister to Haiti.[28]

Soon after Joseph and Paul's meeting, Joseph eagerly introduced Dunbar to Frederick Douglass himself. During his introduction, the accomplished Dunbar quickly won Douglass's trust and respect. Douglass, who held a post as commissioner of the fair's Haitian exhibition, hired Dunbar as clerk, paying him a salary of five dollars per week from his own pocket.[29] Through this connection, Dunbar met Cook.

Cook's college-educated parents had been friends of Frederick Douglass. A remarkably gifted violinist, Cook had benefited from the dignitary's influence, as Douglass aided in raising money to send the young man away to Berlin at age fifteen for tutelage with Hungarian violinist Joseph Joachim.[30] Abroad, Cook had enjoyed the patronage of white audiences who valued his virtuosity and accepted him. Back in Chicago, he participated in the fight for blacks' involvement in the fair.

Despite black audiences' enthusiasm for the fair, organizers had at best disregarded their attendance and participation. Those African Americans who hoped to display their contributions to society had had to make an appeal to Congress for the honor of participation. It had resulted in an exhibit and a special program, "Colored American Day."[31] Douglass advocated the Colored American Day, in part so as to support Will's plan to mount an opera there based on Harriett Beecher Stowe's *Uncle Tom's Cabin*, the 1852 novel still respected at the time for its image of the self-sacrificing Christ-like slave, Uncle Tom.[32]

It is evident that the World's Fair, and others like it, had a far-reaching effect on those who attended. Colored American Day, though criticized by the black press as an unacceptable surrender to the insulting, bigoted system of segregation, found the support of the black public. Figures indicating that more than two-thirds of the day's 2,500 attendees were black proved that efforts to focus on and address the accomplishments of the black world had succeeded in attracting attention.[33]

When Dunbar appeared onstage that day, he read his specially prepared poem, "Colored Americans," using the platform as a chance to speak about the entitlement of the nation's blacks:

> *And their deeds shall find a record*
> *In the registry of Fame;*
> *For their blood has cleansed completely*
> *Every blot of Slavery's shame.*

> *So all honor and all glory*
> *To those noble sons of Ham*
> *The gallant colored soldiers*
> *Who fought for Uncle Sam!*[34]

Confidently, Dunbar proclaimed that the nation's blacks had risen above what he saw as the shameful history of slavery, illustrating their nobility and gallantry. The largely black audience's thunderous applause came directly after hearing that this work had been Dunbar's own creation, a statement affirming his belief in the rights of African Americans.

Dunbar knew as well as did other artists the limitations and risks blacks confronted as they pursued their art. His poem, "We Wear the Mask," published in his 1896 collection, *Lyrics of Lowly Life*, would describe the black performer's challenges as eloquently as it did the general black population's experience:

> *We wear the mask that grins and lies,*
> *It hides our cheeks and shades our eyes,—*
> *This debt we pay to human guile,*
> *With torn and bleeding hearts we smile,*
> *And mouth with myriad subtleties.*

Why should the world be overwise,
In counting all our tears and sighs?
Nay, let them only see us, while
We wear the mask.

We smile, but, O great Christ, our cries
To thee from tortured souls arise.
We sing, but oh the clay is vile
Beneath our feet, and long the mile;
But let the world dream otherwise,
We wear the mask![35]

In the post-Reconstruction era, it appeared that blacks were to wear a metaphorical mask, hiding their suffering and "tortured souls" in order to serve as the national joke and the natural entertainer. Black minstrels were even further expected to don the literal mask of blackface created by whites to signify "black." A projection, it began in the imagination of racist whites rather in the lives of actual blacks. In his poem, Dunbar touched upon the very issues that plagued the souls of America's blacks, and most certainly a sensitive though dynamic performer like Bert.

As a classically trained violinist and composer, Cook had already received the would-be seal of approval, having worked abroad and in New York with Antonín Dvořák, renowned composer of Symphony No. 9 in E Minor, "From the New World." Nonetheless, he faced obstacles in his efforts to pursue his art. In the States he met resistance to his efforts to play, compose, and conduct concert music. He would later shift his focus to composing and working with Negro music, yet without abandoning his orchestral training.[36]

Cook's superior confidence in his skills, and his tendency to be wary of those who might cheat or undercut him, added to the challenges he faced. He had considerable difficulty making things go his way. Not only did he possess a grand vision of taking Negro music into the legitimate theater, which theater managers and producers viewed with skepticism, but he also was intransigent, a result of his natural arrogance and independence. Some individuals, black and white, were inclined to rebuff the outspoken, often irascible artist. Having received his due respect in Europe, Cook was disinclined to tolerate slights or offenses, intentional or not. He was uncompromising and proud.[37]

Cook and Dunbar worked together first on *Clorindy, or The Origin of the Cakewalk*. The brainchild of Will Marion Cook, who would write the music as Dunbar wrote the book, *Clorindy* was a musical about the beginnings of the cakewalk in 1880s Louisiana. At a time when the performances of vaudeville and other forms of theater focused on racial "authenticity" while also harking back to some mythologized ideal of Southern plantation life, black artists like Cook used such claims as a way to create more realistic representations of blacks' own histories and experience.[38] Rather than settling into hyperbolic blackface performance that focused nostalgically on plantation life, Cook aimed for a reflection of blacks' actual postemancipation lives and, importantly, communities.

Years later, Cook would recount glowingly his and Dunbar's efforts to write the show:

> We got together in the basement of my brother John's rented house on Sixth Street, just below Howard University, one night about eight o'clock. We had two dozen bottles of beer, a quart of whisky, and we took my brother's porterhouse steak, cut it up with onions and red peppers and ate it raw. Without a piano or anything but the kitchen table, we finished all the songs, all the libretto and all but a few bars of the ensembles by four o'clock the next morning. By that time Paul and I were happy, so happy that we were ready to cry "Eureka!" only we couldn't make any noise at that hour, so both of us sneaked off to bed, Paul to his house three blocks away and I to my room.[39]

Although written in a seemingly wild and rapid fury, the musical pleased Cook. The piece would be his first Negro operetta, and he had great expectations.

The next day, while working the piano on what he described as "my most Negroid song, 'Who Dat Say Chicken in Dis Crowd?'," however, his mother had a most dramatic response to his creation. She entered the living room, her face covered in tears: "Oh, Will! Will! I've sent you all over the world to study and become a great musician, and you return such a *nigger*!"[40] Shamed by her son's departure from European classical music, Cook's mother could not see or appreciate the merit of music utilizing syncopation and lyrics written in the African American vernacular. Despite Cook's dreams that his musical creation would mark a new era of Negro music moving onto the legitimate stage, he knew that he could hold out hope for only his own generation. Blacks of his mother's generation would not yet be ready for these Negro songs.

Even as Cook wrote the work for Bert and George, who continued to tour in vaudeville, the notion that blacks needed to remain in "their place" held true. When Cook went to Isidore Witmark, a top Tin Pan Alley publisher, to present his pieces, he waited two hours before being given forty minutes to attempt to introduce the new music to him. After the session, Witmark abruptly walked out, flatly refusing Cook and thinking him "crazy to believe that any Broadway audience would listen to Negroes singing Negro opera."[41] Nonetheless, despite this initial rejection, Cook did eventually win Witmark over with his persistence, confidence, and "the sheer extraordinariness" of his music.[42] Subsequently, the show secured the support Cook sought. It would be performed on the Casino Theatre's roof garden, accomplishing a rare feat: landing a Broadway house.

Although Cook and Dunbar had wanted Williams and Walker to star in *Clorindy*, the duo was wrapping up their very successful vaudeville run as the production prepared to mount. So, in the summer of 1898, Ernest Hogan, then the leading black comedian, starred in it in their stead. A hit with audiences, the show disappointed Dunbar, who had hoped the production would surmount stereotype, presenting an innovative image of black life and culture. In rehearsal, they had had to abandon Dunbar's libretto, largely because the uncovered roof garden setting rendered the long lines of dialogue impossible to hear.[43] To Dunbar's dismay, it seemed the story had been replaced with the standard coon imagery that he and others found distasteful.

Although Dunbar himself had written dialect poems, he was conscious of its limitations and would later remind others, "You know, of course, that I didn't start as a dialect poet. I simply came to the conclusion that I could write it as well, if not better, than anyone else I knew of, and that by doing it I should gain a hearing. I gained a hearing, and now they don't want me to write anything but dialect."[44] He was quite aware of the ways that submission to the demands to use stereotype could bind the black artist.

Still seeking to mount a show featuring Williams and Walker, however, Dunbar and Cook collaborated again, on a work titled *Senegambian Carnival*. Evidently an expansion and reworking of *Clorindy*,

Senegambian Carnival featured the stars and showcased a variety of talented performers rather than elaborating a single story. As was common for the period, a musical was typically a series of songs strung together with a number of dance acts. In late nineteenth-century musicals, songs were significant in and of themselves; often there was no link between them, nor a relationship to the overall story. The songs did not drive the story of the musical forward so much as relate or connect to characters the actors in the musical portrayed. Furthermore, with the influence of Tin Pan Alley's pluggers and their efforts to make songs into hits, some musicals included songs simply because an individual performer preferred it over others.[45]

Senegambian Carnival opened on 29 August 1898, in Massachusetts, at the Boston Theatre. It starred Williams playing "a newly rich prospector named Dollar Bill," opposite Walker's Silver King, a con man out to steal his money.[46] Without extant librettos, one can glean the show's content and structure only from contemporary reviews. The musical appeared at times to have a developing story, but was hardly consistent from one location to another, if critics are to be believed.[47] In Cincinnati, a reporter remarked: "The first act is a plantation scene in the South. The darkies are supposed to depict the primitive slave days with the sunset festivities in the slave quarters. They dance and sing to their heart's content."[48] In contrast, in Boston a journalist recalled that "the carnival opens at a steamboat landing on the Mississippi, where an excursion is to be taken north."[49]

Despite such discrepancies, it is clear that the show paralleled vaudeville's format, including a range of specialties, from singing to comedians to acrobats, in addition to the cakewalk finale, by then one of Williams and Walker's most popular presentations.[50] The hit song of the show was "Who Dat Say Chicken in Dis Crowd," a reprise from *Clorindy*.[51] In many ways a coon song, it possessed lines referring to blacks' stereotypical craving for and obsession with eating chicken:

> *Who dat say chicken in dis crowd?*
> *Speak de word agin' and speak it loud*
> *Blame de lan' let white folk rule it*
> *I'se a lookin' fuh a pullet*
> *Who dat say chicken in dis crowd?*[52]

Yet, it also held traits of a black melodic idiom that rendered it distinctive and popular among the songs released as sheet music.[53]

As Bert and George worked together in the company, Bert, as comedian, came to the foreground. His performance seemed to fascinate audiences. Critics, who placed him noticeably out front, verified his obviously outstanding performance time and again. A *Washington Post* critic wrote: "Bert Williams is one of the cleverest delineators of Negro characters on the stage, and has no trouble at all keeping his audience in tears of laughter."[54]

It was during the production of *Senegambian Carnival* that Bert met Charlotte (Lottie) Thompson. A singer in the show, Lottie had met Bert while *Senegambian Carnival* was in rehearsal. Eight years Bert's senior and a widow, Lottie hailed from Illinois. She had been married to a businessman and living in Chicago before moving to New York City to pursue acting. Youthful, though obviously an experienced woman, she possessed a vitality that Bert found appealing, a quiet grace that matched his elegant reserve. She carried herself demurely, yet was extroverted enough to enjoy and desire a life in theater.

If the theme of romance had been acceptable for blacks onstage—during the time, white theater producers and managers barred the topic—at some point, Lottie might have played opposite Bert. Yet, it's likely that, even had the dominant society accepted such a theme, she still might not have pursued such a part for other reasons. Lottie was, in many ways, a private, reserved woman. And unlike George's Ada, Lottie did not have an engaging dynamism onstage that captured the audience's attention. But that hardly mattered offstage: during *Senegambian Carnival*'s rehearsals, she'd captured Bert's.

While courting Lottie, Bert visited her at her sister Carrie's home, in Chicago's Hyde Park. During that visit, he enchanted Lottie's three nieces, Charlotte, Eunice, and Laura, with his amusing stories, doting on them. In the children's eyes, perhaps the most wonderful aspect of Bert's personality was his willingness to make fun of himself. During one visit to the house at Fifty-fifth Street and Cottage Grove, he had worn brown patent leather shoes that caused him excruciating pain. The girls had encouraged him to take them off, which he did. When it came time for him to head home, however, he couldn't get them back on. The next day, he told a tale about the ordeal, full of embellish-

Charlotte (Lottie) Williams. COURTESY OF THE YALE COLLECTION
OF AMERICAN LITERATURE, BEINECKE RARE BOOK AND MANUSCRIPT
LIBRARY

ments. He had walked home carrying shoes in one hand, his cane in the
other. When he got to the elevated train, he happily gave his shoes to
a man who claimed they'd fit him. Riding over to the Loop in shoeless
comfort, he walked over to the Sherman Hotel and, with nary a word
to anyone, went boldly through the lobby and right up to his room in
his socks.[55]

Most likely a tall tale, it nonetheless endeared Bert to the girls, who
giggled endlessly, tickled by the image of the big tall man, shoeless
and shameless. Although a humorous story, it also highlighted the

circulation problem with which Bert had always struggled and would continue to struggle his entire life. He would seldom complain, except when making the story material for a joke, choosing otherwise to suffer in silence.

Lottie's family received Bert happily, and the couple married in New York on 21 September 1899. Bert's mother, Julia, served as a witness.[56] Although they made no public announcement in the press, Bert had certainly made an impression on Lottie's family, who mattered most.

Lottie was a gentle and supportive presence, one that Bert needed in his life. She stepped into the role a seeming natural, elaborating on details about Bert's character in exchanges with journalists. Awed by his intelligence and attractiveness, she was his greatest fan and protector. Over the years, she would always be nearby during interviews conducted in the library of their Harlem brownstone, admiring her husband's incomparable poise. All the while, however, she seemed a somewhat distant spectator to his life and, perhaps, even to her own.

Still, in these early days, as she traveled with the company to perform, she learned to become one of the group. She came to be quite an amusing storyteller. And there was nothing she relished talking about more than her beloved, handsome Bert.[57]

By the time Bert and George's next musical appeared in theaters, they had the Hurtig Brothers, Benjamin and Jules, and Harry Seamon as their producers. The Hurtigs and Seamon had ventured into booking famous vaudeville acts like Sophie Tucker, "The Last of the Red Hot Mamas"; building their own theaters, including Hurtig and Seamon's Harlem Music Hall (which would later become the Apollo); even going into music publishing, from which Bert and George would benefit, publishing several songs with the company.[58] Their management brought distinction to Williams and Walker, as well as considerably more exposure. It also provided means, as Bert acquired his own valet, Chappy (William Chappelle), to assist him during his costume changes.

Moreover, the Hurtigs and Seamon had a connection to Broadway; through their affiliation, the duo would gain at least the opportunity to press for access to the city's greatest theaters, using their mounting popularity as grounds for their breakthrough. Although they had gained increasing prominence, they continued to play theaters around—but off—Broadway, not yet having achieved a cherished dream.

𝒲illiams and Walker's next show, *A Lucky Coon,* another written by Cook and Dunbar, further expanded on the story of Dollar Bill and Silver King.[59] Sensitive to the use of the offensive term "coon," Bert and George offset the effects of the word in advertisements that emphasized class and tact; as always, they included their offstage images, elegant and wearing suits.[60] Thus they emphasized the reality of their dignified demeanors, which countered the characters they played. Opening in late 1898 in New York, *A Lucky Coon* presented a loose story, held together with variety performances, still not quite a complete and continuous narrative. The show describes Dollar Bill's trip to New York City, where he wins $30,000 in the lottery, subsequently coming into a risky situation as Silver King attempts to get his hands on the money. Nonetheless, with Silver King's help, Dollar Bill succeeds in entering "Darktown" (or black) society.[61]

In reviews of *A Lucky Coon,* Williams and Walker received praise as a vaudeville comedy duo, rather than as performers of the old darky stereotypes. In Washington, the *Post* announced, "Williams and Walker are the Weber and Fields of their color."[62] It was Weber and Fields who, working in ethnic comedy as Yiddish comedians, had transcended mere type to elaborate on deeper themes in their comedy. In their "Dutch" act, portraying two Germans, they focused on characters rather than painted caricatures of themselves. Bert and George's "thinking along new lines" had evidently begun to pay off.

Performing before mixed crowds, Williams and Walker were in incredible demand. Based on their opening in New York, their success seemed a certainty as they played to "standing room only" theaters in the Midwest and on the East Coast.[63] As white audiences remained their bread and butter, if only because segregated theaters—though illegal—limited the number of blacks present, the duo also remained mindful of their black public. Through continuous efforts to be a conspicuous, positive presence in the black community, they assured blacks of their loyalty.

In the show, however, George introduced his popular feature, "The Hottest Coon in Dixie." Another piece that worked within the conventions of the coon song, it was a reprise from *Clorindy* and had been performed by Ernest Hogan in that production. It described the dapper character Walker played as he attempted to push beyond the simple meanings of the offensive term and image:

> *Behold the hottest coon,*
> *Your eyes e'er lit on,*
> *Velvet ain't good enough,*
> *For him to sit on;*

> *When he goes to town,*
> *Folks yell like sixty,*
> *Behold the hottest coon in Dixie.*[64]

Regardless of George's reframing of the stereotype through his own endeavor to deepen the character and give it specificity, the lingering images of Zip Coon maintained. For every move that Bert and George made against the stereotypes that had earlier served their venture into entertainment, the constant reminder of their accommodation to those stereotypes persisted.

The duo's own writing efforts produced their next venture. Originally titled *4–11–44*, a legendary number combination used in the gambling game Policy—called "the numbers" today—*The Policy Players* opened in October 1899 at New York's Star Theatre with an all-black cast. Bert and George, eager to write their own story based on the game, developed their script with the aid of Jesse Shipp.[65] Shipp worked on the script, encouraging the pair to rename and rewrite the musical.

In the resulting story, Williams plays Dusty Cheapman, a man who comes into money through his gambling endeavors and wants to gain entrée into high society. Walker, playing Happy Hotstuff, commits himself to realizing Cheapman's aim while also looking out for his own interests.[66] Working with familiar themes, the two developed stage "business," comic bits in keeping with their characters.

The response to the play continued to solidify Williams and Walker's reputation as a comedy duo. A Boston writer raved: "Of course, Williams and Walker come very near to being a whole show. While they are on stage, the audience have eyes for no others. Williams will be remembered as the tall, lean 'cullard' gentleman with the large and hungry mouth. Walker is slick and sprightly, and together they are a pair of 'warm babies'!"[67]

Friends and Partners. COURTESY OF THE YALE COLLEC-
TION OF AMERICAN LITERATURE, BEINECKE RARE BOOK AND
MANUSCRIPT LIBRARY

Perhaps as importantly, some attentive critics recognized Williams
and Walker's ambitions to rise above the coon or minstrel show and
move toward musical comedy and farce: "While possessing the distinctive atmosphere supposed to hover around the modern up-to-date
darky[,] 'The Policy Players' is written more along the lines of farcical
comedies in which white performers play than any other. It surely has
more genuine fun."[68] During the time, the presumed highest compliment paid to blacks would note their successful efforts—although often
still considered mimicry—to mirror white performance. That Bert and
George's comedy could step away from minstrelsy's legacy and toward
farce evidenced their triumph, even if it was still expressed in racial terms.
By the time they mounted *The Policy Players*, a reviewer remarked on

the duo's rise to fame, noting that they "have the distinction of [being] $500-a-week vaudeville stars, and there is no doubt that they command a numerous following."[69]

Black performers like Williams and Walker, Ernest Hogan, and others gained access to broader—still mostly white—audiences, becoming increasingly successful and established. Yet, they faced the possible aggression of a public that could turn on them at any moment. On the one hand, they collected a "numerous following," yet on the other, as highly visible black public figures, they could easily become the focus of disgruntled thugs. Even though their fame and wealth increased with each passing musical, Williams and Walker would soon get a harrowing reminder of their tenuous position.

On 12 August 1900, a sweltering evening during a summer heat wave, a black man named Arthur Harris headed from his home on West Forty-first Street in the Tenderloin to purchase cigars and wile away the hours at McBride's saloon. After several hours, Harris's common-law wife, May Enoch, sought him out at McBride's, calling him home. As she stood at the street corner waiting for Harris to leave the saloon, Robert J. Thorpe, a plainclothes policeman, approached. Assuming her to be a prostitute, Thorpe charged Enoch with soliciting. Harris arrived in time to see when the white man "grabbed my girl," and not knowing Thorpe was a policeman, scuffled with him. During the course of their struggle, Thorpe clubbed Harris. In defense, Harris extracted a knife, cutting Thorpe twice. After the incident, both Enoch and Harris fled the scene. The policeman died the next day, a result of his injuries.[70]

Three days after the altercation, while policemen visited Thorpe's home, unrest mounted and erupted, as extant antiblack feeling rose to the surface. By the evening of 15 August, a riot began, set off by angry whites who heard of another fight between a black and a white. A rumor had circulated that a black man, Spencer Walters, had tried to shoot a white man, Thomas J. Healy, in the area near Thorpe's home. The incident fueled the whites' rage, and those in the neighborhood went out into the streets, attacking random blacks in revenge.[71]

As the majority of white police officers stood back, at best doing nothing to protect the safety of the black population, and at worst contributing to the brutality on the streets, violence ensued. Blacks were chased, dragged from streetcars, and beaten in full view of inhumane policemen.[72] At the time of the escalating violence, George Walker and Ernest Hogan were on the streets and encountered the enraged mob. They and other performers quickly became the focus of that mob, as their fame and visibility motivated a direct attack on them. Recognized as celebrities, they were now destined to be the object of violence because of their blackness. James Weldon Johnson would later write that "the cry went out to 'get Ernest Hogan and Williams and Walker and Cole and Johnson.' These seemed to be the only individual names the crowd was familiar with."[73] Indeed, their fame possessed a terrifying edge.

Ultimately, Ernest and George escaped into the black-owned Marlborough Hotel, but not until after the mob had managed to pull George from a Sixth Avenue streetcar. Bert, lucky to have exited the theater in a different direction, was unhurt. But Ernest and George, as well as others, reported injuries and being robbed at the hands of the angry crowd.[74]

Unprecedented success apparently came with a high price for black artists, who represented the dangerous threat of a black bourgeoisie—and general black population—that was steadily increasing. As the city filled with white immigrants from other parts of the nation and the world, the struggle for resources—from employment to housing to political power—intensified.[75] Performers like Bert, George, and others would not likely forget how fragile their acceptance into society was, despite their impressive salaries and the applause of admiring audiences. As they performed in the days and weeks following the rioting, such thoughts would doubtlessly haunt them.

Yet, shortly after the horrors of the August riot, Williams and Walker gained their true crown of glory with *Sons of Ham*, a show that ran for two years to full houses in all the cities they played, including New York, Boston, Philadelphia, and Salt Lake City. The production opened in September 1900 at New York's Star Theatre to considerable praise and success. Will Marion Cook, J. Rosamond Johnson, Will Accooe, and several other black artists wrote the music; Jesse Shipp completed the book; and Alex Rogers supplied lyrics for the songs.

Sons of Ham concerns Tobias Wormwood, played by Bert, and Harty Lafter, played by George, who pretend to be the sons of a man named Ham. Learning that the actual sons—Jeneriska and Aniesta—are acrobats and away studying but soon to return home, Tobias and

Harty decide to take full advantage of the opportunity to stand in as them so as to inherit. They show up in Swampville, Tennessee, where Ham lives, and succeed in their roles—until the real Jeneriska and Aniesta show up.[76]

Throughout the show, although the performers knew their success depended on the satisfaction of an overwhelmingly white audience, their songs turned attention to the black audience. An example was Ada Overton Walker's feature, "Miss Hannah from Savannah." The tune spoke of a Southern girl who moved north with all intentions of maintaining her Southern pride and distinction. At a time when blacks were moving North in increasing numbers, this would have special meaning for blacks in the audience. The song told her story:

> *Up from the land of the fragrant pine,*
> *Came a dusky maiden to the Northern clime;*
> *She told all her friends, Ah's gwine to see*
> *The diff'rence in the sassiety.*

> *Ah's heard so much 'bout their high-toned ways,*
> *'Bout dem actin' more like white folks ev'ry day,*
> *If dey tries to come it on me too gran'*
> *Ah'll tell 'em who I am—*

The chorus continued with the proud refrain, "My name's Miss Hannah from Savannah, Ah'm some blueblood ob de land-ah!"[77] It bespoke the reality of the so-called "black aristocracy," who separated themselves, as people of distinguished background and upbringing, from common blacks.

As early as the 1880s, black Americans had debated the issue of class distinctions and social gradations in the community. The black elite—often descendants of black political leaders who had gained prominence during the Reconstruction, or of people of color who had been free prior to Emancipation—was cultured, educated, and hierarchical. The population's existence dramatized the fact that there was a range of black experience, overturning the notion that blacks could accurately be discussed as a single undifferentiated mass.[78] In the North, the black aristocracy scorned Southerners as ignorant and provincial, resenting the influx of migrants who seemed to be generally of lower class. In her song, Miss Hannah defended her own Southern breeding even as she critiqued

Northern blacks' uppity ways. Such a song addressed the problem of discrimination existing within and among members of black society.

The production brought in vague images of Africa, and more elaborate sets than the previous shows, all of which added to the audience's enchantment. Evidently, many audiences realized that they had witnessed something altogether new. In Denver, the *Post* declared, "It is seldom that the theater-going public sees a genuine novelty, but [*Sons of Ham*] is one in every sense of the word."[79]

By this time, Williams and Walker had attained their audience—dedicated fans followed them. As a *Dramatic Mirror* critic wrote: "An overflowing house greeted Williams and Walker and their colored company last night, when their new production, *Sons of Ham*, was seen for the first time in this city." Recognized as an "excellent vehicle for the introduction of specialties, songs and choruses," once again it still seemed to be more in the vein of a vaudeville show than a musical with a single central storyline. Nonetheless, with the duo's features, like their singing of such songs as "Zulu Babe," and the added performances of others on the roster, there seemed to be plenty of material to keep their audience happy and satisfied.[80]

And Ada Overton Walker, no wallflower, would make her presence felt. Even after marrying George, she would establish herself on her own merits. In effect, she would be the company's leading lady, blazing across the stage in performances that rendered her a close second behind Bert and George's famously popular antics. She gained further visibility for both her singing and dancing, as she became a central feature in Williams and Walker shows.[81]

In Boston, a critic described the group as "the cleverest aggregation of colored entertainers that ever appeared before an audience in this city." The journalist enthused that the company "in its parts is a revelation, as it displays a class of colored talent never before seen in this city." Holding the audience in the palm of their hands, the performers seemed to control them, for "Williams and Walker were excruciatingly funny, as they always are, but . . . they showed a versatility that was new to a Boston audience." They drove the audiences' reactions, for "[f]rom the time they first made their appearance until they disappeared[,] the house was in a paroxysm of laughter, every song and every dance being encored over and over again."[82] And critics readily saw Williams's particular gift: "It is hard to say which one of the stars made the biggest hit last night, but one would have to see Williams to get any idea of the expressions of his face when he changes from laughter into blank dismay whenever things go wrong against him."[83] Bert was becoming recognized as an actor with range, despite his role as the funnyman of the team.

Even as the duo devoted themselves increasingly to the work of their theatrical careers, they also expanded their pursuits into the nascent recording industry. Between seasons of *Sons of Ham*, which ran from September to June, Williams and Walker performed in vaudeville, still the reigning popular entertainment for the masses. They played theaters in the city, featuring comic songs and their classic roles of country bumpkin and city slicker. Then, in October of 1901, as *Sons of Ham* went into its second season, Bert and George traveled to Philadelphia to record at the studios of the Victor Talking Machine Company.[84] These were disc recordings, rather than the cylinders typically in use then, and Williams and Walker made a significant splash on the scene. They had been well loved onstage and in their Tin Pan Alley sheet music songs. Now audiences would be able to listen to the pair in the comfort of their own homes.

Edison's 1878 demonstration of his tinfoil phonograph first suggested to the public the possibility of "bottling sound."[85] At the time, however, the technology was so primitive that it seemed to be little more than an odd novelty. When Edison returned years later to develop the phonograph, he created an improved machine using removable wax cylinders, a technology that would allow for more permanent recordings.[86] The wax cylinder recordings helped spread the experience of this extraordinary technology to Americans throughout the country. And as stage stars came to prominence, it would be the recording industry that would extend their recognition and fame.[87]

It had been the 1889 establishment of the Columbia Phonograph Company that buttressed the transformation of recording from its more mundane potential use in business (in dictation, for example) to the field of entertainment. With such companies' efforts at promotion, music machines, later termed "jukeboxes," would further open the technology to the public. By the late 1890s, the technology would become affordable to the general public and individuals, taking up residence in private homes across the country.[88] Despite slowly but steadily increasing access, the drive for fledgling recording industry pioneers like Supreme Court stenographers turned Columbia founders Edward Easton and Paul Cromelin to keep their businesses afloat was sufficient to encourage their consideration of black artists.[89] Their desire to build their businesses overcame their desire to maintain segregationist practices or even concern themselves with a solely altruistic aim to promote equality.[90]

When Williams and Walker appeared on Victor, the company proudly announced their arrival, declaring in its catalog:

> The most popular songs of the day are the "Ragtime" or "Coon Songs." The greatest recommendation a song of this kind can have is that it is sung by Williams and Walker, the "Two Real Coons." Their selections are always from the brightest and best songs with the most catchy and pleasing melodies. Although Williams and Walker have been engaged to make records exclusively for us at the highest price ever paid in the history of the Talking Machine business, and although their records are the finest thing ever produced, being absolutely *the real thing*, we add them to our regular record list with no advance in price.[91]

Being the "real thing" was a key criterion in the estimation of a performer's success, especially black performers, expected to play to type. Williams and Walker played "Two Real Coons," shaping themselves to the majority white audience's expectations even in their recordings, yet they gained a degree of control so that they did not simply satisfy the expectation but, more importantly, made inroads by establishing themselves in a new industry.

Although both Bert's and George's voices recorded well, Bert's would be captured on more than sixty recordings over the years, whereas George would later refrain from recording, deciding that the new medium did not best suit or display his talents. On the recordings, Bert's style came across as distinctive, his delivery strong, his deep voice resonant. It was Bert whose recording career would continue to keep him in the public ear, even after he moved out of the public eye years later.

Williams and Walker's burgeoning popularity clearly indicated the public's eager reception of their performances. With each show, the duo won more of the public, allowing them to begin their policy of utilizing all-black casts in large productions. Yet, even during these early years of their partnership, Williams and Walker began to feel the pull of their audiences: their particular demands and varying expectations. What complicated their relationship with those audiences was the knowledge that they consisted of both blacks and whites. These two groups held disparate expectations of the performers.

In a 1928 article on "The Dilemma of the Negro Author," writer James Weldon Johnson would address this conundrum, which would as easily apply to other black artists as well as authors. For the Negro author—and likewise, the entertainer—there were always two audiences: white and black. These two audiences were not only different but, furthermore, "divided," possessing "often opposite and antagonistic points of view."[92] Artists struggled when attempting to satisfy audiences because to capitulate to one was necessarily to ignore or even to reject the other. Each audience, in its own way, limited or at least attempted to delimit the freedoms of the Negro artist. Whites did so by supporting depictions of the Negro as at best an indolent peasant and at worst a brutish menace; Negroes did so by insisting on promotion of only "nice" images of the Negro.

What created the complication with audiences, then, was the nagging issue of representation. Whites and blacks alike brought to performances their own notions of what was an appropriate representation for blacks. Both expected that representation to be "real" or "true" to their notions. Both audiences conflated the representational with the real: they expected what they saw onstage to be a manifestation of "truth." For whites, the coon, and for blacks, the "New Negro." While the mainstream society pressed for continuation of the old black stereotypes in relation to the legacy of minstrelsy with its backward images, the black community pressed for change with concerns about representation.

Blacks' concerns about representation, and their efforts to recreate the image of blacks, developed in response to minstrelsy's legacy. They also came in resistance to the white society's subjugation of blacks during slavery, as well as post–Civil War politics and popular culture following slavery. Southern blacks, who had lost hard-won rights gained after the Civil War and had seen the reinstatement of home rule, struggled to hold their ground against Jim Crow segregation and pervasive violence at the hands of white supremacists. Northern blacks, barred from equal participation in the society, often denied access to public services, and facing economic discrimination from being shut out of white-collar job opportunities, closed ranks in efforts toward self-protection. Although segregation was not on the books in the North, it clearly existed in Northern society, which was largely antagonistic toward the population.[93]

As a result of such exclusion, blacks in the North and the South united under the banner of racial solidarity and self-help. The community had no other options, having been excluded and closed off from opportunities. Through the creation of mutual benefit and historical societies, fraternities, and other organizations, African Americans provided for each other in life and death, motivated by this exclusion from the larger society.[94] They attempted to supply for each other what the white society categorically refused them.

Furthermore, blacks responded publicly to the denial of their humanity. Making a clean break from the burden of history and slavery, they sought to present a new face to American society. In time, this face and image would come to be known as that of the "New Negro."

Although the "New Negro" did not blossom into a movement until the absorption of the concept into Alain Locke's 1925 cultural treatise of the same name, the symbol and idea of the New Negro already existed in black society's notion of representation.[95] Since the term's first use in the Cleveland *Gazette* on 28 June 1895, in which the journalist referred to the "New Negro" as having attained "education, refinement and money" in the effort toward postbellum racial uplift, the phrase was linked to blacks' struggle for self-definition. Further developing from this through the time of Locke's seminal work, the "New Negro" began as an idea, an invention that came into being in the minds of America's blacks. Not yet a conclusive reality in 1895, over the years this possibility of a new self—a remaking of the black subject on his or her own terms—captivated the imagination of leading blacks in the nation.

In the context of the racialized society, black Americans sought to reinvent their public image by reconstructing their public face.[96] The creation of the "New Negro" entailed reframing and reforming the image of the Negro in response to degrading representations existing in the white society: blacks thus aimed to redefine themselves as a people. They endeavored to "reconstruct blackness as a presence," in the face of a white society that, through acts of violence and the denigration of the blacks, conspired to establish blackness as an undeniable absence.[97] Blacks wanted their true faces and experiences known and sought to do this by displaying the very best that black America could be.

The reconstruction of blackness entailed an assertion of a new representation, which required two things: the creation of a "presentable" image and the shedding of the past—the "old Negro," defined in opposition to the new.[98] In order to create a presentable image, blacks had to invalidate the dominant society's notion of the race as childlike, ignorant, and immoral by supplanting it with the reality of blacks as mature, intelligent, and principled. They would do that by displaying exceptional Negroes who would represent the best the community had to offer. With regard to shedding the past, Negroes would have to move away from their history in slavery in order to focus on the possibility of a new future.

By showing the representative Negro, blacks would reform their image in America. Focusing politics on representation or "respectability," black leaders demanded achievement—in business, art, indeed, in simple comportment—that could be utilized as representative in order to defend the rights and dignity of an entire people.[99] Ultimately, this was a reactive view of how the post-Reconstruction black would and could become part of the greater society, by meeting—and indeed, exceeding—its standard of the human being. Bert and George, as phenomenal successes, would be an excellent example of what the race could achieve and would carry a burden of responsibility as representative figures.

The other side of this re-presentation demanded the abandonment of the old Negro's past. This meant a distancing of the race from the history of slavery and the recollection of that experience in order to move forward. Although the "memory" of slavery could not be erased, the "recollection" of it remained needless and unproductive. Alexander Crummell, an African American leader of the period, distinguished memory from recollection: "[M]emory is a passive act of mind . . . the necessary and unavoidable entrance, storage, and recurrence of facts and ideas to consciousness. Recollection . . . is the actual seeking of the facts, the endeavor of the mind to bring them back to consciousness."[100] Crummell and others admonished blacks against the recollection of slavery, insisting that blacks focus on future possibility rather than past degradation. If performers like Bert and George bowed to the mandates of minstrelsy, playing the Jim Crow and Zip Coon characters that originated decades before the Civil War, they risked holding the race back with old Negro images.

Two black leaders, Booker T. Washington and W. E. B. Du Bois, exemplified the focus on the "New Negro." Their work defined the political and intellectual trajectory of black America from the turn of the century through at least the first decade.[101] In their opinions, they expressed the needs and concerns of the Negro in American society in order to advance the race. Furthermore, they addressed both the efforts of common black folk as well as the achievements of artists, specifically discussing Williams and Walker.

Washington and Du Bois held differing opinions regarding the best manner in which to achieve "uplift." Washington's putatively anti-intellectual focus on a narrowly conceived industrial or agricultural education for blacks stood in sharp contrast to Du Bois's support of avowedly intellectual pursuits. Washington's focus on economic development, sacrificing social equality and civil rights in his 1895 "Atlanta Compromise" speech diametrically opposed Du Bois's 1903 articulation in *The Souls of Black Folk* of the need for the American Negro to be wholly accepted into society.[102] Yet both Washington's and Du Bois's views on the future of Negro progress supported the idea of self-help, expressed through the notion of representation.[103] Perhaps surprisingly, despite the seemingly retrogressive images that Williams and Walker presented, they both found the comedians to be crucial to uplift efforts and their contribution invaluable.

Washington and Du Bois would both pen books that addressed the Negro's contribution to American society.[104] Within those histories they would identify Bert and George as leaders important to the black Americans' narrative and trajectory of uplift. Washington would see in the contributions of Williams and Walker the possibilities of "more modern Negro comedy," "a more worthy kind of Negro comedy" embodied through them.[105] He would refuse an easy acceptance of Williams and Walker's role in maintaining the stereotypes and embrace their work in spite of its distance from what might be considered "elite culture." He would claim that they oppose the minstrelsy standard and expectation, leading black comedy into a new modern era and leaving behind minstrelsy's deleterious images. Du Bois would celebrate their achievements, praising Bert and George for their move away from minstrelsy, through which they would ultimately "develop and uplift the art."[106] He would see their work not only as consistent with the idea of representation but also as an example of "a new light comedy" of a new era.[107]

Paralleling the view of Washington, Du Bois would look to the future and see Bert and George as great actors for change.

In another work, Washington would go further to commend Williams specifically for his individual contributions. What might have been a troubling darky performance to some, Washington would describe as "quaint songs and stories in which [Williams] reproduces the natural humor and philosophy of the Negro people."[108] He would conclude that Williams "has done for one side of the Negro life and character just what the old plantation Negroes did for another—given expression and put into a form which everyone can understand and appreciate something of the inner life and peculiar genius . . . of the Negro."[109] In Washington's view, Williams's darky character, far from duplicating the images of minstrelsy, would present the reality of the Negro character and forms of expression. Williams's work would be important not only for its resistance of the stereotype but indeed for its truth: it *was* real, and did not merely "represent" the real onstage.

Washington would also recognize Williams for his offstage contributions, describing him as "a tremendous asset of the Negro race."[110] Moved by Williams's refusal to "whine and complain" about race or the personal indignities he suffered, he would see the entertainer's success as equal to the success of the race. A public figure, Williams would illustrate the capacity of the American public to respect a black man. Washington would thereby take full advantage of the opportunity to hold Williams up as a prime example of the New Negro in action, even if while onstage he appeared in the old Negro's garb.[111]

The views of luminaries like Washington and Du Bois would demonstrate the extent to which Bert and George seemed to fit the new image of the Negro, while indicating also the extent to which the black community's ideas of representation depended on the politics of visibility. Frequently and explicitly, those in the community reminded black performers (and other blacks) that their success or failure affected the future of all African Americans, whether they were entertainers or not. They took those who had greatest success as examples and held them up for others to follow. They believed that change might be possible as a result of those individuals' exposure and access to diverse audiences.

Influential blacks and journalists writing in black newspapers focused on visibility. They assumed that greater visibility would increase black pride and inform those outside the community of blacks' strength.[112]

Presuming most importantly that the presentation of black figures on-stage would be politically efficacious, leaders charged performers with the duty to expose audiences to blacks' reality, which minstrelsy failed to do.[113]

While Bert and George gained bigger and better opportunities, of-fering their greatest contributions to musical theater, they struggled both in defiance of minstrelsy's legacy and also in response to the black community's demands for representation.[114] Although critics like Sylvester Russell of the *Indianapolis Freeman* would attempt to be their conscience, lauding them and at times chastising them for their unac-ceptable accommodation, they would continue to enjoy galloping success with their black audiences, as well as with whites.

Throughout their partnership, while Bert took the fore as comic, George took the fore as spokesman. He reassured the black community of their shared concerns, even as he managed Williams and Walker's business interests. A gifted businessman, he did a stellar job in his role. And with Williams and Walker's thrilling onstage shows and offstage ef-forts to reach out to the black community, they did become representa-tive. Furthermore, being the key comedy team during the years of the surge in black musical theater in New York, 1890–1915, Williams and Walker became exemplary, "the standard against which other comedy acts were compared."[115]

5

From Broadway
to London: *In Dahomey*

ollowing their triumphant two-season run of *Sons of Ham*, Williams and Walker continued to build their reputation in black musical theater, aspiring to nothing less than greatness. Their relationship with producers Hurtig and Seamon had elevated the duo. Even as Bert and George had taken *Sons of Ham* to the stage, they had also established their collection of actors, singers, and dancers as a company. After the production's run ended, the two raced onward with plans, enjoying the afterglow of their success.

Williams and Walker began preparations for their biggest and brightest musical yet with the contributions of their black artist-friends, including Will Marion Cook, who took the fore as the principal composer and conductor; Jesse Shipp, who penned the script and would stage-manage the show; and Alex Rogers, who wrote lyrics. The production would feature the duo as headliners. Nearly as importantly, it would exhibit the talents of a host of others: Cook's able wife, singer-actress Abbie Mitchell; George's rapidly self-distinguishing spouse, incomparable dancer Aida Overton Walker; and even Bert's own Lottie.[1]

Through what appeared to be a combination of grit and gall, the duo would press for a Broadway theater for their musical. After a remarkably profitable tour of the new Williams and Walker show, Hurtig and

Seamon would tap their invaluable connection as employees of Klaw and Erlanger, powerful producers and theater owners. Members of the Syndicate, an alliance of producers and booking agents who controlled theaters not only within New York City but also across the nation, Klaw and Erlanger would grant Williams and Walker unparalleled access to the Broadway stage.[2] And with Williams and Walker's appearance at the New York Theatre between Forty-fourth and Forty-fifth Streets on Broadway, they would make history. They would present "the first full-length musical written and played by blacks to be performed at a major Broadway house," their elaborate $15,000 production, *In Dahomey*.[3]

In Dahomey had begun as Bert and George's ambitious dream to "explore the African background onstage."[4] During their brush with Dahomeans nearly ten years before at San Francisco's Midwinter Fair, both of them had been intrigued by the Africans, and they were curious as to how they might bring their experience with Dahomeans to the stage. Whereas the practical George viewed his and Bert's interaction with Africans most importantly as a chance to consider the onstage possibilities of integrating Africa and America, the intellectual Bert regarded the exchange as an occasion for contemplation. An avid reader, he had often pored over his rare edition of John Ogilby's *Africa*, a 1670 tome tracing the history of African peoples.[5] Ogilby, a "royal cosmographer and geographic printer," had distinguished himself as "a pioneer in the making of road atlases," later becoming a well-established translator and publisher.[6] His *Africa* was a translated collection of prior travelers' narratives, an over-600-page opus, which Bert would have read in archaic, seventeenth-century English.[7]

Providing physical descriptions of the land as well as of the continent's diverse peoples, Ogilby affirmed his text's authoritativeness in its subtitle, which boldly proclaimed, "Being an Accurate Description." Throughout *Africa*, he described extremes of African "bestial" degeneracy and semi-civilization, a seeming verification of the continent's backwardness, yet he also discussed the evident sophistication of African cultures.[8] He characterized Abyssinians as "lovers of Learning and Learned Men." He also remarked that Abyssinian women were "diligent and zealous of literature [*sic*], taking great delight to study the Scriptures."[9] In a discussion of the "Kingdom of Guinea," he described a village so large that "not onely [*sic*] the Kings keep their Courts and

Royal Residence there, but also there is a University, where Scholars Commence, and the Priests receive their Orders and several Dignities; besides a settled Staple for the Merchants of this Kingdom."[10] With such observations, *Africa* devoted attention to the various peoples who prized erudition and progress as Ogilvy envisioned them.

Those observations sparked Bert's imagination. From his perspective, in his hands lay access to peoples and civilizations to which he believed himself deeply connected. "I think that with this volume," he said in a comment that would become well known, "I could prove that every Pullman porter is the descendant of a king."[11] For Bert, the possibilities after meeting true Dahomeans related not only to Williams and Walker's theatrical future but also—and perhaps more importantly—to the history of blacks as a whole. He reflected on what he considered to be the proud history of people of African descent, rather than the shameful history of African savagery promulgated by Victorian notions of the "dark continent." He thereby took his encounter with Africans out of the realm of ethnology and into a more meaningful and personal sense of ancestry.

The choice of Dahomey as the musical's location, influenced by Bert and George's experiences at the Midwinter Fair, was likely to have been shaped also by the lingering effects of Dahomey's resistance to French colonization during the 1890s. Although accounts of the Dahomeans' struggle for power had ended with news of their final conquest by the French in 1894, rumblings had begun again in 1901. "Moslem tribes" reportedly threatened rebellion. They rejected the sovereignty of King Toffa, who had replaced the deposed King Benhazin, then exiled in Martinique.[12] The subject of Dahomey continued to be sensational and would certainly draw the attention of an audience.

Although Bert and George had admirable ambitions to render Africa onstage, by necessity they had to balance those ambitions with the demands of producing a profitable show and responding to white audiences.[13] Throughout the production's run, *In Dahomey*'s creators would continuously alter and adapt the show, hoping to better satisfy their distinct black and white audiences.[14] They would strive to remain loyal to their black audience without alienating the white audience, and to entertain their white audience without degrading themselves and their black audience.[15] As they did so, they would also attempt to render their own aesthetic representation of Africa. They would create a majestic spectacle that countered the prevailing image of the "dark continent."

And, in the absence of "Americanized African songs," to which George had aspired, they would create songs utilizing the African American idiom of ragtime. They would launch a critique directed both inward, toward blacks as a community, as well as outward, to the whites in the audience who viewed the production.[16]

In Dahomey opened in Stamford, Connecticut, on 8 September 1902. From there it made its way to Boston, continuing on tour to such locations as Chicago, Philadelphia, Cleveland, St. Louis, Kansas City, and Minneapolis between October 1902 and February 1903.[17] The musical revolves around characters Shylock Homestead (Williams) and Rareback Pinkerton (Walker), confidence men. Their names feature puns that give clues to their actions throughout the play; "Shylock Homestead," for instance, at once references Arthur Conan Doyle's character "Sherlock Holmes," who had appeared on the literary scene in 1887, and Shylock, the miserly moneylender of Shakespeare's play *The Merchant of Venice*. Nineteenth-century audiences would have been familiar with Shakespeare's Shylock regardless of their education; at that time, everyone from commoners to the elite read the famous bard. Rareback Pinkerton's name references the Pinkerton Detective Agency, established by Scottish immigrant Allan Pinkerton in 1852.[18]

In the musical, Shylock (Shy) and Rareback (Rare), living in Boston, are hired as detectives to locate a missing treasure, and they hope to make financial gains in the process. As they search for the heirloom, they become enmeshed in a black syndicate's fraudulent plan to steal money from a wealthy old man named Mr. Lightfoot and his group of African colonizers. At a time when "syndicate" signified, in its more innocuous form, news agencies that sold features to papers, and in its more menacing form, certain theatrical producers' monopoly of American theater, the term would possess potentially ominous undertones for its audience.[19]

Shy and Rare join the syndicate, traveling to Florida for the second act, during which they search for Lightfoot's treasure near his Gatorville home. Along the way, further antics ensue, dominated by Shy and Rare's animated exchanges. At the end of the second act, the two join the colonizers on their trip to Africa.[20]

In the third act, set in Dahomey, Shy and Rare attempt to endear themselves to the Dahomean king through gifts of whisky. As a result, they are made "caboceers," assistants of the king. Lightfoot, disgusted by the turn of events in Dahomey, ultimately abandons his plan, announcing his intention of returning to America.[21]

During the production's tour, audiences acclaimed *In Dahomey*, and Hurtig and Seamon reaped impressive profits. Throughout the musical's run, the producers would receive returns that more than quadrupled their initial investment of $15,000.[22] With that compelling testament to Williams and Walker's star power, Hurtig and Seamon negotiated *In Dahomey*'s move to Broadway.

The show's move to Broadway verified Bert and George's arrival as a force to be reckoned with on the New York theater scene. Hurtig and Seamon's eagerness to place them in a superior venue, and Klaw and Erlanger's willingness to mount the duo's all-black production in their own Broadway theater, proved that fact.

Nevertheless, reactions of some "established Broadway managers" diminished this heartening sign of possible change. As Williams and Walker's Broadway opening had approached, a *New York Times* journalist had noted a "thundercloud . . . gathering of late in the faces" of unspecified managers. These words suggested not only discontent with the team's success but a deeply menacing reaction to their access to the Broadway stage. The writer explained that "[T]here have been times when the trouble-breeders have foreboded [*sic*] a race war."[23] Such a statement harked back to the very real violence of the 1900 Tenderloin riot. George and Ernest Hogan, as prominent blacks, had then found themselves the object of a white mobs' rage. Now, with Williams and Walker's move to Broadway, they became the focus of angry white mobs and the outraged doyens of the Syndicate.

An historic first for ambitious black entertainers, the company's feat was an ominous sign auguring ill for Syndicate members, who sought to close blacks off from the very theaters that would secure their long-term success. Broadway theaters, with higher ticket prices and more affluent patrons than vaudeville, were every performer's dream, whether that entertainer was white or black. Threatened theater owners and producers who desired to maintain the status quo fought to keep black performers from having access to those venues. They insisted on resisting change, despite the fact that Williams and Walker's success in other city theaters as well as with previous productions attested to their ability not only to survive but also to generate a profit. As the duo progressed in their career, they would repeatedly need to defend their right to Broadway stages, despite the evidence of their unusual success. With *In Dahomey*, however, they reigned at the New York Theatre from 13 February for fifty-three glorious performances.[24]

After their conquest of Broadway, Bert expressed their early frustrations and final achievement:

> Broadway! And Williams and Walker! Williams and Walker! On Broadway! At last! Hallelujah! We're here. It was a pigs in clover puzzle to get here, but we've done it.[25] Maybe you think I'm bringing in this fact pretty often. Even I can see there's a good deal of crowing over it in this article as far as I've gone. But we've got a large-sized crowing fit coming to us all right. If you had any idea how often we've tried for Broadway only to get sidetracked, you'd begin to understand how it hits us. . . .
>
> The way we've aimed for Broadway and just missed it in the past seven years would make you cry. We'd get our bearings, take a good running start and—land in a Third Avenue theater. Then we'd measure the distance again and think we'd struck the right avenue at last—only to be stalled in a West Thirty-fourth Street music hall with the whole stunt to do all over again. We'd get near enough to hear the Broadway audiences applaud sometimes, but it was some one [*sic*] else they were applauding. I used to be tempted to beg for a $15 job in a chorus just for one week so as to be able to say I'd been on Broadway once. I'd have made a daisy chorus milkmaid.[26]

While his words were playful, Bert had most certainly felt the pain of producers and theater owners' resistance to his and Walker's fight for Broadway. Their popularity throughout the city might have been impressive, but it had taken *In Dahomey*'s substantial returns for anyone to be convinced of their prospects.

Bert continued, recalling that some people to whom he semi-jokingly complained called him "a funny chap." He admitted:

> But I wasn't. I was just a sore one. But I've tried one application of the cure-all B[r]oadway for that sore feeling and it's all gone. If the proprietors of that salve want a testimonial from me they can have it for the asking. Maybe the reason we were so long in finding Broadway was because we never thought of looking for it *In Dahomey*. Now maybe you begin to

get on to [t]he reason why I'm feeling happier than a barnstormer that's caught the ghost in a somnambulistic trance.[27]

"Ecstatic" could hardly describe the thrill of achievement Bert got from having finally made it. The theater district and Broadway were far from the same. It was a terrific triumph that Williams and Walker had finally reached their destination.

George, though obviously no less excited, chose to take the path of assured confidence as he recounted:

> It was a narrow path but it led to Broadway. And Broadway (as any good surveyor can tell you), is the centre of the universe. And in that centre is a smaller centre. And we're in it. Some years ago we were doing a dance before an east side audience. They gave us [a] hand, and I called out to them: "Some day we'll do this dance on Broadway!" Then they gave us [a] laugh. Just the same we gave Broadway that same dance.[28]

For George, others' doubt only drove him to further dedicate himself to realizing their dream. He had continued to be an aggressive and demanding businessman, finding Hurtig and Seamon—representation that would meet their needs.

He told a story that explained how the disparaging mockery of one man led him first to disgust, then to a gratifying victory:

> One night I told a New Yorker I believed we were a warm bunch, and that we'd end up on Broadway sooner or later. He didn't say anything but he just hummed two lines of a song we'd made our first hit with. It was: "Oh, I don't know! You ain't so wahm! Day'd oddeh coons as wahm as you-oo!"
>
> I've hated that song ever since. Just the same[,] when I saw that man's face in the second row, on our opening night on Broadway, it did me good.[29]

For George, this tacit recognition of their accomplishment made Williams and Walker's struggle well worth it.

Despite the seeming stamp of approval, theater managers maintained certain segregationist practices during *In Dahomey*'s run. The theater owners recoiled as they witnessed black society's arrival to the theater, decked out for a night on the town and determined to demand the best seats that they could afford. In spite of some blacks' willingness to pay for access to the superior seats of the house, Klaw and

Erlanger drew the color line. Even those who could afford to pay a dollar for such a seat had to accept accommodation in the gallery or forego the chance to see the company perform.[30]

A *New York Times* writer, relieved by Klaw and Erlanger's choice, pronounced the decision "a triumph in fact for all concerned." Yet that choice resulted in the neglect of the duo's most fiercely devoted audience. The journalist chose not to remark on the irony that black musical director James Vaughan's placement at the head of his orchestra stood as the only black presence on the floor of the house, other than the "boys who peddled water in the aisles."[31]

Bert and George had labored to get *In Dahomey* to the Broadway stage, but their work did not stop there. The show would have numerous versions, interpolating new songs, cutting and adding scenes, and creating adaptations made for their varying audiences.[32] Their constant efforts to better satisfy audiences became clear as the show's various versions unfolded. Yet they persisted in their efforts to keep their vision alive.

In Dahomey included elements of the minstrel show, yet was more than this. The show's opening, however, was an obvious continuity of the tradition. It began with a medicine-show quack's pitch selling products to lighten skin and straighten hair.[33] Not only was the "doctor's" stump speech a retention of minstrelsy, but the excited response of the onstage black spectators watching him seemed to reinforce the stereotype of the ignorant, gullible black.

Despite such an opening, which appeared to be mainly concerned with remaining consistent with prevalent stereotypes, *In Dahomey*'s creators balanced the production with a measured degree of parody that directed their attention to black audiences.[34] And black audiences rewarded them for their efforts. During the show, one *New York Times* critic could not help but observe: "At intervals one heard a shrill kiyi of applause from above or a mellow bass roar that betokened the seventh heaven of delight."[35] Indeed, the antics of Williams and Walker as well as the messages of the musical had hit home.

The primary vehicle for connecting to the black audience was through songs, particularly the opening song, "Swing Along," as well as two others titled "Society" and "Leader of the Colored Aristocracy." The first of these spoke about the importance of black pride even though the "white fo'ks a-watchin' an' seein' what you do,/ white fo'ks jealous

In Dahomey, *Medicine Man Showing His Preparation to Turn Colored Folks White,*
1903. COURTESY OF THE MUSEUM OF THE CITY OF NEW YORK

when you'se walkin' two by two."[36] Urging blacks to "lif' yo' head and
yo' heels mighty high," it insisted, "[Y]es, swing along from a early
morn till night."[37] The merry, quick, and syncopated rhythms of ragtime music contrasted with the defiant words of the song, which recognized blacks' desire to retain pride and dignity, though subjected to
whites' scrutiny.[38] Although written in dialect and suggestive of carefree
enjoyment with such lines as "Sun's as red as de rose in de sky," "Swing
Along" maintained a tension throughout that would have certainly communicated well and clearly to the black audience. They would have
been well aware of such scrutiny. Even as they respectfully strove to get
equal access to theatrical entertainment, they constantly found themselves forced to sit in "nigger heaven."

The other two songs critiqued the black elite. The first, "Society," did
so in references to the influence money provided within black society.
The second did so with direct reference to the "hypocrisy" of high society in "Leader of the Colored Aristocracy."[39] In "Society," Lightfoot, a
moneyed man seeking entrée into elite society proclaims:

> *To get in high society*
> *You need a great reputation,*

Don't cultivate sobriety
But rather ostentation.[40]

Focusing on possessions, "A lot of gold laid by in gilt edged stocks . . . a high-toned house that's builded on rocks," he places value on achieving position as a superior in the society.[41] His persistent words indicate the imperative these represent—in particular, his desire for his daughter to marry a royal prince and stand "at the head of the best society."[42]

His daughter's values and hopes, however, stand counter to his own. Within the song, she protests. She declares that the man she loves is himself a prince, although not royalty. Her solo becomes a duet, as she and her beloved pronounce that love trumps entrance into society, for "love is the king!"[43]

"Leader of the Colored Aristocracy" took this subject further with a focus not only on the social climber but also directly on the community:

And then I'll drill,
These darkies till,
They're up in high society's hypocr[i]sy;

They'll come my way,
To gain entrée,
To the circles of the colored aristocracy.[44]

Those obsessed with entering the "colored aristocracy" not only sought to distinguish themselves as superior to others but also willingly participated in hypocrisy. They became counterfeits as they traded in their values for access to high society.

Noting the policing eyes of whites, encouraging blacks' to be proud, and critiquing striving members of the black community, *In Dahomey* spoke in various registers to its audiences. As it maintained these critical elements, the script also focused largely on Williams and Walker, who floored audiences with their effervescent comedy. Their parts as Shy and Rare harked back to their past roles, yet also moved away from stereotypes through further development of their characters.

Bert's Shylock Homestead was reminiscent of Jim Crow as a slow, dim-witted figure in blackface. In the musical, however, Bert created a character that was more than a "type" due to the humanity he displayed through a range of emotions. Extending writer and *In Dahomey* lyricist James Weldon Johnson's criticism about the use of the Negro dialect in poetry—that it "is an instrument with but two full stops, humor and pathos"—one could say that Bert fashioned the Homestead character as a challenge to Johnson's statement.[45] He utilized a range of expression that included those two stops, but by no means ended there.

As Rareback Pinkerton, George was still in part the Zip Coon type. He sparkled with vivacity and nonstop loquacity, dominating in terms of literal presence in the show. Whereas Bert's strength was his terseness and ability to communicate much in few words, George's was the opposite. A smooth talker, he had also become known and appreciated for his dance moves. He played the role with vitality, yet refrained from undignified excess.

Although these characters in some ways leaned on old figures from minstrelsy, in their scenes Bert and George emphasized their inheritance from ethnic comedy. They played to their strength as a comical pair. George focused on his role as the city slicker, in contrast to Bert's subtle depiction of the country bumpkin, which paralleled the immigrant greenhorn. They paced their scenes in a manner that gave full attention to their extraordinary chemistry.

During a long exchange in Act Two, Scene Two, Rare encourages Shy to stay the course throughout their efforts to secure Lightfoot's heirloom. In the process, he relates the story of Nick Carter and Old Sleuth, "the greatest detectives in the world," who never got tired of chasing down leads. He begins:

> Never heard of Nick Carter and Old Sleuth? Why, Shy, they're the greatest detectives in the world. Nick Carter is the only man living that's been shot through the heart forty-one times, and Old Sleuth's been knocked in the head with his arms behind him and a gag in his mouth and throwed in every sewer in the country.[46]

Rare launches into an extensive account of Old Sleuth and Nick Carter's efforts "to trace up some bank robbers." He conjures up the scene for Shy. The detectives traveled by train to the Western town where the robbers were said to be hiding: "Imagine a mountain pass about fifty thousand feet above the level of the sea, a bridge suspended in midair over a chasm one thousand feet deep. A stormy night. The snow falling thick and fast and not a ship to be seen."[47]

Continuing the tale, Rare describes Nick and Old Sleuth, the sole passengers awake on the train. The two were playing pinochle in the smoking car when they heard "Crack, crack, crack, and the whip-like report of a gatling gun." In response to the noise, Rare explains, Nick "was seen to rise suddenly to his feet and take from the hat rack a bottle of rye whisky, take a drink and light a cigar and coolly raise the window to prevent the broken glass from entering the wounds made by the bullets of the bandits." Meanwhile, Old Sleuth "threw a keg of beer out of the window, and the robber ceased firing long enough to secure the beer." The robbers, who had removed the middle span of the bridge unbeknownst to Nick and Old Sleuth, had set the two up to take a plunge to their deaths, along with everyone else on the train.[48]

Luckily, Old Sleuth, "whose hearing was wonderfully acute, said: 'Nick, the middle span is out of that bridge ahead. I can hear the air sucking the broken rails. Something must be done at once.'" No sooner had he said that, Rare claims, than Nick "plunged through the window, caught the telegraph wire, which broke his weight and swung him over the chasm." Nick attached the bell cord to the span, which had been removed and had fallen intact onto a nearby marsh. Then he passed one end of the cord to Old Sleuth, who helped him snap the span in place, saving the lives of the unwitting, still-sleeping passengers.[49]

When the story concludes, the doubting Shy starts in with questions for further clarification:

SHY: How deep did you say that chasm was?
RARE: One thousand feet.
SHY: Then I suppose this Nick Carter, having rubber soles on his shoes, hit himself on top of de head and bounced back in de smoking department of de car and played peanuckle till he got to town.
RARE: Nothing so unreasonable as that occurred. An artificial lake at the head of the gap used as a reservoir became flooded and burst its banks. The torrent of water swept through the chasm and carried Nick to the town thirty miles away and landed him on the platform of the depot just as the train pulled in with Old Sleuth standing on the cab of the engine smoking a Childs Cigar.[50]

As Rare supplies rapid-fire details, Shy continues to question the story, at times backing up to mention a line delivered earlier:

RARE: The robbers, after securing the beer that Old Sleuth threw out the window descended to a valley twenty-six thousand two-hundred and six feet below.

SHY: By actual measurement?

RARE: Yes, by actual measurement, and after drinking the beer lay down to collect their thoughts.

SHY: How many robbers was there?

RARE: Three.

SHY: I believe that part of the story.

RARE: What part?

SHY: The part where the three robbers, after drinking a whole keg of beer between them, laid down.

RARE: Nick Carter opened his satchel on the platform of the depot and took out an airship while Old Sleuth, unscrewing the top of his walking cane, removed a large electric light plant.[51]

With that, Shy is ready to finish the conversation, recognizing that "them robbers was up against it," yet not quite believing his partner's account of Nick and Old Sleuth's feat. As Shy and Rare begin to walk off the stage, Rare promises to tell Shy the rest of the story. Shy, however, has had enough: "You ain't going to tell me the rest, cause I'm jist naturally ashamed to listen at you."[52]

Throughout *In Dahomey*, as Bert played Shy, he deepened the usually simplistic darky role to create a fuller fleshed-out character. He introduced a new aspect to the classic dimwit, adding a dimension that audiences applauded not only for its humor but also for its illustration of his talents as an actor. His Shy was dubious and contemplative, rather than outrageously obtuse.

As he depicted the character in his typical slow-moving, yet more reflective manner, Bert communicated his minimal lines with profound expression. Mime became his most useful tool. Its focus on physical and mental control, training "the body and mind together to become an instrument of expression," challenged Bert to elevate his acting above the burnt cork.[53] Countering the makeup that flattened features and resisting the typically frenetic vaudeville performance style, Bert became a mime. He made "every part of the body . . . perfectly flexible and controlled by the study of movement."[54] More than merely concentrating on the importance of gesture, which constitutes only part of the mime's work, Bert paid attention to the body as a whole. When he did so, he enriched his character as well as the scenes in which he appeared.

A reviewer raved about a moment in the play during which Bert led the audience through a range of emotions during an exchange with George's character:

> This bit of pantomime of Bert Williams did not occupy two minutes. It began on a note of laughter and it ended on one. It was not elaborated and did not seem striven for. There was no slow faltering and working up of "pathetic" by-play. Any actor could have done that. But this [N]egro actor had his audience shouting with laughter one instant, and the next, with a few peering glances, an intent attitude, and a wonderful manipulation of his lips, he almost made you want to cry. The laughter ceased abruptly, something caught you at the throat, the eyes pulsating, hotly for a second—and then you were laughing again.[55]

Through mime, Bert displayed an emotional and performative range that belied the boisterous performance style of minstrels or the broad physical comedy of vaudeville. Although the performance was comedic, beginning and ending in laughter, it was also dramatic, touching upon Shy's emotional depth. Although Bert played the familiar Jim Crow character, his singular performance enabled him to step a bit out of the heavy shadow that the stereotype cast.

Through Bert's most significant solo performance in the musical, his character would come to have a name: the "Jonah Man." In a song with the same title, Bert introduced this new stage self, a persona for which he would be known throughout the remainder of his career. Not merely miserable or unlucky, the unfortunate Jonah Man was contemplative. He communicated the experience of the wretched. When Bert played the Jonah Man, he did so with control, enabling one to take a journey from near-tears to laughter *with* him, rather than merely to laugh *at* him:

> *My luck started when I was born,*
> *Leas' so the old folks say.*
> *Dat same hard luck's been my bes' frien'*
> *To dis very day.*
>
> *When I was young, Mamma's frien's—to find a name they tried*
> *They named me after Pappa—and de same day pappa died,*
> *Fo'-*

CHORUS

I'm a Jonah. I'm a Jonah Man,
My family for many years would look at me and den shed tears.
Why I am dis Jonah, I sho' can't understand,
But I'm a good substantial, full fledged, real first-class Jonah Man.[56]

Baffled by the misfortune of his existence, the Jonah Man described his experiences in plaintive and subdued tones.

Years later, Bert would describe who he had become onstage:

> I am the "Jonah Man," the man who, even if it rained soup, would be found with a fork in his hand and no spoon in sight, the man whose fighting relatives come to visit him and whose head is always dented by the furniture they throw at each other. There are endless variations of this idea, fortunately; but if you sift them, you will find the same principle of human nature at the bottom of them all.[57]

Bert had developed a fundamental idea, which he would use to find experiential common ground with his audience. The key to his success was the creation of a realistic persona.

The character did not exist in a vacuum: his every action and statement had to be deeply considered. "I must imagine an idea and find out the way it would strike him [the Jonah Man]," Bert explained. "[W]hat he would do and think about it at any particular moment . . . in any particular frame of mind."[58]

Despite Bert's reliance on a stereotype to shape the Jonah Man, the character in no way lacked depth. He discussed his aims and method:

> I try to portray the darkey [*sic*], the shiftless darkey, to the fullest extent, his fun, his philosophy. Show this shiftless darkey a book and he won't know what it's about. He can't read or write. But ask him a question and he'll answer it with a philosophy that has something in it. . . . There is nothing about the fellow I *work* that I don't know. I have studied him, his joys and sorrows. Contrast is vital. If I take up a lazy stevedore, I must study his movements—I have to, he's not in me—the way he walks, the way he crosses his legs, the way he leans up against a wall, one foot forward.[59]

Through Bert, the darky became new with his meticulous representation. He depended on his many performance techniques, combining movement with character development in order to form a multidimensional person of contrasts. In addition, he incorporated pieces of his own imagination. The Jonah Man thus became an extension of both reality as well as the fertile mind of an artist.

In attempting this depiction, however, Bert risked reinforcing the stereotype. But he took responsibility for the darky figure's new shape. The Jonah Man was not a mere holdover from minstrelsy, he insisted, but a new creation. As Bert said elsewhere, "Minstrels . . . are a thing of the past because there is no more minstrelsy. To cork your face and talk politics is not minstrelsy. There are no more men like 'Daddy Rice,' the originator of minstrelsy."[60] Trying to distance himself from minstrelsy's legacy, Bert revamped the old persona. Rather than a two-dimensional exaggeration, Jonah Man became an embodied expression of Bert's innovation. By reinterpreting the type, Bert encouraged audiences to accept this new idea, and himself as an artist.

He talked about his character's effectiveness in relation to his own theory of comedy:

> Troubles are funny only when you pin them to one particular individual. And that individual, the fellow who is the goat, must be the man who is singing the song or telling the story. Then the audience can picture in their mind's eye and see him in the thick of his misfortunes, fielding flatirons with his head, carrying large bulldogs by the seat of his pants, and picking the bare bones of the chicken while his wife's relations eat the breast, and so forth.[61]

The Jonah Man, a reality-based person, often became the butt of Bert's jokes. A specific person with whom the audience could relate, he was paradoxically also one at whom the audience could laugh. Bert's comic subject was close enough to the audience so that his experience resonated, yet distant enough so that the audience could laugh at him at will. Maintaining a delicate balance between the two through attentive characterization, Bert created a character for whom an audience nearly wrote the material themselves. For, if they could already picture the amusing situations in which the character might find himself, they could be—in fact, already were—prepared to laugh at these situations when they became comic material.

Through Bert's unique performative style as Jonah Man, he garnered the lion's share of the critics' attention. Despite Bert and

George's equal and balanced work together, Bert appeared to be the key performer in the production. A *New York Times* journalist declared unequivocally, "He has the genius of the comedy in full measure. Walker is an able second, but distinctly a second."[62] The *New York World* spoke specifically about George's lesser importance: "George Walker was funny, but his business was principally that of a foil."[63] Yet another writer averred that "Williams must be given the greater part of the night's success."[64] Bert established himself as comic with George's able assistance, yet it seemed that the audience had placed him notably in front of his partner. *Williams* and Walker it was.

In reviews, some white critics recognized Bert's genius in spite of—or perhaps even because of—his heavy burnt cork makeup and subtle nuances in performance. Others, however, ignored it or explained it away. Addressing Bert's comic success, a very appreciative reviewer wrote:

> Williams, in particular, had electric connections with the risibilities of the audience. He is of serious, depressed turn of countenance, dull but possessing the deep wisdom *of his kind*; slow and grotesquently [sic] awkward in his movements. He holds a face for minutes at a time, seemingly, and when [sic] he alters it, bringing a laugh by the least movement.[65]

Although writers often did value Bert's skill, the persistent legacy of minstrelsy frequently shaped the white public's reception of his performances. And an obsession with authenticity influenced critics' appreciation. Repeatedly, white critics expressed the notion that Williams and Walker's characters *were* real, even *were* themselves, rather than a fiction. Writing about Williams's "kind," the journalist wrote as a superior, differentiating between himself and Williams. Bert was not merely a character in blackface, he was also a comedian with a black face, of a "kind" different from the writer himself. When some critics penned reviews, they exposed their own contradictory reactions to Bert's onstage efforts with their tendency to focus on race. These contradictions would continue to surface throughout Williams and Walker's career.

Black critics wrote about *In Dahomey*, at times more concerned with the show's implications than with the performance itself. After the production opened on Broadway, a production by the black

Smart Set Company gained access to first-class theaters in 1903. *New York Age* theater critic Lester Walton addressed the importance of the matter: "If but one show was successful it would mean much for the future of the negro on the stage; if both failed[,] colored theatrical aggregations would find their prospective status by no means enviable, and would signify the continuance of colored shows at second-class theaters for an indefinite period."[66] These apparently material concerns proved the importance of visibility politics among influential blacks.

Walton insisted on performers' assumption of responsibility for their representations. He encouraged actors to recognize the influence of their onstage performances. He emphasized the empowering potential of the theater for blacks: "The stage is the medium by means of which ideas—whether true or false—are disseminated; where many opinions are molded. . . . The stage will be one of the principal factors in ultimately placing the negro before the public in his true and proper light."[67] The greatest exposure to the "true" Negro, for those white audiences who seldom encountered him or her in their daily lives, would be through the theater, Walton believed. Consequently, he demanded that actors take their roles seriously. Black performers themselves would have to display the proper image in order to turn audiences away from minstrelsy's traditional derisive and belittling representation of blacks.

Walton expressed optimism about the influence the Negro theater could wield when in the hands of responsible actors. He confidently delimited the requirements to be met by Negro theater in order to achieve its goal—in his view—of uplift and the "effacement" of racism:

> With colored performers of high moral character and ability assuming character roles in wholesome plays[,] there can be no doubt as to what the effect will be. Plays possessing those elements that will serve an iconoclastic purpose in the dissipation of false impressions regarding the negro race as a whole; plays mingled with farce, yet dramatic interest, and embodying true and admirable negro characters; plays worthy of serious consideration and appealing to the most prejudiced, are the kind that will certainly assist the race in its fight for right and just recognition.[68]

In Walton's view, the individual performer's public comportment, the material performed onstage, and the subsequent success or failure of a show all contributed to the success or failure of the "race's" agenda.

Hopes for racial advancement and social equality intimately connected to the performance of the actors. Onstage became merely one location of the actors' performances on behalf of the race. The performance began with each person's acknowledgment and acceptance of this broad understanding of his or her role in representing the community. It continued with the actor's portrayal of realistic theatrical roles onstage and included their proper offstage deportment. All elements helped to produce the best image of the race, thereby inspiring the people and winning over even the "most prejudiced."

Walton, however, neglected to consider the power and persistence of racist thought. He imagined that blacks could erase preconceived notions about race on which the culture depended, creating entirely new possibilities. Yet, as minstrelsy's incorporation of blacks had shown, mere visibility did not counter the weight of history. The burden of the performer, contrary to Walton's view, was largely externally defined.

Bert, mindful of the tensions between his onstage role as the darky and his actual intelligence as a contemplative, dignified man, took Walton's challenges to heart. He would never simply turn his back on them. As he performed his fastidiously rendered Jonah Man, he strove for excellence onstage. He also strove to remain attentive to his role as a public face, sensitive to his responsibility. Despite his efforts, some black critics, such as Sylvester Russell of the *Indianapolis Freeman*, would at times question his allegiances.

D espite Williams and Walker's challenge to please their audiences and Bert's concern about his own role, the duo would celebrate their biggest opportunity to date: a tour of *In Dahomey* in England. In April of 1903, the company of sixty-plus members sailed from New York City on the *Urania*, attracting the curiosity and attention of journalists in the city as they boarded the transatlantic ocean liner.

On that day, a crowd of "the elite among New York's colored population" stood at the dock, bidding the company farewell and gracing the members of the chorus with gifts: boxes of candy, baskets of fruit, and bouquets of flowers. Watching the dramatic send-off, a writer disparaged the party: "The scenes at the dock were ludicrous in the extreme. For almost every one [*sic*] in the company a salt water voyage was a distinct novelty, and each had prepared for it in a different way. Some of the men wore ulsters—despite the warm weather—and had binocular glasses swung over their shoulders. Golf caps were the prevailing style of headgear, and nearly every man and woman carried a steamer chair."[69]

While some journalists took the opportunity to mock the company's inexperience with international travel, suggesting that the black performers were misplaced on the elegant transatlantic ship, Bert himself would take it in stride. "All of us, down to the members of the chorus," he divulged, "pushed out our chests and shoved our hats back on our heads and walked up the gang-plank trying to look just as if crossing the ocean was an old story. That was the way we *tried* to look, but at least half of us in our hearts felt we might never put our peepers on America again."[70]

Regardless of such glibness, the emotionalism of the moment was difficult to ignore. Journalists watched as "[f]inally, the last good-by[e]s were said, the visitors returned to the pier, and the Aurania [*sic*] began to draw slowly away from the land. There was much waving of adieux and some tears shed."[71]

Critics stateside guessed at the Williams and Walker Company's chances for success. One black critic insisted on their good prospects:

> The combination of Williams and Walker will surely take in London, where there is interest in everything American and where there is more-over little of the anti-negro spirit in evidence here. The colored race is more esteemed in Great Britain than here on account of the distance "which lends enchantment," probably, and Senegambian swells [fashionable people] are well received in good society. Without this prejudice to battle against, and with a goodly equipment of American humor to exploit, they ought to come in for a long run. It is not likely, however, that King Edward will invite the dusky stars and their wives to dine and lead the cakewalk.[72]

Although not knowing what to expect, but hoping for the best, Bert would later admit, "George Walker, my partner, and several of the leading members, to say nothing of myself, hoped everything would end right, and we thought we had reason for the hope, but we knew it was not the surest thing in the world." He averred, "We thought we would make a hit in England. We felt we had a good show and were positive we had some good people, and were confident we would have a successful trip. But—" he began jokingly, "well, I think most of us made our wills before we started."[73] Williams and Walker would become the first black theatrical company to appear in London. The pressure to succeed was intense.

N orman J. Norman, the American producer responsible for bringing the acclaimed musical comedy *The Belle of New York* to England, had determined that he would bring a Negro show to London. *The Belle of New York* and his later venture, *The Chinese Honeymoon*, which generated significant returns for him in the States, gave proof of the possibility that a production like *In Dahomey* might succeed.[74] In London, excitable critics thrilled to the arrival of "the real thing": a musical comedy "written and composed by negroes."[75] Fascinated by the performers, all of whom had "negroid blood in their veins," critics declared that London would enjoy authentic black entertainers, instead of white imitators in blackface.[76] The fixation on authenticity persisted.

The company would perform on Shaftesbury Avenue, which in 1903 was the theatrical center of the West End of London. The theater district had been moving westward for years, and the Shaftesbury Theatre was the first to open on the avenue of the same name. By the time Williams and Walker performed, the theater district of the Victorian era, which had been centered on the Strand, had given way to Shaftesbury Avenue. The avenue "became synonymous with bright lights and commercial entertainment as much as 'Broadway' implies the New York equivalent."[77]

Although London was the welcome home of musical comedies, the company arrived unsure about the audience's tastes. Bert and George's memory of their previous failed performance in England years before troubled them. On opening night, all members of the cast were nervous. Bert would explain, "We had been told all sorts of stories about the roughness of the London audiences, and were warned to wear steel armor under our costumes, and all that sort of thing. Of course we knew it was exaggerated, but we were a little bit fearful just the same."[78]

Among the things the company would change for their six-week run in England was the use of dialect. Bert would later admit, "Once or twice I turned loose a little broad 'coon' talk on them, but they couldn't understand all the words and lost the point of the jokes." As a result, they decided to shift away from dialect, and to focus on "straight English."[79] One important element that remained the same, however, was

Bert's use of burnt cork. People claimed that "it would be fatal for me to appear in cork," he said." They thought it would be puzzling to the English audiences, who wouldn't understand it, but Bert ended up standing firm: "For about ten minutes they had me going, but all of a sudden I got sort of bullish myself and stopped listening to suggestions."[80] He remained as convinced as before that in blackface, his comic skills were on best display.

Bert's fears about the audience response were not entirely off-base, however. A *Daily Mail* writer acknowledged that on opening night there were "[t]hose who had come to scoff," but also stated that those same spectators "remained to laugh."[81] Still, all the while, there were those in the audience who questioned the show's vision of African American life, complaining that "[i]nstead of white coats, large-brimmed hats, colored bandannas, cotton dresses, we have *aggressively* smart dress coats, diamond studs, and Paris millinery."[82] Evidently, the play's very modern concern with fashion and international trends seemed threatening to critics. In Bert, those with a lack of imagination and desire to find a "type" would note his "real negro charm," even while others would see in his performance that "touch of pathos which is the true test of the comedian."[83]

The response was generally positive on opening night, and the audience received the company with "hearty laughter and abundant applause."[84] Up until the unfortunately puzzling ending, that is. *In Dahomey*'s creators had been eager to present a face of the African continent unfamiliar to white audiences. Admittedly, however, the continent was not personally known to the writers themselves. Spectators read the show as "a musical comedy of 'coon' [African American] life"; it seemed that the conclusion, with its representation of Africa, was bound to confound.[85]

The third act finished with a tableau of Dahomey, an imaginative rendering of Africa. The tableau should have been familiar as a "pantomime," a common presentation during the Victorian era that featured a transformation of the stage using ornate costumes and sets to create a unique spectacle. Surely the final scene should have qualified as pantomime, resplendent as it was with rich greenery and the creation of a swampland. An extravagant scene, it included company members dressed in camouflage costumes. Without a doubt, *In Dahomey* had transformed the stage into Dahomey, the cast members into Dahomeans.[86]

Notwithstanding the writers' attempt to impress audiences with this wondrous transformation of setting, London audiences became confused. They could not make sense of the mystifying creation presented. Although this image of exotic Africa was to some extent certainly shaped by then-current perceptions of the African continent, the conspicuous absence of the most powerful images—Africa as anticivilization and the African as savage—left a void in their understanding.[87] The actors had created their own image of Dahomey, and audiences struggled to absorb—but most often seemed to resist—that vision. One critic declared that the point of contrast focused on by the show's writers must have been the African's dignity in his own land versus the "absurd aping of white men's ways which is perhaps the most pathetic thing in regard to the 'colour problem' of the present day."[88] The writer disparaged blacks in America while also upholding an image of the African as a noble savage. Another misread the representation of Dahomey in a different direction: as an attempt "to indicate a return to primitive barbarism as the ideal of the negro race."[89]

Ultimately, in order to placate the perplexed audience, the performers changed the ending of the show. They scrapped the cast's trip to Africa and finished *In Dahomey* instead with the outdated cakewalk. In London, the dance was a rage. A reviewer for the London *Era* would later happily announce, "A real cake-walk has been introduced into *In Dahomey*, at the Shaftesbury Theatre, by the Negro comedians, Williams and Walker. This item was omitted on the first night because it was believed that the dance had had its day in London. The number of letters received by the management requesting its introduction proved this idea to be incorrect."[90]

The abandonment of the script not only undermined but overturned the magnificent vision of Africa that *In Dahomey*'s creators had struggled to represent. Audiences' expectations foiled the company's attempt at rendering their version of *In Dahomey*. And as the creators submitted to the audience's demands, they took a regrettable step back from their interpretation. They would later decide to cut the third act and initiate the play with a prologue taking place in Africa.

By serving the public, however, the company also benefited. To audiences, Bert and George remained "irresistibly comic" in a show where all the black performers entertained with "zest and abandonment . . . : teeth gleam, voices ring, eyes beam, and they dance with their whole bodies in apparent ecstasy of enjoyment, alive to the finger-tips."[91]

Bert's use of pantomime, as well as that of others in the cast, received considerable attention as a critic remarked, "Some members of the company are equal to the best exponents of the art in France."[92]

Focusing on Bert alone, writers expressed appreciation of his method. One journalist noted Bert's comical pessimism, stating that "he gets most of his droll effects by quaint byplay and wonderful facial expression, showing the instinct of the true comedian."[93] Another remarked that "[b]y quiet methods Mr. Williams keeps the audience in a constant roar of laughter," declaring him "an actor of great comic power and observation."[94] Bert's critics, in agreement about his success as Shy, recognized that the "sad earnestness with which the lengthy misanthrope copes with bad fortune and the treachery of friends is full of fine humor."[95]

George drew applause as "the embodiment of fun and good humour," being an entertainer "whose jolly face, general alertness, and exhilarating manner make for general cheeriness."[96] Furthermore, his dancing with Aida "was of the most delightfully free and graceful manner."[97] Time and again, the pair received encores as they danced for the public.

In spite of whatever confusion audiences had experienced, they thoroughly enjoyed the production. On 24 May, a journalist reported on the publication of the show's music by Keith, Prowse, and Company. The writer lauded *In Dahomey* for its "instantaneous" success, Williams and Walker for their status as a "trademark," and Cook for his music, which was "being whistled and sung [all] over the town."[98]

Barely a month after their arrival, the company's fortunes soared. King Edward VII wished for a command performance, and with haste the company went to Buckingham Palace. They performed on the ninth birthday of his grandson, the Prince of Wales. The gathering was a garden party of more than 150 guests, and the Williams and Walker Company mounted *In Dahomey*, sets and all, on the palace grounds.[99]

Jesse Shipp, the company's stage director, fussed about, taking care of every detail so as to put on the best possible show. Bert recalled that "[Jesse] had pitched in early in the morning and helped the carpenters and the electricians: he fixed the footlights and he rounded up the 'props.'"[100] Hard at work, Jesse barely stopped to talk as various representatives from the palace came down to the sets to ask how things were progressing. When one particular individual asked him if he had any problems with how the English did things, Jesse blew his top. He went into a litany of complaints about this, that, and the other.[101] In retrospect, Bert wished that the question had been posed to someone else, because Jesse was given to speaking his mind; he did not fret about "knowing his place" as a black man. Opinionated and outspoken, at times even rash, he readily vented his spleen. Still, Shipp couldn't have possibly acted so poorly, Bert hoped.

No sooner had "God Save the King" begun to play than the nervous cast spied through the curtains the procession of their audience. Everyone would sit on the lawn, save the queen mother, the king, and the queen, who had chairs in an area nearest the orchestra. As the members of the company spoke in whispered exclamations about the impressive audience, Shipp remained distinctly unimpressed—that is, until it dawned on him that the man he had been "roastin' the country to" was the king himself.[102]

Bert, however, being a reserved and judicious individual, had more than a moment's hesitation that afternoon. When determining whether or not to sing the show's "Evah Dahkey is a King" for the performance, he wondered, would the King have a sense of humor about a song that claims the possible royal lineage of the common person? And a black one, at that?

With words by Paul Laurence Dunbar and E. P. Moran, "Evah Dahkey is a King" was a song in the Negro dialect. The first verse spoke of the "mighty cur'ous circumstance dat's a-botherin' all the nation,/ all de Yankees is dissatisfied wid a deir untitled station." Relating the irony of a "democratit" people infatuated with and happy to wear titles if only they can "snare 'em," the singer observed a "[pe]'culiar thing/ When a dahkey starts to huntin' he is sho to prove a king."[103] The singer also observed that, looking into his own history, the Negro would most certainly discover a connection to royalty, a statement echoing Bert's remark when reading Ogilby's *Africa*.

Throughout the song, the comparison of blacks to whites continued as the singer declared, "Evah dahkey has a lineage dat de white fo'ks can't compete wid,/An' a title, such as duke or earl, why we wouldn't wipe our feet wid." Announcing that nothing less than the position of king could satisfy the black man, the singer followed with a line that would have concerned Bert during his command performance: "Fu a kingdom is our station an we's each a rightful ruler."[104] Undercutting the traditional notion of monarchal authority as unique and inherited, the song claimed the right of all Negroes to a kingdom and to power. The thought of performing such a song, even playfully, worried Bert, but he went on with it, nonetheless.

In the end, the king enjoyed the show. He remarked flatteringly about the company, though it came in terms that infantilized its members: "To me . . . the great attraction of this negro musical comedy is that the performers play with such zest. They seem to take as much delight in it as the children themselves."[105] The company had made an obvious impression, which trickled down to other London audiences, who would demand to see the production the king so praised.

Following the performance at the palace, "the band kept up the refrain and all the little princes and princesses gave imitations of the 'cakewalk.' [The] noble Briton [was] having taught to his children the 'cakewalk'." With the encouragement of guests, the cakewalk took off all over again, and London became "cakewalking crazy."[106]

Aida, who had once instructed New York's elite in the dance, reprised her role as she taught British society how the cakewalk was done. Taking the fore as instructor to uninitiated Britons, she played a crucial role. She confidently established herself as an authority and as a teacher, saying: "Society, which is now learning the cakewalk, has had the advantage of years of training by the best masters of dancing and of the bodily graces. Its members whom I have instructed, therefore do cakewalking easily."[107] She also defined for the public the meanings of the dance, once viewed as merely the highfalutin expression of slaves. Speaking with the London *Tatler*, she explained: "In early days the dance was performed with greater dignity—was less of a dance and more of a walk. The Ethiop[ian] was in sooth [*sic*] a picturesque fellow. He went about his task with an inborn sense of beauty."[108] She discussed the dance in terms emphasizing grace and dignity not generally attributed to a race often described as uncivilized and unrefined.

Elsewhere, when asked point-blank to define the cakewalk, Aida would declare it a dance "peculiar to our people" and distinctly of American origin, attentive to influences that led to the dance's creation.[109] Even as she instructed her students she told them, "Think of moonlight nights and pin knots and tallow dips, and of lives untouched by the hardness of toil, for I tell you there was sunshine in the hearts of those who first danced the cake-walk."[110] Rather than look upon black Americans' past in shame, Aida proudly insisted that students ponder the Negro's experience. She urged them to reflect on it constantly as they endeavored to achieve the elegance of the original dancers. Describing the cakewalk as a "gala dance," she conferred on it the same urbanity that the elite would have granted any other stately dance.[111]

The company's performance for the king would linger in their memories, but none would be as moved by the experience as Bert. He would later say, "It was the proudest moment of my life . . . to appear before my sovereign, for I am British born, hailing from the Bahamas. When I remember how he laughed and applauded, I feel good, I can tell you. The King kept standing up to see better."[112] Bert's comment held considerable irony, for while he identified as a Bahamian British subject, he in no way acknowledged a tie to black Bahamians. Primarily concerned with the honor exemplified by the king's demand to see *In Dahomey* and the king's fascination with the company's performance, Bert recognized only the privilege of being in the imperial leader's presence. He overlooked the experience of black Bahamians who continued to fight for survival as he toured abroad. A new migration to the States had begun at the turn of the century as impoverished Bahamians sought economic opportunity, moving to Miami, Florida, mainly for work in agriculture.[113] Like the Williams family, they often moved permanently, hoping for an improved standard of living, despite the reality of racial discrimination and segregation in the South.

While other Bahamian subjects of the king suffered at home or struggled stateside, Bert sang the praises of his sovereign. For him, the encounter would become the definitive experience of his life. He would return to it repeatedly as a manner of articulating what it meant to be a "star," that is, interacting with and performing for illustrious audiences. He would also utilize it to express his frustrations as he faced racial discrimination in America. King Edward VII, as an audience to Williams and Walker, would confirm blacks' entitlement to a standard of treatment far superior to that which they received. It would also corroborate Bert's belief that the baffling racial practices of American democracy represented an isolated and backward view regarding blacks' place in society.

Whereas George would use a different tone, Bert expressed his excitement about the command performance with great humility: "We were treated royally. That is the only word for it. We had champagne from the Royal cellar and strawberries and cream from the Royal garden. The Queen was perfectly lovely, and the King was as jolly as he could be and the little princes and princesses were as nice as they could be, just like little faeries."[114] For George, although the command performance had been an honor, he chose to speak casually of the nobility. He thereby subtly affirmed his viewpoint by using diminutive terms to refer to the children, although royalty, rather than feeling compelled to use honorific titles.

After their performance for the king, the company's run at the Shaftesbury Theatre continued through Boxing Day (26 December 1903). Following a few weeks of downtime and preparation, they then began a tour of the suburbs and cities of England. The tour continued into the late spring when a new company took over.

Before the new company toured, Bert and George themselves would thrill audiences repeatedly. Aida would distinguish herself in the role of Rosetta Lightfoot, the rebellious daughter, as "the life of the whole company."[115] Her exceptional performance would cause one writer to describe her as "one of the best [dancers] we have ever seen."[116] The London *Royal Magazine* would go on to declare her "the leading 'star' lady of the Williams and Walker Company . . . a born actress who could shine in serious parts, and even Shakespearian drama."[117] Additionally, Lottie, though no Aida, would perform her lines as Mrs. Stringer, the confidence woman, "in an incisive manner and with just the right amount of spirit."[118]

Although their command performance would be the most magnificent time of their journey aboard, Bert and George would have yet another unique opportunity. While in Edinburgh, Scotland, they and eight other men of the company were initiated into Freemasonry in Lodge Waverley, No. 597, on 2 May 1904. Officially proposed and seconded by James Halliday and William Gordon, members of the Edinburgh Lodge, they were subsequently passed on 16 May. They then took the second degree and raised to the third degree on 1 June of that year. Unlike the Freemasons in the United States, even those in the Northern states, Scottish Freemasons, at least those members of Bert and George's lodge, upheld principles regarding antidiscrimination and race. And indeed, the Scottish Masons would hold considerable sway at a crucial time in the years to come.

By the time the production returned to the States, *In Dahomey* had enriched the show yet again with new songs and fresh scene changes. Importantly, a Boston reviewer observed that Will Marion Cook had "succeeded in lifting Negro music above the plane of the so-called 'Coon' song without destroying the characteristics of the melodies."[119]

Williams and Walker Company Members with Scottish Masons: Bert Williams (seated, far right), George Walker (seated, second from left), James Halliday (center), William Gordon (standing, extreme left). COURTESY OF THE GRAND LODGE OF ANTIENT FREE AND ACCEPTED MASONS OF SCOTLAND

Given its new prologue and structure in two acts, it seemed like an entirely new production to spectators. The company's return to the States was done with great fanfare as the writer explained, "There is no need of an introduction of Messrs. Williams and Walker, as they are too well known in this city from their work in previous pieces, but it is doubtful if two comedians were ever more deserving of praise than now. They have the only organization in the country that is producing a real colored opera."[120]

A black writer discussed the importance of *In Dahomey*, which by 1905 had been playing for three winters. His words, like those of Lester Walton, illustrate the idea that the proper presentation of blackness or black life would be sufficient to create a new image of blacks in the minds of the white public:

The play . . . introduced the American public to another side of the varied, yet admirable character of the American Negro, who insists on entering every field of art, and becoming master of it. It is impossible to write down the history of the progress of this heterogeneous, yet indivisible people, without including these young men, *In Dahomey*, or Williams and Walker, just as you please.[121]

Asserting the New Negro concept of black improvement and achievement, the journalist wrote Williams and Walker as heroes, central to the tale of racial uplift and progress. Presenting African American history, the writer designated a place for the black entertainer and, specifically, for Williams and Walker. Such a role would come with considerable responsibility, which Bert and George would face as they moved on to their next big production.

6

First Class All the Way

$\mathcal{H}$aving appeared on Broadway, before the monarch of England, and throughout the States with their production of *In Dahomey*, Bert and George insisted on being in a completely new league as performers. By the time *In Dahomey* had closed, they'd established themselves and, consequently, now had a "unique position in the world of entertainers. Of the five thousand colored players in the country, they alone [had] really national reputations."[1] They performed onstage, in recordings on Victrolas, and, in a manner of speaking, in the parlors of families across the country that still enjoyed Williams and Walker sheet music as home entertainment.

Other black performers, such as songwriters Bob Cole and the Johnson brothers, also made remarkable strides in show business. Cole and Rosamond Johnson had signed with musical publisher Joseph Stern in 1901, and in 1906 would stage their own all-black musical, *The Shoo-Fly Regiment*. Entertainer Ernest Hogan continued to tour and perform in his own shows and in 1905 starred in *Rufus Rastus*. He had distinguished himself as the "highest-priced" single black vaudeville performer in the nation. Others graced the stage, but these were the performers who dominated musical theater.[2] Surpassing them in visibility as well as access to top theaters were Williams and Walker. They were the performers who proved that Broadway was possible for black musical comedies—a "unique position," indeed.

In 1904, Bert, George, and, importantly, Aida, had begun a mutually beneficial relationship with a black-owned music publisher, Attucks Music Publishing. Named to honor Crispus Attucks, "black protomartyr of American freedom" and the first casualty of the Boston Massacre of 1770, the company had been founded by Cecil Mack (a.k.a. R. Cecil McPherson), who had written songs for *In Dahomey*.[3] Leading performers, Bert, George, and Aida, along with composers Jesse A. Shipp and Alex Rogers, were "mainstays" in the company's catalog.[4] With the support of the commercially successful company, the entertainers moved away from the racially incendiary coon songs of the times and toward more realistic representations of black American life. They achieved this despite the company's need to appeal to both whites and blacks, as well as to introduce songs performed by both races.[5]

As Williams and Walker gained national visibility, they exploited their position, demanding more control of their artistic contributions. Always a man of vision as well as the businessman of the pair, George took the fore in leveraging the team's incredible achievements. Although onstage Bert stayed steadily in front, offstage George made a distinctive name for himself—as well as for Williams and Walker. No sooner had the company returned from its domestic tour with *In Dahomey* than George created the Williams and Walker Glee Club, made up of company members.

By the summer of 1905, the group traveled to Boston to perform for Booker T. Washington and his wife. There they enjoyed refreshments, games, and the society of the most powerful black leader in the nation. The Glee Club sang an assortment of songs that gave "not merely the plantation and folk songs in which the race is especially expert, but also music of a classic order," demonstrating the black performers' contribution to racial uplift.[6]

George, seen as "somewhat of a philanthropist as well as a comedian and actor," was fashioning himself into a "large-hearted and sympathetic" man.[7] He offered the Glee Club to the artistic community on behalf of both himself and his partner. Through the Club, members sought "not merely the acquisition of money and fame, but also their [members'] development along artistic, personal, and moral lines," which was increasingly a refrain in George's discussions with the black press.[8]

Driven to see Bert and himself take greater advantage of their opportunities through the Williams and Walker Company's fortunes,
George pushed for them not only to remain on Broadway with their
next show but also to move from second-class to first-class theaters. If
successful, the Williams and Walker Company could demand and earn
considerably more money from their performances than ever before.

Unfortunately, despite the duo's unprecedented success, they faced
mountainous obstacles. When Bert and George met with Hurtig and
Seamon, the managers informed them that if they had any intentions of
making their next show a reality, they would have to find new financing.
For Williams and Walker's new show, *Abyssinia*, the duo envisioned
elaborate costumes for their cast that numbered more than one hundred, spectacular lighting, and even a manmade cascade.[9] It would be
more "pretentious and costly than any other [production] they had attempted."[10] Hurtig and Seamon refused to provide the investment that
such a production would require. Regardless of *In Dahomey*'s track
record, the managers continued to question the possible success of a
large-scale black production, particularly one requiring more than double the investment of *In Dahomey* itself.[11] Yet, even as Bert and George
moved forward to secure another investor, Hurtig and Seamon vied for
control, suing the duo in July 1905.

A harrowing and unpleasant affair, the suit took Bert and George to
the Supreme Court of New York County as their former managers
sought to prevent their move to other representation. At the same time,
though, it averred Bert and George's incomparable qualities as performers. Arguing about the "extraordinary efforts" and the "extraordinary risks" they assumed to provide for Williams and Walker's
production, Hurtig and Seamon cited their incalculable loss without
these "special and unique performers whose performance cannot be
duplicated."[12]

Declaring that "Bert A. Williams is the subject of imitation by many
performers, but is absolutely without an equal; that his rendition of
com[ed]y lines and songs, facial distortions, dances, walks and gestures
convey an extraordinary and peculiar humor to the observer, which is
inimitable and difficult of description," they testified to the team's
matchless virtuosity, even as they aimed to maintain control over the
trajectory of Williams and Walker's career.[13] Far from ignoring George,
they attested to his "special and distinctive reputation for his dancing in
which he is unexcelled."[14] Yet, perhaps even more essentially, they

homed in on the relevance of the duo as a *duo*, whose names "are always coupled and mentioned together, and when reference is made to one, the name of the other will also invariably be mentioned."[15] Williams and Walker were irreplaceable, the plaintiffs cried. Both apart and, of course, together.

Required to file proof of Williams and Walker's profits in the three years preceding the suit, Bert and George showed gains of about $40,000 each per year. They eloquently illustrated their business's lucrativeness.[16] Hurtig and Seamon then claimed that without Williams and Walker's business, the managers would suffer inestimable damages. With such proof, it might have seemed that the managers would win their case. Yet, despite the efforts of their attorney, Hurtig and Seamon did not regain control. The judge ultimately declared the duo free to pursue new management.

Williams and Walker's accomplishment was truly remarkable. At a time when black Americans' rights were at best overlooked and at worst outrightly denied, when lynchings of African Americans ran rampant, in part inspiring W. E. B. Du Bois to organize the Niagara Movement in an effort to secure blacks' "full political, civil, and social rights," Williams and Walker had dared to seek redress.[17] Five years prior to the formation of the National Association for the Advancement of Colored People (NAACP), the organization that would wage legal battles fighting for social justice for blacks, the entertainers had utilized the courts for recourse—and won.

The judgment in their favor was even more noteworthy considering that their recent annual earnings of $40,000 each placed them financially in the same class as influential whites. That year, the House had proposed that Vice President Charles Fairbank's salary be increased to $15,000 annually, and the Senate proposed that U. S. District Attorney Henry Lawrence Burnett (of the "Southern District of New York") receive $10,000 per year, "the highest salary ever allowed a United States District Attorney."[18] Given that the black performers' success had previously made them the object of a white mob's rage and the influential Syndicate's anger, it would seem their earnings might, at minimum, invite scorn. Regardless of their exceptional affluence as part of the first generation of black stars, however, the two unbelievably commanded the consideration of a New York Supreme Court judge.

Never ones to rest on their laurels, Williams and Walker quickly sought a new manager, securing Melville Raymond, a businessman well connected to the theatrical Syndicate. Before plunging into staging their production, however, the two appeared in vaudeville. They had become so successful that they received offers to appear in big-time at Hammerstein's Victoria Theatre.

Vaudeville had continued to reign as the premiere national entertainment and would become even bigger with New Yorker Sime Silverman's first December 1905 issue of *Variety*, the vaudeville bible.[19] Over the years, as vaudeville's reach had grown, it had developed into two distinct tracks: "big-time" and "small-time." Compared to "big-time," "[s]mall-time was ... [the] minor leagues": a place where performers would hardly want to stay long on their way to the majors.[20] The budgets for big-time theaters were high; they offered lavish productions with stars headlining the attraction. Big-time vaudeville theaters featured only the most well-known entertainers, like Sarah Bernhardt ("The Divine Sarah"), the cherished French actress; small-time vaudeville offered lesser names for cheaper prices. Whereas big-time theaters typically gave two performances a day, small-time vaudeville did four, five, or even continuous performances.[21] Hammerstein's offer for Williams and Walker to play the Victoria, then the city's leading vaudeville venue, confirmed once again that Bert and George had made it as major names.

Despite Williams and Walker's legitimacy, another performer, the white Southern monologuist Walter C. Kelly, drew the color line. He refused to appear on the show's bill with the team. George laughed in reaction to the incident, deciding, "The man is foolish.... The day is past for that sort of thing. Both white men and black men have a right to earn a living in whatever manner they find most convenient, providing they injure no one else." He dared to remark, "I do not think I will be thought conceited if I point to the fact that Williams and Walker are pretty well established, while Mr. Kelly's fame is still somewhat in retirement." Then, in his audacious style, he added a flippant comment: "Of course, if [Kelly] is looking for a little advertisement, he will probably get it at our expense, but it is pretty small work at best."[22] In the end, the show went on without Kelly.

While George appeared glib, even cocky, about such situations, Bert was less inclined to take them in stride. He hated being the center of such controversy, and even though he and George were hardly responsible for Kelly's actions, George's provocative statements made him uncomfortable. While George could rise above such attitudes and react with an air of nonchalant superiority, Bert felt these cuts deeply, as evidenced by his profound taciturnity. In their efforts to have their demands as top performers met, George kept coming back to the table with dogged determination and limitless perseverance. Bert found himself often willing to back down—to George's undoubted frustration. "No, I never was much of a business man," Bert would later admit. He elaborated on how they worked:

> Walker generally arranged the contracts. He was suave; one of those oily fellows, and so persistent. Walker used to insist on having things decided his way—OUR way. . . . In a business deal where the other party decided against us, I was usually willing to consider it settled rather than argue. Not so with Walker. He would talk on and on. "Arguing," he called it, and little by little the other side would begin to be convinced.[23]

Although in this instance, making things go George's way also usually meant Bert and George's way, the different styles of George and Bert would mean that they were not always as united as Hurtig and Seamon would imagine.

With George's increasing frankness, he seemed to receive endless offers to share his views with the public. Never one to miss a chance to expound in the press, George spoke on behalf of himself and his partner, sharing a vision

> [t]o erect in New York an Ethiopian Theatre where the plays produced by black men may be staged, and the songs of black people may be sung. The contemplated national theatre will be the center of the musical life of the Afro-American people; singers will here be trained; the old songs of the race, which have been worth so much, both in slavery and freedom, will be preserved to generations to come; embryonic actors will be given a chance to either develop or convince the management that there can be no development; a school of music, in which ambitious men and women may study, and at the same time, come in direct contact with the music of the stage, will be opened; indeed all things that touch the artistic side of the life of this people will have its center here.[24]

Although the Ethiopian theater would never actually come into being, George's vision of this imagined institution would symbolize the depth of his commitment to the artistic future of African Americans. More than that, it would place him at the helm, shoring up his own position as a race man who had the interests of black people at heart.

When the black-owned Pekin Theater opened in Chicago the year following George's 1906 interview, owner Robert "Bob" Motts would affirm his role as "a leader among the colored people in that part of Chicago," a position George would have craved for himself.[25] Motts, a local visionary who used his own money to support his venture, not only imagined the venue but also "remodeled the place, constructing a little bijou theater, complete in all its details."[26]

George would later go on to speak about Motts's achievement in relation to his own goals: "Chicago is the only city in the country that has a distinctive colored theatre, and it is our ambition to make money enough to build them in other cities, because they can be made a great force for education. I wish we had such a theatre where we could train negroes to realize that a colored person has parts worthy of serious notice by himself and by others."[27] He thus created his vision not only on behalf of Williams and Walker but also for the benefit of the black community as a whole.

By far the greater part of Williams and Walker's contributions continued to be *on* the stage. *Abyssinia*, a musical partly set in Africa, was even more grand than *In Dahomey* had been. This would seem to have boded well as the Williams and Walker Company went into rehearsals of the new production. The relationship between Bert and George during this time, however, seemed to grow surprisingly cold. As George prepared the cast and crew for the new show, Bert hung back, appearing at the theater only for the first dress rehearsal, having been given updates from Alex Rogers on the show's progress.[28]

In truth, as opposites differing not only in manner but also in interests and tastes, Bert and George appeared together little except onstage. Having by this time established themselves, the need to present themselves as a pair in public had lessened significantly. They were like McIntyre and Heath, the leading white blackface comedy duo: a dynamic, well-suited pair onstage, but distinct individuals with separate lives offstage.[29]

While George had gained standing in and among the company and before the public, Bert had retreated. He spent his time at home with Lottie, reading the translated poetry of Persian writer Omar Khayyám and the philosophy of Goethe in his vast library, or socializing with a few friends and his father, Frederick, at a local bar.[30] There were few people with whom he most shared himself. His father, a proud man who had held great ambitions for Bert ever since he saw him on a platform spieling, perhaps knew best Bert's inner yearnings.

On Sunday evenings, Bert would go to Matheney's Café, on 135th Street and Seventh Avenue. There he would meet with a few others—Chris Smith and Jim Burris, songwriters famous for the tune "Ballin' the Jack"; Henry Troy of the Williams and Walker Company; and singer-comedian Tom Fletcher. They would talk late into the morning, telling stories, even locking up for the owner when they left.[31]

Often, Bert brooded alone, developing a habit of chain-smoking and heavy drinking that matched his weighty reflections. The habit would have haunting consequences for him, although at that time it soothed his troubled soul. It was George, on the other hand, who created a public face and a standpoint for Williams and Walker, locating himself at the center of the community of black entertainers. Over time George established himself more—ever the dandy. The reserved West Indian, however, with a few exceptions, found himself far from that center. At times, Bert was even in isolation.

With his natural reserve, which some read as "downright snobbishness," Bert would have needed to reinvent his offstage self to become the representative Negro the black American community demanded.[32] Not knowing this, or being incapable of doing so, he remained distant.

Nonetheless, there were some ways in which the two actors participated together as they worked with the Williams and Walker Company. Knowing that the eyes and ears of the world were upon them, they wisely set a structure for the comportment of company members, which they laid out in a booklet. "I don't suppose there is a theatrical in the world that is so strictly disciplined as ours," Bert later claimed. "We can't afford to let our people do anything wrong—it would spoil all our efforts to build up a decent reputation."[33] Although desiring to maintain a degree of levity about the circumstances, Bert and George knew what was at stake as they explained:

> We do not by any means wish to make you inmates of an asylum, nor do we wish at this time to seem to attack your deportment or behavior, but, knowing that the bond of prejudice is drawn so tightly about us, and that the eye that sees everything we colored folks do is every [sic] ready to

magnify and multiply many times over the value of the most innocent deed committed by us, we write you this letter to warn you to so conduct yourself that your manner and mode of life will disarm all criticism and place you above reproach.[34]

Creating rules and a list of penalties for transgression, Williams and Walker protected themselves by setting monetary fines that would be used "for the immediate use of members of the company who many be in need of assistance."[35] Having faced countless indignities while on the road, they held no illusions with regard to the realities: "Dressing rooms kept from them, refusals to work from stage hands, and the thousand and one little incivilities born of prejudice . . . the things which a negro company must expect to face until it has made something more than a name for itself."[36] These incivilities continued even after a company made a name for itself, as was obviously the case with Williams and Walker.

byssinia opened on 20 February 1906 at the Majestic Theatre in New York. At that time, it was a six-scene story, but like *In Dahomey*, this musical comedy would change shape during its run, as its creators adapted and tightened the script to a four-scene play. Yet again, Bert and George worked with representations of Africa, with a book and lyrics written by Jesse Shipp and Alex Rogers. The musical program, directed by James Vaughan, was an integration of African and African American music. In fact, the program itself declared, "The overture to *Abyssinia* is a blending of native African and American negro melodies, and although foreign to the thematic material of the play, is nevertheless intended to suggest its character."[37]

The subject matter reflected recent events. In 1896, Abyssinia (now Ethiopia) gained the distinction of being "the only African country to emerge victorious from Europe's late-nineteenth-century scramble to colonize Africa." It had remained sovereign in the face of Italy's attempt at conquest.[38] Abyssinia had a powerful place in the imagination of America's blacks: the black press had written about King Menelik's successes during the time with pride and defiance.[39] The focus on Abyssinia underscored the triumph of black "self-determination" and "African resistance," particularly at a time when blacks in the States struggled against a prejudiced and segregated society.[40] In *Abyssinia*,

Williams and Walker gestured to this as they retained historical accuracy within the play. The show included a king named Menelik, the nation's capital of Addis Ababa, and Abyssinian words within the script itself.[41]

The play centers on characters Jasmine Jenkins (Williams) and Rastus Johnson (Walker), tourists who travel from their home in Kansas to Abyssinia. "Ras," moneyed by having recently won $15,000 in the lottery, uses $900 to pay off the mortgage on his land in Kansas. With another portion of his winnings, he bankrolls a trip abroad for a group that includes his aunt and members of a Baptist congregation. Together, the group travels to Europe and then extends its trip to Abyssinia after oil is discovered on Ras's land.[42] During their time in Abyssinia, Ras and "Jas" become entangled in a web of confusion, at the height of which

> Ras is mistaken for a rebel chief, and Jas, trying to protect his friend from the officials, grabs a vase from the market stall. The official then charges Jas with theft and explains that the penalty for such a crime is the loss of the offending hand. . . . The emperor's daughter [later] reveals the misunderstanding, and Ras and Jas are freed. As they leave, they sing to their newfound friends.[43]

As was true of *In Dahomey*, *Abyssinia* avoided overt romance in its storyline: "Negro shows had to be particularly careful. No serious love interest could be included. No 'suggestion' was allowed."[44] During the time, a concern about propriety reigned. For blacks, performing "niceties" onstage meant that they could not include romantic themes.[45]

Aida, by this time a well-established dancer and choreographer who could use her national reputation as a forum, would express her frustration about these constraints. From her beginnings with Williams and Walker as a model in a simple tobacco ad, she had become a celebrated singer and a master teacher of the cakewalk, both in the States and abroad. Even more importantly, she had become an advocate for blacks in theater. She wrote about "The Color Line in Musical Comedy":

> You haven't the faintest conception of the difficulties which must be overcome, of the prejudices which must be soothed, of the things we must avoid whenever we write or sing a piece of music, put on a play or a sketch, walk out in the street or land in a new town. . . . Every little thing we do must be thought out and arranged by negroes, because they alone know how easy it is for a colored show to offend a white audience.[46]

Educating the audience as to the obstacles black entertainers faced, Aida insisted, "No white can understand these things, much less appreciate them." To illustrate her points, she explained that although she had worked in musicals over the past ten years, "[T]here has never been even the remotest suspicion of a love story in any of them. During those ten years I don't think there has ever been a single white company which has produced any kind of musical play in which a love story was not the central motive."[47] The standard was different for blacks. It limited the artists' options, forcing them to work with and, where possible, around constraints. Black writers and actors remained fully aware of the proscriptions created by white producers, theater owners, and audiences.

Nonetheless, by oblique tactics, the Williams and Walker Company contradicted the standard for black musical comedy. They subtly incorporated romance into the show. Foregrounding George's real-life marital status—Aida was the female lead in the production—they worked against the current.[48] The play includes a scene between Ras and the emperor's daughter, Miram, during which the couple converses about Ras's home. In the scene, the usually smooth Ras is reduced to a nervous would-be suitor who alternates between discussion with Miram and asides directed to the audience.[49] *Abyssinia*'s creators and performers found their own means of surmounting and challenging the conventions of the time.

*A*udiences hungered for another Williams and Walker production. In Boston, a critic wrote that the Globe Theatre was "jammed last evening—jammed is the only word, that will describe the audience which filled every available spot where the stage could be seen."[50] In New York, "A large audience greeted *Abyssinia* enthusiastically and showed its unmistakable approval of the splendid production."[51] In Philadelphia, even as a critic showed less excitement about the book and lyrics, the journalist admitted that *Abyssinia* was carried "upon a tidal wave of tumultuous laughter and applause. In fact, at times one couldn't hear the play on account of the approval of the audience."[52]

As before, it was Bert, over George, who dazzled the audience. A New York critic even complained, "[T]here was altogether too much of Walker and too little of Williams in the performance."[53] Throughout one performance of the play, audiences cried out Bert's name, hoping to get an encore right in the midst of the play. The writer described their mania for Williams: "One of us, as likely as not an Astor or a Vanderbilt, shouts, 'Bravo, Williams!' as though he were acclaiming [Enrico] Caruso [a famous Italian tenor] at the opera."[54] Bert was not merely the main funmaker. In Toledo, the *Blade* would declare him "a whole show in himself."[55] In an even more telling indication of Bert's reception, "The Divine Sarah" would watch the show from a box and later head backstage to meet Bert. There, she proclaimed him to be "the greatest comedian I ever saw—white or black."[56]

In *Abyssinia*, Bert again received the greater share of attention in a scene that afforded him the chance to incorporate dramatic range into his role. His crucial scene was also the climax of the musical. During it he, as Jas, awaits judgment for theft of the vase. If a gong strikes three times, Jas will lose his right hand as the cost of his crime. If it strikes four, he has been found innocent. Before the judgment, Bert sings in the voice of the pitiful Jonah Man, powerless and trapped by his continuing plagues of unbearable misfortune. He begins "Here It Comes Again." intoning:

> *Here it comes again—plague take it—here it comes again!*
> *But when that feelin' comes astealin'*
> *'Taint no use to complain.*
>
> *I thought that Jonah spell was passed*
> *But I was figgerin' too fast;*
> *My dream it was too good to last*
> *Dog bite it! Here it comes again.*[57]

Through the song, Bert sets the stage for what ensues. At the end of the song, the gong begins to ring. A *Chicago Tribune* reviewer described the scene:

> Three strokes and then a long pause. The look of fatalistic hopelessness on the face of the listening victims simply convulsed the spectators last evening. And when after a pause, the fourth stroke was heard, Jasmine seized that good right hand of his and, his face broadened out into the inimitable Williams grin, the climax carried the house off its feet. The applause was deafening, and shouts came from every part of the house.[58]

Bert had done it again. He'd drawn his audience to his side and pulled them out of their seats with his triumph. As before, he relied on gesture and expression to convey what words could not and did not. Critic Mollie Morris would aver, "From the moment Bert Williams appeared in the desert [set] carrying his shoes 'because his feet didn't hurt' until the close of the last act his every word and look called for laughter."[59] He defied the burnt cork that flattened features just as it did the dimensions of black characters and illustrated his unhindered ability to communicate both wordlessly and effectively.

In spite of such nods to Bert, *Abyssinia* received less critical acclaim than *In Dahomey*. This was perhaps because *Abyssinia* was an artistically ambitious production whites thought "too arty" for a show by blacks.[60] As one disgruntled critic wrote: "White people must always form the bulk of the colored man's audiences and do not care to see their own ways copied when they can have the real thing better done by white people almost any week in the theatrical season."[61]

Much of the music, again written by Will Marion Cook, was in an operatic style. Some writers objected to this. One critic would get at the heart of the matter, remarking to the detractors: "[N]o doubt when you entered the Majestic Theatre last evening you was [*sic*] in a reminiscent mood or tuned up to see and hear a performance similar to an old-time negro plantation minstrel." He continued with a defense of Cook and *Abyssinia*: "Prof. Will Marion Cook is a master composer and has developed negro music up to a standard of quality superior to the average comic-opera score. It is true a few numbers are reminiscent, but this is true of the music of all our later day composers."[62] White critics seemed reluctant to consider seriously the elements of the show that questioned or contradicted the legacy of minstrelsy. They chose to emphasize those elements most consistent with the tradition. They wrote the rest off as imitative. Here, the dilemma of the Negro artist was obvious. The creators of *Abyssinia* received criticism for ambitions that were apparently better left to white artists.

A Boston reviewer emphasized the elements of the show containing "characteristic ragtime tunes, the dancing that goes with them, and much Negro humor."[63] He disregarded the operatic music utilized, suggesting that the two and their company should stick with the Negro melodies and traditional music typical of their race. He thereby barred musical idioms other than ragtime.

A critic from the *New York Evening Post* stated his case even more plainly. "[T]he music is at times too elaborate for them and a return to the plantation melodies would be a great improvement upon the 'grand opera' type, for which they are not suited either by temperament or by education."[64] Regardless of the credentials of those who selected an operatic musical style for the production, the writer rejected that possibility. The critic reinforced a belief in the realism of plantation melodies, clear holdovers from minstrelsy, as blacks' traditional music. Seeking a familiar black representation, the reviewer enjoyed the cast most "[w]hen they sang and danced with negro quaintness and abandonment."[65] Favoring a theatrical performance of the timeless Old South myth, the critic interpreted all other influences as imitative and unsuitable for blacks.

Following a performance in Chicago, another critic remarked on the work as too ambitious and un-Negro to be entirely acceptable:

> [T]he music is technically good, though unsuitably operatic. . . . The producers seem to have said to themselves, "Now we'll show these white folks that we can do things on the stage just like they can"; but who cares if they can? And a majority in the audience is sorry they do. For there is barely a trace of negroism in the play.[66]

In this way, yet another journalist critiqued the show for its lack of characteristic elements from minstrelsy, creating a divide between authentic and inauthentic black performance. Although technically capable, these entertainers were artistically transgressive. Even as Bert and George sought to define themselves artistically, creating a higher standard for their performance, reviewers sternly criticized them. It was a poignant reminder of the limitations set by the white general public. Their conceptions of the black entertainer were shaped by minstrelsy's mocking caricatures.

Despite this limiting view of black performance, not everyone was a disconcerted critic. Carle Browne Cooke of the *New York Morning Telegraph* enthusiastically noted that this "so-labeled 'musical comedy' . . . [was] really, in justice to its able producers, a modern negro-comic-opera." Cooke declared, "Instead of giving a poor performance[,] the Williams and Walker company gave the best 'first night show' Monday eve that has ever been given by a similar aggregation in years."[67]

ith the debate between the limiting views of the white public and
the more progressive critics raging during *Abyssinia*'s run, a
strong-willed George would press on and state his own perspective.
While reviewers lauded Bert as a familiar character though a talented
actor, and criticized the musical as an "aping" of the white man's ways,
George would stake a claim for the future of the company in particular
and black entertainers in general. Regardless of the public's refusal to
acknowledge the Williams and Walker Company's inroads, he would
stress that in *Abysssinia* they experienced "the greatest success we ever
had." He would attribute that success to "our knowledge of how to
please an audience[:] we must give them the real negro character.
Few negroes will burlesque their own race; in fact, we don't have to be
burlesqued if we stick to nature. . . . We know that when we try to act
like white folks, the public won't have us; there are enough bad white
actors now."[68]

Seeing the uniqueness of his company's contribution, George would
argue that "[t]here is no reason why we should be forced to do these
old-time nigger acts. It's all rot, this slap-stick-bandanna handkerchief-
bladder in the face act, with which negro acting is associated. It ought
to die out and we are trying hard to kill it."[69]

In a challenging voice of defiance, George would address the means
by which change would come. He discussed the role of Ethiopian theaters, which he had previously talked about at length, as places

> where negro boys and girls can be taught to respect themselves, their
> qualities and their abilities. You can't get the best out of a boy by telling
> him that his hair should be straight instead of kinky[,] that his nose
> should be classic instead of flat. Nor can you expect a colored girl to re-
> alize the best there is in her if you make her believe that a black skin can-
> not be beautiful.
>
> . . . We are trying to encourage the development of this [theatrical en-
> tertainment] our greatest talent.[70]

George spoke as a commanding, unequivocal activist. Positioning himself as a forward-thinking contributor to racial uplift, he would continue
to distinguish himself as a courageous advocate.

During *Abyssinia*'s run, in around April 1906, Bert and George returned to the recording studio. It was Columbia they went to this time,

however, rather than Victor. In their first session, they would record a duet from *Abyssinia*, "Pretty Desdamone," with George singing the lead. For George, it would be his last recording, whereas Bert would continue to record with Columbia throughout his career. He would also go on to record his most famous piece, "Nobody."[71]

"Nobody" was an Attucks Music Publishing song later interpolated into *Abyssinia*. It would become the most popular song of Bert's career. In future recording sessions, Bert would develop his unique performance style, moving away from singing tunes the way he had in his 1901 recordings. He would instead begin to half-recite and half-sing them.[72] "Nobody" would supplant "The Jonah Man" as Bert's foremost song detailing the life of the unfortunate character he played onstage.[73] The song began in a speaking voice:

> *When life seems full of clouds and rain,*
> *And I am full of nuthin', and pain,*
> *Who soothes my thumping, bumping brain? Hmm?*
> *[he sighs] Nobody!*
>
> *When winter comes with snow and sleet,*
> *And me with hunger and cold feet,*
> *Who says here's 25 cents, go ahead get something to eat?*
> *Nobody!*[74]

As Bert sang, the echo of his own voice rang out in woefulness and sad acceptance. No melodramatic tone manifested resentment. Rather, it appeared that even as he framed each question, the character knew there could be only one answer: "Nobody!" Slowly, he worked through the song as though his misfortune were certain.

In the chorus, Bert mimicked the wail of a slide trombone that led each line, the protracted lamentation of a man who could not understand his fate. This section of the song, rather than the verses, he sang:

> *I ain't never done nuthin' to nobody,*
> *I ain't never done nuthin' to nobody no time,*
> *Oh, until I get something from somebody some time,*
> *I'll never do nuthin' for nobody no time!*

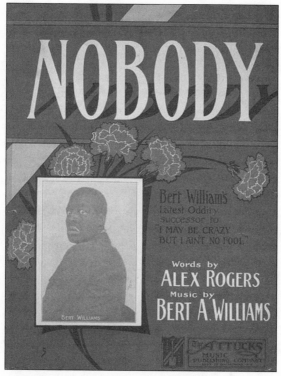

Sheet Music, "Nobody." COURTESY OF THE LESTER S. LEVY
COLLECTION OF SHEET MUSIC, SPECIAL COLLECTIONS, SHERI-
DAN LIBRARIES, THE JOHNS HOPKINS UNIVERSITY

If at any point Bert dropped his defeated tone, it was in the chorus. In that section of the song, he came nearer to a complaint than at any other point. Each line acknowledged his blamelessness and his continuing invisibility. Although responding to the trombone, his wail went out as a promise to voice his pitiable experience to the listening world.

As if to further underscore his misery, in the second verse the character recounted the failures of presumed friends, his abandonment when in dire need:

> *When summer comes all cool and clear,*
> *And my friends see me drawing near,*
> *Who says, uh, "Come in, have some beer?" Hmm! Nobody. . . .*

When I was in that railroad wreck,
And thought I'd cashed in my last check,
Who took the engine off my neck? Not a soul.

Forgotten, then, by friends who were unreliable even in fair weather, Bert painted his character as wretched. Within this verse, however, his "Hmm! Nobody" began to register a more disgruntled tone at the refusal of "friends" to acknowledge him. When he finally stated, "Not a soul," the clipped tones of his words dramatized the sentiment of a man about to change his ways. Then the final chorus came:

I ain't never done nuthin' to nobody,
I ain't never done nuthin' to nobody no time,
Until I get something from somebody sometime,
I'll never do nuthin' for nobody no time!

In this well-loved song, the character moved from recounting his experiences to deciding to change his behavior as a result of his exclusion. As the Jonah Man singing "Nobody," Bert had created his trademark, guaranteeing repeat performances both in the recording studio *and* on the stage.

Columbia, far from making a case for the unusual elements of the Williams and Walker's offerings, plugged the recordings as coon harmonies. This would continue even as Bert returned several times in the following months to record more tunes, stepping away from coon songs and punctuating the songs' lines with asides and comments. In much the same way that the sheet music of Gotham-Attucks (Attucks having merged with Gotham Music Publishing in 1905) had moved away from the lyrics of typical coon songs, the substance of Columbia's recordings also shifted. With the commercial success of and interest in the subgenre, however, the epithet continued. The 1906 recordings included music not only from *Abyssinia* but also pieces written expressly for Bert, often by Bert himself. Through these forays, he made a name for himself as a recording artist. He would not return for several years to record again, however, and when he did, it was always as a solo performer—without George.[75]

The fortunes of Williams and Walker would seem to have been magnificent as they performed in vaudeville and musical theater and then recorded with Columbia. As the *Abyssinia* run wound down, however, problems surfaced. Aida would sever her connection with the company for reasons "veiled in mystery." While George would claim that Aida was ill and, in one writer's words, "simply resting at their New York home from the fatigues of an arduous season," others would have different ideas. "At front," another journalist wrote, "it is admitted that there was some slight jar between the Walkers, and that the soubrette had taken herself off without standing on ceremony and to the great chagrin of the management."[76]

George, a socialite still popular with ladies, enjoyed his fame. Notwithstanding his marriage to Aida, the shameless philanderer found other women to keep him company.[77] He constantly both sought and attracted attention. During their time spent on the road, Aida had most certainly been neglected by the well-loved headliner of Williams and Walker, humiliated by his unabashed adultery.

In addition to the troubles with Aida, problems with Melville Raymond, Williams and Walker's manager, surfaced. The team sought to separate themselves from Raymond, even as rumors circulated that Raymond's failure to secure first-class houses was at the heart of the team's dissatisfaction. Bert and George quickly came forward to clarify matters. Although they and Raymond certainly had "strained relations," their problems had nothing to do with the issue of playing to first-class theaters, they insisted. Rather, Raymond had not kept up his end of their agreement. They went so far as to announce that, if necessary, they would "lay all the facts in the case bare, and leave the decision to the public."[78] Undoubtedly, George's voice boomed loudly in that line, as he threatened to expose the reticent and irresponsible Raymond.

By mid-September, Williams and Walker went to court to dissolve their agreement with Raymond. Subsequently, following Raymond's plunge into bankruptcy, Circuit Court Judge Hough placed *Abyssinia* in the hands of receiver James Barton.[79] When moving on to their next project, Bert and George would get yet another manager. That time, at George's insistence, they would secure more of the details of their contractual agreement.

No doubt, George was a savvy businessman. Lest his flash be mistaken for lack of substance, however, in a personal interview he happily revealed the role his extravagant clothing played offstage. In short: "Dress [was his] stock in trade . . . part of his method of making business."[80] It was an advertisement on behalf of Williams and Walker rather than an ostentatious display. It was also, he reminded the reporter, what his audience wanted: "The general public expects to see me as a flashy sort of darky and I do not disappoint them as far as appearance goes."[81] Skilled at playing his part, George accepted the role, then went still further and mastered it. Offstage, he drew the spotlight and kept himself in it.

It could be no surprise, then, that concerned African Americans would write the team, urging them to reconsider their role, as did Albert Ross, professor and Kansan. Although he readily admitted that he was overstepping his bounds as a spectator in giving advice, he did so respectfully. He had observed that the Williams and Walker name "is magic to our people, the characters you bring out in your plays . . . have the effect of [being] ideals which almost every negro boy and girl, however far distant in the backwoods, seems [sic] to pounce upon, imitate, emulate and follow as the standard."[82] Such fame came with great responsibility. Ross asked that the team consider the importance of "[b]ettering mankind, uplifting your fellowmen." Include a "prominent character," like the recent black Rhodes scholar Alain Locke or Harvard orator Roscoe Conkling Bruce, he suggested, in addition to their "old plantation Negro" and "ludicrous darkey" types.[83]

To their credit, Williams and Walker responded kindly to Ross's letter. They explained their situation, which they described as nearly a predicament. They depended on the satisfaction of "the non-sympathetic, biased and prejudiced white man" for the larger part of their success. At the same time, however, they felt compelled to address the desires of black theatergoers who wished to see characters that "remind [them] of 'white folks.'" Williams and Walker had to shoot for the average. "[W]e must draw from the mass and not from the few," they maintained. Regrettably, they could not hope to feature the Lockes and Bruces of the world in their performances. They were all-too-rare. Williams and Walker had to "use characters most familiar to-day."[84]

Although the team responded to Ross as a unit, the autumn before, George had unilaterally addressed the public in an article on his history in show business. He presented himself as the man with the plan, one who wanted to originate new opportunities for blacks in show business. He informed readers that, in the early days, "How to get before the public and prove what ability we might possess was a hard problem for Williams and Walker to solve."[85] As he watched "[b]lack-faced white comedians . . . make themselves look as ridiculous as they could when portraying a 'darky' character," he knew that black performers could do better.[86]

Expressing distaste for the theatrical convention of blackface, George remarked on the "fatal result" that black performers "imitated the white performers in their make-up as 'darkies.' Nothing seemed more absurd than to see a colored man making himself ridiculous in order to portray himself," he admitted.[87] This was a difficult path to tread, particularly since his partner used the despised cork. George plowed ahead, however, arguing in Bert's defense: "[He's] the first man that I know of our race to attempt to delineate a 'darky' in a perfectly natural way."[88] George relied upon the black audience's appreciation of the difference Bert's performative style made when playing the loathsome stereotype.

Echoing the views of black critics who laid out the performers' challenge as representatives of the race, George insisted on his belief in the entertainer's representative role:

> Williams and Walker have labored hard to bring to the front people of their race who possess theatrical, musical, and some artistic ability. . . . The love, the humor, and the pathos of the black race in this country afford a field for wide study, and I am sure the stage is the place where the character of the African race can be studied from a real artistic point of view, with special advantages to all lovers of music and theatrical art.[89]

George embraced his and his partner's role in racial uplift, even as black critics sought to define it.

Before their next show, Bert and George secured new management, this time taking up with F. Ray Comstock. Comstock, who would push for the Williams and Walker Company's placement in first-class theaters, would agree to Bert and George's equal interest in managing the company. Their contract placed greater control in Bert and George's hands. They alone would determine "the plays, music, lyrics, costumes, actors, and stage crew," as well as their tour itinerary. Moreover, detailing their earnings for seats, they ensured that they would make from a minimum of twenty-five cents to a maximum of one dollar and fifty cents each.[90] Furthermore, their agreement put them into a relationship with the Shubert brothers, Lee and Jacob (a.k.a. J. J.), theater owners, producers, and rivals of the Syndicate.[91]

George had been the one struggling to persuade theater managers and their producers of the Williams and Walker Company's potential for success. He had negotiated for first-class, higher-quality theaters, declaring, "Either first-class houses or tents."[92] Although no hard-and-fast definition for "first-class theater" existed, a 1905 legal case had described it as "a theater . . . for productions of the highest order." Ruling out venues for "popular price" entertainments, including melodrama, vaudeville, and burlesque, the New York court had determined first-class theaters to be defined by price (ranging from one dollar and fifty cents to two dollars) as well as by type of performance, generally musical comedies and drama, called "legitimate theater."[93]

Courageously drawing the line against second-class theaters, George had triumphed. When Lester Walton remarked on Williams and Walker's "great fight," which later became a "winning fight" to play in first-class theaters, he would insist "that they can draw crowds, composed of both white and colored theatre-goers, to the best houses as they did to the second-class theatres."[94] He would demand that the theatrical community acknowledge their influence.

White members of the press kept close watch on these developments as well. One journalist announced, "After a rather uphill fight to satisfy their ambition, it seems as if Williams and Walker, the dusky comedians, were finally about to be exhibited at two-dollar prices. . . . Since their return from London[,] Williams and Walker have nursed an almost uncontrollable ambition to play in the better class of houses, but they have hitherto been doomed to disappointment."[95] Witnessing the Williams and Walker Company's move to first-class theaters, the critics acknowledged their feat.

After triumphing in that struggle, however, Bert and George would continue to face the dilemma of how to serve their black audience. Having gained access to superior venues, such as Atlantic City's Savoy Theatre, even breaking the color line as the first black act to play St. Louis's Garrick Theatre and Washington, D.C.'s Belasco Theatre, they would often perform in theaters where managers continued to exclude blacks from prime seating. Just as was true during *In Dahomey*'s run, potential audience members would not be permitted to secure such seating even if they had the means to pay for it.

In a less-than-subtle remonstration about the ordeal, critic Walton would comment: "The writer . . . thinks the question of accommodating the colored citizens is a serious one, as Williams and Walker would not be in the musical comedy business today had they not received the loyal support of their race."[96] With a reminder that the performers were accountable to their black audience, Walton would demand allegiance to the audience who had made Bert and George the successes they had become. He wanted them to use their influence to change the order of things in the theatrical world.

Perhaps partly in response to their audience's needs, two months after the opening of their next production, *Bandanna Land*, the Williams and Walker Company would hold an extraordinary sixteenth anniversary celebration of the two founders' collaboration. A journalist would write that on that night in the theater, "Every seat in the two upper floors was occupied two hours before the performance. At 6 o'clock so crowded was the gallery that the police were detailed to prevent more from going in."[97] The overpopulated upper floors would be partitioned for blacks, and for this particular performance, both the gallery and the balcony would be set aside. The event would be not only for Williams and Walker but also for their audience. They would perform old songs, announce well wishes from other performers, and give speeches.

Comedian Ernest Hogan's telegram, read aloud, would reaffirm Williams and Walker's contributions, while positioning Hogan himself as the duo's elder: "Sixteen years ago I tried to open your eyes to the great future of the Negro actor. I am glad you have taken advantage of the advice, because no other Negro artists can claim such a glorious record you have all to be proud of. The credit is yours and you have sixteen more of very hard work before you."[98] Bert and George would recall the shared history between themselves and their audience. With the supportive statements of other entertainers, they would make their place clear.

Bandanna Land opened on Broadway on 3 February 1908.[99] With a setting in and suggestive of the American South rather than Africa, as was true of their previous shows, it invited audiences to speculate about the authenticity of the production. Because of its focus on "Southern Negroes" as represented "by the humorists of their own race," to some critics the musical seemed to be more genuinely the work of blacks.[100] As in several of their previous musicals, the subjects of money and status surfaced as themes.

The story tells of Skunkton Bowser (Williams), who stands to receive an inheritance from his father's employer. A group of Southern blacks, led by a "scheming lawyer" named Mose Blackstone, creates a realty syndicate in order to purchase a piece of land, competing with a railway company for possession. Quickly, however, they discover that they have insufficient funds for their purchase. Encountering Skunkton, the heir, they bring him and his friend Bud "Bon-Bon Buddy" Jenkins (Walker) to their town. Subsequently, Bud inveigles Skunton into letting him handle his financial affairs. As a result, the syndicate buys the land, afterward selling half to the railway company. Blackstone's plan is to make even further profit by causing such disturbances on their own half of the property that the company will gladly pay an inflated price to possess it. In the end, Skunkton and Bud overturn the syndicate's plan, selling the land themselves and turning a profit.[101]

In theaters filled to capacity and offering standing room only, audiences thrilled to the performance of the Williams and Walker Company. Williams and Walker's roles as "the principal entertainers" received praise time and again, with Williams's "refined, apparently natural and thoroughly effective" style lauded as being well matched by Walker's "astonishing clothes, [dancing] with vigor and grace, and [singing] with much heartiness."[102]

Moreover, not only was the general public thrilled, but Williams and Walker's peers in the profession were impressed. At a "professional matinee," such celebrities as Fields and Weber, and George Cohan, actor and playwright, gave their support. "I think Williams and Walker have at last hit 'em" was a comment overheard during the show.[103]

The highlights of the show included segments led by Bert, George, and Aida, who had returned from her previous retirement. By spring of 1908, however, it did not include Lottie, who had taken a hiatus from work on the stage due to ill health. During the months the show performed and toured, she would continue to convalesce in her and Bert's New York home.[104]

As *Bandanna Land* continued its run at the Majestic Theatre, Bert hired his friend John Nail, of the black-owned firm Nail and Parker, "to hunt him a suitable piece of real estate." It's likely that Lottie, the prudent and more financially savvy of the two, pressed him to do so. She was the "household policeman," as she called herself. Bert, respectful of the "watchdog of the treasury," as he described Lottie, appreciated her interest in real estate as much as she valued his in books.[105]

After several weeks, Bert bought a building at 146 West 99th Street, "to be used for dwelling purposes."[106] It would become his and Lottie's new home, one the recovering Lottie would cherish. While he was on the road with shows, she would remain at home, the two of them staying connected with nightly telephone calls.[107] Through his purchase, Bert thus became one among the many blacks who moved to Harlem during the period. By the end of 1908, George Walker, Bob Cole, Lester Walton, and Ernest Hogan would all move uptown.[108]

The migration to Harlem had begun in earnest at the turn of the century. Real estate developers, in anticipation of subway construction extending up Lenox Avenue to 145th Street, had overbuilt the area.[109] Their speculation had cost them: their buildings lay vacant.[110] By 1904, Philip A. Payton, Jr., a black real estate agent who owned the Afro-American Realty Company, saw an opening. He proposed that apartment building owners open their empty properties up to affluent black residents. Landlords, compelled to consider their bottom line, took him up on his proposal.[111] As James Weldon Johnson would note, "Economic necessity usually discounts race prejudice—or any other kind of prejudice—as much as ninety per cent, sometimes a hundred."[112]

Week after week, the *New York Age* advertised the opening of new apartment buildings for rent in Harlem. Increasingly, they appealed to "select" colored families by trumpeting "the cheapest" rooms in the "finest" apartment houses.[113] With time, John Nail had joined this enterprise, creating his own successful real estate business.[114]

Bert's agent plunged into the New York real estate market on his behalf while Bert strove to earn his keep. Although he had no song to top "Nobody," his role onstage offered another display of his unsurpassed acting through his use of pantomime. His contribution was an incomparable poker pantomime, during which he played the entire piece literally "close to the vest." He ran the full gamut of expressions as he mimed a card game of many players: "[H]e pantomimed the draw, the study of the hand, the bets, the suspicious looks, the raise, the call, the disgust of the loser."[115]

First, Bert shuffled the cards for numerous players and dealt them out. Subsequently, he studied his hand and looked over his shoulder quickly, protecting his privacy from an imaginary player who tried to spy. He then conveyed satisfaction as he realized he had a good hand. Just as quickly, he controlled his telling facial expression and contained his joy as he looked at the other invisible players. He placed his bet, but, following it, his look of satisfaction dropped a little as he "saw" others raising the bet. He slowly studied his cards again, calculated figures in his head, and studied his cards yet again. After that, he counted the money he had laid out before him, peered at his cards, and confidently pushed forward his entire pile of cash and coin. He laid his cards out, but within seconds, his grand smile faded as he glanced at the winner's hand.

Against the weight of blackface, Bert played out the various emotions of numerous characters. He retained subtle bodily movements while successfully communicating a range of expressions to the audience. He did all this as if in defiance of the makeup that marked him, all to the audience's pleasure and applause.

At the end of act two, George, resplendent in his most magnificent costume of the evening, sang "Bon Bon Buddy," dancing to its infectious refrain:

Bon Bon Buddy, the chocolate drop, dat's me,
Bon Bon Buddy is all that I want to be,
I've gained no fame but I ain't 'shame I'm satisfied,
With my nickname, Bon Bon Buddy, the chocolate drop,
dat's me.[116]

Perhaps for the first time, George's song offering was more popular than Bert's. The song reflected the character and sparkle of both his onstage and offstage characters. He displayed his singular dancing skills while performing an act that placed him alone at center stage.

The final act of the show featured Aida's contribution, a performance of the *Salome* dance, which was a "craze" in 1908.[117] As a serious modern dancer, Aida quite appropriately performed the then-popular *Salome*, based on the biblical story in which the virgin Salome agrees to dance for her stepfather, King Herod, "in return for the head of John the Baptist, a man who had wronged her and her mother."[118] For Aida, however, performing this dance as a black woman was very risky. *Salome* was a notoriously seductive veiled dance performed often in revealing clothing that either tantalized or scandalized audiences. Aida knew that

Sheet Music, "Bon Bon Buddy." COURTESY OF BROWN
UNIVERSITY LIBRARY

her choices throughout the performance of this dance would be crucial
and needed to be above reproach.[119] The black woman of her era strove
for respectability and dignity; she could not afford to reduce herself to
a sexual object.

Toward that end, her performance, described in detail in the program, focused on her acting of the scene, as well as her choreographic
interpretation. With regard to her costume, a critic noted that "Aida
Walker appears to wear little, but to those close down to the front there
was plainly visible the form of trunks over her form. Then, again, the
veiling which was worn was heavy and covered her particularly well."[120]
When she danced, she displayed a range of emotions, all meant to direct the audience's attention to her performance, rather than to titillate

them. It began with her reviewing the scene at the banquet hall when "[t]he intoxication of the dance possesses her—the realization of her power as a seductive woman—the sheer joy of dancing . . . mounting into rapture when John's head is brought to her." Her emotions then shift to fear, horror, and finally, frenzy, as she becomes fully aware of her awful act.[121]

To one critic, the *Salome* dance was "one of the chief features of the performance."[122] Another critic resisted its significance, flippantly stating that "a question might be raised as to the color of the daughter of Herodias."[123] Although in a later scene, Bert would perform a burlesque of the dance that might be interpreted as nullifying the significance of Aida's contribution, her performance had made inroads for the black female dancer and choreographer.

As the three leading artists made their mark onstage, a dignified guest made his mark, gracing the performers with his presence during opening week. Booker T. Washington "took a seat in the balcony" while the comedians performed, having made an impromptu stop at the theater on the way to his hotel. One by one, audience members learned about his presence, and their excitement continued to grow until Bert and George had to stop their onstage exchange and send an attaché of the house to discover what the commotion was about. Upon discovering that the great leader was in the balcony, they invited him to take a box, but he declined, claiming he was comfortable where he had been placed.[124] A favorite of both common folk and dignitaries, Williams and Walker reveled in their singular status.

When responding to *Bandanna Land*'s story and its focus on black American life, both black and white reviewers alike considered the onstage image to be the same as reality. Lester Walton reflected on two particular scenes in which deeply meaningful exchanges occur between Bert and George's characters:

> In the first act when Bert Williams produces an old pocket Bible his mother has given him years ago to keep, and George Walker looks at it and states his mother also gave him one which he kept in his trunk, the sentiment was strictly Negro, and the thought occurred to me that in the colored contingent there were few whose mothers had not given them in early life just such a book to keep and read as had mothers of the two stars.[125]

In the face of stereotype, Walton affirmed the truth of the scene. He insisted that black audiences recognized these elements as familiar, also verifying that Williams and Walker first and foremost related to their black public. In his discussion of the scene, Walton focused on the verisimilitude of the onstage moment so much that he spoke of the experience within the play as that of Bert and George rather than that of Bert and George's *characters*.

He continued with a discussion of another scene:

> [I]n another act when George Walker names the property in question "Bandanna Land," after a handsome handkerchief which he sees and causes him to grow reminiscent and recall the days when his dear old mother wore just such a handkerchief there was displayed another bit of sentiment that should have been appreciated by many in the house. I am glad to see that the day has come when our big actors have reached the point where they find it a pleasure to introduce in their shows some little character-bits that bring out strictly Negro traits and customs of which the race should feel justly proud.[126]

Walton regained perspective, indicating the role-playing involved in George's part. Nonetheless, he considered the performers' connection to their black audience, assuming that it was a relationship more intimate than that of the white audience. To him, the realism of the scenes emphasized the black audience's privileged relationship to Bert and George, being members of the same community.

Various reviewers from the white press focused on realism or referred to the legacy of minstrelsy in order to assess Williams and Walker's show. Attentive to the responses of white and black audiences alike, a journalist for the *Brooklyn Daily Eagle* also noticed the divide between them:

> The piece is naturally full of songs and dances for the principals and those are the things which arouse the white spectators to something like a fury of applause. The touches which portray the life and character of the ordinary negro arouse quick and hilarious laughter among the colored auditors, pretty good evidence that the authors and actors have told the truth.[127]

The writer surprisingly distinguished between measures of white and black enjoyment, believing that the former group's enjoyment depended on plentiful entertainment, whereas the latter's depended on a presentation of the "truth."

Other critics described the performers as "natural," and "spontaneous," denying consideration of the blacks as professional entertainers. Rather than attributing skill to the actors as masters of their art, they assessed the company's work from the height of scornful superiority. In one such review, a journalist characterized *Bandanna Land* as a "negro minstrel show," encouraging the reader to "[i]magine a negro camp meeting devoted entirely to mundane frolic, wherein a colored person of some distinction—Bert Williams—blacks up to make himself real REAL and REAL black!"[128] The writer took the play's references to the South as an invitation to read the show as a literal continuation of minstrelsy, despite the fact that Bert Williams alone wore blackface.

*W*hereas George, who played the confident dandy onstage, could export the "badness" of this character to his offstage self in interviews and articles, Bert could not do so without costs. A darky character like Bert's was caught in the middle of the debate over what was "true" Negroness—the Negro's "real" speech, manner, and intelligence. The debate encapsulated the historical African American struggle for self-definition and reminded blacks that this struggle had still not been won. When George maintained the manner of the dandy in his discussions and business dealings, he gained the admiration and respect (although sometimes grudgingly) of those who watched this brazen man in action. Bert, on the other hand, would be pressed by expectant black audiences to distance himself from the darky figure, convincing them of his concern for the image of blacks.

In response to concerns about Williams and Walker's connection to their audience, George assured readers:

> [W]e want our folks to like us. Not for the sake of the box office, but because over and behind all the money and prestige which move Williams and Walker, is a love for the race. Because we feel that, in a degree, we represent the race and every hair's breadth of achievement we make is to its credit. For first, last, and all the time, we are Negroes.[129]

This was George's assurance that, despite Williams and Walker's success and their move to higher-class theaters, they had not forgotten their home, or their "folks." George dropped any possible suggestion of pretension and spoke in a register that, as before, acknowledged who "their people" were. As if to settle the matter once and for all, George declared that Williams and Walker were, "first, last and all the time, Negroes."

George thereby answered any questions their readers might have regarding Bert and George's appreciation of the black audience. He took the opportunity "to testify to the loyalty of the colored people, and to thank them for their patronage, their encouragement and their sympathy. We try to the extent of our little utmost to deserve it, and perhaps in a day to come it may be provable that we have tried."[130] Allying Williams and Walker with blacks and recognizing their debt to the community, George attempted to recuperate any status ironically lost through their move to the first-class theater that simultaneously secured their position among blacks.

Bert also endeavored to position himself in relation to blacks. One such opportunity came when he agreed to an interview discussing the team's success. From his mouth, however, the words did not resonate with quite the same power as they did from George. Claiming that he and George based their performances on a yearlong study of "the Negro character" that they undertook while living in the South, Bert stated that it was through observation that their performances gained their virtuosity. As if to make a case for his worthy subject, he then declared, "The American Negro is the natural minstrel." For a performer who would insist on the study his characterizations required, Bert's subsequent repeated remarks about "native" humor and "natural voice" were surprising.[131]

In his aim to speak of "the Negro," Bert separated himself from the subject, rendering his West Indian identity tacitly obvious. After all, he could not speak of prior or intimate knowledge, but rather, he depended on the examination of his subject. Despite whatever sincerity he might have felt or expressed, his comments seemed forced and unnatural. They seemed far from the earnest, though urgent, statements of his partner.

Bert did become impassioned about the race, but seldom during interviews. On one unusual occasion, when asked "if all great negroes did not have white blood in their veins," he erupted. "White blood make a black man any smarter!" he shouted. "I guess not! Why, what kind of white blood do we get! The very worst and lowest and meanest there is. And when a man with some of this in his veins becomes famous do you say the bad white blood did it—the blood of a race of . . . scalawags—or do you say black blood did it in spite of the corpuscles from some poor white trash."[132] As a mixed-raced man frequently called to account for his success in racial terms, Bert exploded in response to the then-dominant idea that his best aspects resulted from his "white blood." Daring to speak out, he challenged the assumption that the blood of a white man bestowed finer qualities on the black. Furthermore, he countered the belief that whiteness conferred dignity and respectability upon a man. He proposed the view that black blood could, indeed, account for the superior achievement of an individual plagued with "bad white blood."

As he calmed, he stated his case for black actors, insisting: "We can do . . . on the stage [that] which white people . . . know we can do. We eat and live and feel and love and understand as well as any one else. And we can play just as well—that is, in our own kind of way. I say give us a chance, and Williams and Walker and a lot of other 'coons' will surprise this town and . . . others."[133] In his defense, Bert took the voice of Shakespeare's Shylock, speaking in terms that implicitly referenced the character's famous monologue. Through his words, he addressed the humanity of blacks as well as the right of black actors to express the fullness of their experiences.

Between seasons of *Bandanna Land,* Williams and Walker appeared in vaudeville, making the most of their visibility from the show. Although they used material from their production, they still got big laughs, and enjoyed receiving "the largest salary ever paid to colored vaudeville performers": $2,000 per week.[134] This placed them clearly in the same league as McIntyre and Heath, the leading white blackface comedians. In this interim period, they also used their clout in the New York black theatrical community to create an organization long in the making.

In 1906, George had attempted to create a society for black entertainers, calling on performers "to come forward and give a hand." His efforts, however, had resulted in failure. Despite being an inspired idea as a location "where all professional colored people can meet and exchange views and feel perfectly at home," as well as for "those who seek to improve themselves in their art," the club never got off the ground.[135] In July 1908, however, the Frogs was born.

Named after Greek playwright Aristophanes's play, "The Frogs" was by no means an accidental choice for the society's name. Aristophanes (c. 448 BCE–c. 388 BCE) had been known as the greatest ancient comic writer, with plays that combined political, social, and literary satire. *The Frogs*, his great play produced one year following Euripedes's death, "laments the decay of Greek tragedy, which Aristophanes attributed to that writer."[136] Although it was a comedy, *The Frogs'* focus on the crisis of art resonated with the preoccupations of these black artists, whom some audiences imagined as comedians first, and artists after, if indeed at all.

With George's home, by now on West 133rd Street, serving as headquarters, he placed himself at the center of affairs. He offered himself for nomination as president, later stepping up to take the post. The other positions read like a who's who of black entertainers: J. Rosamond Johnson, writer-composer, as vice president; Jesse Shipp, playwright and Williams and Walker's stage director, as treasurer, and R. C. McPherson (Cecil Mack), composer, as secretary. Bert was head of the Art Committee. While the Frogs sought to promote the relationships of those in the theatrical profession with those outside of it, it also concerned itself with the achievements of those within the profession. Members aimed to make black entertainers' successes and contributions well known to the black public.[137]

When the Williams and Walker Company returned to theaters after the summer to continue its run of *Bandanna Land*, Bert and George still faced resistance to their ambitions. They attempted to ensure that their shows remained in first-class theaters, after having fallen from such placement during the previous season. As they approached a run scheduled for Garrick's Theatre in St. Louis, Missouri, however, the resident manager expressed his worries to theater owner J. J. Shubert. He was concerned that Williams and Walker's appearance would "absolutely undo everything we have done here to regain our first class prestige and will simply take away our standing in this community."[138] He requested that Shubert reconsider his decision.

In his response, Shubert wrote plainly: "What we are after is money and I do not think Williams and Walker will hurt the house in the slightest degree. . . . I only wish I had more shows like Williams and Walker to put in there, and I am sure you will find that you will make more money out of them, more than out of anybody else."[139] The risk was significant, but so was the chance for gain, which would be necessary for so large a production. As these battles continued, so did tensions between displeased black audiences—who were in some cases still barred from the better class of setting in theaters—and the theaters' managers.

Little did Bert and George know, however, that their challenges were only beginning. Just before Christmas of 1908, Lottie, who had taken time off from performing the prior season, decided to retire from the stage due to continuing ill health.[140] Although at the time her decision was temporary, it would bring an end to performances with the dual partners of the Williams and the Walkers. She would not return to the stage. Not very long after that, George himself would suffer greatly, drastically changing the future of them all.

While performing in Boston, George took the stage to sing his by-then trademark song, "Bon Bon Buddy." As he danced, he began to sing uncharacteristically, "in a thick-lipped manner, droning out the lyrics." Cast members, amused, initially imagined that he was improvising a new joke. Afterwards, they learned he had taken ill. While onstage, George had suffered a stroke.[141]

In the weeks following the performance, George discovered that he had contracted syphilis. Highly contagious, sexually transmitted, and incurable, syphilis was the AIDS epidemic of its time. It had become a dark shadow over society, a taboo subject that no one dared to mention. As George fought the sickness, struggling to continue to perform, he began to suffer a physical and mental collapse. His mind began to deteriorate, and his bodily control weakened, which foreshadowed the dementia and paralysis that would follow.[142]

The night of George's final performance, in Louisville in February 1909, Chappy, Bert's valet, watched a heart-wrenching scene. George approached his partner.

"Well, Bert," he announced, forlorn, "I'm going to leave you."

In uncharacteristic emotion, Bert nearly broke down in tears. Finally, he turned around, replying, "No, you're not. I'm going to leave you." Shuffling onto the stage, he went into his act.[143] Devastated, he resigned himself to the one thing of which he still remained certain: the show must go on.

George would eventually depart for a sanitarium in Michigan and attempt to recover. Although he claimed a "slight indisposition" that would keep him away from the stage for only a short time, his February performance would come to mark his retirement from the stage.[144]

Aida eventually donned George's dapper clothing. She wore the elegant hat, the sharp suit, and took to the stage to play the irrepressible, vivacious Bud Jenkins. A powerful performer, she honored her husband well. And, as she sang "Bon Bon Buddy," she reminded audiences of her own extraordinary vitality. She lit up the stage with her solo performance.

Eventually, Bert would be forced to stand alone. Not only would he perform without George, but he would also need to find a way to carry on the Walker—and the Williams and Walker—legacy. As George had written the December preceding his retirement, Williams and Walker was meant to be seen "in the light of a race institution."[145] Yet he, not Bert, had been the team's race man. He, not Bert, had been the public face of Williams and Walker, the one who assured the black public of the team's commitment to their black audience, above all. If the Williams and Walker "race institution" were to continue, it would now be up to Bert alone to keep the vision alive.

3

Bert Williams—
A Show in Himself

7

The End of an Era

Although Bert hesitated to take George's place as a race man, he did take steps toward changing his image. However, he would never come to fill George's shoes. Indeed, as he approached the public, especially the black public, his presence at times most served to remind audiences of George's obvious absence. Williams *without* Walker. It also revealed the manner in which Williams could—and would—go on without Walker.

Bert did not become George, but he did become—or attempt to become—a different version of himself. He worked outside of his usual vein of reserve and inner reflection. With improvisation and innovation, he began to take on new roles—roles that had become available as a result of the reality of George's debilitating sickness and absence.[1]

As Bert approached his public, he asserted himself in two unusual ways. In interviews and articles, he first established himself as an historian, a knowledgeable resource for information on African American theater history. He drew from his vast personal experience in the profession as well as from the extensive reading he pursued as an autodidact. Once an inquisitive child and now a contemplative adult, Bert created a public self-image that belied the blackface darky he played onstage. Secondly, he took on the role of visionary, imagining the future of black theater. He expressed his vision of Negro theater with creativity and passion, yet, unlike his partner, he refrained from thrusting himself into the spotlight.

A month prior to George's retirement, Bert gave an interview during which he discussed his concerns regarding "The Dramatic Stage as an Upbuilder of the Races." From the start, he refused to indulge in joke- or storytelling. For the interviewer, Veronica Adams, meeting the comedian was anything but the typical interaction with a black performer. Bert claimed that "he didn't know any funny stories," and quickly moved on, speaking with grave intention. At the same time, Bert highlighted his status as an experienced performer: the interview took place at a theater, apparently between curtain calls. Bert thus encouraged Adams, a white journalist, to see the interrelatedness of Bert Williams the comedian and Bert Williams the intellectual.

Adams seemed to accept Bert's self-presentation. She noted early in the article that Bert spoke with as much seriousness about his work as did David Mansfield or Robert Bruce Mantell, both established white dramatic actors of the time. From the outset, she acknowledged that Bert considered "the development of the dramatic instinct among his people one of the chief educational agencies for his race."[2] As Bert began the interview, he subverted the expectation of his audience by diverting the focus from the typical course of a performer-interviewer exchange. Despite Adams's incredulity at the tenor of their conversation, she avoided commenting to Bert about his surprising seriousness.

In editorial statements, however, Adams compared this entirely different offstage Bert Williams with his onstage character. With no outward indication to her interviewee, she grappled with these two images: "I had expected to find the typical negro comedian. I thought when I was taken back to his dressing-room that I would find a grimacing, sluggardly actor, who would entertain me with ... frivolous chatter."[3] Throughout the interview, although Adams listened to the actor's words, she continued to editorialize. She telegraphed her disbelief at the turn in conversation. This disbelief persisted throughout Bert's discussion of drama and the Negro, when she described him as speaking "in a tone and manner that belied the shambling appearance he affects in *Bandanna Land*."[4] Bert was no bumbling, ignorant darky character, no classic minstrel in which to find reassurance. Despite Adams's apparent success in her battle to reconcile the two Williamses, at times she still could not contain her disbelief.

To the white general public, the onstage character seemed to be Bert's "true" representation. Bert brought Adams into the theater setting perhaps to juxtapose these images and to force her to acknowledge these distinct selves. Between his comments, Bert left the interview to take an encore onstage, returning to pick up his serious subject. The difference between the character and the actor should have been simple—and clear.

Adams, however, tended to resist. Her parenthetical comments evidenced her difficulty in reconciling the disparate images. They illustrate how the fixation on authenticity shaped audiences' reception of Bert offstage. With time, though, the discrepancy either resolved itself or Adams finally adjusted to reality. She eventually settled into the interview and her actual exchange with the performer.

As Bert proceeded to explain the importance of the theater for the African American community, he demonstrated immediately his competence as a resource: "In the olden days, when the church and the stage were allied, the drama was a potent agency for the instruction of the people."[5] Throughout the interview, he elaborated his points on the history of theater. He discussed it in the context of the black community, thereby broadening the subject in order to display his vast knowledge:

> The church seized upon the instrumentality of the stage to bring home to the people the great lessons of life. . . . If we see a thing we carry the instructive effect for years, whereas we might forget it inside five minutes if we only read it. Religion spread its doctrines of charity, faith and hope and love for your neighbor through the drama[,] and the stage became the right arm of the church.[6]

Illustrating his intelligence, Bert presented himself as the complete opposite of the vapid comical character he portrayed onstage. At the same time, he demonstrated through his words an understanding of historical facts that had bearing on the profession that he knew best.

As he continued, Bert looked back: "In fifty years [the Negro] has made strides. He is working out his destiny with a heavy burden on his shoulders."[7] He had seen, from his vantage point as performer, the race's efforts toward changing its image. Speaking as an informed witness to much of that history, despite his origins, he affirmed the race's advances.

In his discussions of theater history, Bert acted as the keeper of memory. Whether or not his story told things as they were, it did verify his place. He could never replace George, but he could stake a claim as an expert resource, particularly in the wake of George's absence.

In the coming years, Bert would further affirm his exceptional knowledge of African American theater history and locate himself as central in it, despite his Bahamian background. He would establish his relevance even though he had "defected," in colleague James Weldon Johnson's words, to the "white stage."[8] Pointing to his forebears, such as Sam Lucas, the first black man to have a leading part in a white company, playing the title role in *Uncle Tom's Cabin*, and Ira Aldridge, the black Shakespearean actor, he would honor those esteemed actors. Importantly, he would see the great actors in relationship to himself, as men who "preceded me by years in being 'featured' in white companies."[9]

As a visionary, Bert used his imagination to elaborate an image of Negro theater. Whereas George had imagined a series of "Ethiopian" theaters concerned with work by, for, and about blacks, Bert envisaged a different picture of the future. In Bert's conception, the comedian and the tragedian of Negro theater had parts to play not only on the stage but also in the larger society—not only in black society but also in society as a whole.

While he discussed the black actor's representative role, however, he delicately addressed his own. He was careful not to overextend himself or position himself as a leader. Aligning his vision with a political agenda, he spoke in (Booker T.) Washingtonian terms:

> The negro actor will . . . take rank with the negro teacher in the negro school. Booker Washington will then have strong allies in his work of elevating the social standard [sic] of the black man. The tragedian or the straight comedian will carry the word of Tuskegee Institute to every village and hamlet and into every home, white or black. Companies of purposeful players will not only uplift the black man, but they will, through the presentation of proper plays, aid toward a more perfect understanding between the races.[10]

Espousing Washington's view of blacks' responsibility for their own improvement, Bert proposed a new direction for the theater. Using Washington's words, he invoked the concepts of black self-help and uplift. He supported the view that blacks who were individually working to change their own particular circumstances, yet also concerned about the community as a whole, could make improvements for everyone.

Furthermore, Bert envisioned this work of the theater reaching beyond the black community alone. Actors would "carry the word of

Tuskegee Institute," explicitly uplifting blacks, and therefore reaching both blacks and whites. Through the creation of art, actors would aid in the mutual understanding of the races. By representing the best the race had to offer and presenting "proper plays" displaying the dignity and humanity of blacks, actors would educate the public.

Discussing future opportunities on the stage, Bert predicted, "The day is not far off when the traveling negro dramatic company will come to town as often as the negro musical or minstrel company." Optimistic, Bert stated a hope for the day "when the colored performer can be something more than a minstrel man, a song and dance artist, or a slap stick gent."[11] As he looked into the future, Bert simultaneously remembered the present limitations placed on performers.

Nonetheless, as Bert continued to consider the future of black theater, he saw the possibility of new roles. They would move beyond characters like "the man at the door, the coachman or the waiter," and toward "the negro who rises above the menial and gains position in business or a profession."[12] Viewing the insistence on old roles as restrictive, he criticized both the stasis of the roles and the stereotypes themselves. He thereby made the risky move of creating a vision of Negro theater that might exclude himself.

Far from leaving his own contributions behind or classifying himself as the minstrel man of a bygone era, however, Bert instead discussed his efforts toward change. Even as he played the Jonah Man, he committed himself to "nailing down a plank of virtue," elevating both the character and his aims.[13] Although his critics might declare his character a retrogressive detriment to the race, he nonetheless saw his work as related to his forward-looking goals.

Bert thus left a space for himself to take part in the community while also avoiding appointing himself as a figurehead. He depended on the development of a collective consciousness among blacks but refrained from proposing collective action. Despite his professed personal interest in the uplift of the race, he insisted on the importance of individual, rather than collective, effort. That would be the means by which substantial change would be effected. Elsewhere, he continued to discuss his desire to uplift the race yet defined his role "to uplift it, not as a mass, it is true, but by showing individuals what it is possible for them to accomplish."[14]

Although Bert located himself in his vision of the future, his words belied a sense of conflict. His Jonah Man, although dignified and deep, still derived from a stereotype. The blackface role could be freeing, but it could also be limiting. A reflective man like Bert would not be able to deny this conflict. "Once, like Eddie Foy [a vaudevillian and star of musical comedies] I fancied myself playing Hamlet," he would confess. "But I discovered that pigment in the skin makes all the difference. Did I break my heart of it? Not at all," he claimed.[15]

Bert did, however, think about his dreams. He pondered about his character. Although he did not "break his heart" over the restrictions, he did feel conflicted. It was evident from his difficulty, try as he might, to find a place for himself in his own vision of the future.

He believed that the great American play should be "the story of the struggle of the negro to rise from meniality and servility to a position of independence, portraying the difficulties that seem almost insurmountable, keeping always in mind a certain omnipresent prejudice against him."[16] In Bert's mind, the American story was a Negro story, entailing the struggle from slavery to freedom and the fight for the American ideal of liberty. In truth, the story was also his own. Bert was the Negro who struggled for independence, the figure who fought prejudice to achieve freedom.

Clarifying his point, Bert urged his readers to consider blacks' experiences. He could have easily been speaking specifically about his own:

> When we picture the negro on the stage we think of him singing, laughing and cutting up. That seems to be his nature. But has it ever occurred to you that under his mask of smiles and this cloak of capers there is hidden dire tragedy? God surely has been good to the black man to make him take his lot with a smile on his face and a joke on his lips. Has the dramatist appreciated his every opportunity?[17]

With well-chosen words that implicated even himself in his statement— as part of the "we" who pictured Negroes as cut-ups—Bert questioned the audience's assumption that blacks were "natural" comedians. He pointed to a "mask of smiles," thereby troubling the idea that blacks knew nothing of suffering amidst their humor and hilarity. Rather than focus on the mask, Bert insisted that the dramatist look beyond it to understand the fount of strength that enabled the Negro to smile through pain—that enabled Bert to smile through pain.

Bert's statement referred to his friend and colleague Paul Laurence Dunbar's famous poem, "We Wear the Mask." Giving voice to the bifurcated personhood of the black subject, Dunbar had spoken about the mask that blacks wear in everyday life. It "grins and lies," covering the pain they endure. Whereas Dunbar declared the continuing need for the mask to hide blacks' pain from the world, Bert suggested the dramatist's exploration of both the surface and below. In his view, the theater's work would expose blacks' humanity. Bert thus created a case—and a space—for the black actor as well as himself. He simultaneously recognized the black community as he also referred to himself.

As he attempted to convince this audience, a white readership, to embrace a new idea about blacks as artists, Bert presented a challenge. Who would be the dramatist to pen the complex emotions the Negro felt? Who would unmask him and see the truth of his experience? By issuing this audacious challenge, Bert took the vanguard as an artist who considered not only the future of the race but also the future of the arts.

Illustrating the standard to which he aspired, he fleshed out his vision by citing a quintessential playwright: Shakespeare. In the mid- to late-nineteenth century, Shakespeare's works had been popular texts for audiences of disparate classes and education. Integrated into the culture and contextualized so as to respond to its audiences, Shakespeare's work "was not only domesticated; he was humanized."[18] His work was accessible to audiences who knew the texts well enough to recognize puns, parodies, and malapropisms during performances that hardly honored those texts as sacred.[19]

By the turn of the century, the establishment of categories of high and low art contributed to the sacralization of Shakespeare.[20] At the time of Bert's writing, Shakespeare was both commonly known and acknowledged as brilliant. The playwright of Negro drama would therefore be a genius, the Negro's story being worthy of the greatest possible talent.

The challenge would then be to train an actor—Bert used renowned Shakespearean actor Edwin Booth as an example—who would be worthy of the great dramatic role. Bert thereby proposed not simply the creation of plays appropriate for black theater but, significantly, the training of actors who would be well suited to them. His vision of the future theater was now complete.

Throughout Bert's discussion of Negro theater, he drew an optimistic picture of possibilities—and struggled to defend his own contribution. With each further elaboration, he revealed his own as-yet unrealized ambitions. Unlike George, for Bert, imagining the future Negro theater would entail the difficulty of determining his place.

Despite the challenges, Bert's endeavors to address the public helped him to establish a new voice. As historian, he stepped into a more comfortable role as educated expert. He proved himself to be a repository of knowledge, then went even further to place himself in the history of African American theater. As visionary, he faced a more knotty subject: envisioning the future, he risked placing himself in the past, even as he attempted to validate his identity as both entertainer and educator.

Whatever his success in actually achieving validation, Bert would at least verify his independence from Walker. He would continue his work without George's public voice. Williams had moved on without Walker, but negotiating the vast white and black worlds and audiences alone was still a daunting prospect for him. Without George, "he felt like a ship without a rudder."[21] Although audiences and critics alike had praised and respected Bert's work over the years, he now faced both the professional obligation to pick up where he and his partner left off and this personal challenge to present himself to his public.

After George's retirement, Bert's first move was to deny its finality: he promised reporters that, when George recovered, the two would work together again.[22] When he negotiated an exclusive three-year contract with F. Ray Comstock, the agreement included both the possibility of George's return to the stage as well as Bert's own pursuit of solo opportunities.[23] With the new contract intact, Bert took his next big step: a solo turn in vaudeville.

Although vaudeville never became a mainstay for him, it was to become significant for his life as a solo performer. It would afford him the spotlight and uninterrupted attention, except, perhaps, when audiences cheered for encores. Additionally, it would permit him to take greater control of his work. Bert would have license to think exclusively of himself without considering other cast members. It would also keep him performing before black and white audiences alike. In vaudeville, Bert displayed particular mastery as a "single" and affirmed his status as a top artist and original performer.[24]

A famous entertainer like Bert performed in nothing less than "big-time" vaudeville. Regardless of a theater's status as big-time or small-time, however, vaudeville audiences expected the same from all performers: nonstop entertainment. In vaudeville theaters, particularly small-time, audiences enjoyed a dynamic relationship with performers, as well as a large degree of influence. Vaudevillians, dependent on the audience's reception for their success or failure, recognized that even in big-time, audiences often voted with their feet—walking out of the theater in the middle of a substandard show or act. Entertainers knew well that all acts had to prove their worth and skill.

At each show, even when playing only hours apart in the same theater, acts had to substantiate their right to be on the bill. Headliners also had to prove themselves: each time out, they had to perform for a new audience, maintaining and reaffirming their star power. No one could argue against the audiences' influence. They had paid their money, and they demanded satisfaction. Recognizing their power, theater magnate Oscar Hammerstein II called the intimidating, mysterious crowd the "big black giant."[25]

Although the audiences made demands of vaudevillians, performers eagerly sought the chance to grace the vaudeville stage. As vaudeville actor James Fitzpatrick explained: "The vaudeville manager . . . invests in nothing but the four walls of the theatre. . . . People do not go to vaudeville theatres to see the stage set or hear the orchestra play or admire the manager."[26] It was the performer alone who drew vaudeville's audiences.

Despite being undeniably tough, vaudeville's audiences were also kind. One performer remarked:

> They were critical, and they had a right to be, as paying customers. But they were more often than not friendly, too. They applauded frequently, though not overzealously, even when they had not been thrilled or amused especially, but because they may have sympathized with the fellow "up there" who was trying to make a living. . . . The vaudeville audience did not look for moral or spiritual uplift. It distrusted what it considered hifalutin or highbrow. . . . What the vaudeville audience wanted most was good straight entertainment. . . . They wanted variety, and vaudeville gave it to them—variety of which there was no apparent end.[27]

Always, amusement was the bottom line. If performers pleased audiences with the myriad types of entertainment displayed, the audiences would show their support for the hardworking man or woman on the stage. Performers knew to provide "good straight entertainment" that kept audiences happy, and a successful vaudevillian would have to work hard to stay on top and keep them laughing.[28]

For Bert, the issue of what constituted good material was a matter of experience and study. In an interview with Lester Walton, the comedian would discuss his viewpoint regarding humor and what constituted a joke. He highlighted superiority and its importance in joke telling, explaining: "One of the funniest sights in the world is a man whose hat has been knocked in or ruined by being blown—if provided, of course, it be the other fellow's hat! All the jokes in the world are based on a few elemental ideas, and this is one of them."[29] When the butt of the joke was someone else, one had not only the chance but also the right to laugh. This position of superiority, of the person witnessing rather than experiencing the misfortune, created a distance that enabled the witness to see the humor in the situation.

Continuing, Bert described a friendly setting in which the superiority-inferiority dialectic maintained:

> The sight of other people in trouble is always funny. This is human nature. If you will observe your own conduct whenever you see a friend falling down on the street, you will find that nine times out of ten your first impulse is to laugh and your second is to run and help him get up. To be polite you will ask him if he has hurt himself, but when it is all over you cannot resist telling him how funny he looked when he was falling.[30]

Recognizing the importance of universality, relying on the specific instance yet the universal truth, Bert sought comical common ground. In his philosophical observations, he found truths that could be transformed into comical moments to suit white and black audiences alike.

Bert hoped to avoid the expectations that white audiences might have had for the black comedian and actor. He expressed the difficulty of doing his own material while working against the demands of the audience:

> Just think what I have to do to "git by." The Caucasian believes every colored man is a "coon," that they are all alike, that they should not live in a modern way. This is a mistake. We have as many differences as the white man and no one characteristic covers us all. Do you think because I have an African strain in me, that I ought to stick a feather in my hair and go out there and shoot up things?[31]

Although he worked in comedy, Bert demanded freedom. He refused the representations of the black man as primitive. He dared the audience to look at their biases, to recognize their prejudicial ideas about the black man. He also expressed his concerns about being given the space to pursue his interests on the stage. Always, Bert's performance included deliberation and preparation. While performing comedy, he wished to do so with dignity. In the vaudeville environment, Bert would get that chance. Yet, as was often the case, it came with a price.

Reminiscences of various white vaudevillians testify to the camaraderie the performers enjoyed. Although constantly traveling and frequently low on cash, they supported each other and provided a type of makeshift family for one another.[32] When on the same bill, they rode the train together, ate meals together, and shared lodgings.

But this was not so for African American performers. In big-time vaudeville, no more than one black act was included on a bill. Managers, concerned about their white family-oriented patronage, were anxious about black fans dominating the audiences, so they kept the performers to a minimum. As a result of these executive decisions in big-time vaudeville, led by such power brokers as B. F. Keith, Edward Albee, and Willie Hammerstein, black vaudevillians had little chance to develop the camaraderie as a group that whites enjoyed on the circuit. When Bert performed in big-time vaudeville, he knew that the color line created a divide between him and the other players.[33] He experienced it not only as he looked at the show's bill but also elsewhere.

Especially on the road, Bert depended on the saloons as chances for socialization. When the Volstead Act would pass in 1919, prohibiting "the sale and manufacture of alcohol," it would devastate his social life.[34] Saloon life was crucial not only to his personal well being, but also to his career as an actor, which necessarily relied on relationships. His heavy drinking had probably started in part as a means to justify taking up a seat.

As he would tell his friend, Chicago drama critic Ashton Stevens, "[T]he saloon [is] the only club in which a man of my color [can] meet a man of your color. And I like my friends; like to be with them; like to be seen with them."[35] Some saloons, however, weren't "particularly cordial." Those "heavy" saloons, as Bert termed them, made life hard. He suffered grave humiliation, which he'd at times attempt to avoid by saying in his "best London accent: 'Sorry! I thought Mr. Stevens was here.'"[36] But some unpleasant scenes were unavoidable.

Buster Keaton would recall in his memoir that, "Although the theatrical profession was the first to break through the color line, throughout

my boyhood and youth [ca. 1900–1920] you never saw whites and Negroes on the stage at the same time."[37] Keaton recounted a story his father told that speaks to the isolation that Bert, as a black performer in
big-time vaudeville, must have felt:

> When Negroes were allowed in white saloons at all they were restricted
> to the end of the bar farthest from the door. Pop ignored this the night he
> walked into the Adams Hotel bar in Boston, which was conveniently situ-
> ated, being directly behind Keith's Theatre. Bert Williams, who was again
> on the bill with us, was standing, as required, far down at the other end.
>   "Bert," said Pop, "come up here and have a drink with me."
>   Bert looked nervously from one white face at the bar to another, and
> replied, "Think I better stay down here, Mr. Joe."
>   "All right," said Pop, picking up his glass, "then I'll have to come down
> there to you."[38]

Although they were in the North, far removed from de jure segregation, custom demanded the practice of segregation, perhaps even Bert's
formal address of Joe Keaton, a colleague, as "Mr." Despite his position
as a leading act on the circuit, his fame, and his respectability, Bert was
aware of the limits to his freedom. That reportedly nervous look he
gave "from one white face at the bar to another" indicated the constant
challenges he confronted when deciding when to assert his rights and
when to accept what others decided was his proper place.

As Bert went into big-time vaudeville, he knew the sacrifices it entailed. He also knew that he'd have to prove himself all over
again—as a single. He took the stage in May of 1909, performing in the
leading vaudeville house in Manhattan, Hammerstein's Victoria. Even
though he was a top name, he met resistance. It has been said that blacks
did not find camaraderie among performers in big-time vaudeville. The
controversy that ensued because of Bert's presence proves this.

The White Rats, a white vaudevillians' organization that was "part union
and part fraternal order," instigated the controversy. They protested Bert's
status as headliner. Initially founded in 1900, the White Rats had aimed to
protect and defend the interests of performers against managers who controlled bookings.[39] After making some significant strides—for example,
the end of commissions—the Rats dwindled in number then died, only to
return years later.[40] Still focused on the dignity and identity of the artisan

as "skillful, independent, and manly," they rebelled against what they understood as B. F. Keith's feminization of vaudeville.[41] The organization rejected women and African Americans and determined that it would do whatever necessary in order to "make us financially independent, free, and estimably respected in the eyes of our professional brothers."[42] Their goals excluded protecting a well-paid black performer like Bert, whose success was viewed as pernicious by the White Rats.

Intimidated and infuriated by Bert's success, the White Rats reportedly attempted to get him billed as a regular act instead of a featured act. As a regular act, Bert would receive only a fraction of the publicity, pay, and performance time that he would have as a featured act. He would have only a few minutes to perform, rather than a more substantial block of time (from fifteen to thirty minutes), and he would hold an inferior placement on the nine-act bill, rather than next-to-closing, which was the coveted spot. Despite Bert's prior agreement with Hammerstein's, the managers, perhaps unnerved by the pressure the organization placed on them, dropped the plan to bill Williams as a headliner.

A writer for the *New York Age* regretted that Bert did not secure his proper standing as headliner and admonished him for remaining mum: "Colored comedians of high standing can do much by fighting for their rights; for after all the theatre manager is going to give the most consideration to those who are the strongest box-office attractions; and during his fly in vaudeville Bert Williams is one of that number."[43] It seemed to the journalist that Bert had power, perhaps more than most. He should have taken the managers to task for their refusal to honor his contract.

Although the writer did not continue further along these lines, he registered his dissatisfaction with the comedian's inaction. Referring to Bert as among the "colored comedians of high standing" along with Ernest Hogan (up until his untimely death from tuberculosis that May), the writer imagined that Bert was among what *should have been* an influential group. By failing to do what was within his rights, Bert undervalued not only himself but also other black comedians.

As if the debates surrounding Bert's appearance were not enough to create anxiety, he also faced his own nervous tension as a seasoned performer stepping back into solo performance for the first time in sixteen years. After *Bandanna Land* closed, Chappy, Bert's valet, continued to work for him. He recalled the comedian's terrible fretfulness the first time out in solo performance: "[A]lthough Bert wasn't to go on until 3:45, he was completely made up and pacing about the stage at 2."[44] Prior to that day, Bert had decided that he would not perform his hit song

"Nobody." Despite the fact that from the first time he sang the song in musical theater it had been a popular piece, he had been determined to do his act without it.

Chappy, however, "without [Bert's] knowing it . . . slipped the music to the orchestra leader and told him to play it as a cue song. Well, when they heard 'Nobody,' the crowd went wild, and Bert had a cinch after that."[45] "Nobody" had become Bert's trademark song, and even the mere sound of its chords was enough to get audiences excited to hear him.

In vaudeville, Bert continued to perform in the same slow-paced, deliberate style he had used in his shows with George. He resisted the hectic pace of the bill, with its slew of competing, varied performers. On the stage, as a masterful, confident entertainer who knew that his audience eagerly awaited him, he relished his time. The one thing he did do that paralleled vaudeville was to offer variety. His performance included comic songs, "lies," and dancing.[46]

"Nobody" was Bert's trademark, but his "lies," as he called them, were the pièce de résistance of his performance.[47] In short lies, or stories, Bert incorporated details of black life. His subjects included everything from the marital relationship and family to work, church, and casual barbershop talk. They affirmed a world almost entirely black, making few references to the larger society beyond.

Many of the stories featured "ole Spruce Bigby," a savvy, proud man from a rural area (presumably the South). He spoke in dialect and was full of observations and always compelled to have the last word:

> Somebody was bragging the other day and saying that he had seen a twelve story building started in St. Louis in one month and finished in the next.
>
> Old Spruce Bigby said: "Dat aint nothin'. When I wuz livin' in Chicago I'd be goin' to work of mornins an' see 'em layin' de foundations of a buildin' an' when I'd be comin' home at night they'd be puttin' folks out fuh back rent."[48]

In such a tall tale, Spruce, though an older rural man, remained attentive to the modernization of society. Using a storytelling style that echoed Joel Chandler Harris's popular Uncle Remus tales, Bert's Spruce Bigby harked back to the image of the old entertaining and philosophical Negro whose remarks tickled audiences. He also cited the reality of urban blacks, however, who struggled to survive in the cities despite the promise of modernization.

Another tale addressed work, humorously treating the issue of protecting one's pride:

> When old Spruce come home the other evening[,] he says to his wife,
> "I ain't goin' to work fo' ole man Grimes no mo'."
> "Whut's de matter?" asked his wife.
> "Aw, on account uv a remark he made to-day."
> "Whut'd he say?"
> "He say, 'Spruce Bigby, you needn't come back to work tomorrer, nur de nex day, nur none a de rest a de days.' An' I don' like none a dat kind a hintin' roun' so I jes quit."[49]

At a time when the city's blacks struggled to maintain a decent standard of living in the face of stiff competition for jobs—especially from white immigrants—the joke would have resonated well. Many blacks lived on the borderline of deprivation or poverty while striving to retain their dignity. Blacks in the audience would have recognized this concern.

At the same time, Bert's choice to turn the tale away from urban blacks toward a rural character also took advantage of regional biases against Southern blacks, providing the distance that would render Spruce a suitable butt of a joke. Whites in the audience who expected to see the common black stereotype could rest assured with the seemingly familiar image of Spruce.

Finally, in a story that referenced black attitudes about the political scene, Bert painted Spruce once again:

> Spruce Bigby is a foxy old rascal. It was near election time. As usual there was [sic] the Republican and the Democratic candidates for Governor. One of the white politicians asked Spruce:
> "What do you think of Brown?"
> "I think he's a good man," replied Spruce.
> "Well, what do you think of Green?"
> "I [t]hink he's a good man," answered Spruce.
> "Ah, come on now," said the politician, "who do you think has the best show?"
> "Barnum an' Bailey," said Spruce.

Although a rural, uneducated man, Spruce was politically conscious. Suspicious of both candidates, despite the fact that Republicans (the party of Abraham Lincoln) would have held more meaning for blacks whether

Southern or Northern, he revealed his knowledge that neither held substance. Referencing Barnum and Bailey, Spruce tacitly suggested that as long as both insisted on putting on a show, he would rather see a proper circus. Significantly, Bert's character dared to say this before a white man.

Bert ended his turn in vaudeville with a "dance of indifference, a laconic dance, if you will."[50] Here, he innovated. Although generally he was not a smooth dancer in the manner of George, he had created his own memorable moves. An "eccentric" dancer, in the language of the day, he gave his performances a unique stamp.[51]

For Bert, the dancing became part of the darky character he portrayed. Like pantomime, dancing was important. "I don't believe there are any limitations to what can be expressed through this medium [of movement]," he would explain.[52] So, at the end of his act, he used movement as "his instrument," utilizing it "to play on, to express the odd and intimate traits" of his character.[53] He "raise[d] one knee waist high with his foot back underneath him, and then hitch[ed] the other foot up to it, traveling across the stage." With that "trick step," he took his exit, leaving the audience crying for more.[54]

Despite the dispute over headliner status and Bert's own attack of nerves, he was a "scream." In vaudeville's argot, he "made good." A critic declared him "the hit of the bill, despite the attempt of the 'White Rats' to make him only a small part of the program."[55]

Bert's skyrocketing success as a solo act would help him to afford his own car. It placed him alongside those Americans who could luxuriate during the increasingly popular Sunday drive, although Bert himself had an appetite for speed.[56] Regardless of the controversy surrounding his appearance at Hammerstein's, Bert continued to have access to big-time vaudeville, the accolades of audiences, and the wealth it offered.

As important as the fame and the money, however, was the presence of George, who returned to the city to visit Bert as he performed in vaudeville. It was a heartening—yet tragic—sight. Accompanied by an attendant, George was barely recognizable. "[H]is head nodded involuntarily, his legs shook, his lips were parted by a meaningless smile, and his words were uttered hesitatingly and without direct purpose." In the eight months since his onstage stroke, George's wretched decline had accelerated.[57]

On 21 October 1909, an advertisement in the *New York Age* boldly announced the upcoming appearance of

THE FUNNIEST MAN ON EARTH
BERT A. WILLIAMS
THE BIG FELLOW OF
WILLIAMS & WALKER
IN THE NEW MUSICAL PLAY
"MR. LODE OF KOAL."[58]

The ad could not possibly express Bert's trepidation. Although years of being before the footlights had proven his impressive onstage skills, offstage Bert still was lesser known than his very public partner. As he moved on to this new stage of his career, he both reestablished himself as a performer and also reintroduced himself as an individual.

While George, under his mother's care in Lawrence, Kansas, attempted to recover, Aida secured a starring role in Cole and Johnson's upcoming musical, *Red Moon*, and Bert took a chance as a new solo star.[59] Though without Walker, there would only be half of the famous duo, producer F. Ray Comstock offered Bert his own show. In fact, although he wished George well, Comstock had removed thoughts of him from his mind. As Comstock stated, Bert had "demonstrated beyond a doubt that he is one of the funniest comedians living, and is fully capable of heading a show alone."[60]

A three-act musical comedy with a large black cast and crew, *Mr. Lode of Koal* evoked Williams and Walker's previous productions. To the black public, it must have seemed indicative of Bert's determination to continue in the Williams and Walker tradition, despite his short-term run in vaudeville. They couldn't ignore significant differences, however: George's retirement, Aida's decision to perform with other companies, and Lottie's continuing absence from the stage loomed large.

Nonetheless, Bert endeavored to bind his company together as a family. A month before their 1 November 1909 opening, they indulged in "field day exercises" in Kansas City. They ran races and played baseball as well as other sports in an event planned for company members alone. Bert, pitching and captaining a baseball game, ushered in the fun, satisfied to see his company's smiling faces. He did, however, refrain from playing with too much vigor. He had to be careful of his feet, which, with their continuing circulation problems, often gave him grief.[61]

A fantasy perhaps influenced by the popular productions of *Wizard of Oz* and *Babes In Toyland*, both produced and then remounted as revivals on Broadway, *Mr. Lode of Koal* plays out the dream of Chester Lode. The play's title, a pun, doubly referred to Bert's continued use of blackface in the title role as well as to Chester Lode's unfortunate experience as the reluctant ruler of Koal.[62]

Chester imagines himself shipwrecked on the mythical island of Koal. After island people discover him, they replace their missing monarch, Big Smoke, with him. Although Chester tries numerous times to escape, he never succeeds.[63] The first act establishes the story that unfolds, culminating with the title character eating somniferous berries. In the second act, Chester dreams as a result of having eaten the berries. The indigenous people carry him in as a substitute for Big Smoke, and then Chester sings, after which others in the cast perform musical selections. The last act opens with Chester awakening. By the end of the play, the real Big Smoke, whose kidnappers release him, returns, making Chester his servant.[64] Desperate to get away, however, Chester searches for a means of escape. When he makes his dash, "he casts in his lot with the audience, and the last seen of him is a memory of flying coat tails, white gaiters and rolling eyeballs as he disappears up the aisle of the theatre."[65]

Critics agreed that *Mr. Lode of Koal* was a less-than-stellar production, but a successful star vehicle for Bert that demonstrated that he could succeed as a solo act.[66] It was a "moderate hit."[67] Bert maintained his former style in the show, working slowly and deliberately, infusing Chester with the Jonah Man's melancholia. Through the musical, he mainly carried the Williams and Walker torch. Perhaps that is why *Mr. Lode of Koal* appeared to be an extension of the Williams and Walker legacy rather than Bert's self-innovation that would reintroduce him to the audience as soloist. He performed apparently unremarkable songs that were, however, deemed entertaining because Bert Williams sang them.[68]

Woven into the plot, the song selections built on the story and further developed Chester's character. "That's Aplenty" centered on the antics of a man caught in the wrong place at the wrong time:

T'was in a hencoop one dark night I stopped to rest myself,
and to my great surprise I spied some pullets on a shelf,
I tried to shake hands with a hen, when some buckshot passed my head,
I dropped my bag and turned around to the gen'man said. . . .

CHORUS:
Mr., Mr., Oh, listen like a friend,
No use to argue, just let the matter end;

Excuse me boss, if wrong I've done,
There ain't no use to shoot that gun,
Just move that much so I can run
Thank you! That's aplenty, plenty. . . .[69]

As the unfortunate man caught at the losing end of what would seem to be a good opportunity, Bert replayed the Jonah Man. He also reiterated the familiar image of the chicken-stealing black on the run from the powers that be. Additionally, he continued his characteristic dancing, made famous in the duo's cakewalk performances years before.

Bert's monologues, the numerous chorus selections, and dance numbers assured audiences that *Mr. Lode of Koal* was similar to Williams and Walker's work. The production even included some of the previous members of the Williams and Walker Company as well as music written by the duo's longtime associates Jesse Shipp and Alex Rogers. It provided the black press with hope that Williams and Walker's work had not ended, despite George's absence.

The show also proved that this "big fellow" was indeed "a show in himself." Bert gained considerable attention as he worked without George. He may have lacked the able support of his "foil," but he nonetheless showcased his skill and captivated his audience.

Describing audiences won by a gesture, a joke, a dance step, or an expression, white critics often continued to comprehend Bert's performance within the legacy of minstrelsy. Attempting to identify the wonder of his magical sway over audiences, reviewers still spoke of authenticity. In racialized reviews, the critics classified *Mr. Lode of Koal* as a show featuring the black man as the "natural" entertainer, seeing in Bert the very embodiment of "blackness" for white audiences' enjoyment. In their more extreme readings, they even translated the show into minstrelsy as a performed darky joke book.

Reviewers envisioned themselves as representative of their audience. An individual "I" became a spectatorial "we" as they re-created the theatrical experience for absent readers and defined the show for would-be spectators. Their interpretations created meaning, and those meanings existed beyond the reach and control of the show's creators and performers.

First, some critics praised Bert while underplaying his skill and framing the performance in stereotypical terms. An Ohio reviewer noted that "his *apparent spontaneous* funnyisms proved the magnet that caused much laughter," while a New York critic described them as "*unpremedi-tated* funnyisms he simply can't help."[70] Lauding Bert's seemingly un-controllable actions and normative humor, these critics emphasized the idea of the black entertainer as a "natural" entertainer. They reduced Bert's skill to an expression of his unconscious and his inherent ability. It was as though he were subject to the whims of his unconscious rather than being in control of it himself. Such critics refused, in understated terms, to permit Bert conscious choice. They located power, even dur-ing the performance, beyond the performer himself.

Reviewing Bert's gestures and dances, a Chicago *American* critic re-lated them to the writer's own beliefs about race, using racialist terms to talk about the comic's gifts: "There is no other funny man on the stage who can do with his hands and feet what Williams can do with his. They are racial, those hands and feet."[71] With such words, the writer en-visioned Bert as a literal embodiment of blackness. Noting "racial hands and feet," the critic spoke to an audience that apparently needed little further description to decode his meaning. Blackface was a me-tonymy for the black body, a body believed to possess a manner of movement that highlighted its difference and strangeness. Blackface makeup marked Bert as a caricature for the audience's facile reading. The critic seemed to believe that Bert performed as he did because of an inherent racial difference. The authenticity of Bert's racialized move-ment consequently made him incomparable onstage.

The critic's reading of Bert's movement suggested a kinesis of race. If the critic could describe Bert's movements as "racial" and expect the audience to understand, it implied the existence of a common lexicon that made these "black" movements intelligible to readers and critics alike. Gestures and dances reified blackness in a language that existed apart from the spoken word.

In Boston, a *Globe* reviewer remarked appreciatively of Bert's "suave and sugary African humor."[72] He now turned the racialist ideas toward the "dark continent," envisioning "Africa" in the *Mr. Lode of Koal* pro-duction, despite its absence from the show's story or songs. For the writer, it was Bert himself who connoted Africa, which had little to do with any actual reference made within the musical. The description therefore reminded readers of Bert's race. More importantly, however, it informed audiences that Bert's performance was appropriately "black."

If these references to authenticity demanded that blacks' representa-tions be "true," then announcements of the "Africanness" of Bert's humor were promises of genuineness. "Africa" was the repository of blackness, and "African" was the symbolic superlative of "black," presumed to be its truest representation. If audiences wanted to see authentic blackness, then there could be nothing more authentic than the "African."

Finally, in a review that escalated racialized commentary, a critic remarked on what he found to be the incoherence of the production. In the process, he explicitly discussed the show in the language of minstrelsy:

> Does one expect unity and logical flow of incident in a "darky" joke book? The chances are that one would let the gaudy-colored affair lie peacefully on the railroad newsstand if he suspected such an impertinence. When we succumb to the surreptitious desire for the broad tang of "nigger" humor, we want no disturbing atom of intelligence busy-bodying about. Our mental dissipation—and joke book—must be complete. "*Mr. Lode of Koal*" is a sort of physical embodiment of such a joke book. We see the jokes, so to speak, in the flesh.[73]

Rather than assess the apparent flaws of the show in an artistic critique, the writer discussed it in racialized terms. Thus the show was "gaudy-colored," containing "nigger" humor and "no disturbing atom of intelligence." Minstrelsy, which emphasized the ignorance and excessiveness of blacks, supplied the language of both disdain and hilarity in which to critique the production.

Literally constructing black people as jokes, the "physical embodiment" of a joke book, the critic transformed performers into a darky joke book that the white audience, succumbing to a "surreptitious desire," read. The joke, then, was obviously on those who performed. In fact, their every action amplified the joke they embodied. Being jokes "in the flesh," the black figures gracing the stage were the material at which the audience laughed. Representing *Mr. Lode of Koal* as a joke book rather than a musical, performers as minstrels rather than comic actors, the journalist created an image of a show that minstrelsy's fans—even if they were hidden or secretive—would enjoy.

More than anything, it seemed that as long as Bert played the blackface character, critics would see the darky. As a vehicle for Williams, *Mr. Lode of Koal* featured his patented humorous antics, which were as funny as ever. Yet neither he nor his show could surmount the stereotypes critics associated with black performance. Bert's vision of blacks' opportunity in the theater had apparently not yet arrived.

Other black shows on Broadway, however, like Cole and Johnson's
Red Moon, attempted to go beyond black stereotypes with greater success. *Red Moon*, a musical comedy, portrayed two different American
minority groups, Native Americans and African Americans. It had
opened at the same theater, the Majestic, at which Williams and Walker
had opened *Bandanna Land*. Moreover, it had enjoyed a tour of nearly
a year as well as an enthusiastic reception by blacks and whites alike.[74]

frican American reviewers responded with differing degrees of
encouragement and criticism to Bert's performance. As before,
they considered it in relation to its importance for the black community.
They implied that Bert's achievement was not important merely for him
but also for black theater, directly linking his work to the race. Like
many white critics, these reviewers fit Bert into their own agenda. In
this instance, their concern was with ideal representations of the race.

Thomas Swann, of the *Indianapolis Freeman*, wrote a glowing commentary on Bert's success in the West, having lifted the musical to the
level of an artistic statement:

> It has what may be termed the spiritual sincerity of symbolism. *Mr. Lode of
> Koal* is the reflection of the individual quality of the men and women who
> actually portray the play rather than a drawn-out rendition of the creator's
> theme. Here is portrayed the true fundamentals of all art, the correct idea
> which proceeds from the quality of individual genius, from a deep sense of
> feeling and love for the work—from the fullness of its art sense.[75]

In a reversal of the white critic's darky joke book reading, Swann's commentary distinguished *Mr. Lode of Koal*'s cast as artists. Instead of
embodying jokes, they constituted genius and their participation manifested the brilliance of the show itself. The artistic excellence of the production possessed no parallel and was "without model or shadow."[76]
Being no minstrel show, then, the play contained "the true fundamentals
of all art" and was a sincere expression of "feeling and love."

According to Swann, not only did Bert serve his audience as an
artist, but he also served the black community as a political leader:

> By his persistency in staying before the footlights, in every part of the
> great Republic of the New World, and displaying his powers as an artist,
> he has compelled men and women in every station in life to "Stop, look

and listen!" By this token he has made a contribution of inestimable proportion to America's most perplexing sociological problem.[77]

More than an artist, Bert was an activist. Not only did he perform, he also made a statement. His words onstage equated to an exhortation, his artistic excellence to an effective call to action. Bert's call was to address "America's most perplexing sociological problem," which was the problem of racial discrimination.

In the writer's view, Bert challenged his audiences in performances that made them not only laugh but also reflect: "With him in the spotlight there is always something doing, and it is all giltedge. He not only makes you giggle—he makes you think."[78] Both comedian and activist, Bert did work onstage that was also work for the race.

Taking Bert's success as a sign, Swann subsequently determined that "we are nearing this day of better things."[79] He decided that Bert's achievement would effect change. If Bert could succeed in being taken seriously as an actor—and presumably as a man—other blacks in society could as well. Swann envisioned the fate of the race as being closely linked to that of Bert.

Yet another critic saw the show as a harbinger of a new era in Negro stagecraft and optimistically bade farewell to the "slap-stick buffoonery of the past."[80] Again, as before, Bert and company embodied progress. This reviewer, like the other, imagined activist possibilities through the production itself, for "if the characters created by the coming forth of *Mr. Lode of Koal* are accepted in New York it is but a step further when such great comedians as Mr. Williams and others I might mention will be seen from under cork in spectacular, fantaies [*sic*], fables and travesties."[81] In effect, he put debates about representation to work, proposing new political interventions through Bert and his company.

Such black critics mobilized the notion of representation as political activism and spoke on behalf of their black public. Focusing on the idea of representation, they asserted their opinions and announced their expectations of Bert. Writing in the declarative if not the imperative, the journalists emphasized the importance of activism and intervention. Moreover, they implicitly introduced the idea that the maintenance of Williams and Walker's legacy would require Bert's commitment to both.

Although black critics may have had better motives than the white critics did, they also assessed Bert's performance in terms of their own concerns about race. The black critics simply turned attention to their concern about proper representation, whereas white reviewers highlighted continuities that dated back to minstrelsy's stereotypes. Ultimately, the finer details of the show and performance got lost among prevailing debates in white and black society about the role of the black actor. Although *Mr. Lode of Koal* did display Bert's talents, he could not escape the larger discussions that defined the meaning of his work and contributions.

D uring the *Mr. Lode of Koal* tour, the show faced the contradictory criticism of reviewers, and the company itself experienced great difficulties. When securing accommodations in Iowa, for example, proprietors prohibited them from rooming in hotels. The company had made no plans in advance, so the managers at the theater where they were performing had to seek housing for the cast and crew among local black residents.[82]

The sixty-odd members of the company found food and shelter during their stay, but the *Age*'s Lester Walton did not easily disregard such egregious mismanagement. He criticized the irresponsible booking agent: "Knowing the prejudice that exists relative to feeding and lodging colored performers, the advance agent should make it his business to see that the members of the company secure proper accommodations."[83] Although at the time Walton did not indict Bert in the near-fiasco, he soon came to place blame on the entertainer as well.

When *Mr. Lode of Koal* closed quickly after a run of less than thirty weeks—far short of a full season—Walton wrote again. He acknowledged the limited critical success of the show but claimed that critical response had less to do with the show's closing than did poor management. This was due to F. Ray Comstock's neglect and, by extension, Bert Williams's apparent acceptance of that neglect. Walton wrote disdainfully:

> It would require a long stretch of imagination to picture the *Mr. Lode of Koal* Company playing in second-class theatres of the Stair and Havlin Circuit [a large chain of cheaper popular-price theaters] with George W. Walker of the famous team in the saddle. But in such houses the company has been playing for the past two weeks. Last week in Philadelphia Bert Williams was seen for the first time in many years in a second-class Stair and Havlin house—the National Theatre, and this week the booking is equally as bad—Blaney's Amphion Theatre, Brooklyn.[84]

In Walton's view, Bert's refusal to "[compel] Mr. Comstock to live up to his contract and keep him in first-class theatres" caused the unfortunate fall of the show to second-class theaters. Although Walton recognized Bert's skill as an entertainer, Walton insisted that "he misses his old partner—George Walker—more for the business than the artistic end."[85] With George gone, it seemed that Bert had much to learn about the business of theater. In his unskilled hands, he had perhaps even tarnished his and his partner's legacy.

Having received no further bookings from Comstock, after *Mr. Lode of Koal* ended, Bert returned to vaudeville. Yet again: controversy. As before, the White Rats objected so vociferously to Bert's designation as headliner that the managers—as before—lost their nerve. The circuit owners, Percy Williams and Willie Hammerstein, who had initially admitted that Bert would headline, rescinded their offer amidst the White Rats' protest.

In writing that was more openly critical than the previous year, a journalist for the *Age* decried the influence of the White Rats, who evidently believed "that the progress of the colored vaudevillian should be retarded."[86] The reporter noted, however, that in a subtle act of resistance the managers indicated who the headliner really was.

Maude Raymond, a singer-actress who had recently finished a run in the Broadway musical *The Young Turk*, was also on the bill. At Hammerstein's Victoria Theatre, although promoters created posters featuring "Maude Raymond" on the first line as headliner, they wrote Bert's name, which appeared second, twice as large and with the reference, "the greatest and most original comedian in the world."[87]

Although the managers had backed down at the White Rats' insistence, they indirectly highlighted Bert's placement on the bill: "In electric lights in front of the Victoria Theatre 'Bert Williams' can be seen at a distance, and in the lobby of the theatres his pictures are conspicuous everywhere. It cannot be recalled that a 'headliner' has ever received such barren honors as Miss Raymond, but the unwritten law of the White Rats has not been violated."[88] The managers honored, perhaps only in appearance, the White Rats' mandate. While the critic wryly acknowledged that Bert did ultimately receive his due, he also recognized the regrettable and cowardly manner in which the managers chose to give it.

Journalists didn't miss the irony that Bert's vaudeville colleagues appreciated his talents even as they resisted his status on the bill. The *New York Morning Telegraph* observed, "The other performers on the program hurried to the front of the house to catch Bert Williams. Those who could not get out in time crowded into the wings."[89] The *New York Age* journalist noted the disparate reactions of these white performers who "congratulated [Bert] and pronounced him great," yet all the while sought to "draw the color line." Furthermore, he denounced the discrimination against Bert not only as signs of "Negrophobia" but also as un-American activities that advanced one group with the objective to retard another.[90]

The audiences' reactions were perhaps even more ironic and contemptible. The *Age* reporter noted the "hearty ovation" the audience offered Bert, yet recognized that those whites who became "hysterical" watching the comedians' funny antics were also often overheard remarking, "Gee, too bad he's colored."[91] Despite the writer's disinclination to comment at length on the remarks, he registered surprise at the audience's ambivalence. Audience members who, in one moment appeared to be with the comedian in their laughter and in the next became critically distant and drew the color line, shocked and disturbed the writer.

When laughing, audience members had perhaps displaced the mask they normally wore, which typically separated them from the black performer onstage. Their laughter encouragingly suggested the solidarity that laughter and humor inspired despite racial differences. In the post-performance moment, however, those audience members again donned their masks, thereby declaring difference and reestablishing distance. In effect, they denied the extent to which Bert, while performing, had "won" them, irrespective of his race.

Even as the White Rats aggressively resisted Bert's work and status as an artist, others also engaged in lesser forms of resistance to him. White audiences, though laudatory, were also critical and self-conscious in ways that had little to do with the performance's quality and nearly everything to do with their own racial perceptions. Additionally, performers also respected Bert while they simultaneously wished to deny him his right to treatment as a major box-office attraction. Despite having had access to big-time theaters and offers that welcomed his skill, even Bert could not altogether avoid controversy as a result of his race. In his next big move as a solo act, he would continue to enjoy the respect of many fans, while at the same time, he would incur the wrath of others who hated to see the heights to which his inimitable skill could take him.

8

Ziegfeld's Follies

When Bert's run with *Mr. Lode of Koal* ended, he informed the company of his intention to appear "in a big colored production next season," hoping "to see many of those present with him when the season opened."[1] As he moved on in his new career without George, however, he decided to step away from the heavy responsibilities of managing a large company. He plainly lacked George's business skills, and he preferred solely to perform rather than also to manage others. Additionally, other offers, such as a $1,000 per week contract from the Moss-Stoll circuit of variety halls in England, proved to Bert his desirability as an individual performer.[2] At first, Bert had been directionless and lost without George, but with time he had found his feet. Sadly, even as Bert's star continued to rise, George's would wane.

Bert and the theatrical community missed George, but they all needed to move forward without him. Aida, though devastated by George's continuing decline, did not have the means to afford the luxury of retiring in order to care for him. She balanced her continuing work on Cole and Johnson's *Red Moon* with her efforts to care for George, who spent time at his relatives' homes in Kansas, and then sought treatment in Michigan sanitariums.[3]

The Frogs also moved on. When they met at Bob Cole's home in May of 1910, they addressed new business matters and elected officers in George's absence. Bert became president; his longtime friend, playwright Jesse Shipp, took the post of first vice president and treasurer; and critic Lester Walton became second vice president. John Nail, Bert's former real estate agent, took the position of financial secretary, while R. C. McPherson, composer and music publishing entrepreneur, became corresponding secretary.[4] Although through their work they continued to honor George's vision, they resolved to do so accepting the fact that he would not return to serve.

As little as a month after Bert's announcement to the *Mr. Lode of Koal* Company, he received and accepted an offer from Florenz Ziegfeld to perform as a featured act in the *Follies of 1910*.[5] Ziegfeld was a singularly brilliant producer, the kind who could put performers on the theatrical map.[6] His *Follies*, a famous all-white revue, was an established New York institution soon to become a national institution. It had inspired acerbic pundit, Dorothy Parker of *Vanity Fair* to lampoon its display of "glorified" American showgirls.[7] If Bert joined the *Follies* ranks, he would make history as the first black entertainer to perform in Ziegfeld's sensational *Follies*.

Performing in the *Follies* would in many ways prove to be a terrific boon to Bert's career. He had numerous hurdles to jump before he could pursue it, however. The first was his contract with F. Ray Comstock. Although their agreement had ended in disaster with *Mr. Lode of Koal's* early closing, Bert was still bound to a three-year contract with the feckless producer.

Comstock refused to allow Bert's release from his contract, threatening to seek an injunction to restrain him from pursuing work with others. Pointing to the details of the contract, Bert's $300 per week salary with a share of profits, Comstock argued that any move for separation on Bert's part would indicate a flagrant disregard for their binding agreement.[8] In the end, Bert filed a complaint through his lawyer, declaring that Comstock broke their contract. Closely following that action, Comstock filed a countersuit, claiming that Bert had been the one to break it.[9]

Bert's complaint included mention of his show's less than thirty-five weeks of bookings, the numerous expenses Comstock racked up unknown to him, Comstock's failure to share any bookkeeping or accounting records with him, and the fact that the two partners could no longer come to any agreement. Most importantly, however, he addressed Comstock's unacceptable booking practices.[10]

The contract stipulated that Bert would be booked only in first-class theaters, in which the best seats cost $1.50. In court, Bert enumerated the second-class houses in which he'd been booked, where the top seats cost only $1. They included the Grand Opera House in Philadelphia, a city in which Comstock's associates, the Shuberts, had first-class houses, and the Lyceum in Cleveland, where Comstock himself had a first-class theater. Bert argued that the show's losses had come from Comstock's booking practices, which were in breach of contract. "[T]his sort of treatment, and this method of booking the attraction [with scattered stops in far-flung cities, requiring extensive railroad travel] resulted in practically loss after loss. In every second-class house that we booked, we lost money."[11]

When it came to booking, Comstock insisted that he had secured for Bert a full, thirty-five-week season. It seemed, however, he could not deny the bookings in second-class theaters. Bert then charged Comstock with lying about the season's length, claiming that he had been booked for only twenty-seven weeks.[12] Comstock failed to prove the court otherwise.

Bert, articulate and confident, declared the damage done by the show's early closure:

> It is fatal to the prospects of a performer, particularly one who is part owner of a production, to close his tour in the middle of the season. This not only advertises the fact that he and his play is [sic] a failure, but it injures him in his profession and with owners of theatres where the play is to appear later in the season. It leaves the time of the theatres open, with the difficulty of filling the time, and all blame would fall upon me if it had gone out in the profession that I had refused to continue performing in the middle of the season.[13]

Recalling the responses of critics like Lester Walton, who had blamed Bert for the show's mismanagement, Bert had definite grounds for his statement.

Ultimately, Bert had to admit that, due to the show's losses, which were "nineteen weeks out of a total of twenty-seven," he owed Comstock $5,500. He was also indebted to creditors of the firm of Comstock and Williams. "To indicate ... good faith," however, he had begun to pay Comstock back. He had paid Comstock $325, from the $1,100 per week he had earned in vaudeville. Even as he made efforts to pay off his debt, however, Bert averred that he continued to be dissatisfied with Comstock and his business practices. In conclusion, Bert stated, "We cannot get along in this business venture and I will not continue in business with one who had confronted me with nothing but losses."[14]

By December 1910, the judgment came through: Comstock would have no further hold on Bert.[15] Bert was free. Whereas Comstock had failed to make a compelling case, the usually retiring Bert had fought back, arguing and winning in a fashion akin to George. In George's absence, the reticent Bert had spoken up, showing himself capable of managing his affairs.

Onward he moved, pursuing work with the famous Flo Ziegfeld.

Florenz Ziegfeld, Jr., son of the founder and president of the Chicago Musical College, had established himself in the legitimate theater as a daring impresario with a talent for headline-grabbing publicity stunts.[16] He and his common-law wife, French actress Anna Held, frequently staged outrageous exploits.[17] Their greatest claim was that Miss Held bathed daily in forty gallons of milk delivered to their New York suite. To back up that claim, they timed a milk delivery to coincide with the arrival of members of the press, whom they'd invited to witness Anna luxuriating in her "French beauty secret."[18]

A perfect match, Flo and Anna both devoted themselves to capturing the attention of the press. Ziegfeld's publicists promoted him as "the P. T. Barnum of the theatre."[19] Held, with Ziegfeld's backing, became a sensation in the shows that he crafted especially for her. Despite Anna's rather feeble abilities, she had an engaging style, and she tested the boundaries of acceptable theatrical performance in her racy acts.[20]

It was Anna who initially suggested the idea of the *Follies*. She reportedly remarked to Florenz, "Your American girls are the most beautiful in the world, if you could only dress them up chic and *charmant* [sic]. You could do a much better revue than the *Folies-Bergère* in this country."[21] With that suggestion, Flo began his *Follies of 1907*, which would be officially rechristened the *Ziegfeld Follies* in 1911.[22] Although it was not the first revue staged in the States, from its initial installment, the *Follies* was the grandest and most glamorous, aided by "the Ziegfeld Touch."[23]

A variety show including comedians and chorus girls, the *Follies* could have been considered vaudeville. From the start, however, between Ziegfeld's connections and his concept of the show, he endowed the production with a style that encouraged its affiliation with legitimate theater rather than vaudeville. Benefiting from a relationship with theater owners Klaw and Erlanger, who produced the *Follies*, Ziegfeld reclassed his venture. Having begun in legitimate theater producing Anna Held's musical comedies, he elevated his revue to meet its standards.[24] At the time of the *Follies of 1907*, Klaw and Erlanger paid Ziegfeld a salary of a mere $200 per week but footed a bill that altogether was reportedly upwards of $17,000 per week.[25]

From its first year, Ziegfeld's revue played the roof garden of the New York Theatre as a "major attraction" throughout the summer of 1907. Its status as "major" was because previously, such runs had been unusual. Most theaters in this era prior to air conditioning closed between the beginning of June and Labor Day. Ziegfeld's *Follies* was the first Broadway show to run straight through the summer.[26] Although not a remarkable success in its first New York edition, the *Follies* gained notice, particularly during its extensive tour, which ensured its continuation as an annual revue.[27]

The creators of the *Follies of 1907* had the Parisian revue in mind when realizing their show. Ziegfeld dubbed the New York Theatre's roof garden the "Jardin de Paris" and created an environment in which the audience would be able to watch the performance while eating, drinking, or smoking at tables facing the stage.[28] For the first five years, the structure of the *Follies* also reflected this Parisian connection, using the "compère" (fatherly figure) and "commère" (motherly figure) characters characteristic of the European revue. A third character led the compère and commère through numerous sketches and acts, all satirizing the events of the year.[29] The essential difference between the continental revues and the *Follies* was that Ziegfeld utilized American performers, drawing talent from minstrelsy and vaudeville.[30] Over the years, the structure of the revue would shift to the chorus and showgirls, reducing stage time for comedians.

Before plunging into his work with Ziegfeld's *Follies,* Bert first had to jump his next hurdle. This time, however, it was with the able assistance of Flo himself. As when Bert performed in vaudeville, controversy followed him as he approached his new endeavor. Ziegfeld had taken a considerable risk offering him a contract. Not only did the comedian's addition make him the sole black among an all-white cast, but it also put him in the company of a bevy of white chorus girls.

It would seem that Klaw and Erlanger, having chosen to align themselves with the sensibilities of white audience members, would not accept Ziegfeld's radical idea. After all, they had been generally timid about supporting black performers, despite having mounted Williams and Walker's *In Dahomey*. Surprisingly, however, Ziegfeld's producers backed him in his choice. Instead, it was the performers who balked, although none spoke openly and publicly about his or her protest.[31] Ziegfeld staunchly supported his new cast member despite the protest of others in the company. He declared Bert to be indispensable.

Flo's decision to hire the talented and already-famous Bert was not the only means by which he showed his distaste for racial discrimination. Years before, when James Weldon Johnson and his brother, Rosamond, had had a meeting scheduled with Flo, they traveled to his apartment, which comprised an entire floor in the Ansonia Hotel. Stepping into a free elevator, they informed the operator of their destination. He refused to move, however, telling them to take the service elevator. Unwilling to accept the substandard treatment, they told the hotel manager about their appointment with Ziegfeld and the elevator boy's refusal to carry them in the passenger elevator. Haughtily, the man affirmed that the boy had been complying with hotel policy.[32]

When James Weldon and Rosamond called Flo to explain their inability to keep their appointment because of the elevator boy's refusal to serve them, he told them to wait. Immediately, he descended and then had a heated discussion with the manager, who remained insistent about the policy. Disregarding his protests, Flo led James Weldon and Rosamond into the passenger elevator, ordering the operator to take them up. When their session was over, he called the elevator back up and rode down with them to the lobby. Flo, a man given to acting independently, did not countenance the high-handed directives of others.[33]

Throughout Bert's tenure in the *Follies*, journalists of the African American press would chart his progress. They would laud his achievements and critique white critics, their loyalty to Bert and hopes for black performers' future prospects inspiring them. His move to the *Follies*, however, would come with significant challenges.

The year before Bert's start in the *Follies*, Lester Walton had complained about the management's racial intolerance. At the box office, a black "high government official" had been turned away, having been told that the show was sold out. Undeterred from seeing the performance, he decided to buy tickets from a "speculator." While outside, however, a "colored attaché of the house" informed him that he should not attempt to buy seats: blacks were no longer welcome in the theater.[34]

The rejected patron asked Walton when theater managers Klaw and Erlanger had changed their policy regarding the admission of blacks. Walton discovered that an incident that had occurred ten weeks prior had been the impetus for the change. A few black men seen flirting with several white women during the show had infuriated white male on-lookers, who sought to have the men expelled from the theater. An altercation ensued when the black men refused to leave. Subsequently, the theater changed its policy regarding the admission of blacks generally. Walton summed up the story: "Since that time a colored applicant for a ticket to the Jardin de Paris has been getting a reception at the box office akin to that usually accorded the first act on a vaudeville bill—very much à la cold storage."[35]

With Bert's precedent, he increasingly faced continuing demands to be mindful of his black public, an audience that would remain sensitive to the decisions he made. In some ways, Bert would seem to fail to meet their needs. Even after his inclusion in the *Follies of 1910*, for instance, his black public would be unable to secure tickets to the show. "When several members of the race applied for tickets during the first two weeks of the show and were informed that all seats had been sold, the word went out that colored patronage was not desired, and few sought admission during the balance of the company's stay in New York."[36] As was true the year before, blacks in New York had no access to the *Follies* when performed at the Jardin de Paris, regardless of Bert's status and that he had a black following in the city.

In later years, James Weldon Johnson would speak of Bert's move to the *Follies* as a "defection" to the white stage, placing on his shoulders the burden of responsibility for "the sudden stop to what had been a steady development and climb of the Negro in the theatre."[37] The reality is that the "term of exile," from 1910–1917, during which blacks no longer played Broadway theaters, came largely as a result of the untimely deaths and retirements of numerous performers.[38] Ernest Hogan had passed away in 1909, George had retired, and in 1911, Bob Cole would die. Without the leading performers who had proved the viability of black theatrical productions, Broadway's doyens would no longer be persuaded to finance such ventures.[39]

In spite of such setbacks, the evolution of black theater did not stop. Rather, it continued instead in Harlem. During that term of exile, theaters like the Lincoln (located on West 135th Street) and the Lafayette (at Second Avenue and 132nd Street) would open up, becoming the "new Broadway" for black entertainers. Outside of Harlem, Motts's Pekin Theater in Chicago would invite New York black performers, like Will Marion Cook, to work on productions. In addition, the creation of black touring companies, such as Sherman H. Dudley's Smart Set Company, would afford leading black talent new opportunities.[40]

At the time that Bert joined the *Follies*, however, many of these developments were in the nascent stage. In response to criticism, he justified his choice: "The colored show business—that is colored musical shows—is at a low ebb just now. I reached the conclusion last spring that I could best represent my race by doing pioneer work. It was far better to have joined a large white show than to have starred in a colored show, considering conditions."[41]

Ironically, Bert explained that his decision to move away from all-black productions was tied to his feelings of responsibility to his black public. He took on the *Follies* as a pioneer, he said, opening up the frontier as a black man performing in a high-profile show among whites. Although his role in relation to the black community only partly factored in his decision—at that time, opportunities on Broadway for all-black companies were rarer than before—he underscored his link to other blacks.

Regardless of his rationale, Bert had an extraordinary chance. The *Follies* provided high visibility and regular work: a summer season in town, and a season touring on the road. Furthermore, that road tour would exclude locations in the South, a stipulation upon which Bert had insisted, and with which Ziegfeld had agreed.[42] It also gave Bert the means to share his success with his father, for whom he opened up a poolroom and barbershop in Harlem.[43] Most important, it brought him closer to the vision he was developing.

Bert's unspoken ambition was to perform a dramatic role on Broadway in legitimate theater. As he dared to pursue that ambition, he began to gain the will to take risks alone. Although conflict was anathema to Bert, a man admittedly inclined to back down, now he leapt at this chance. Despite his distance from the black public, despite the controversy that ensued, he continued. As Bert pursued his vision, one he would later express publicly, he would also claim to have the interest of the black community at heart. Such statements would become increasingly important as his absence from his black public continued.

The atmosphere on the Jardin de Paris roof garden was high class. Members of elite society, such as the Vanderbilts and the Rockefellers, would gather at the roof garden for their summer entertainment: to see and be seen.[44] Paying a premium for tickets, enjoying food and drink while taking in a show, these spectators differed significantly from those in vaudeville. With time, the opening of the *Ziegfeld Follies*, rather than the weather, became the indicator of summer's arrival in New York City.

By 1910, Ziegfeld's revue had already begun to turn its attention toward "scores of young women, beautiful in features and form, brilliant and showy cossumes [*sic*], luxurious scenery and surroundings."[45] While the *Follies* leisurely displayed its glamorous girls in captivating presentations of pulchritude, the segments between those parades increasingly featured swiftly paced variety acts.[46]

Bert was scheduled to have a large role in his first *Follies*. Ziegfeld had meant him to enjoy "all the prerogatives of a stage supported by his own aggregation. Williams was to feel as much at home and be permitted to conduct himself in just the same way as when touring *In Dahomey*, surrounded by fifty or sixty people of his own color," a Cincinnati journalist wrote. That arrangement, however, was deeply unpalatable to the cast. "They refused absolutely to bow and scrape and make way for the negro comedian or to place themselves in such a position during the performance as to give the impression that they were supporting him or were subservient to him."[47] The cast pressured Ziegfeld, threatening to strike, so Bert instead had to perform his vaudeville act.[48] Although not the star of the show as originally intended, he still received considerable and enthusiastic attention.

Various reviewers believed that Bert was "the real star of the evening."[49] The *New York World* announced, "He has more real talent than all the rest of the cast combined."[50] A *New York Sun* headline lauded Bert as the "funniest" in the show, and the theater critic avowed that "only two of his predecessors had succeeded in creating anything like the same degree of merriment."[51] *Chicago Evening American* journalist Constance Skinner insisted that Bert was "not one of the *Follies*.

He is the wisdom of the show. He was wisdom and wit before F. Ziegfeld ever committed a folly."[52]

Critics couldn't get enough of Bert, like Ralph Renaud of the *San Francisco Chronicle*. Because Bert had "such a colossal reputation to live up to," Renaud wanted more. Despite the dearth of Bert, he declared the comedian to be "a scream."[53] In New York, the *Evening Post* reviewer was left hungry for more of Bert's act, writing that he should have performed longer and remarking that "the uproar which greeted him was fully deserved."[54]

Audiences applauded two new songs that Bert performed, "Constantly" and "White Folks Call It Chantecler, But It's Just Plain Chicken to Me." "Constantly" was a pained Jonah Man character song. Frederic Hatton of the *Chicago Evening Post* noted how Bert "chronicles with many drooping glances, turning down of mouth corners and graphic gestures of those huge but eloquent hands another of those adventures of misadventure which he does so well."[55] Another Chicago journalist, Ashton Stevens, went so far as to pronounce the song a classic, "creaming with dismal fun, a minor epic of hard luck. It was slow-gaited, lopperjointed Williams at his deadliest. His funer[e]al joy in that song laid us out, and we forgot that we were dead only when we waked to applaud for more."[56]

Half-singing and half-reciting with a forlorn sigh, Bert played his Jonah Man character.[57] He supplemented his expression with gestures, which deepened the somber tones:

There is a word called misery, and misery loves company,
That's the reason why it chases me . . . constantly.
My landlord never bothered me befo',
Always said that my rent was sho',
But now he just knocks on my do' . . . constantly.

Bert's first-person recitation increased the plaintiveness of the piece, his "constantly" a resigned sigh of a hopeless man. While he spoke, a trombone slid in empathetic tones. The chorus confirmed his state:

Good luck, eyes me, spies me, guiles me . . . constantly.
Bad luck seeks me, sneaks me, greets me, constantly.
Some times I feel like a bird in the tree,
Flying around, so gaily and free,
But it seems hard luck clipped my wings for me . . . constantly!

Exemplifying Bert's theories about a good song, the lyrics told a story anchored in his character. The song detailed the regrettable travails of the singer. The chorus, furthermore, personified his misfortune. It expressed the wretchedness of the character's experiences. Bert performed a second verse, escalating the tale:

> To prize fight once I thought I'd try,
> I was to fight a man that they called Kid Nigh[?],
> The man just kept his fist in my eye . . . constantly.
> The fight only had about six rounds to go,
> There I was, and I needed the dough,
> But the referee just kept picking me up off the flo' . . . ooh, constantly!

Life literally beat the character in "Constantly," similar to the figurative beating the singer of "Nobody" endured.

As true of Bert's other songs, the chorus contained variations, continuing the story rather than merely repeating earlier phrases. Building on his preceding verse, Bert took his character's story further:

> Good luck, eyes me, spies me, guiles me . . . constantly.
> Bad luck seeks me, sneaks me, greets me, constantly.
> That man he sho' did have the knack,
> Of just shooting 'em in, like the jig of a jack,
> When he'd hit me in the stomach, I'd bulge out in the back. . . .
> Constantly!

As in "Nobody," in which an "enjine" from a railroad wreck ended up on the Jonah Man's neck, the suffering in "Constantly" was extreme. Here, as in "Nobody," the Jonah Man recounted his tale with dramatic, reluctant pacing.

Hatton wrote that "the Williams artistry in all of its clean, clear, certain human appeal" improved the show.[58] Although he did not consider these Bert's best songs, he stated that "they exact from the singer a proportionately greater exehibition [sic] of technique."[59] The "human appeal" of which Hatton wrote was broad, not narrowly related to race, despite Bert's use of burnt cork. In songs like "Constantly," he embodied the complexities of this lugubrious storyteller while also removing Bert Williams, the actor, from the frame of the performance.

Bert's other new song came during a burlesque of a popular French play, *Chantecler*. His role as "the Blackbird" called for wearing a top hat and tuxedo jacket with a feathered tail and bird feet.[60] He emerged on-stage breaking through an egg and sang "White Folks Call It Chante-cler, But It's Just Plain Chicken to Me." Despite being a coon song complete with the chicken theme, it had a parodic tone, mocking whites' pretentious language. A sample of the song reveals the satire:

> *White folks call it chantecler,*
> *But it's just plain chicken to me;*
> *And the last time you were one of those,*
> *You wore it fricassee;*

> *They may call coffee "demitasse,"*
> *And "croquette" is another name for hash;*
> *You may call a barn fowl Chantecler,*
> *But it's just plain chicken to me.*[61]

Of course, the satire competed with the audience's expectations. Hatton, having admired Bert's other offerings on other terms, read this one in fa-miliar racialized language, stating that the comedian "epitomizes the love of the colored race for chicken. To see his hands reach out for the fowl is to have a new comic understanding of all the stories of the temptations of A.M.E. parsons in the vicinity of the hen coop."[62] Despite the potential for an alternative interpretation, the song could not successfully compete against the powerful stereotypical images found everywhere from car-toons and articles, to greeting cards and postcards.

The slippage that occurred in the space of a single critic's review in-dicated the persistence of racial stereotypes. It demonstrated the ap-parent unconsciousness with which individuals perpetuated these notions. In one fell swoop, Bert provided a "new comic understanding," yet also reified extant ideas about blacks as both chicken-thieves and pseudoreligious hypocrites. These contradictions revealed the tena-cious racialist terms in which audiences could and did interpret black performance.

Although loathe to incur controversy, Bert did act in a rather risky boxing sketch with Billy Reeves. The players added "A Street in Reno" to the show following "Great White Hope" Jim Jeffries's 4 July ignomin-ious defeat against black heavyweight champion Jack Johnson, in Reno, Nevada.[63] A send-up, nonetheless, the sketch could not have failed to strike a nerve with some people in the audience. The brazen, confident

Bert Williams in Scene from The Follies, *1910.* COURTESY OF THE MUSEUM OF THE CITY OF NEW YORK

Johnson, married to a white woman at a time when intermarriage was illegal in most states, had talked tough and made good. Spectators, white and black alike, had believed in the high stakes of the bout; the despair of many whites matched the pride of blacks who watched Johnson pummel Jeffries in the decisive fifteenth round.

"'Johnson wins' was a bulletin that disappointed and saddened 30,000 men, women, and children who thronged Times Square," began a *New York Times* article.[64] The sadness quickly escalated to violence, however, as enraged whites took their racial fealty to homicidal extremes. These eruptions, following viewings of fight footage or after the exultations of blacks, indicated that racial hatred seethed very close to the surface. In Texas, Illinois, Nebraska, Arkansas, Georgia, New York City, and other locations, the eruptions cost lives.[65] No wonder that, despite its levity, the Reeves-Williams fight scene was not as popular as Bert's songs.

Ultimately, reviewers turned their attention to Bert's other offerings. Chicago critic Ashton Stevens declared Bert's songs free from "the remotest stench of the tenderloin," avoiding "the 'flash nigger' telegraphing to his 'ma-baby.' There was just simple man-fashion humor, kindly infectious humor, humor that made humans of us all."[66] Critics continued to police Bert closely, evaluating him on the basis of his "cleanness." Evidently, he passed the test. Stevens's "flash nigger" comment referred to the Zip Coon role. Fond of and lucky with the ladies, the Zip Coon's sexual insatiability rendered him less than manly—and less than human—in Stevens's view. Ironically, the dandy character had gained its meaning through stereotypes that whites created during minstrelsy, yet the writer placed the responsibility for the unacceptable role on the black actor himself.

Bert's rich approach to performance humanized his character. In his "infectious" performance, he stepped away from stereotype. He created a local color black persona, which Stevens affirmed, proclaiming Bert "the Mark Twain of his color. His humor knows no limit, save that it invariably stops far back from the frontier of the indecent."[67] His material was clean. More than that, however, it was thoroughly realistic, the work of a master storyteller who knew his subject well. Nonetheless, reviews also had the potential to undermine Bert's performance as they assessed his work in racial terms.

After Bert's *Follies* run, critic Sylvester Russell decided that Bert "will only be a hero by contending for his own show next season and by either contending for the best of everything or accepting nothing."[68] If the entertainer could succeed in the *Follies*, he could certainly do even better on his own terms, Russell thought. Declaring Bert "our most noted brave soldier, but timid actor," Russell demanded boldness and ambition in the vein of the comedian's "domiciled partner," finding Bert himself to be a terrible disappointment.[69]

Lester Walton, however, so often Bert's advocate, spoke admirably of him. In a column following Bert's move to the *Follies*, he reassured readers that the performer wore "the same sized hat as heretofore," certain to note that Bert still went to his favorite barber.[70] Walton thereby informed readers that Bert had not become self-important and that he continued to associate with others in Harlem. Although Bert performed with and solely for whites, Walton tacitly stated that he was still accessible to the black public as one of the race.

Despite Walton's comments, Russell's concerns could not easily be ignored. Russell saw Bert as sorely lacking the courage of George Walker. He saw in Bert cowardice, his willingness to await opportunities a sign of his lack of motivation, that he had "no back bone." In an interview with Ashton Stevens, Bert had expressed his hope to play "this

old rheumatic character of mine in a white production," but also admitted, "it will take time."[71] Content to wait on the audience's adjustment to
his presence onstage with whites, Bert stated that he had it put into the
contract that he would not appear onstage with white women. Keeping
in mind the fearless but ailing George, Russell was not only unimpressed but disgusted by Bert's remarks.

George's health worsened daily. By August, he would have a nervous
breakdown, transferring to a sanitarium in Islip, Long Island, as he
neared the end of his fight against syphilis.[72] Meanwhile, in Russell's
view, Bert seemed to be squandering his time when he should have
been "writing a Negro play in which to star."[73]

Perhaps in response to African American critics' skepticism, Bert
would eventually reassure them of his satisfactory experience in the
Follies cast, proving the appropriateness of his decision:

> I am certainly treated with the greatest respect by all the members of the
> *Follies of 1910*. More so than with my own people. I enjoy the work, and
> there is never a hitch. When I call for a rehearsal of the orchestra for a
> new song, the orchestra is right there on the spot and the management
> pays for it. I have one of the swellest dressing rooms on the first floor and
> it's a peach. I travel in a Pulman [*sic*] stateroom and the men of the com-
> pany and press representatives seek my company. I am greatly pleased
> with the *Follies of 1910*.[74]

With such words, Bert attempted to diffuse concern about the controversy around his joining the show. He tried to dispel the idea that he
might have been uncomfortable in the company and, more importantly,
that colleagues discriminated against him. At the same time, he indicated that he had not lowered his standards or expectations by agreeing
to join the *Follies*. Furthermore, he averred that the *Follies* cast treated
him with greater respect than had his "own people," a sign of his turn
away from all-black productions.

Although some members of the *Follies* had sought to exclude Bert
from the company, he would indeed receive a significant welcome. As a
member of the cast, he got an invitation to participate in an Actors' Field
Day, a benefit to support the Actors' Fund. He joined such Broadway
lights as George Cohan, who opened up the fairgrounds in a parade;
Marie Dressler, a famous vaudevillian who in 1914 would team up with
Charlie Chaplin in *Tillie's Punctured Romance*; and Annie Oakley of

vaudeville fame. The day included races, baseball, and games. Bert made his contribution with Billy Reeves, "boxing for the championship."[75] His move to the *Follies* had not been easy, but he found some comforts and made his mark.

G s Bert joined Ziegfeld's cast, he recorded four numbers from the revue for Columbia. Promoting the star with a full-page ad in its November supplement, the label moved entirely away from racial references, proclaiming Bert a "World-Famous Comedian."[76] Standing alone as a featured performer held exclusively by Columbia, Bert would become a major asset of the record label. The press release trumpeted the label's achievement:

> Through an arrangement recently concluded we have acquired the sole right to record and reproduce the absolutely unique and inimitable art of Bert Williams, one of the greatest comedians the stage has ever known, and the highest priced artist in vaudeville in America at this writing.[77]

Extolling Bert's skill as comedian and artist, the label focused on his singular contribution to the world of entertainment. Despite the end of his partnership with Walker, Bert clearly reigned supreme as a top comedian who "has since been a headliner [in vaudeville] whenever booked."[78] Describing Bert's gifts, the release declared that his "humor is of that genuine sort that relies on no clap-trap, horseplay or stage-setting for its effect. It goes straight to the mark by a direct appeal to the intelligence through the sense of humor and perception of the grotesque and the ridiculous."[79] Bert produced nothing less than "masterpieces" in Columbia's studio, reflecting "with the last degree of faithfulness every trick of expression and vocal inflection that goes to form the sum total of the comedian's entertaining strength."[80] These recordings proved to the public that Bert continually honed his talents. He developed his style further as he emphasized storytelling over singing. A gifted artist, Bert often required only one or two takes for a successful recording.[81]

The most distinctive song Bert recorded was "Play That Barber Shop Chord," which had actually been one of his vaudeville selections before his *Follies* performance. Although all four recorded pieces would be strong sellers, "Play That Barber Shop Chord" would remain in the

Columbia catalog for eighteen years until 1928.[82] At the time of its release, barbershop harmony, now defined as "four-part harmony," was associated with "extemporized noisy tune-making" and the bastardization of legitimate musical forms.[83] "Play That Barber Shop Chord" popularized it in a song that "ameliorat[ed] the term [barbershop harmony] . . . disseminating it into the American mainstream."[84]

Bert belted out a quick-paced ragtime piece. With exuberance that was characteristic of the upbeat, syncopated music, he described a "kinky-headed lady they call Chocolate Sadie" who would go to see "a swell colored fella" named Bill Jefferson Lord play piano in a rathskeller.[85] Throughout the performance, Bert cried out as Sadie, requesting that Mr. Lord "play that barbershop chord." The narrator served only to set the stage for the character, depicting her adoration:

> *She heaved a sigh,*
> *every time she could ketch his eye, she'd cry,*
> *"Mr. Jefferson Lord, aw, play de barbershop chord!*
> *It's got de soothin' harmony,*
> *It makes an awful, awful, awful hit wit me!*
>
> *Play dat strain, aw, please, play it again!*
> *'Cause Mister when you start, the minor part,*
> *I feel your fingers slippin' and agrippin' round my heart!*
> *Oh Mr. Lord! Dat's it!*
> *Dat's the barbershop chord!"*

In the repeated exultations of Chocolate Sadie to her "Lord," Bert created an ironic location of black religiosity. The rathskeller became the underground chapel for Sadie's conversion, as Lord's ministrations seized her heart. Sadie's name, indicative perhaps of her Southern identity, suggested this song's observation of Northern urban black society's move to secularism or—worse—a sacred profanity. Ragtime, whose music had originally been associated with vice—bordellos and smoky taverns—thus became transformed. It was a new religion whose minor key and catchy rhythms drew audiences into it, whose musicians became Lord of all and sent the eager audiences into a type of religious ecstasy. As if to emphasize that point, Bert closed the song with an exclamation as Sadie: "Oh, goodness me!"

oward the end of the year, Lester Walton interviewed Bert about participating in the *Follies*. As before, Bert expressed his Booker T. Washingtonian conservatism that centered on independent action, perhaps to turn attention away from the idea that he was an activist for blacks. He toed the line between an acknowledged relationship to other blacks and an individualistic view of his work: "When I became a member of the *Follies of 1910* I well knew that my success would be due to the tact I displayed. I realized that it was up to me to be a success or failure."[86] Bert took responsibility for whether or not he was successful, well received, or rejected. In spite of the known intransigence of certain cast members, he refrained from shifting responsibility to them. He deflected attention away from the issue of discrimination and focused on his own ability to affect the outcome.

As he spoke, Bert explicitly linked his view to that of Washington, remarking, "Booker T. Washington is the acknowledged leader of our people, but the ten millions of colored people in the United States must not sit idly by and expect the eminent educator to do it all."[87] Bert believed that each person had to take responsibility—as he had done— and contribute to the struggle for change. Espousing Washington's philosophy regarding blacks' rights, Bert posited that the individual efforts of millions of people would bring the greatest degree of change for the race as a whole.

Bert then declared, "I believe that the Negro is bound to get on top eventually, but it will be by pursuing a conservative policy. . . . All races who have been down have managed to get on top only after much perseverance. I am positive we will overcome the obstacles in our pathway of progress, but it will be step by step and not in bounds."[88] A telling statement, in light of his radical crossing of the color line in the *Follies*.

In spite of the resistance he faced personally, Bert maintained hopefulness regarding future change. "There are many rights being denied us to which we are justly entitled," he admitted. "But we must remember that the only way to get them is to strive inch by inch to realize our ambitions."[89] Though not an overwhelmingly optimistic statement, it contained his belief that ambitions could be achieved against all odds, even though white society refused blacks' rights. Bert's success, his profound hope for change, and his role as a leader perhaps obligated him to speak with optimism on behalf of those who experienced bigotry on all fronts.

Struck by Bert's composure, Walton elaborated on the entertainer's admirable achievement. He brought Bert into the fold of the black community by focusing on the "diplomacy and tact" required in order for Bert to pursue a successful career in the *Follies*. Bert's composure in handling his position had as much significance as his work itself, Walton claimed. At the same time, for breaking into the *Follies*, Walton called Bert a "Daniel Boone." That accomplishment was work "in the interest of the colored performer."[90] Thus, Walton linked Bert's move to his apparent activism.

On Bert as diplomat, Walton introduced the matter of tact. Presenting him as an illustration to others, Walton insisted on Bert's service to the community even though he did not assume a role of leadership. As an example, he used Bert's conduct during the very tense situation resulting from his acceptance of Ziegfeld's offer. He stated that Bert's handling of the animosity of whites, who were angry and jealous about the development, had resulted in alleviating tensions. The mere thought of placing a black man in the midst of "a big Broadway production costing over $50,000, in which were over sixty female white performers," had been enough for some to threaten to boycott. Keeping this in mind, Bert had determined that he would insert a clause in his contract stating that "at no time would he be on the stage with any of the female members of the company."[91]

Recognizing the sensitivity of the issue, Bert had used diplomatic methods preemptively, quelling others' qualms about his participation in the show. As if to testify to Bert's success, Walton verified that Florenz Ziegfeld and Manager Rosenbaum had both pronounced the comedian among the most popular members of the show. Worries about the audience's reception of the actor had been unfounded. Walton continually underscored Bert's sensible handling of a potentially explosive issue. Bert had demonstrated his thorough awareness of the politics of respectability in this delicate situation. With a final statement on the issue, Walton pronounced, perhaps wryly, "While his efforts at diplomacy would not warrant his appointment as Ambassador to the Court of St. James, yet it would not surprise me greatly if he qualified as Minister to Liberia."[92] Furthering his notion that Bert's work reflected well on the black public, Walton urged his readers to view Bert's achievement as crucial to the race's efforts toward equality.

At the same time, however, Walton would continue to have some concerns about Ziegfeld's *Follies*. Chiding Ziegfeld for failing to consider the black audience, he would state:

> Mr. Ziegfeld should now be more favorably impressed with the colored clientele and when he produces *Follies of 1911*, in which Bert Williams will be one of the leading attractions, he should show a more magnanimous and charitable disposition toward the colored residents by giving them an opportunity to see the production so that they can maintain their erstwhile enviable position among the residents of other cities.[93]

The tensions around Bert's choice would therefore continue, as Walton and other blacks waited to see how Ziegfeld—and Bert—would ensure that the black community be properly served.

Matters seemed depressingly inauspicious for those whose hopes rested on Bert alone. At best, Ziegfeld's managers had been selective about serving blacks. They acknowledged their patronage only when the *Follies of 1910* cast performed at the Grand Opera House in New York during "what is considered the worst week in show business—the week before Christmas."[94] Blacks not only had turned out for the performance but had in fact ensured the show's success. Yet managers still had not been compelled to reconsider their generally exclusive policies.

Despite the challenges of this phase of Bert's career, his life seemed filled with wondrous opportunities. Then the inevitable happened. On 6 January 1911, at only thirty-eight years old, George William Walker died. He had spent his last moments in the presence of his beloved mother, Alice, for whom Aida had sent weeks before, so that she might be by her son's side until the last. At the time of George's death, Aida herself had been in Cincinnati, touring with the Smart Set Company.[95] When the news of George's passing went out, Aida, Bert, and Jesse Shipp, among others, were the first to receive the telegrams.

The news devastated Bert. He knew that the loss meant the end of a life as well as the certain end of an era for both himself and black theater. "From the day we became partners we were never separated, never had any difficulty of opinion, and no harsh or unkind words ever [were] passed between us," he recalled. "When George became ill, I knew I could never even thing [*sic*] of securing anyone to take his place."[97]

During their sixteen years together, the two had been more than a mere comedy duo. Williams and Walker had shown that from humble beginnings in the rough world of the medicine show, a black performer could become a leading light. With George, the enterprising businessman, at the helm, they had proven that blacks could excel on Broadway. George, the man who seemed never to fear anyone or anything, had demonstrated that, with defiance and persistence, one could hit unprecedented heights.

George's funeral was held in New York on 9 January, attended by Bert and Lottie, Aida and Alice, dozens of admirers who crowded the chapel, and hundreds of others who could not gain entry. Aside from the throngs who sought to pay their respects as George's body lay in state, friends and colleagues offered condolences with wreaths and flowers, displaying how well-loved George had been. Bert's wreath read "My Dear Old Pal," and others, sent from the Frogs, the Colored Vaudeville Benevolent Association, the Clef Club, and the Smart Set Company, indicated George's centrality in the black theatrical community.

George was not only loved by those in the arts, however. Lester Walton declared that "the business man, the minister, the doctor and the lawyer [all] vied with each other in paying homage to one who, by his deeds for good, had challenged their admiration and won their respect."[98]After the funeral services, George's mother traveled with the body through Chicago to Lawrence, Kansas, where hundreds of other friends and fans met them at the train station.

Critics and fans shared their sentiments about George's uniqueness and at times went further to detail what made him even more praiseworthy than Bert. In the plainspoken Sylvester Russell's words, George was "bold and fearless enough to stand up for what the services of Williams and Walker were worth. He rarely ever received encouragement, not even from his partner, who wilted at Walker's exhorbtant [sic] demands as the price for their services."[99]

Another stated explicitly the distinction between the two performers: "Williams and Walker are names quite familiar to the public. Williams is with us. His art is an asset to his profession. Walker's art is an asset to his race and his profession."[101] With reference to Walker's exceptional work on and off the stage, writers articulated the loss in words that evidenced their belief that the community would never be the same.

Lester Walton elevated his description of Walker, yet refrained from judging Bert: "[T]he stages loses [sic] . . . a black Napoleon, who was no dreamer; one who dealt in the realities of life; who was a race man in all that the phrase implies; who was a gentle, yet a resolute leader, whose influence has done more to dignify the colored performer and the profession he represents than all others." The memorials written for George, who was fast becoming immortalized after his death, made the question more pressing than ever: How would Bert memorialize his legacy?

*I*n an incident that boded ill, shortly after George's death, during a performance in Washington, D.C., the black public again saw its patronage all but disregarded. Bert, silent, seemed unconcerned about their needs. Critic R. W. Thompson of the *Indianapolis Freeman* described blacks who were "compelled to climb to the roof of the National Theater, and then . . . obliged to content themselves with seats in the fathermost [*sic*] corners, where it was difficult to see or hear anything that was being done on the sides of the stage. The first five rows and all of the center section were sold only to white patrons."[102]

Pressure mounted on Bert to act as George might have done. Ominously, Thompson reported that many of those "self-respecting colored people" had declared that they would never return to endure such conditions in the theater again. As black fans struggled for access to Bert's performances, they hoped that he himself would take action on their behalf. Nothing changed, however. And while they wondered about the depth of Bert's commitment to the black community, Bert continued to receive affirmation of his popularity with the larger—mainly white—audience.

Even as black audiences had at best limited access to Bert in the *Follies of 1910*, white audiences across the country gained greater access to him. While the company was on the road with its western tour, Bert had planned to leave from San Francisco to begin preparations for the next year's production. No sooner did theater managers discover his intention to depart before the *Follies'* performance, however, than they protested. They compelled Ziegfeld to request that the comedian stay and perform in town. This occurred in Salt Lake City, Denver, and other cities, ultimately requiring that the entertainer carry out the entire western tour.[103] Evidently, certain audiences' demands would not be ignored.

The next year's production, crowned *Ziegfeld Follies of 1911*, remained high class. Bert enjoyed an augmented role in the *Follies* that year, introducing the various segments of a three-act show throughout the evening. He shuffled onto center stage and began the production with the words, "What is the plot of the *Follies*? Nobody knows. What is the moral pointed out by the *Follies*? Don't ax me—nobody knows."[104] These lines had particular significance. Later in the evening, he would return as "Nobody" in a burlesque. Of course, the reference also reminded the audience of Bert's most famous song.

Once again, Bert made a considerable impact in the show. That year, he had an undeniably central role. A writer for the *New York Evening Mail* went so far as to attest, "In the advertising Mr. Williams' name ends the list, when it should lead all the rest, for it is a Williams show."[105] His significant contributions to the show included a burlesque and a sketch with comedian Leon Errol.

In the burlesque *Everywife*, he portrayed "Nobody," a chorus figure in the satire of a Greek morality play. The *Follies'* version chronicled the vicissitudes of married life, entailing Everyhusband's encountering "Rhyme, Drink, Gamble, and the varied attentions of the Great White Way, and . . . meeting with Reason" after Happiness leaves the home.[106] Throughout the piece, the wisdom of Nobody held together the short play, leading the audiences as they observed the couple's travails. Such a role permitted Bert to "display his pleasant gifts as an actor and entertainer."[107] Evidently, the comedian had an opportunity to stretch himself a bit more, developing a role in which he would provide more than a mere laugh. His interludes between scenes and "explanatory remarks" provided "the only bright spots in this portion of the performance," according to one critic.[108] The comedian stood before the curtain—it served as the background. With "no accessory of any sort," he delivered his brief monologues so well that "the interest was maintained and the requisite spirit of fun imbued."[109]

Critics enthused most about Bert's sketch with Leon Errol, who was a new addition to the *Follies*. The *New York Herald* reviewer stated that Bert, with Errol, "brought down the house" in this skit.[110] A critic for the *Evening Post* wrote that Bert had provoked "the heartiest laughter" as a "leader in the fun."[111] Most importantly, in Bert's work with Errol, he found a capable foil. It was a pairing that would demonstrate how well Bert could move on in his onstage efforts without George.

In "Upper and Lower Level," Bert was a red cap charged with the duty to help British tourist Errol find his train to New Rochelle during the chaotic construction of the new Grand Central Station in New York City.[112] A *New York Morning Telegraph* journalist commented that "[t]his travesty on conditions at the Grand Central station was a gorgeously humorous conceit, and Williams made it excruciatingly funny."[113]

Ziegfeld Follies, *1911. Bert Williams as a Porter, Leon Errol as a Tourist in Skit about the Chaos at the New Grand Central Station.* COURTESY OF THE MUSEUM OF THE CITY OF NEW YORK

The set required the construction of girders high above the stage, as the two characters had to make their way to the upper level of an imaginary Grand Central Station. Throughout the scene, Errol played a loquacious tourist, making the most of his frenetic energy—his strength was physical comedy. This was the perfect foil to Bert's methodical, taciturn plodding as the porter. Like the energy of George's smooth-talking dandy, Errol's talkative tourist made for the perfect balance.

Ashton Stevens described the scene: "Like the guide that precedes the Alp climber, Mr. Williams has an English tourist on the other extreme of the rope around his waist."[114] The tourist frequently stopped to chat, moving nervously at the risk of falling from the girder. Finally he did, at a point where a nearby sign read "160 Foot Drop." Stevens explained that Williams "casually pulls him [Errol] up, and as casually drops him again." He thus spared him from "what Mr. Williams described as the 'chasm.'"[115]

The tension in the sketch eased and then built up again in moments between the falls of Errol's jumpy tourist. The instant Bert secured him again, he asked, "Porter, have you a match?" In response to the request, Bert, as porter, immediately began to search his pockets, letting go of the rope. He thereby initiated a second drop, from which he caught and saved the tourist again. After that fall, Errol followed up his previous comment: "Never mind the match, Porter, I broke my pipe."[116]

Settled on the girder, Errol and Bert then engaged in a long exchange for about fifteen minutes. The exchange centered on Bert, with Errol asking him questions about his life.[117] A segment included the following:

ERROL: You have a wife and family, I suppose?

WILLIAMS: Oh yes sir; I's married an I'se got three chil'un.

ERROL: Is that so. Ah, that's very commendable.

WILLIAMS: Yes sir, so it is.

ERROL: What are the names of your children?

WILLIAMS: Well I names 'em out de Bible. Dar's Hannah and den dar's Samuel and de las' I name "Iwilla."

ERROL: Iwilla? I don't remember that name in the Bible.

WILLIAMS: Sure 'tis. Don't you 'member where it say, "IWILLA RISE"?[118]

The joke centered on Bert in this segment, mocking his character's use of the Bible—erroneously—to determine the names of his children. As this practice of biblical lots was thought to be historically common among African Americans, such a joke was race-specific.

An important aspect of their exchange was that the role of comedian and straightman passed back and forth between Bert and Errol. When the joke focused on Bert, Errol set him up for his joke and Bert delivered the punch line. Although it may have appeared that Bert was simply the "butt" of the joke, it was actually in these set-ups that he, as performer, took focus from his partner onstage. In other words, he became the lead while Errol played the supporting role. He drove home the comical lines with his subtlety and control.

At other points throughout the scene, however, Errol's fidgety, maladroit character became the center of attention. His restless body drew focus, and the difference between his activity and Bert's relative inactivity further increased the comical contrast between the tourist and porter. Unlike Bert's scenes with George, in which George's long monologues created further opportunities for Bert's drawn-out punch lines, Errol got laughs with his own antics.

As the scene continued, the two climbed higher in search of the tourist's train. They then rested again, at which point Bert withdrew his lunch. He informed Errol that his wife unfailingly provided him a delicious meal, and stated that it would be ham and biscuits that day. The nervous Errol turned to look, knocking the porter's lunch box right off the girder. Bert's reaction? A slow nod, a subtle tapping of fingers on his knee, and a serious, lingering look at Errol.[119]

Throughout the scene, tension mounted and diffused, never failing to build again, even after the prior long exchange between the characters. After the porter's lunch fell from the girder, the tourist promised a good tip—a mere five cents, which the porter accepted with a look of disgust. Soon after, Errol fell again, this time at the "288 Foot Drop." As Errol fell, the rope continued to uncoil as though he had indeed fallen into the chasm, while Bert remained expressionless. Guffaws of laughter exploded from the near-hysterical audience. Even when the rope pulled tight, evidencing that Errol had fallen several stories, Bert never lost his poker face.[120]

The porter then took action, griping about the "Five cents!" and untying the rope that connected him to the tourist. No sooner did the rope drop down than he took up the tourist's suitcase, flinging that into the chasm as well. A sound effect indicating an explosion went off as Bert stared out into the distance and cried, "There he goes, way up!" Finishing his commentary, he said, "Ah, here he goes, now he's near the Metropolitan Tower. Ef he kin only grab that little gold ball on the top—um, he muffed it!"[121] The scene with Errol's third fall satisfied comedy's "rule of three's": once a joke or gag is used more than once, it has to be used three times for full comic effect. Bert's once-quiet, reserved porter had the last word and the last joke, entirely at Errol's expense.

Bert held center stage. This scene was one in which "[t]he white man literally becomes the black man's burden," and Bert's reversal supports that point.[122] Controlling Errol's movement and his fate, Bert took him in hand and led the unwitting tourist through the maze of Grand Central Station. He overturned the usual onstage relationship between black and white, revising it for the skit. Bert also ensured that he played to his strengths, with pacing and timing that worked best for him.

The full skit had not been part of the original show script. Rather, Bert had created it himself. He had had a mere skeleton of an idea from which he and Errol developed the sketch: the *Follies* had written "Five cents!" as the comedian's only line.[123] It had taken his and Errol's improvisation, rehearsing in a spare dressing room, in order to devise characters and subsequently begin to create dialogue. Developing a short line into an entire scene, Bert demonstrated his skill in crafting a comical story while also creating an alternative role to play onstage. Where possible, he took advantage of the chance to build up a character in a scene that did not rely on the submissive role that "black porter" might have connoted for white writers and audiences. Years later, Errol would describe Bert as "always most resourceful," playing a dominant role in the development of their scenes.[124]

$\mathcal{A}$s in his first year, some critics appreciated Bert's work while others grappled with his identity and achievement. After witnessing the Grand Central sketch, a Boston journalist claimed that the entertainer "proved that he is a really skilful comedian who can do better work than is usually given him in musical plays."[125] Ashton Stevens vouchsafed Bert's considerable talent as actor, quoting John Barrymore, another member of Broadway's leading acting family: "I'd be proud to play in a company supporting Bert Williams." Furthermore, Stevens honored the actor, claiming, "And . . . I'd be proud to write the play if I had enough wit."[126]

Several critics' statements revealed their efforts to reconcile their image of Bert while acknowledging his talents. A Boston critic praised Bert as having "lost none of his powers as a humanly comical darky."[127] For audience members, this character's inherent humanity mollified his blackness, embodied through makeup, dialect, and gesture. As spectators noted all the markings of blackness, holding them in the foreground, they also seemed to register what made the character human, i.e., civilized, familiar, and "like one of us."

Compelled to recognize Bert's talent, yet often drawing attention to race, some writers struggled with the latter's relevance. As the *New York Morning Telegraph* sang Bert's praises, its writer commended him as he also telegraphed race: "Whether serious, grotesque or just simply funny, this dark-skinned man demonstrated again that he is one of the most finished actors on the American stage."[128] Was Bert's success in spite of or because of race? In a similar way, an *Evening Post* writer declared, "It is very doubtful if there is a more amusing actor of the kind, black or white, on the stage to-day."[129] Extolling Bert, both of these writers spoke of him as uniquely talented: a standout. All the while they also read his race, if only then to disavow its relevance. He surpassed his race, they seemed to say, illustrating his worthiness as not solely a comedian, but an actor; not merely any actor, but one of the best.

A final quotation most expressively demonstrated writers' struggle to assess Bert. After a positive review, a critic wrote that Bert received from the audience "a bigger hand than any of the others, in spite of race, color or previous condition of servitude."[130] Citing the Thirteenth Amendment, the writer revealed an apparent anxiety regarding either Bert's shocking success among an all-white cast, his domination of the show, or his popularity with the audience. Although the writer may have written facetiously, the reference to the Thirteenth Amendment was no simple joke. The parallel between Bert's historic achievement of integrating the *Follies* and the historical mandate freeing the slaves was unavoidable.

The critic continued: "[W]hen he has finished his evening's work he makes the need of a White Hope on the Jardin de Paris stage as imperative as Jack Johnson did in the squared ring."[131] Boxer Jack Johnson's winning career had not only inspired the need for White Hope Jim Jeffries but had also inspired in some whites the need for retaliatory race riots. Despite the lightness of tone, the fight and riot references stood out, having occurred just the year before. As the members of both Ziegfeld's *Follies* and Bert's audiences adjusted to his presence on the stage, they would continue to negotiate this space between recognizing Bert Williams as an artist and as a black man.

*W*hile Bert's white critics evidenced anxiety with regard to reconciling his artistry with his blackness, his black critics faced the challenge of appreciating his individual work as being representative of the black public despite its occurrence outside of that community. That year, Lester Walton appeared convinced that Bert was making a definitive move away from black shows:

> Despite the fact that Mr. Williams is no longer associated with colored productions, and for that matter it is not likely that he will be again soon, the members of his race are evincing no little interest in his movements, fully appreciating that even if he is not at the head of a colored show and providing work for many colored Thespians that his success as a performer, nevertheless, affects the race to which he belongs, either directly or indirectly.[132]

Walton's words exposed his thinly veiled criticism of Bert for having moved away from his black audience and colleagues.

At a time when there was still work—although not generally on Broadway—for black performers, Bert's absence was palpable. The Smart Set Company's *His Honor the Barber,* in which Aida appeared, continued to perform, even enjoying a short run on Broadway at the Majestic Theatre. Resourceful black actors, such as "Jolly" John Larkins, had determined to establish their own companies in order to have artistic control over their work.[133] Jesse Shipp, after a brief stint working with Negro baseball team the Brooklyn Royal Giants, had gone to the Pekin Theater with a new script.[134] Although work in black theater still seemed possible, Bert had turned away.

Such tension as Walton expressed belied the admiration that characterized his descriptions of the entertainer the previous year. It also revealed the complicated relationship that Bert's black audience had to him. Even though it remained to be seen if Bert would retain a commitment to the black public, Walton believed that blacks would remain interested in the performer's activities. Walton's words, however, also suggested the possibility that Bert would fail his black audience as his fame outside of their domain increased. Further complicating Walton's relation to Bert was that, though a dramatic critic, Walton had to write about the show based on hearsay. He devoted no space in the column to complain about the continuing exclusion of blacks from the Jardin de Paris, but the policy had not changed. This is obvious from the language in which Walton wrote about the *Follies,* remarking that Ziegfeld's show "*is said* to eclipse all previous efforts," and that it "is said" to have been larger than his other shows.[135] As though keeping opinions on more problematic issues in check, however, Walton then highlighted the encouraging decision that the lionhearted Ziegfeld made in supporting Bert:

> [I]t must not be forgotten that someone gave him the chance to do the shining, and it is here where Florence [*sic*] Ziegfeld, Jr., comes in for congratulations, compliments and the like. It was Mr. Ziegfeld, who a year ago decided to take Mr. Williams into the *Follies of 1910,* despite the protests of a bunch of weak-kneed friends and prejudiced white performers, who excitedly informed the producer that to put a colored comedian in a show with a large galaxy of white performers would never do; that such a step would create consternation and provoke a race controversy.[136]

Elsewhere, Walton continued to utilize Bert as a representative figure, expressing his discouragement about the small number of black successes on Broadway. Bert had been one of the few who had excelled, and Walton appreciated the actor's accomplishments, as opportunity for blacks often had a trickle-down effect. If Bert crossed the color line, this would be good news for others. As before, however, Walton qualified his statement: "Although Mr. Williams is traveling with a large white production and may not be so closely associated with members of his race as when he was at the head of a colored show, the fact remains that he is a colored man nevertheless and is regarded as such, thereby reflecting great credit on the race of which he is a member."[137] Seemingly obliged to honor Bert's achievements, perhaps only because he was a member of the race, Walton insisted that others should respect him as well. Walton also saw the need to acknowledge that a reader might have rejected Bert because of his retirement from black theater. Even as Bert's success had value, it came with a cost, as it created distance between him and the black public.

Anticipating the resistance of an audience that might have questioned Bert's move away from the black community, Walton gave them reason to reconsider the artist. He emphasized that "[n]o colored performer has ever reached the position now occupied by Bert Williams." He detailed the greater work Bert had done independently: "[Williams] is now playing in theatres in which it was never possible for Williams and Walker to secure booking."[138] Walton anticipated the reaction to Bert's move from black theater, which evidenced the journalist's own sensitivity to Bert's position as much as the possibile sensitivity of Walton's readership.

Following along the lines of a Booker T. Washington and, indeed, Bert himself, Walton opted to read the actor's individual success as a type of racial activism. He linked Bert's work to the future of all blacks: "[I]f it is true that races are nowadays elevated by the work and success of individuals and not so much by the efforts of the masses, then the heights reached by Bert A. Williams in the theatrical world is not alone his success but that of the Negro."[139] In case he had not adequately persuaded his audience, Walton conceded: "That he is not the star of a colored organization is deeply deplored by hundreds of citizens of color, but it must not be overlooked that conditions at this time warrant his actions in becoming connected with a white production."[140]

Through this commentary, blacks continued to observe Bert during his second year in the *Follies*. They reconciled the remoteness of his performative successes with the possibility of those successes' beneficial effect for the black community. As Bert pressed on, he would repeatedly face pointed criticisms and raised expectations while he pursued the pinnacle of solo performance.

9

Opportunity
Knocks

Before the *Ziegfeld Follies of 1911* finished its tour, Bert confirmed his long-term commitment to the revue, signing a three-year contract. He thus became the highest-salaried member of the *Follies*, a sum of $62,400 a year with an agreement that he would have a principal part in the shows.[1] Not only had he crossed the color line by becoming part of the lavish all-white Broadway production, but he had also ensured his steady work as a leading member of the cast. He had shown that blacks who break through to "The Great White Way" can triumph and stay. The black press heralded his accomplishment to readers, echoing Bert's excitement. Although he had not yet realized his deepest ambition, his achievement seemed to be a sign of good things to come.

Then, on 1 April 1912, Bert lost his champion. His father, Frederick, died of chronic endocarditis, at age sixty-one. An infection of the heart's inner lining, endocarditis was a complication resulting from vascular disease, damaging his father's already weak heart.[2] Although Frederick had been hospitalized for several weeks, his doctors and Bert alike had been powerless to help him. Perhaps in honor of his father, Bert pressed on with his ambitions, further moving toward realizing his dream of a dramatic role.

The theatrical world seemed to respond to Bert's wishes when the "bishop of Broadway," David Belasco, sought him in the months following the death of Bert's father.[3] Called the "bishop" because of his austere manner and cleric-like dress, complete with black suit and white collar, Belasco had begun his career as an actor in California. He had moved to New York in 1880, working there as a theater manager. A decade later, he started leasing his own theater, thereby beginning his career as an independent producer.[4]

Belasco's innovations with staging and set design created a new standard for theatrical productions, and his gift for turning little-known talent into stars became legendary. It was he who had transformed actress Mrs. Leslie Carter into "the American Sarah Bernhardt."[5] Even more important to Bert, it was Belasco who had groomed vaudevillian actor David Warfield for the dramatic stage. Belasco was unique, "the first American producer whose name, regardless of star actor or play, attracted patrons to the theatre."[6] By calling Bert to his office, he had declared him "ready."

Bert, nervous and excited, had hoped for this moment. Over the years, he'd wished that the countless comparisons made of him to other actors would invite just such a chance. One critic had favorably compared Bert to Warfield, a former dialect comedian, declaring them both great artists.[7] Another stated that Bert rang "a note of pathos" as true as did Joseph Jefferson, of the prominent American theater family, who brought Washington Irving's *Rip Van Winkle* to life in his most famous role.[8] Although Bert had never played a dramatic part, in his shows he had always savored dramatic moments, displaying his exceptional skill through pantomime and the expressive delivery of his lines.

As Bert approached Belasco, however, he feared wasting the producer's time. He spoke of his journey to Belasco's office: "You know—me visiting Belasco. All dressed up. So warm now, I had to tear the suit to get back to earth. As I tore it I stood on the pavement and said to myself, out loud—'that's the ape part—tearing its clothes.'"[9] Fearing himself unworthy of meeting the esteemed dramatist, sensitive as to how he would appear—an inelegant ape approaching a great man— Bert disparaged himself. He mimicked the ape that he believed white audiences saw in him.

Although Belasco did not name a specific play in which he would feature Bert, during the meeting he expressed an interest in presenting the comedian. Overwhelmed, Bert agreed to his proposal without hesitation. He cherished the offer, saying that "Mr. Belasco's recognition of me made me happier than anything else in my whole life."[10] In interviews, he began to speak of his hopes to play a dramatic role: "Now that I have realized all my early ambitions to amuse and entertain, I'd like to do something a little different. I know I can make them laugh. Now I want to show that I can make them cry."[11] Bert wished for the opportunity to fully develop a dramatic character and dared to voice that wish.

"I want sometime to do a whole piece," he said, "to interpret one of my race as sympathetically as Mr. Warfield did the Jew in *The Auctioneer*."[12] Warfield had portrayed with compassion Simon Levi, a benevolent hardworking man struggling to provide for his wife and adopted daughter.[13] The play, a sentimental comedy, had allowed Warfield room for both comic and dramatic acting.

Bert went on to say, "[I]f I could interpret in the theatre that underlying tragedy of the race, I feel that we would be better known and better understood. Perhaps the time will come when that dream will come true. I will never cease to hope that it will."[14] Bert sought to realize the "mutual understanding between the races," of which he'd previously spoken. Stepping into the spotlight as a dramatic actor rather than a comedian, he hoped to promote a deeper image of the Negro and his own experience. Working with the producer who had made Warfield famous and respected, Bert hoped to have the same success. Those hopes had perhaps rightly rested on David Belasco, the man best equipped to guide his transformation. With Belasco as his new champion, Bert might have made this dream come true. Work in a dramatic role on the legitimate stage could take him beyond the darky character, showing a new face to the world.

According to Belasco, his rare consideration of Bert came after much deliberation. He attested, "I found myself wondering whether I might not discover and develop a negro player competent to portray great tragic characters before a modern audience."[15] Subsequently, he wrote, "Upon mature consideration, however, the chances for success of such a player came to seem very dubious."[16] Continuing to reflect on the possibility of a comedian whom he could groom for such a role, he then remembered having seen Bert. That memory heartened Belasco.

Soon after their meeting, however, contractual concerns began to plague Bert. After all, he had just signed the three-year contract with Abe Erlanger. Anxious, he sought advice from friends, who advised him to discuss the matter openly with both Belasco and Erlanger. It had seemed that Bert intended to pursue it, by first negotiating a way out of his contract.[17]

Bert, however, never actually carried it out. As his colleague concluded, "Williams'[s] aversion to controversy or argument prompted
him to plead timidity." Bert felt indebted to Erlanger, whom he believed
had "taken a chance" on him. Although a lawyer friend insisted that Erlanger's decision had been good business sense, not charity, Bert never
lost his sense of duty.[18] Perhaps following his previous aggravations in
court with Hurtig and Seamon, Melville Raymond, and F. Ray Comstock, Bert was reluctant to risk facing litigation. Despite Belasco's efforts to encourage him, Bert withdrew.[19] He never actually brought the
issue of his contract up with Erlanger. Nor did he broach the subject
with Belasco himself. In the end, he abandoned the endeavor and returned for the next season with the *Follies*.

As the company—Bert included—prepared for the *Ziegfeld Follies of
1912*, the theatrical community debated Ziegfeld's unknown reasons for
starting the season in the fall rather than the summer, as per usual. Various critics lay responsibility at Bert's feet, claiming the cast's unwill-
ingness to accommodate him. In defense of Bert's character, previous
manager Jack Shoemaker penned an editorial for the *Age*. Although
Shoemaker's aims were admirable, he provoked the ire of some blacks.
First, he made grand statements about Bert's generous charity to his
now-deceased partner. Second, he claimed that Bert's respectable behavior was "white."[20]

Within a week, Aida Overton Walker herself responded. Still a force
to be reckoned with as a prominent, forthright woman who had since
taken her own company into vaudeville with terrific success, Aida
vented her feelings.[21] She was outraged that Shoemaker had misrepre-
sented her late husband, "depicting him as a charity patient." In truth,
she argued, Bert had done his duty as partner and friend by paying
George his portion of their shows' profits and covering funeral expenses. Furthermore, she complained, "[I]f the only way left Mr. Shoemaker to show Mr. Williams['s] WHITENESS is by showing that he has
done his duty to his partner, I think it a poor way of impressing the
readers of The [*sic*] Age of Mr. Williams'[s] finer points as a man."[22]
Once again, Bert had been drawn into the center of a debate, one that
alienated him from a former colleague.

*O*n light of his recent losses, Bert's return to Ziegfeld's *Follies* must
have been triumphant. He had secured a lucrative contract, assur-

ing his place in the revue. He played various roles, but his most memorable was that of a cabman, in a skit with his new comic foil, Leon Errol.[23] Although *Variety* reviewer Sime Silverman remarked that the "comedians . . . are wasted" in the show, it appeared that Bert nonetheless thrilled audiences.[24] A *New York Tribune* writer judged his scene with Errol "[o]ne of the most successful."[25]

In his sketch with Errol, Bert played a cabby, and Errol was his drunk fare. "The curtains opened to reveal the oldest living horse in New York City, 'Nicodemus,' an equally battered cab, and a shabby driver, Bert Williams, stationed in front of a set painted to resemble a view of Seventh Avenue at Forty-seventh Street."[26] The scene began with Bert cleaning the cab while his horse, played by two actors, appeared to be ailing. After a few minutes, Leon Errol entered, dressed spiffily in coat and tails and obviously drunk.

The cabby saw him as easy money and planned to take advantage of him:

WILLIAMS: Where do you want to go, boss?
ERROL: I wanna go sebalabaloo.
WILLIAMS: Oh, you want to go to Seventh Avenue?
ERROL: Yesh, I wanna go sebalabaloo. Y'know wher' tis?
WILLIAMS: Oh yes, I know where 'tis. Git in an' I'll drive you dar. I know where 'tis all right. It's fur![27]

As the discussion continued, the joke was on the drunk, because the audience could plainly see that the actors already were on Seventh Avenue. Meanwhile, the horse threatened rebellion at the suggestion that he would travel far. Reassuring the horse, Bert turned to him, whispering, "Oats, Nicodemus, Oats." At that, the horse's attitude improved.[28]

Preparing to depart, Errol began his effort to board the cab. As in the previous year's skit, he utilized his skills of physical comedy, falling as he attempted to enter. It was only when he took the cab lamp in hand to light his way that he successfully boarded. Then, he cried goodnight to his driver. The scene closed with the decrepit horse slowly taking off.[29]

That year's skit shifted attention to Errol, whose physical comedy stole the scene. With less dialogue to ground it, the sketch took shape in the slurred sentences of Errol's drunk. Although the contrast between his and Bert's characters heightened the humor, Bert's quietly deceptive cabby took a backseat to Errol's stumbling. Although the setting established an ironic scene, the exchange lacked the topical bite of their Grand Central Station sketch of the year before. Nonetheless, critics noted Bert's "solemn demeanor and droll wit."[30]

(W)hile the skit may not have been the highlight of Bert's performance that year, he enjoyed other memorable moments on-stage. When Walton wrote about Bert's participation in the *Follies of 1912,* he thought the comedian's best piece was "Borrow from Me," a song that Bert would record the following year for Columbia. Walton believed the artist should have had better offerings and should have collaborated with his previous songwriters.[31] But many of them, like Will Marion Cook, who performed with James Reese Europe's Clef Club Orchestra, had moved on to other work in black productions and beyond.[32]

Being a revealing choice as the strongest of Bert's offerings, "Borrow from Me" was an unusual piece. In it, Bert called attention to himself in a first-person song.[33] Generally the "I" in Bert's selections was the "I" of the Jonah Man, but in "Borrow from Me," Bert retained his own voice. When referring to himself in the song, he incorporated his own viewpoint in a performance that might have seemed otherwise disconnected from his offstage self.

A short introduction with a quick tempo led into the song, which then slowed before he began:

> *I met a manager here on the street yest'rday,*
> *Says, "I'm got a great part for you to play,*
> *And I'm so sho' you can get up in it right away,*
> *I want you to just listen and see now how sweet this sounds;*
> *I'm going to take out in a day or so,*
> Uncle Tom's Cabin, *you know, it's a marvelous show,*
> *My cast is most complete you know,*
> *But I thought I'd like to have you to play the bleedhound."*

Unique in its reference to performance itself, the story seemed to address Bert through its mention of acting. It did so obliquely, however. The "I" who spoke did so in dialect, rather than in the comedian's actual offstage voice.

Regardless of his indirect approach, Bert made an unusual statement through his song. He came out from behind the mask of the blackface darky to speak about himself. Communicating directly to audiences, whom he assumed would care to know not about the classic stereotypical character but rather about Bert Williams himself, he dared to recount his frustrations: managers who undervalued him and roles that disgusted him. He allowed himself, the performer rather than the character, to take center stage.

Rather than protesting the suggestion of the manager, Bert as narrator/character responded with an overtly ironic statement. He remarked, "Well, bring me the Czar of Russia, just have him come on over here, and blacken up and play Uncle Tom's part," continuing with other outlandish proposals such as casting "the Statue of Liberty to play Miss Eva." Stating this nonchalantly with no dramatic tones, he refused the substandard offer. He used hyperbole to state his case and to express his profound dissatisfaction.

A musical interlude followed, after which Bert bemoaned the situation in which he frequently found himself because of his willingness to help others financially. He then offered a challenge to any future borrowers:

> *Every time they get a plan,*
> *Where they think that they might need a man,*
> *Who they'd like to have lend five or ten,*
> *Seems like they just test my generosity;*
>
> *I loaned my coin out day by day*
> *To different brothers who took oath, they say,*
> *But these few words I wanna say,*
> *for fear there's any present want to test me;*
>
> *If you'll bring me the stone that David slew Goliath with,*
> *And from the apple Adam ate, just bring me the co',*
> *Bring me a leaf, from the very same tree,*
> *That the dove carried that branch, back to Brother Noah;*
>
> *Bring me that lion that let Daniel live,*
> *And the whale that swallowed Jonah in the sea,*
> *If you can bring everything that I'm asking you to bring,*
> *Then, oh boy, you can just borrow from me!*

Bert's outcry gained even further meaning in light of his experiences while touring. Notable blacks, like Blind Boone (John William Boone), a musical prodigy who toured the country playing piano, often invited themselves backstage and Bert would hold an "unwilling reception" for them. Although strangers, they assumed that their common fame was reason to meet the performer.[34] Many such blacks displayed little respect for him, indicating their belief—in Bert's opinion—that he "ain't nothing. He's only a nigger, just like me."[35] Their expectations that he welcome their constant intrusions were enough to make him wish for his own individual space apart from the collective. The lyrics of "Borrow from Me" were Bert's self-aware comment on his treatment, a song directed to blacks, though sung in the presence of whites.

Ever since he began performing in Ziegfeld's *Follies*, Bert had made strides for the benefit of the "colored performer." Yet for two seasons, Bert had never been onstage with white women. In the *Ziegfeld Follies of 1912*, however, he "convinced the white performers that a colored person is human and can be cultured and refined just like the Caucasian." In that year's production, the comedian had lines with women and in two acts was on the stage with principals.[36]

Bert had once again broken through, crossing what had been defined as the color line. As always, his achievements merited close observation, as they were the yardstick by which advances of the entire race would be measured. With this knowledge, Walton affirmed that Ziegfeld was a true gentleman who believed that "art knows no color line."[37] Walton subsequently expressed hopes that Ziegfeld would eventually cast Bert in a big show with a full white cast.

Still, if Bert's appearance onstage among white women seemed to bode well for change, white critics' shifting expectations of Bert tempered such optimism. Even as critic Rennold Wolf interviewed Bert for an article in which he declared the performer "The Greatest Comedian on the American Stage," he fixated on the question of humility. Emphasizing the fact that Bert had not lost his modesty, he explained that Bert "never obtrudes himself upon the whites in the organization, and keeps within his dressing-room when not actually engaged in a scene."[38] Although Bert was part of a theatrical community, critics expected him to limit his involvement and interaction. Wolf praised Bert for his self-exclusion, noting his practice of declining invitations from his colleagues because of his sensitivity to the possible protests of strangers. This seemed to be most admirable to Wolf, thereby indicating the depths of Bert's humility. Although his success in the *Follies* repeatedly led him to new heights, Bert would always be expected to balance it with self-deprecation.

*A*fter several successful seasons, Bert bowed out of the *Ziegfeld Follies of 1913*. Rumor had it that he would play the part of "Friday" in Klaw and Erlanger's production of *Robinson Crusoe*.[39] Despite various reports about the upcoming show, it never materialized—at least not with Bert in it. In 1916, a nineteen-year-old Al Jolson would play the role of servant Friday in the Shuberts' Broadway production.

Still, Bert didn't return to the *Follies*. Instead, he teamed up for a performance with the Frogs, pursued a run in vaudeville, and returned to Columbia to record more songs. But there had been a significant change in his home life that was likely the cause of his break: the death of his sister-in-law Carrie, and the subsequent relocation of three little Chicago girls to his and Lottie's Harlem brownstone.

Bert and Lottie, without children of their own, welcomed Charlotte, Eunice, and Laura as their adopted daughters. The three girls had first met Bert when he and Lottie got engaged and he visited her mother's house in Chicago. From the first, they had admired his gentle nature and attentiveness. Now, as they joined the Williamses, the girls would come to relish Bert's tendency to spoil them.

He became "Uncle Eggs" to the girls, singing in a gentle baritone unlike his stage voice, plucking out tunes he composed on the parlor piano as they and Lottie listened. Although when he played late into the night, Lottie at times became, in her words, "a drowsy critic," the girls loved it. They also loved when he showered them with gifts.[40] They were well matched to the mild-mannered man. "Life with Uncle Eggs was wonderful all the time," Charlotte would recall. "It was like living with Santa Claus. He never raised his voice; he was never angry."[41] He would tell stories about his father and read "serious books" to them from his book collection. His library included a vast range of rare works in beautiful bindings, from Oscar Wilde's *Epigrams* to Thomas Paine's *Age of Reason*, as well as an unexpurgated edition of *Arabian Nights*.[42]

Their years together would strengthen their bond, even as Lottie, whom he called Mother, continued to care for her "boy." A frugal manager of household affairs, Lottie would take both Bert and the girls in hand, parsing the money he made out to him with the exception of his

Lottie Williams. COURTESY OF THE YALE COLLECTION OF AMERICAN
LITERATURE, BEINECKE RARE BOOK AND MANUSCRIPT LIBRARY

indulgences of books and cigarettes. At this point, Bert was a careless
smoker, too often "as likely to place . . . a smouldering ember on a rare
book as any other object."[43] At home with Lottie and the girls he found
solace, although he still liked to pass his spare time out in the saloons
or on the street talking with other men.[44]

Just as Bert surrounded himself with his family, he also reunited
with other blacks in performance. The year before, he had stepped
down from his presidency of the Frogs, with Jesse Shipp succeeding

him in the office. Now, he returned to support their onstage efforts.[45] He delighted his black public when he decided to team up with Aida and comedian Sherman H. Dudley, of the Smart Set Company, for a performance of the Frogs. A "stupendous undertaking, involving the expenditure of hundreds of dollars," the ballyhooed tour began in New York, sweeping through Philadelphia, Baltimore, Washington, D.C., and Richmond.[46]

A history-making event, the show featured an array of stars. As a prominent comedian, Bert was a top draw, but he was one among numerous entertainers, both veterans and neophytes, on the stage. He also joined former members of the Williams and Walker Company, such as Alex Rogers and a young man named Charles Gilpin. Additionally, he shared the stage with other leading black performers, like Sam Lucas, "dean of the colored theatrical profession," who had made history as a black man in a white company, playing the title role in *Uncle Tom's Cabin*.[47]

Without a doubt, Bert was the main attraction, in part because his move to the *Follies* had put him out of the reach of and thus further sought after by his black audiences. With the Frogs' tour, black audiences in Washington, D.C., and Richmond had the pleasure of seeing the most famous black comedian of their time. The Frogs ensured that there would be no "Jim-Crowing" of theaters, selecting venues large enough in size and open enough in policy that black audiences could view the performance in comfort.[48]

With her avid interest in the security of the profession and her husband's status as a founding member of the Frogs, Aida offered to participate. Although it was rumored that she and Bert would do a turn together for old time's sake, she chose to perform without him. In the time since George's death, she'd had little contact with Bert, and it seemed they had grown distant. Refusing to travel in the company's special Pullman rail cars, in which Bert and Sherman traveled, Aida arrived at the performance independently. There she sang two numbers and presented a dance with Jesse A. Shipp that the audience loved.[49]

The Frogs' Frolic took the surprising structure of a minstrel show, with Jesse Shipp as an interlocutor. All the performers had a hand in the proceedings, which audiences—black and white—thoroughly enjoyed. While the bill came in three parts, each with assorted acts in each section, it was a minstrel show in name only. Songs, dancing, and sketches, including that which Dudley and Bert presented together, having momentarily joined as a duo, steered away from stereotype. Their fans loved their uproarious skit, in which Bert dressed up in drag wearing a slit skirt so as to play a "dusky damsel," awaiting Dudley's visit as a gentleman caller.[50]

Throughout the tour, Bert affirmed his connection with his most loyal audience, showing up to honor them with his most unusual presence. He would not return to such a performance again. Nor would Bert again cross paths with Aida. The Frogs show would be the last time they performed together—and possibly the last time he even saw her.

After the Frogs' tour ended, Bert had a solid run in vaudeville during his busy year off from the *Follies*. Offered $2,000 per week for his appearances, he distinguished himself as the highest paid black performer in show business.[51] Although it is frankly arguable which year was his biggest, having from the very beginning always performed as a headliner (whether covertly or overtly), 1913 was a good one. After his hiatus, fans had welcomed him back.[52] During the run, the comedian took the stage during the notoriously "low ebb" that began in the theatrical world just before Christmas. Despite the dates of his engagement, managers had to turn several hundred patrons away for lack of seats.[53]

Bert performed at the Palace, located "at the northeast corner of Forty-seventh Street and Broadway."[54] Having opened on 24 March 1913, the theater was not yet even a year old at the time that he graced its stage in December. Although the Palace had opened with a loss—which encouraged competitor Willie Hammerstein to declare, "I give it six months"—it would later become known as "New York's premier vaudeville theatre."[55] Its fortunes turned for the better after "the Divine Sarah" (Sarah Bernhardt) reigned there in a booked-solid seventeen-day engagement during the spring of 1913.[56]

Intending to live up to its name, the Palace had plush box seats, ornate wall ornaments, glamorous marble in the inner lobby, and crystal chandeliers.[57] As its influence in New York City grew, mesmerized performers and audiences alike would proclaim it the "Taj Mahal of vaudeville," the "Mecca of every vaudevillian." Entertainers aspired to perform at it because it was, in the words of vaudevillian Sophie Tucker, "to American performers what a command performance is to a British actor. Something to live for. Something to boast about all the rest of your days."[58] A theater of moderate size, the Palace held 1,736 seats and was small enough to encourage intimacy between performer and audience, as compared to later theaters such as the 1919 cavernous Capitol downtown, a 5,300-seat house.[59]

Jack Benny recalled the Palace as "the theatre every actor was nervous about."[60] It could make or break a performer: a flop could mean being shut out of big-time vaudeville. If a booking went well, however, it would lead to extended engagements in other big-time venues. To state it succinctly: "It made millionaires and bums!"[61]

On Monday, 26 December 1913, the day of Bert's opening, the theatrical world showed up at the Palace for the first show: the matinee. "Everyone in show business that was in town seldom missed that performance—and that included everyone who could give an artist a job."[62] That afternoon, the sidewalk in front of the theater, nicknamed the Palace Beach or "the Beach," was populated by innumerable vaudevillians from big-time to small-time. They would congregate, sharing their experiences at the Palace and elsewhere, gossiping about other performers.[63]

By the time evening came, Bert and others on the nine-act bill, in keeping with the vaudevillian edict, were prepared to provide nonstop entertainment. The buzzword "variety" was crucial: "No two acts in a show should be alike."[64] George A. Gottlieb, the booking agent for the theater, believed in the exacting science of planning the bill.

That night, Herbert's Leaping Dogs opened the show. A customary opener, it was a "dumb act." Such acts typically opened so that the show could start on time while also permitting late arrivals to seek their seats without spoiling the performance for others. That night, the opener was "exceptional." It included a parade of the animals and a number of new tricks, including "high-diving" and "loop-the-looping."[65]

Second on the bill was a "typical vaudeville act," which was meant to "settle" the audience.[66] Prince Lai Mon Kim, Chinese Tenor, dressed in a "flowered coat with flappy sleeves," spoke with perfect enunciation and without dialect. A good follow-up to the opener, he sang in "a rather agreeable tenor."[67]

Charles Grapewin and Co., described as a "hardy perennial," was third.[68] In a position meant to build the show to a dramatic crescendo—most often climaxing in a hilarious headliner comedian—the company offered a comedic sketch. This piece had the audience guessing "what is to come next."[69]

Gertrude Vanderbilt and George Moore followed. They presented their piece to a house that was "in a pleasant frame of mind."[70] Gottlieb wrote that it should be a "corker," a "name." Thrilling the audience to great expectations of the performances to come, the fourth act offered "the first big punch of the show," still building excitement for the acts to follow.[71]

The "big act" of this half of the show was provided by Miss Odiva. A known performer, she was big not only for her fame but also for her act's size: she used numerous seals and performed "aquatic feats" in a tank. The audience welcomed her, as evidenced by a reviewer's note that she did the Travilla Brothers "the honor of 'lifting' their idea." She performed with an "irrepressible" and "garrulous" announcer who seemed to have been given to excessive commentary, but she herself nonetheless offered a strong performance.[72] Just as Gottlieb demanded, this act was a novelty. Above all, it provided the audience something to talk about during the intermission.

Because it "must not let down the carefully built-up tension of interest and yet it must not be stronger than the acts that are to follow," the first post-intermission act was challenging to schedule.[73] It had to start the second half of the bill off strong and stimulate the audience's excitement. That night, Florence Tempest sang, incorporating numerous costume changes, "from her boy's clothes to a ravishing ball gown of white, for her final song." This, combined with a dance with two young men "that might have been more spirited, but could not have been more graceful," seemed to satisfy the audience.[74]

In the seventh place, Morris Cronin and His Merry Men entertained with "illusions, acrobatic comedy and juggling." "[S]mall bits of surprise and the constant succession of unexpected flashes" held the audience's attention.[75] Being the full-stage act Gottlieb demanded, it fit the bill exactly. And as performance by an established name, it encouraged audience enthusiasm.[76]

Bert, as headliner of the show, came in the number eight slot, next to closing. As vaudeville increasingly focused on comedy performance, comedy acts most frequently occupied this headliner position. The audience waited all show long for this performer. Usually a single, it could just as likely feature a woman as a man.[77]

Beginning with curtains closed, a single spotlight trained on center stage, Bert crept his white-gloved hands through the opening of the curtains in hesitant movements. Little by little, taking his time, he revealed himself. His arm, his shoulder, then finally his entire body

Bert Williams as the Jonah Man. COURTESY OF THE YALE COLLECTION
OF AMERICAN LITERATURE, BEINECKE RARE BOOK AND MANUSCRIPT
LIBRARY

slowly and apprehensively pushed through the curtains "with awkward
reluctance" until he completely stepped through them. Wearing a wig of
kinky hair and blackface makeup, he was clad in his classic Jonah Man
outfit. He wore an old ill-fitting black coat that once had tails, which had
been cut. A white collar "obviously false and unconnected to a shirt—no
cuffs protruded at the wrists" peeked out at his neck. The white gloves
he wore entirely covered his hands. His jacket hung over too-short pants
that exposed his ankles, shrouded in black socks. Dusty shoes, too
large for him, but not clownish in appearance, encased his long feet.[78]

With this beginning to his performance, Bert established the comic situation, giving his audience *permission* to read his bodily movements as intentionally comical. Warming them up for the performance while also demonstrating his control as performer, he established his performance space. Stepping into the area before the curtain and standing in the spotlight, Bert created a break in the action of the hectic vaudeville show, calling attention to his departure from the vaudeville vein. By doing so, he moved toward a new presentation of his presumably culturally and historically predetermined character.[79]

Bert had once discussed blackface as a way of losing himself behind a mask: for him, the mask could symbolize the possibility of multiple identifications.[80] With its "excess symbolism," it could "embody conflict and . . . endow it with hyperbolic excess."[81] Although the ritual of blackface and the legacy of minstrelsy appeared rigid and inflexible, their meanings were not. The mask could signal not the limiting of interpretations but rather the multiplication of them, as Bert created his own unique character.

There is no doubt that minstrelsy persisted into the vaudeville theatrical space. Nonetheless, with Bert's performance, there was at least the possibility of intervention, if not successful subversion, of the stereotype he played. Within that small but significant space, Bert pursued his work, thereby manipulating the mask. Onstage he wore the old Negro's garb, yet to some degree he adjusted that garb. A writer for a theatrical magazine commented on Bert's inspired onstage presentation:

> One phase of Bert Williams' [sic] acting that depicts him as a true artist is his "nice" exaggeration; his sleeves are too short, his shoes too big, but not too short or too big. Imagination, and taste, govern his make-up. It is a misconception of what is comical to appear on the stage in a pair of well-fitting boots, if one is a clown, but it is a tedious misconception, and makes for a tedious evening, to appear in shoes a yard too long. There is a nice point between which it requires subtlety to gauge, and which, when rightly gauged, proves the man a comedian sensitive to comic values instead of a minor criminal.[82]

If the minstrel role had historically called for uncontrolled, grotesque expression of an imagined blackness, then Bert displayed a muted, subtle version of that expression. According to the reviewer, it was "imagination, and taste" that dictated his choices. Subtlety combined favorably with Bert's emphasis on slow and deliberate movement. The critic affirmed, "It is by this element of subtlety that Bert Williams shows an original mind; subtlety of costume, of manner, of voice, of movement especially—even his feet are subtle sometimes, an unobtrusive commentary on what is going on over the footlights. It is the lifespreading touch in all his work."[83]

During his performance, Bert used manifold techniques as he sang and when telling his stories, addressing his disparate audiences of whites and blacks. Joke structure "calls for three people: in addition to the one who makes the joke, there must be a second who is taken as the object of the hostile . . . aggressiveness, and a third in whom the joke's aim of producing pleasure is fulfilled."[84] As a joke teller who served not a dual but a divided audience, Bert stood betwixt and between two audiences. A protean figure more unstable than his slow-moving characterization would suggest, Bert shifted his identification with those audiences. As a trickster, he would tell jokes in which the third party became the co-conspirator or co-hater of the butt of the joke.[85] At differing times, he placed whites and blacks in that position.

"The Darktown Poker Club," one of the songs Bert performed that night, took its story from the classic minstrel theme of the urban black male poker club. "The Thompson Street Poker Club," an illustrated series popularized in *Life* magazine and collected for publication as a single volume in 1899, was undoubtedly familiar to audiences.[86] The series recounted the card-playing antics of a group of blacks that ranged from a local minister (Rev. Mr. Thankful Smith) to a professor and elders in the church. The willful violence of the characters, however, undercut their seeming respectability. These blacks would protect their "rightful" wins of card games with the weapon of choice, the straight razor. Characters spoke in a heavy "Negro" dialect, while the narration utilized Standard English with a slightly sardonic tone.

Cartoons accompanying the stories either depicted the aged, kindly "Uncle," familiar from images of Harriet Beecher Stowe's Uncle Tom character in *Uncle Tom's Cabin*, or caricatures with protruding lips and large, round eyes. The series featured blacks as an anthropological curiosity. The narrator's commentary highlighted the peculiarity, ignorance, and violence of his subjects. The cartoons gave white readers a glimpse of blacks in their "natural habitat," exposing the degrading terms in which they referred to each other and the deceit that characterized their relationships with one another.

Images like those published in the *Life* series surfaced in the print media generally and were not simply evident but omnipresent in newspapers and magazines that ran regular series. Presumed to be authentic representations of black humor, despite having been written by whites for whites, these kinds of sketches, cartoons, and jokes appeared regularly in publications.[87] *Life* had the company of literary journals, including *Harper's, Atlantic Monthly, Scribner's Monthly, Century Monthly,* and *North American Review,* all of which recycled the imagery, stereotypes, and degraded dialects of minstrelsy. *Harper's* printed stories between the 1870s and 1920s, running at least two stories per issue that centered on the antics of an ignorant and amusing black character/caricature.[88]

"Darktown Poker Club" was Bert's most popular song of the night, distinguished from the others as his "best bet."[89] He would later record it for Columbia in 1914. The lyrics were "the dictum of a darktown sport to his fellows at the poker table, after he has lost his roll in the game as played 'according to Mr. Hoyle.'"[90] When Bert performed the song, he used accommodationist masking as his technique to address audiences. "Accommodationist" described humor that "was first initiated, directed, and shaped by the slavemasters themselves, and only later appropriated and reclaimed by the slaves."[91] In *accommodationist masking,* Bert entertained white audiences, yet carved out a space for himself. He represented something familiar, encouraging the audience to respond pleasurably with recognition.[92] Yet he also created variations of the presumably familiar, thereby complicating its meaning.

With the extent of the stereotypical scene familiar to whites—to whom "The Thompson Street Poker Club" had been presented as though a slice of black life—Bert's song would seem to be another page added to the book.

He spoke his song in a low and rumbling voice:[93]

> *Bill Jackson was a hold up [?]*
> *He joined the darktown poker club,*
> *Then cussed the day they told him he could jine;*
> *His money seemed like it had wings,*
> *If he held queens someone had kings,*
> *Each night he would contribute all his coin.*

He says, "I think I'll play 'em tight tonight,
No bobtailed flush will make me bite,
When I go in, my hand will be a peach"—Hah!
Till he'd gone in and lose his pile,
He got kind of broodish after a while,
One night he got up and made a speech. . . .

Throughout this entire section of the song, Bert used the slightest of gesticulations, all close to his body. He emphasized select words as he spoke. A flutter of his hand might convey the image of Jackson's money taking flight; a tight mouth with pursed lips, Jackson's new resolution about how to play the game. Perhaps more importantly, his narrator's laughing aside, "Hah!" betrayed the amusement of one who looked on knowing that he himself had nothing to lose. Bert built the tension of the song, using understatement to increase it. By presenting a narrator to lead into Jackson's words, Bert quickly developed a character through which to speak the lines.

Although Bert alone was on the stage, as he looked out at the audience each person would feel as though he said the words only to him or her. The no-one-in-particular to whom he spoke became each individual in the audience. Through his minimalist approach, the single spotlight, the minor movement, he drew the audience to him rather than projecting himself outward. His talents gave credence to the theory that the audience is "not so much a mere congregation of people as a body of thought and desire. It does not exist before the play [or performance] but is *initiated* or *precipitated* by it; it is not an entity to begin with but a *consciousness* constructed."[94]

Despite the fact that Bert did not address the audience directly, he created the role audience members would play. By doing this, he influenced their consciousness. By the very intimacy his presentation form created, he bridged the gap between them. Engaging them as they focused to catch his subtle bodily gestures, changes in intonation, and lingering delivery, Bert then worked against the grain in an uncustomary—even antivaudevillian—style. Yet, the audience willingly joined him in it.

As Bert continued the song, he moved away from narration, becoming Bill Jackson, who gave the foiled cardplayer's speech to his fellows. Looking out into the audience, Bert spoke to them as if they were the others at the table. He pulled the audience in, creating a scene of characters, although he was the only person onstage:

Says [Jackson], "You see this brand new razor,
I had it sharpened just today,
I want to tell y'all some new rules to follow hereafter,
When we play.

"Keep your hands above the table when you're dealing—please,
And I don't want to catch no aces down between your knees,
Don't be making funny signs or tip your hands,
And I don't want to hear no kind of language
That I don't understand.

"Stop dealing from the bottom, cuz it looks so rough,
And remember that in poker, five cards is enough!
When you bet, put up,
'Cause I don't like it when you shy,
And when you're broke, git up,
And then come on back by and by.

CHORUS

"Pass the cards to me to shuffle, every time before you deal,
Then there's anything wrong, why I'll see.
Not gonna play this game no more according to Mr. Hoyle,
Hereafter, it's gonna be according to me!"

Embodying the suspicious loser, Bert displaced the threat of violence onto another character, which he played as distinct from his position as the narrator. Although this did not alter the stereotypical story that he told, it did demonstrate his skill at playing multiple roles in the space of a single story. The comedian's delivery, even when portraying a character as menacing as Jackson, tempered the representation.

Establishing rules for the game, Jackson both threatened those at the table and created terms meant to be fair for all. He both rejected the cheating of "Mr. Hoyle" yet elected himself as the unbiased observer. His ironic exclamation indicated the greater likelihood that, rather than fairness all around, Jackson himself wanted the upper hand. That was the joke of the verse.

Following a short musical interlude, Bert began the next verse, returning to his role as narrator. Staging the scene of the card game, he further developed the sketch, playing first the narrator and subsequently Bill Jackson, the character in whom he finished the song:

Now, seated right by in the clan,
There chanced to be a one-eyed man,
Bill watched him from the corner of his eye;
The one-eyed man would deal and then,
Would cost Bill Jackson five or ten,
Finally he got up with a sigh.

"Aah," he says, "I think that it is a shame,
But there's cheating going on in the game,
And honestly, I-I don't wanna name the guy;
But where I may not call his name,
If I think I catch him cheating again,
I'm gonna take my fist and close his other eye!"

As he sang this last verse, the dramatic exaggeration turned toward a specific figure: the one-eyed man. Although the verse closed with Jackson's physical threat, it was without recourse to the straight razor. The song also avoided the degrading terms of "nigger" and "coon" found in "The Thompson Street Poker Club"—even if the *Life* series used the words to suggest verisimilitude in the conversations of black characters. The final verse resolved the song into a joke as the chorus repeated—evidently for the one-eyed man's benefit—the rules of play that Mr. Jackson intended to enforce.

Even this accommodationist role left room for Bert's mastery. He removed the story from caricatured representation by his controlled physicality and embodiment of both narrator and Bill Jackson. He transformed the song into an opportunity to display his talent in playing multiple roles. While utilizing the stereotype, he moved a step away from the characteristic representation.

That night at the Palace, Bert exhibited the "gift in which he was supreme," honoring the audience with two terrific tales, which he called "lies."[95] Two of his best known were "You Can't Do Nothing Till Martin Gets Here," about an African American preacher who, caught in the rain on the way to service one evening, takes shelter in a haunted house, and "How? Fried."[96] Bert approached the first story using the technique of in-group referentiality. He illustrated the idea that "the comic frame should enable people *to be observers of themselves while acting*. Its ultimate would not be *passiveness,* but *maximum consciousness.*

One would 'transcend' himself by noting his own foibles."[97] His nod to blacks in the theater's gallery, this approach critically studied their behaviors and figures of significance simultaneously.

In essence, in-group referentiality was intragroup humor. Fair game for the black-on-black joke included the rural black, the pretensions of the developing black middle class, the "urbane" black, and religious leaders, among others. These jokes differentiated between the "ignorant" Southern country black and the presumed Northern "sophisticate"; reminded certain blacks of their history, thereby deflating their self-aggrandizement; and exposed the hypocrisy of individuals and institutions.[98]

Some of these jokes would seem ironically consistent with prevailing stereotypes. Perhaps the white members of Bert's audience laughed thinking that their apparent "rediscovery of what is familiar" signaled a joke for which they were the ideal audience. Indeed, this made performances before mixed audiences risky because "[i]rony can only be employed when the other person is prepared to hear the opposite, so that he cannot fail to feel an inclination to contradict."[99] Yet this risk did not deter Bert from utilizing the technique to call black audiences' attention to their own practices. After all, Bert was "Signifyin(g)," crafting new interpretations out of old intragroup images. Through indirection, he participated in a rhetorical strategy that allowed him to critique blacks' understanding of their own traditions. He created "[r]epetition, with a signal difference."[100]

Remaining center stage and using "no gesture which travelled more than six inches," Bert warmed up to the story as he proceeded:

Uncle Ben was a preacher who preached all around through the small towns near where I lived at. He preached, naw, well, he didn't call 'em towns, he called 'em cities. Any place where there was a general sto', fo' houses and a barn, to him, was . . . a city. He was on his way to uh, preach one Sunday evening, and a heavy storm overtook him, and he stopped at de fust brother's house he got to.

As narrator, the comedian pointed immediately to the pretensions of Uncle Ben, a country preacher who had aspirations to shepherding a larger flock. Being an itinerant minister who served various congregations, Ben perhaps believed himself more influential than he was, which the narrator quickly indicated with his pointed reference to what Uncle

Ben termed a "city." He did so ironically, however, with the narrator's ostensible desire to tell the story right, correcting himself as necessary.

In the next section, Bert embodied both Uncle Ben and the resident, playing out their dialogue. In an earnest manner, yet with a slight degree of irritation, he declared as Uncle Ben, "What can you do fo' me? . . . I just can't go no further, that's all there is about it. You gotta do somethin'." This exchange, in keeping with Bert's introduction to the minister's predicament, evidenced the preacher's pretension yet again, as he descended upon the owners of the first visible house and made demands.

Reflectively, the resident declared that he had hardly enough room in the small house for his own family. He then suggested that the preacher stay at his second house around the bend, which he and his family didn't use because "it's ha'nted." To that, Uncle Ben responded, "Well, I'll tell you my brother, I carry the scripture in my pocket. And I am sho' that with that upon my puhson, I need be in no fear of the spear." Bert thus established the anticipation of the challenge to the preacher's faith that would ensue.

Subsequently setting the scene in the supposedly haunted house, Bert described Uncle Ben lighting a fire, getting comfortable in an easy chair, and opening his Bible. The performer then pantomimed the minister extracting his Bible, from which he read aloud and dramatically in character, "It says here, in de fust chapter of de fust book, 27th verses, as to where—." Playing the narrator, Bert interrupted his line as Uncle Ben to explain that "right den a little kitten come on down the steps." As Uncle Ben, Bert displayed the surprised but pleased reaction of the preacher seeing the cat, which turned only to slight alarm when the kitten "then went on over to de fire, and reached in an' got some hot ashes, and washed his face wid 'em, and come back and sit down 'side of [Uncle Ben]."

Retaining the dignity of the character, the narrator remarked with emphasis that Uncle Ben "turned over to the *middle* of the scriptures [to] commence reading again." The unnerving behavior of what seemed to be an ordinary house cat had evidently made its mark. He then turned the pages of the pantomimed text, announcing, "Well it says here, in the 19th book, 14th chapter, and 27th verses, as to where—." This time, Bert interrupted the scripture reading to describe a cat "the size of a bulldog" that went directly "over to the fire and got hisself some hot ashes, washed his face wid 'em, and come and sit at the other side of [Uncle Ben]." Multiplying the characters he played in the story, Bert then spoke as the angora cat to the kitten: "Well, what're we gonna do?"

The kitten responded: "We can't do nuthin' until Martin gets here."

Building the drama of the narrative, Bert then conjured the picture of a more nervous Uncle Ben who, still silent, had by this point observed two talking cats self-cleansing with hot ashes. The narrator subsequently described Uncle Ben turning the pages to the *rear* of the Bible: "As it says in de last book, de last chapter, de last verse—." This was his final word before a cat the size of a Newfoundland dog descended the steps. Bert suggested its enormity with the sound of the cat walking down the stairs, "Kablup, kablup, kablup, kablup."

Increasing the tension, Bert portrayed Uncle Ben watching the cat, which "[w]alked on over, reached into the fire, and got hisself some live coals—ashes wasn't warm enough fo' 'im—washed his feet and come and sit down beside the angora." As soon as the "Newfoundland cat" sat, it said to the angora, "Well, uh, shall we commence on him now, or . . . what shall we do?" The angora, mum, shook its head, but the kitten answered with the now-familiar line: "We can't do nuthin' 'til Martin gets here."

Uncle Ben had apparently seen enough. With no more response than "Hmm," he "got up and put on his coat. Put his scripture away. Said, 'Well, when Martin gets here, you all just tell him I been here, but I'm gone!'"

"You Can't Do Nothing Till Martin Gets Here" called out the black community, who would recognize the image he conjured. In twentieth-century African American humor, the black preacher had become a popular butt of jokes, demonstrating "[t]he decline of the sacred world view." Even these once-protected figures came under fire.[101] Joke tellers like Bert shot down the old images of the sacred minister by drawing attention to his humanity.

A history of the mockery of the black preachers existed among whites as well, however. His presumed pretensions as an exalted man of the cloth were fodder for degrading references to his impropriety and unscrupulous practices. As seen earlier within "The Thompson Poker Club" series, the black minister often appeared within such stories as exemplary of the hopelessly corrupt black. This, coupled with the persistent representation of blacks as superstitious and, therefore, inordinately afraid of ghosts, made Bert's performance risky.

Despite the existing biases of a white audience, however, Bert told this story, and by focusing on the development of the ghost story, he moved attention away from a stereotypical representation of this figure. Critic Heywood Broun avowed that in Bert's performance, he "did not tell the story as a comic anecdote. By voice and pantomime, he lifted it to the stature of a true ghost story."[102] From the very seriousness with which Bert told the ghostly tale, he captured the attention of his audience rather than merely mocking the character he played.

Broun elaborated, "Of course we laughed at the message which was left for Martin, but it was more or less defensive laughter, because we knew in our heart that the preacher of the story had outstayed us by at least one cat."[103] Uncle Ben's contradictions elevated the humor, removing the focus from the stereotypically terrified black to the universally frightening experience of being in a truly haunted house. The pomp of the small-town minister, who insisted that he works in cities, only showed his lack of cosmopolitanism. His firm, dignified denial of superstition and fear resulted in the further hilarity of the conclusion when he finally did head for the hills. The quick finish, the speed with which Uncle Ben made his final decision after patiently waiting and watching, also added a punch to the narrative's ending. Placing the joke on Uncle Ben, Bert refused an emphasis on ridiculous behavior that would simply reinforce the stereotype.

For the second tale, "How? Fried," Bert used the technique of unmasking to tell the story of an ex-slave who outsmarted the devil with his gift for perfect recall. Essential to Bert's humor, unmasking gained further power for the comedian's ability to utilize the technique effectively before mixed audiences.[104] His extended "lie," "How? Fried," indicated Bert's manner of "revealing the gap between appearance and actuality."[105] He did so in a story that said a great deal about the importance of memory, the experience of slavery, and the black struggle for power.

The story began:

Uncle Benjamin, who lived, uh, right close to us had the most marvelous memory of any man I ever seen in my life. Never seen a man who could remember so much. No matter what happened. Any time, any place, he knew all about it. One day he was sitting down out on the porch and I asked him how he come to have such a memory. And he told us this.

As with the previous tale, Bert framed the story, setting up the exchange and scene that anticipated the central part of the narrative. He used a friendly and leisurely tone; one might imagine the character actually sitting on his porch, telling the story to those who had gathered round. The narrative's structure echoed the Uncle Remus folktales penned by Joel Chandler Harris. This perhaps created in the audience a comfortable expectation of a story of plantation life, "befo' de wah," which had recurred in minstrelsy.

As Bert continued, this appeared to be the case. He spoke as Uncle Benjamin, relating that his "great-great-grandfather had the most marvelous memory of any man in the state of Kentucky." A slave owned by a colonel who had him ride in the back of his coach, "[h]e would remember so good that six months, a year, after that time, he [the colonel] would ask him, 'What did so-and-so say Sam?' Sam could tell him. That's how I comes to have my memory."

Responding as though to a member of his imaginary audience who had apparently never heard this story, Bert as Uncle Benjamin queried, "[D]on't you know that my great-great-grandfather had such a marvelous memory that they had a fuss over him?" He then proceeded to explain, "De devil come to this mountain and says, 'Colonel,' says, [*sic*] 'I want that coon.'" According to Uncle Benjamin, the colonel had refused, and the two had argued for over an hour about it. Finally, the colonel decided, "Well, if you can catch Sam where he don't remember, why take him!"

As Uncle Benjamin, Bert then explained in an aside: "Well suh, c'ose you know, Sam didn't have nuthin' to do around the plantation. He was one of the famous few. He just go out every mo'nin' and rake the dead leaves off the lawn, where the gentle zephyrs had blowed 'em the evenin' befo'." With a subtle motion, he conjured the movement of the breezes on the Colonel's plantation.

Picking up the story, Uncle Benjamin described Sam raking the leaves at the plantation one day when all of a sudden the devil appeared: "Sudden, like that, in the guise of a man." Their conversation was short, as the devil asked Sam, "Do you like eggs?" To which he responded— after looking at the man for a minute—"Yassuh!" Just as suddenly, the devil disappeared.

Returning to the narration after the exchange, Bert, as Uncle Benjamin, perhaps stroked his chin, thinking back. Then he set the stage for the next scene: "Well, lemme see now . . . that was ten years befo' de war. Well, after de war, let me see, oh about twenty years after de war, why Uncle Samuel was, uh, out plowing the little field that he had that the colonel had give him so he could take care of his family. Out plowing amongst his corn on this morning. Now remember now, this is thirty years since de war."

He continued to describe the scene as he added that Sam sang his favorite hymn, "Didn't the Walls of Jericho Fall When the Bugles Sounded?" Bert, in character, then sang the lines: "Didn't the walls of Jericho, didn't the walls of Jericho, (get up to me) didn't the walls of Jericho, fall when the bugles sounded?" This built up the drama of the scene as Bert's baritone voice rang out during the a cappella segment.

Cutting off abruptly, Uncle Benjamin declared, "And, just like that, the devil appeared before him again and said, 'How?'"

"Uncle Sam said: 'Fried!'"

After a short beat, Bert laughed deep, hearty guffaws, in character.

An unmasking tale, "How? Fried" spoke of survival and resistance. Although reminiscent of nostalgic slavery stories by Harris and others, including Thomas Nelson Page, whose 1887 *In Ole Virginia* harked happily back to slavery, the details of the story undercut such a reading. Its treatment of the issues of memory, the life of the slave, and power, told through Uncle Ben and Sam, were a remarkable change.

First, within the logic of Bert's story, memory had the effect of countering the dismembered past of slavery and its consequences. In Uncle Ben's tale, Bert overturned the notion that slaves and their descendants had lost their histories and memory. Ultimately, the story characterized memory not as sacrificed, but spared—even spurred throughout time. In the present, Uncle Benjamin possessed information: "No matter what happened, any time, any place, he knew all 'bout it." In the unnamed narrator's commentary, memory signified not only remembering but also knowing and being a keeper of knowledge. Transcendent, Uncle Ben's knowledge included the past and the present, here and anywhere.

Furthermore, Benjamin knew about his own past and family, aware of a great-great-grandfather who not only existed, but from whom he specifically inherited his memory. Because in African American history generally, and in the slave narratives in particular, the subject of family history included the motifs of loss and unknowability, this was an important detail. Innumerable blacks had lost families through the institution of slavery. That Uncle Benjamin could trace a family tree back into slavery challenged the notion that blacks only experienced loss and instead underscored the importance of oral, unwritten history. Perhaps through this story and others that preceded it and him, Uncle Benjamin knew that his own memory was an inheritance. More valuable than material possessions, this inheritance enabled him to remember his family history and legacy.

Finally, the focus on his ancestor Samuel's memory highlighted the idea of memory not as trivial but, rather, as survival-oriented. Samuel's memory made him vulnerable to being overtaken by the devil, but finally strong when he outwitted him. It made him a slave because of his master's dependence on him, but also finally free when he came to have his own land after the war.

Using Benjamin, Bert questioned the idea of black degradation through slavery. Benjamin rewrote history—and possibly his family history—when he said, "Sam didn't have nuthin' to do around the plantation. He was one of the famous few." Bert overturned the image that slaves had been broken through their life on the plantation. The understatement signified the possibility of preservation and, more than this, did so in a tone that ironically referenced the reality of slavery.

The subsequent line, "He just go out every mo'nin' and rake the dead leaves off the lawn, where the gentle zephyrs had blowed 'em the evenin' befo'," revised the timeless myth of the Old South of magnolia trees and pristine plantations. Bert replaced this myth with an image of dead leaves covering the allegedly verdant land. He then went a step farther as he placed the slave within this picture, highlighting the figure who daily preserved the mythic pristine image, each day raking—or cleansing—it of the decay that plagued it every night.

On the issue of slavery and freedom, Sam appeared to be relatively free, but even in this story slavery hardly provided leisure. First, the master carried Sam on the back of his coach so Sam could be continually interrogated about what others said. Second, the master compelled Sam to write his reports. Yet even as these facts called attention to Sam's status, they ultimately took a backseat to the way in which Sam's duties in fact undermined the master's appearance of control.

The struggle for power came last. Although Samuel's apparent trustworthiness earned him land so that he "can take care of his family," that was hardly the happy ending of this story. The audience would not have forgotten that the master had willingly made an as-yet-unresolved deal with the devil. In that exchange between master and devil, the colonel placed Sam's soul in his own hands—unbeknownst to him—when he said, "Well, if you can catch Sam where he don't remember, well, take 'im!" The potential power of darkness within the slave's world—the master—did indeed abandon his hold on Samuel, but only so that Samuel could face a greater evil.

The devil, though powerful, could win Samuel only by inveigling Samuel himself, however. Perhaps Samuel's ignorance that his own soul hung in the balance yielded that final laugh of satisfaction from audiences. Yet could it be that the evidently ignorant Samuel did not merely happen to remember, but actually knew that his memory was his power? If that was true, then Samuel's singing "Didn't the Walls of Jericho Fall When the Bugles Sounded?" as a prelude to his unwitting fight against the devil was not coincidental but telling. The black audience would recognize it, and white audiences would likely know the biblical story: the Israelites circled Jericho for seven days, after which time they blew their bugles, bringing down the walls with the sound alone—and with the power of God. In Bert's concluding line, then, he tied the song to the import of the story. The seemingly unwitting, but *actually* knowing, trickster-slave used the mighty power of God and good to triumph over the power of darkness in both the mortal and immortal worlds.

After his selections, Bert performed his encores. He knew that the audience would hardly allow him to leave without performing his signature Jonah Man song, "Nobody." Although proud of its success, he would tire of its popularity and the constant requests he would receive for it. "Before I got through with 'Nobody,' I could have wished that the author of those words and the assembler of the tune had been strangled or drowned or talked to death," he admitted, joking. "For seven whole years I had to sing it. Month after month I tried to drop it and sing something new, but I could get nothing to replace it, and the audiences seemed to want nothing else."[106]

In a move that likely combined his disinclination to recite the song with his final need to perform it, Bert reluctantly delved into a pocket, from which he pulled out a small notebook. Deliberately, he searched the pages, stopping when he seemed to find his place.[107] He then began his doleful song, "reading as if with difficulty and making 'mistakes,'" which the audiences loved:[108]

> *When life seems full of clouds and rain,*
> *And I am full of nuthin', and pain,*
> *Who soothes my thumping, bumping brain? Hmm?*
> *[he sighs] Nobody!*

> *When winter comes with snow and sleet,*
> *And me with hunger and cold feet,*
> *Who says here's 25 cents, go ahead get something to eat?*
> *Nobody!*

As Bert sang, his "omnipresent sense of reluctance" was subversive.[109] Indeed, perhaps even more than the words themselves, his delivery further expressed his resistant pose. A critic wrote that Bert "twirls and untwirls himself in languorous contortions, his profound bass—overcast with gloom and fit for dirges—all the while unrolling the curious grievance which is the subject of the piece."[110] Although humor was the comedian's object—and indeed, at the end the audience "roars with laughter"—he established a method of deferring audience gratification. Delaying their satisfaction, he proved his control over them, even as they demanded his encore.

Still not satisfied with his first encore, the audience compelled the entertainer to give his cheering public more. He did his poker pantomime as the final piece of his performance. His choice of a silent encore may be seen as a further act of control, even though it came in response to the clamoring audience. In performing pantomime, Bert avoided the dialect-bound speech of his character in order to demonstrate his artistry. He utilized the means of a silent but eloquent vocabulary of movement in order to do so, with a focus on conveying "realistically emotions, dramatic episodes, human situations, and activities without the use of words," which the pantomimic performance style demanded.[111] In his short segment, he became a specific character engaged in "literal mime" that created objects as a "vehicle for the story."[112] Mime permitted him to use his body and, ironically, even the mask of blackface to create a new type and level of expressivity onstage.

After thirty-three minutes of entertaining, Bert finished his performance. Even then, the audience still screamed for him, hoping for more time. Overwhelmed by their incessant applause, he exited the stage. Once Bert was safely ensconced backstage, the Three Types closed the show. When booking the final act, vaudeville booking agents anticipated that many in the audience would miss the start of that act as they continued to cheer the headliner. They also knew crowds would likely leave before its finish, having already seen the star. Never could that have been more true than on this night. Bert had not merely pleased the public, but he had also illustrated his mastery as a comic artist. When he returned to the *Ziegfeld Follies of 1914*, however, he wondered if his clout there would continue after his absence from the production.

10

War at Home
and Abroad

hile Bert took his break from the *Follies*, Ziegfeld's production had undergone a dramatic transformation. It had moved from the New York Theatre's Jardin de Paris (roof garden) to the New Amsterdam at Forty-second Street, a final confirmation that the show had "arrived."[1] A luxuriant space suitable for the impresario's increasingly resplendent spectacle, the magnificent New Amsterdam had been built in 1903, and Flo himself played a role in redesigning it when he took it over from Klaw and Erlanger in 1913. Boasting art nouveau interior design, the New Amsterdam flaunted paintings of Shakespeare, Homer, and the famous characters in their works under its vaulted ceilings. A state-of-the-art theater with perfect acoustics and superior stage facilities, it was the most advanced in the nation.[2] Even the theater's exits exemplified opulence, as gleaming bronze and hand carvings graced the elegant staircase and banisters.[3] The *Ziegfeld Follies'* move to New York's "theatrical jewel" ensured that the show would remain spectacular.[4]

By 1914, more than ever, the structure of the *Follies* had become the product of harried writers and librettists who attempted to accomodate a broad range of talent as well as the demanding Flo. Every year, the cast expanded, as the list of principals shifted and changed. Every principal on that list, from fifteen to twenty men and women or more, had to be served. There were comics, like Bert and Ed Wynn; singers, like Rita Gould; and dancers, like Ann Pennington. On top of that, Flo, a perfectionist whose investment in the *Follies* increased yearly and within five years would reach between $110,000 and $140,000, insisted on having a firm hand in all of the show's affairs.[5]

Writers and librettists who developed the show began around February in preparation for the June opening. They worked tirelessly and were on constant call—literally. Flo telephoned his team with new ideas numerous times a day, even as they worked far into the night crafting scenes. As *Follies* writer Channing Pollack explained, Ziegfeld "devotes his life to the annual revue that bears his name. He works while you sleep." While they worked with Ziegfeld's contributions, writers also had to face the process of "threshing out everybody's ideas," producing more material than would ever be used in a single show.[6]

The *Follies*, however, always demanded numerous rewrites after that. Furthermore, those rewrites required improvisation. As Pollack averred, "The *Follies* has got along for years without an 'orderly procession,' and without an 'orderly procession' it is now packing the New Amsterdam."[7]

Frequently, in efforts to keep up with current events, and in light of changes in world affairs, the writers jettisoned scenes and wrote new ones. Often the cast list was still developing as the writers penned the book, and they responded to directives to draft material for new principals around a prop or a theme. Moreover, when old-timers returned in May from the latest edition's tour, without fail they "received their parts, and went off into corners to read them, returning in the throes of melancholy." After the principals individually edited their parts to their satisfaction, rewrites began again.[8]

In the later *Follies*, even more so than in 1911 when Bert and Errol had developed their "Upper and Lower" sketch, scrappy comedians had to provide for themselves. Not to do so would mean having substandard material or, worse, no material at all. In Atlantic City tryouts, if a scene failed to get a laugh, it got cut from the show. All actors benefited from having top-notch material that was tailored to suit them.[9] For Bert, retiring by nature and unaccustomed to having to write for himself, the *Follies* could be a foreign, perhaps uncomfortable, environment. In black musical theater, Bert had always depended on his script writers like Paul Laurence Dunbar and Jesse Shipp, other black entertainers who understood—and shared—his ambitions. They penned star vehicles with him in mind while allowing him to elaborate further on his roles. In the *Follies*, with writers ill equipped to create material for him, Bert had to depend on his own resources. He not only had the constant burden of having to take responsibility for himself but also had to push to get his scenes placed well in the show.

Bert had once said that he believed comedians had to be "constantly on the lookout for fresh material, funny incidents, funny speeches, funny traits in human nature."[10] His comic material developed from steady observation. The fast-paced environment of the *Follies* was anathema to this approach. Although Bert did actively seek material, he also saw the importance of developing it through constant, deliberate work. He could never satisfy himself with its rapid-fire development:

> I have studied [humor] all my life. . . . It is a study that I shall never get to the end of, and a work that never stops, except when I am asleep. There are no union hours to it and no let-up.[11]

Moreover, as his material was character-based, Bert needed considerable time onstage with it. He tended to work up to his punch lines rather than simply rattle them off. His characters were individuals whom the audience followed and came to know. As the quick scene changes of Ziegfeld's *Follies* allowed less time for his particular approach, he had to find a way to adjust—or he would otherwise end up underserved by the show's writers.

In spite of the challenge of securing quality material, Bert found himself in the spotlight at the opening of the *Follies* season. The *Ziegfeld Follies of 1914* continued to enjoy the patronage of prominent members of New York and Broadway society, including actress Grace George, author and dramatic critic Clayton Hamilton, and actor Robert Hilliard, cherished leading man. That year, Ziegfeld delivered with a program that pleased.[12]

Although the show focused more than ever on the chorus girls, Bert still wielded power as a category unto himself. Critic Amy Leslie described the show as being dependent on him. Leaning its decorative beauty on Bert's "black and Herculean shoulders . . . the *Ziegfeld Follies of 1914* sweep across the empty promises as if there never had been another revue."[13] The *New York Mail* crowned its review with the subheading, "Bert Williams Proves a Regular Cut-Up, as Usual," praising him for having "kept the applause going right through the rest of the show."[14] A *New York World* critic reported that Bert "convulsed" his audiences with laughter.[15] Perhaps the most laudatory remarks were those of the *Globe* writer who admitted that "[i]t is difficult to resist the temptation to overpraise this man. He is a real artist. Every year he improves."[16]

Some hungry audience members praised the show but still craved more of Bert. Sime Silverman of *Variety* noted: "Mr. Williams didn't do much here . . . Many probably regretted Williams did not have more opportunity in the comedy."[17] The *New York Times* also remarked on Bert's conspicuous absence, as he was "in the piece in spots, but he has less to do than usual, although he makes the most of his opportunities."[18]

Bert's most successful contribution was a skyscraper scene with Errol. They created a variation on their 1911 "Upper and Lower" sketch. Amy Leslie described the 1914 scene as "even more ludicrous" than the earlier sketch, set on "the 1313th story of a new sky-scraper in the course of construction."[19]

The scene began with Leon Errol, who was lowered into the scene on a girder, and then called out to be anchored. The tentative Bert, nervous about the extreme height, appeared to be making his way along a beam that seemed "millions of feet from everything." Soon after, the two began to argue about how many whistle blows should signal the engineer to stop the girder's movement. Later, as they worked together Bert slowly caught a rope and hauled Errol in. No sooner did he do so, however, than the work stoppage whistle sounded. Immediately, he abandoned the line, leaving Errol dangling in midair as Bert turned to enjoy lunch at his leisure. After building up the tension in their scene, Errol fell off the girder, struck by lightning. Following the fall, and as the curtain lowered, Bert blasted the horn those three times that he had demanded as the signal to stop.[20]

Again, Errol was the butt of the joke but, more than before, the central player. Praising the scene, the *New York Telegram* acknowledged "an irresistibly comic bit of acting by both men," but the *Evening Sun* believed that Errol "tried to be the star comedian."[21] The *Evening Sun* critic stated that, although Bert had to accept the minor role, "it was Mr. Williams, and *not* Mr. Errol's acrobatic efforts, which made the audience realize that the spirit of comedy in its truest sense is still alive in this weary world."[22] In the opinion of Charles Darnton of the *Evening World*, the roles needed to be reversed. "If he [Bert], instead of Errol, were swung about in the air the present situation would be much funnier."[23] Although, as before, the scene involved an exchange between Errol and Bert, this time Errol's physical brand of comedy dominated— or, at least, threatened to dominate—the scene. In this instance, his role resulted in scene-stealing, or at least eclipsing Bert, so that Bert played the foil.

Errol, previously only a comedian for the revue, had become staging director for that year's *Follies*. His move to a position of influence showed in his high visibility throughout the production. Critics noted that "he appears in all the important scenes," an effect of his unprecedented sway.[24] He dominated not only his scene with Bert but, as the lead comedian, also in the rest of the *Follies*.

As Bert attempted to develop quality material for his performances in the competitive *Follies* environment, Ziegfeld turned to black entertainers for his most engaging idea that year. *Darktown Follies*, an all-black revue written and staged by J. Leubrie Hill, a former member of the Williams and Walker Company, was enjoying terrific success.[25] The show had begun at the Lafayette Theater, bringing Broadway up to Harlem, and inspired "the nightly migration to Harlem in search of entertainment."[26] Hill thrilled to its wonderful reception. After its run at the Lafayette, *Darktown Follies* played Hammerstein's in an abbreviated form. By 1914, it had moved to the Bijou Theatre on Broadway, which had been "reopened as a regular playhouse for colored patrons." Although whites managed the theater and the box office, most other workers were black, including the female ushers.[27]

Ziegfeld, impressed by *Darktown Follies*, bought some of Hill's acts for use in his own revue. This may have been a decent choice in a time of the outright theft of black cultural production, but Hill was deeply disappointed that Ziegfeld had chosen not to break the color line. Although Hill's dancers instructed Ziegfeld's performers, the impresario did not invite them to appear in his production.[28] White producers like Ziegfeld could and often did co-opt acts, reproducing them as if they were their own without crediting or involving the creators. The reality of such practices indicated the powerful divide between white and black performance worlds.

Ziegfeld utilized the show's first-act finale and various songs in the *Follies of 1914*. The finale, "At the Ball," entailed the cast's formation of an "endless chain" passing in front of the footlights as well as behind the scenes while both singing and doing "ballin' the jack," an African American dance.[29] One of the songs, a duet called "Rock Me in the

Cradle of Love," which in Hill's show had demonstrated the encouraging fact that the tacit ban of black romantic plotlines had been jettisoned, also became material for Ziegfeld's show.[30] These selections furthered Ziegfeld's focus on his chorus girls—with whom his interest increasingly lay—rather than with his hired comedians.

A s critics across the nation unhesitatingly dubbed Bert "one of the greatest comedians America has ever produced," some of them appeared to know or sense his frustrations. "Every time I see Mr. Bert Williams, the 'distinguished colored comedian,'" Percy Hammond of the *Chicago Tribune* admitted, "I wonder if he is not the patient repository of a secret sadness." As the compassionate critic watched Bert within the elaborate settings of the *Follies*, he thought that "sorrow concealed, 'like an oven stopped,' must burn his heart to cinders." An almost unwilling witness to Bert's doom, "to sing the shoddy songs from the Broadway hymnal and to utter the commonplace jests from the Broadway joke book against the fleshly [*sic*] background of a Broadway chorus," Hammond regretted Bert's pitiable fate. He believed there should have been more opportunity for the performer "of first rank," who should "fix his fame in the more permanent foundation of the drama."[31]

Others articulated a wish to see Bert take on a dramatic role of substance. A *New York Telegram* writer decided that "his comedy [was] so deft and natural that he won anew his right to the title, 'the colored David Warfield.'"[32] Imagining Bert as equipped for the transition to drama, the writer declared Bert a "sterling artist." The critic further legitimated Bert as an actor by citing the successful vaudevillian-turned-dramatic actor.[33] This reviewer and others watched Bert attempt to find the best way to get more visibility and display his skills in the *Follies*. As he continued to build his career, Bert resisted the underutilization of his gifts and skills, endeavoring to fit his pace and style into the *Follies* format.

The harsh winds of change on the *Follies* set affected Bert deeply, however, and his predicament saddened him. Nonetheless, he was loathe to express his feelings about it. Although in the past, Bert had been taciturn about his feelings, he did speak up. When he did so, however, he turned his attention to what he called the "American phase," instead of Ziegfeld's *Follies*. He addressed his personal experiences with America's baffling practice of segregation.

Rather than reveal his "thwarted aesthetic yearnings," Bert discussed his frustrations with the American scene while socializing among blacks in the casual setting of a bar. On the road with the *Follies*, he attempted to associate with his colleagues, but it had often proven difficult to do so. Even when given the exceptional opportunity of staying in an upscale hotel, custom required that Bert use the freight elevator around the back. Moreover, he still encountered "heavy" saloons hostile to black men—even famous ones. While in Chicago, he stopped in at the Stratford bar and decided to speak his mind.

Although Bert was among other blacks, they were American. Could they—would they—understand as he agonized: "This may sound snobbish, though it isn't; I'm not a native of the United States, but a West Indian, and I must take solace from my philosophy so long as I earn my livelihood in this country." America's stance on segregation, and its status "as the only civilization in all the world where a man's color makes a difference, other matters being regarded as equal," made him distressed and resentful.[34]

Bert had not forgotten the differing circumstances in Great Britain. In London he had sat "in open lodge with a premier of Great Britain," and he had entertained the king in a command performance.[35] He bristled at the fact that in the States he was "often treated with an air of personal and social condescension by the gentleman who sweeps out my dressing room or the gentleman whose duty it is to turn the spotlight on me." The irony of America's history of fighting to defend the principals of liberty and equality and its simultaneous maintenance of segregation upset Bert deeply. His comments came perhaps as an effect of his recent decision, despite his feelings and experiences, to seek U.S. citizenship.[36]

Bert's immediate audience, though black, did not entirely empathize with him. The writer admitted, "Such tears as I may have felt impelled to shed were lessened however by the mean reflection that Mr. Williams receives from the public $1,000 each week."[37] This point rang true: Bert may have suffered humiliation from the substandard treatment he received despite his stardom, but he still did very well for himself financially. As the *Ziegfeld Follies of 1914* went on tour, Bert, Lottie, and the girls moved to a three-story townhouse on Seventh Avenue in Harlem. Bert splurged on alterations, providing the house with "all modern conveniences." He ensured that the ten-room brownstone would be a comfortable home.[38] He did, indeed, enjoy a remarkable life as a top star. Yet, even as he followed his continuously shining star, another would fall before its time.

On 15 October 1914, a front-page announcement, clearly indicating the *New York Age* editor's shock, screamed: "Aida Overton Walker is

Dead." Aida, "The Most Brilliant Exponent of Thespian Art" died suddenly from "[c]ongestion of the kidneys" at age thirty-four. Aida had been confined to her bed two weeks prior. Friends, many of whom had not even known that she had been so confined, expressed their shock. Honoring her memory, the *Age* declared, "No colored woman in America was better known or had a more brilliant list of accomplishments in her particular sphere."[39] It was, indeed, an illustrious career, although it had been much shorter than the black theatrical community had hoped or expected.

Following George's death, Aida had never stopped performing. Although she had been a crucial part of the Williams and Walker Company, after her separation from it she had proven her ability to stand on her own. After George passed, she signed a contract with the Smart Set Company, promoting her career as a soubrette and dancer/choreographer in the company's productions.[40] Through her work with the company, she had built her reputation and fame as the "brightest star among women on the Negro stage."[41]

Aida had also furthered her solo career. Creating her own small company of dancers, she had gone into vaudeville, taking what appeared to be a "small-time" show and raising it to its proper level of big-time vaudeville. Meriting a strong placement in the show, she proved that she had been more than merely the wife of George William Walker.[42]

Eventually, Aida had reappeared as a headliner, after which Walton announced that her "real artistic ability puts her in a class with Bert Williams."[43] In such endeavors, she utilized relationships with black performers that she had developed during her years in the profession. James Reese Europe, part of the community of black musicians and president of the famous Clef Club, served as the music director and band leader for her company's vaudeville performances.[44]

Aida had proven herself to be a gifted dancer and choreographer, mastering a variety of dance forms. She took her interpretation of *Salome* to Hammerstein's Victoria as a singular sensation in 1912.[45] Hammerstein himself had deliberated long and hard about the chosen dancer before selecting Aida for the coveted opportunity. He had observed her dancing and was certain that she would "fulfill every anticipation he . . . held out for her."[46]

Critics compared Aida favorably with her white contemporaries, including "Barefoot Classical Dancer" Isadora Duncan. In Aida's elaborate revival of "The Dance of Salome," she had focused on artistry.

Selecting a modern dance costume and imbuing her performance with deep expression, she had conveyed a story by focusing on an aesthetic interpretation of the dance.[47]

Yet Aida Overton Walker would be missed for more than her performances, just as her husband had been. In a 1908 editorial that had appeared in the *New York Age*, "Opportunities the Stage Offers Intelligent and Talented Women," she had defended the theatrical profession as a reputable pursuit for decent black women. Insisting on the importance of maturity and commitment to the profession, she asserted that young women could do service to their race as successes on the stage.[48] As courageous as her husband, the outspoken Aida had dared to speak her mind throughout her career in the public eye. Furthermore, after a point at which the future of black theater seemed dim, she had persisted by working within it. For this and other choices, she had garnered the respect of the black public.

Due to Aida's beloved status in the community, her family decided to allow her body to lie in state so that admirers could pay their respects. The pallbearers included such well-known members of the theatrical community as Alex Rogers, James Reese Europe, and Henry Green Tapley, who had joined the Masons with George back in 1903. Bert was conspicuously absent from the list, and reporters made no mention of his whereabouts at the time of Aida's death or funeral service.[49]

After the many years that the Williamses and the Walkers had spent together building the company, Bert's absence was a disturbing indication of how cold the relationship between Aida and him had grown. Bert's earlier burlesque of Aida's artistic *Salome* performance in *Bandanna Land* had not endeared him to her. Even more damaging for their relationship were the 1912 comments of Bert's manager, Shoemaker, who had disgraced her husband's memory. Perhaps knowing or sensing that her family would not welcome him, Bert stayed away. While others spoke of Aida as a leading exponent during the cakewalk craze, dance teacher to both American high society and the English aristocracy, Bert remained deafeningly silent.

*O*n 1915, Bert continued his work with the *Follies* as a featured act in the company of comic Ed Wynn, singer Ina Claire, and newcomer to the revue, W. C. Fields, among others.[50] Bert's opportunities in the show lessened, however. A *Boston Evening Transcript* reviewer described that year's comic segments in general as "shorter than they used to be," indicating that the *Follies* provided the comedians with increasingly less attention onstage.[51] Despite these obvious limitations, Walton would revere Bert as one "doing pioneer work . . . blazing a way for himself and others."[52]

One of Bert's remarkable appearances was a skit in which he played Thomas, "West Indian apartment house hallboy." While working in his characteristic style, he had adjusted himself to the *Follies'* faster pace. The scene established him as a tireless switchboard operator fielding innumerable tenant calls. *Variety* set the scene in its review:

> Bert Williams is on a couch at the curtain. It is about one a.m. The switchboard gets busy, the tenants (mostly women) and the callers (mostly men) go in and out when they are not overworking Williams at the phone. He knows them all. It is the class of apartments that may be found all over the west side of Manhattan, between 42nd and 125th Streets. One young woman, as she exits, impresses upon the bell boy he must tell anyone who calls up she had to retire with a severe headache. "Everybody?" asks Williams. "Yes, everybody," replies the girl. "Even the old gentleman?" he inquires. Answering the phone, Williams in response to supposedly a question as to the whereabouts of one of the female tenants says, "Oh, she has gone out with her fie-nance-cier."[53]

The rare scene allowed Bert to develop a character throughout the course of the sketch. Moreover, for the first time he played a West Indian onstage. Rather than playing a black American—or a darky—he returned to his roots. Although he still performed in blackface, Bert created a character that was altogether new to his audiences, referencing his background without leaning on stereotype.

Whereas the tenants in the segment entered and exited constantly, Bert's constancy as the figure onstage created a distinct pacing for the scene. Conversing with them or with imaginary callers on the switchboard, he used the various exchanges to expand on his role, working with fewer lines. A quick-witted character, the hallboy made comments to the many tenants and callers. He shaped the scene, which turned on his actions, the joke consistently at others' expense.

Bert had always loved storytelling and character building. James Weldon Johnson, reminiscing, would say that he got "more satisfaction, it seemed, out of being considered a great raconteur than out of being a great comedian; [he was] extremely funny in his imitations of the West

Indian dialect."[54] Bert would tell his stories onstage, in recordings, and in the newspapers.

Yet Bert would perform the West Indian accent only once onstage. At a time when American blacks often viewed West Indians as problematic—their cultural difference being a tension that made them alien in the Harlem community—Bert embraced this self onstage.[55] He affirmed his difference through this sketch. He also displayed another face in the assortment of selves that hid behind his mask of burnt cork.[56]

During the show, Bert performed one song that he would record for Columbia that year. After that point, however, he would never record his own songs again and seemed to have stopped writing altogether.[57] The 1915 recordings would include eight titles, all produced during the late summer and fall.[58] "I'm Neutral," his song performed in the *Follies*, echoed the building aggression of the Great War and the United States' relationship to the numerous nations by then embroiled in it:

> *Somebody hopped the Kaiser, and I don't know the reason why,*
> *A Frenchman took a swing at me and dug a trench right 'neath my eye,*
> *A Russian saw my color, and he hollered "Kill the Turk!"*
> *Then the Allies all got my range and started in to work,*
> *But I'm neutral!*
> *I am, and is, and shall remain!*[59]

Although it would be nearly two more years before President Woodrow Wilson would ask Congress for a declaration of war with Imperial Germany, the United States' precarious position was evident even then. Wilson attempted to maintain trade with the powers at war, but eventually, with the increasing losses sustained by the nation, this position would become untenable.[60]

As Bert struggled to develop satisfactory material, a recent addition to the *Follies*, juggler W. C. Fields, noted Bert's difficulty in getting the overextended writers to develop suitable material for him.[61] The writers didn't seem to know what to do with Bert's particular and unique talent, which was so different from the other vaudevillians Ziegfeld hired. Fields learned from this sad example. In his first year, the writers did not actually write anything for him. They stripped his scene down to a single pool table, removing the window dressing of waiters and dancers usually found in a pool hall.[62] He then developed his own material for the set. His scene was a hit, which would be immortalized that year in his first silent film, *Pool Shark*. Rapidly, Fields would move up through the ranks of the *Follies* as a success, despite never quite being in agreement with the exacting Ziegfeld.

As Bert's own difficulties increased, he witnessed others' advance in Ziegfeld's enterprises. One of those rising in the ranks was a young African American from the old Williams and Walker days, Will Vodery. A friend of the family, Bert had stayed at the Vodery home whenever he passed through Philadelphia.[63] His and Will's work together began when, during *In Dahomey*'s run, Bert had composed a song that he had needed written in musical notation. Vodery stepped forward confidently, claiming himself capable, and wrote out the arrangement before Bert's eyes. His excellent job convinced the duo to take him back to New York with them.[64]

Despite Bert's maturity compared to the relatively inexperienced Vodery, an incident in 1915 illustrated the veteran performer's fragile ego at a time when his career with Ziegfeld seemed to be in decline. Scheduled to rehearse with Vodery during their Atlantic City tryout—the first performance attended by Ziegfield, not to mention a theater "full of notables"—Bert failed to begin singing his piece as the music began. Quickly, Vodery realized that Bert had forgotten the lyrics as the actor faltered, even after they started up again.[65]

Panicked, Vodery asked Bert what was wrong. Bert walked out to the end of the footlights, where he peered out. "Something's wrong with this music!" he cried. The pressure was on the new composer/arranger, who wished to defend himself without embarrassing Bert. The comedian argued that the score be rewritten, and Vodery agreed to try, although he well knew that nothing had been wrong with the arrangement.[66]

Only after the dress rehearsal finished did Bert address Vodery again, cornering him backstage. "You helped me out of a jam, Buddy! You covered me fine."

Vodery remained unimpressed: "Yes, but what's the big idea?" he queried.

Bert gave an unsatisfactory explanation, then smiled and concluded, "Hell, if a friend can't kick you in the pants, who the hell can?"

In the end, Bert pulled his performance together after an all-night rehearsal with the musician. His song went on as a hit, and Vodery, initially mortified, forgave Bert.[67]

Although Bert's audiences knew nothing of his early season mishaps and still responded excitedly to him, it was hard to miss the changes that were occurring in the *Follies*. A critic for the *Dramatic Mirror* expressed it well. Although the comedians provided amusement, "in the end, it is 'the third on the left' or 'the fourth from the right' that remains our most vivid impression of the production": the showgirls.[68] W. C. Fields continued to write his own material. Bert, however, would continue to remain often dependent on the writers.

The writers of the *Ziegfeld Follies of 1916* opted to celebrate Shakespeare's tercentenary and featured Bert as Othello in a "Travesty of Othello."[69] Audiences "greeted [Bert] with uproarious laughter," although he was "hardly screamingly humorous."[70] The joke for the sketch lay in a scene with Desdemona, played by another male. In an exchange, Bert asks, "Who have you been running around with lately, Desperate-money?" To which Desdemona responds, "Not a single soul, excepting the 72nd Regiment."[71] When Othello attempts to murder Desdemona, "he takes a stuffed club to Desdemona after strangling does no good." As another reviewer described it, "it only irritates her."[72] This was Bert's "broadest chance," in the words of the *Variety* critic, but the comedian "seemed to work too slowly in this bit."[73]

Bert's limited horizons in the *Follies* would eventually lead him to seek other ways to expand his domain, starting work in the nascent motion picture industry. The first movie house screening had taken place at Koster and Bial's in New York City in April of 1896. Vitascope, "the latest marvel," had enjoyed the promotion of Edison, who had agreed to attach his name to the new machine, "in order to secure the largest profit in the shortest time."[74] It had debuted to great applause as audiences viewed the shorts, films "of waves pounding a beach, of boxers flailing at one another, of 'pickaninnies' [black children] jumping up and down."[75] Such bits of entertainment, interesting as they were, did not, however, tempt the public to return for seconds. With few quality films from which to select, and the difficulty of running and maintaining the projectors, the entertainment of moving pictures did not quickly "take."[76]

On top of these challenges, Vitascope investors, who had spent thousands of dollars and counted on monopolizing the developing industry, learned that amateur inventors could easily create their own version of a projector, thereby avoiding copyright issues.[77] This early period of the film industry was "The Lawless Film Frontier," characterized by fledgling movie men's innumerable attempts to make money with an influx of machines, including "projectoscopes, motorgraphs, animotoscopes, kinematographs, cinemetroscopes," and others.[78] Its promoters pitched to the young entrepreneur who sought independence and "the surest immediate money-maker ever known."[79]

By 1905, the "first American motion picture theatre" had opened in Pennsylvania. In only four years, 8,000 more flooded the nation, and by 1915, the movies competed for the audiences who patronized theater, from burlesque to legitimate.[80] They attracted both lecture-hall audiences and vaudeville spectators.[81] Although motion pictures would begin as a novelty, later becoming an addition to small-time vaudeville shows, they quickly gained momentum as a feature in and of themselves.

Although it seemed that the new entertainment form might be a promising means of presenting new images of blacks, early films simply recycled the pernicious stereotypes that already circulated throughout society. Films like *The Dancing Nig* and *A Nigger in the Woodpile*, created and distributed by such prominent companies as Essanay and Biograph, indicated the extent to which the film industry's representations would continue to perpetuate the already-prevalent images of blacks.[82] But no film so effectively expressed how influential and injurious this new medium could be as *The Birth of a Nation*, which previewed in Bert's hometown of Riverside, California, on 1 January 1915. There it played under its working title, *The Clansman*. The film had been based on Thomas Dixon's novel and play of the same name.[83]

The Birth of a Nation was a glorious and wretched achievement of American cinema. Glorious, because it utilized all known cinematic techniques, as well as D. W. Griffith's unparalleled skill, resulting in a filmic masterpiece. Wretched, because in its telling of the Civil War and the Reconstruction period, it perpetuated many of the more damaging images of blacks. Furthermore, it presented the Ku Klux Klan as heroes in the story. The film "directly led to the rebirth of the Ku Klux Klan; KKK Imperial Wizard William Joseph Simmons announced the revival of the Klan simultaneously with Atlanta's opening of the *Birth of a Nation* on 6 December 1915."[84] Even worse, the film told the story with an unequalled technology that President Wilson himself was rumored to have said "is like writing history with lightning."[85]

Despite such ominous signs, like other stars of his time, Bert sought opportunities in film. He was cast in *Darktown Jubilee*, becoming the first black to appear in a film.[86] *A Natural Born Gambler* followed, which was reviewed in *Moving Picture World:*[87]

That celebrated poker game which Bert Williams has so often played in pantomime on the spoken stage, is the inspiration of this two-reel comedy. The characters are all colored persons of the male sex and they are all addicted to gambling. Williams attempts to annex the roll of a swell sport from the city, but the game is raided, and when last seen, the natural born gambler is sadly dealing out imaginary hands behind bars of a prison. The business of some of the scenes could be improved, but Bert Williams's skill at pantomime shows up well on the screen.[88]

Although far from a radically different take on his standard character, interestingly Bert was the only person in the film who wore blackface. As the lightest-skinned actor in the film, Bert wore burnt cork that marked him unmistakably as a black man, a convention carried over from theater. Also, as if to dramatize the distinction of his woeful character, the burnt cork telegraphed difference, even between his role and that of the other black actors. It distinguished him as the deepest comical character: the central character of the film.

Bert's next movie, like *A Natural Born Gambler*, dramatized one of his well-known comic stories. Entitled *Fish*, it featured Bert as a boy who, after hours spent digging for worms, wants nothing more than to fish for the afternoon. Returning home to get his fishing pole after collecting his good supply of worms, he discovers that he has a pile of wood to cut. Tiptoeing away, he leaves his family to the chores—his father and younger brothers as well as his mother, who undertakes the washing.

After a short while spent down by the fishing hole, he catches a big fish, then decides to head home. On his way, however, he sees a house on the top of a big hill. He starts toward it, hoping to sell the fish for Sunday dinner. Following a long trek to the top of the hill, Bert is dismayed to discover that the owner does not want his fish. Moreover, after a long argument, the owner sends his dog after him.

Bert works his way down to the bottom of the hill. No sooner does he reach it than he sees the owner beckoning him back. Hopeful, Bert clods up the hill again, only for the owner to shout that he does not want any fish next Sunday, either! In the meantime, Bert's mother has missed him and traces him to the house. She leads him home and back to the woodpile.[89]

As a filmic version of a story Bert told in performance, the picture seemed only to toy with the possibility of recording the comedian's extant bits. Not only was the now forty-two-year-old Bert improbably playing the role of a "boy," he was also barely extending himself in the performance of this character. Although he had hoped that motion pictures would offer him something new—a dimension of performance that had been unavailable to him onstage—it appeared he would merely repeat his previous performances. Although talk of a series of two-reel comedies featuring Bert created a buzz in the world of entertainment, the difficulty of distributing his image throughout venues in the segregated South discontinued that plan before it even had the chance to begin.[90]

All hope would not be lost, however, in blacks' efforts to have their dignity acknowledged in the theatrical world. On 5 April 1917, *Three Plays for a Negro Theater* opened at the Garden Theater in Madison Square Garden, which heralded an encouraging sign of the possibility of dramatic—as opposed to comic—theater for blacks. Years later, playwright Ridgely Torrence would admit that the all-black cast had suffered from stage fright, petrified that "Negroes trying to be serious before an audience of white people who had never known them on the stage except as clowns, would be jeered and hooted off the boards." Few in the cast would allow members of their families to attend the performance, fearing the shame of the "certain boos, bad eggs, and catcalls."[91] These beliefs, prevalent among neophytes and experienced actors alike, most certainly did have a legitimate basis. With the reality of black caricature and the continuing legacy of minstrelsy still shaping blacks' images, the cast faced formidable obstacles.

The series of one-acts approached black life in America with gravitas, led by some of the former members of the Williams and Walker Company, including Alex Rogers and Jesse Shipp, and former colleagues, such as J. Rosamond Johnson. Working together, the veterans strove to lay a new foundation for black performance on Broadway. Cast, crew, and critics alike knew its import. A writer for the *New York Sun* described the opening as "epochal for the negro plays and players, as it represented their emancipation from the inertia and prejudice which has heretofore kept them from a general hearing."[92]

That night, the production made history. Although Torrence was a white playwright writing about black experience, his works realized what Bert had only dreamed about. The plays featured substantive characters who faced the tragedy of shattered dreams and the struggle to survive in the face of deprivation. They utilized the unique history of blacks in America, treating that history with respect. Furthermore, they elevated the black experience in works that dignified the African American experience.[93] Following the seven-year term of exile, during which productions created and performed by African Americans had been all but driven off Broadway, the plays had heralded a new era in black theater.[94] Moreover, they had made a hit on the Great White Way.

The playwright and his cast would have little opportunity to see their achievement discussed in the press, however, as the following day the United States entered the Great War. Although America continued to enjoy the diversions that popular entertainment offered, the production closed soon after its opening. At a time when the populace as well as the nation's leaders insisted on the need to affirm patriotism, it seemed that the plays' weighty issues could no longer get a hearing. The public turned away from the plays' troubling and frank articulation of racial injustice in American life.[95]

Since the 28 June 1914 assassinations of Archduke Franz Ferdinand and his wife in Sarajevo, the international conflict had been escalating. Although the United States had maintained fragile neutrality with the belligerent nations, Germany's steady and repeated threats of unrestricted submarine warfare, which had resulted in the sinking of the ocean liner *Lusitania* nearly two years before, prompted the nation's declaration of war.[96]

The American sentiment regarding the war had previously been to maintain neutrality in both thought and in action. When the call to action finally came, however, African Americans pushed for the allowance of their participation. Although racial discrimination in the nation had not only persisted but even increased, those who dared to support the Great War agreed with Du Bois: society could change if the black man would "put himself into the turmoil and work effectively for a new democracy that shall know no color."[97]

Without illusions, and with varying degrees of passion, black journalists and spokesmen insisted on the importance of supporting the war effort. The *Age* would write that "the Negro has a case in court upon which his life depends and which he cannot afford in any way to jeopardize. He should not let his rights go by default. Neither can he afford to weaken his claim to any of those rights by a non-performance of duty."[98] With the question of duty having been raised, the general

Bert in His Military Uniform. COURTESY OF THE YALE COLLECTION
OF AMERICAN LITERATURE, BEINECKE RARE BOOK AND MANUSCRIPT
LIBRARY

population of African Americans believed they had to stake a claim for
blacks in America's democracy, while also proving their loyalty.[99]

Even before the declaration of war, states had participated to some
degree in the buildup of resources through National Guard units. Bert
joined two regiments, in Illinois and New York, and was designated as
captain for both.

In the fall of 1916, the Fifteenth Regiment of Infantry of the New York
National Guard, established as the "first negro regiment to be organized

in the State," marched through Manhattan. Bert, as captain and inspector of small arms, had the honor of leading the regiment in a parade before Governor Charles S. Whitman and thousands of cheering blacks.[100]

The entertainer took his place behind the colonel and before the marching men, astride a gray "charger." No sooner had the band begun to play "Onward Christian Solders," and the lines started their advance, however, than Bert's horse dashed ahead, "ears straight back, tail out, and feet flying." Bert could do little more than clutch at the saddle until the horse stopped, well ahead of the band. The restless beast waited, but eventually began its race again, just as the parade turned south onto Fifth Avenue.[101]

The animal made straight for the motion picture cameras recording the event. The cameras captured Bert's every expression, as well as the various movements of the agitated horse. Finally, with the help of two mounted policemen and a traffic cop, they gained control of the horse. Bert hurriedly slid down from the saddle "and planted the well-known Williams feet on the pavement with more emphasis than he ever waved them over the footlights."[102]

Bert's misadventure with the unruly horse should have completely shattered the offstage self he meticulously presented. Yet he dared to let himself laugh at the unfortunate incident, saving face by hiding his mortification under a smile. Later, telling the story to Lottie and his nieces, who had entirely missed his appearance and wondered where he'd gone, Bert affirmed his sense of humor: "On my way down, my horse just turned out of the parade and went down in a subway entrance. I talked to it when it left the parade and I talked to it down there in the subway, but I never did find out why it wanted to go there or why it didn't want to come out."[103]

Despite his humorous account, Bert's experience must have pained him. Not yet an American citizen—he would be naturalized in 1918—he would remain in the States as others fought abroad. For Bert, there would be no moments of valor on the battlefield, no heroic tales from the front. This hometown parade would be as close as Bert would come to military service.

Members of the 15th Regiment were called to arms only four months after the declaration of war, eventually training and heading to France. Known as the 369th Colored Infantry Regiment, or the "Harlem Hellfighters," in time they were honored for their service and heroism abroad.[104] James Reese Europe, a lieutenant in the 369th, would be among those fighting alongside French troops after the 369th was denied the right to fight side by side with white Americans.[105] When the regiment returned in 1919, they would march to the city's deafening cheers. In the meantime, Bert would remain at home, performing and, increasingly, striving to speak out about race relations in the States.

In a patriotic revue that held none of the controversy of *Three Plays for a Negro Theater*, the *Ziegfeld Follies of 1917* went on as planned. That edition saw Bert teamed up with neophyte Eddie Cantor, his new comic foil, in a much-lauded scene. Later, Cantor would reflect on his relationship with Bert, admitting: "When I was in my teens, I became the hottest fan Bert Williams ever had. . . . When we were introduced at our first rehearsal, I was overwhelmed."[106] Meeting his idol terrified Cantor, who described Bert as "a tall, handsome man with a light skin and an air of aristocratic aloofness." Yet, at the same time, Cantor recalled Bert as kind: "[H]e flashed me a warm smile, put out his hand, and said, 'Young man, you and I are going to be good friends.' My doubts as a newcomer were dispelled. It wasn't so much his words—I'd heard them before. It was his voice. It rang true."[107]

In their rehearsals together for the show, Cantor had "camped all over the stage." Bert, in his "almost professorial manner," spoke to Cantor in the privacy of Cantor's dressing room. "Look, son, don't push too hard," he advised him. "You can afford to underplay this character because the situation almost carries the scene." Bert protected the ego of his colleagues, mainly because of the delicate politics of relationships between whites and blacks, but also because of his own sensitivity toward others. As Cantor explained, "So disarmingly did he phrase criticism, it seemed almost a compliment. 'I see what you're trying to do,' he'd say, 'and that's good, but I think you'll find it might work a little better if you try it this way.'"[108]

A notoriously high-energy performer, Cantor often seemed to need guidance. W. C. Fields, who had watched Bert and Cantor at work together, saw the overeager Cantor hamming it up as Bert unsuccessfully attempted to get him to play their scene smaller. After rehearsal, he beckoned Cantor over to him: "You don't have to bang that line over, boy. When you're onstage with Bert Williams, there's no other place for the audience to look except at you and Bert. You don't have to grab the audience by the collar." He then took time to show the energetic performer how to use "gesture rather than volume."[109] Both senior performers took Cantor under their wing even as rumors circulated regarding Bert's imminent departure from the *Follies* to pursue other endeavors.[110]

In Cantor and Bert's scene, the *New York Herald* described Bert as a porter who "has a son just home from college who has taken a degree in dancing and tries it on the father."[111] Cantor, however, provided a more complete account: "Bert was playing a porter at Grand Central Station. I was his son, who was about to arrive home from college. Bert had bragged to the other porters that I was a big strong, husky football hero, and they were all on hand to get a look at me."[112] Unfortunately, the son turned out to be thin and effeminate. The exchange between the two lasted ten minutes, with Bert's pouting son embarrassing him with his childish antics. It ended with Bert ordering Cantor to "[p]ick up those grips. Today is my graduation and your commencement."[113]

For the *New York Times* critic, the sketch was a wonderful idea, although it was unfortunately botched by the writers:

> Here surely was an opportunity for a scene of real humor between the illiterate father, dubious as to the value of a college education, and a representative of the haughtily superior second generation. But the authors missed their chance completely, and made the character of the son an unwholesome and objectionable type, too frequently portrayed on the local stage.[114]

Bert's "artistry can illumine even the most simple declarative," the critic commented. According to the *Times*, Bert had not been the guilty party.[115] For yet another year, Bert was both beloved by audiences and underutilized in the *Follies*. Furthermore, even though he would record two songs, enjoying his record label's praise of him as "just as much funnier as he is days older since his last Columbia records," he would receive little public attention for the selections.[116]

As his star seemingly began to dim toward the end of the year, Bert started to speak more openly about his experiences in America and in the *Follies*, garnering attention for his offstage pronouncements. His words would take on a darker tone, even as he aimed to remain optimistic. By this time, he would have heard about the violence and near-riot that occurred in July when his friend, musician Noble Sissle, was in South Carolina for training and did not remove his hat fast enough to satisfy a store manager standing behind a counter.[117] He would have also known about the bloody July riot in East St. Louis, which began in the shadow of economic and political discord.

White workers' labor disputes had failed, and as the disaffected men blamed black southern migrants, an outburst of aggression exploded on 28 May, when union organizers beat blacks who were walking the city streets.[118] The rancor further deepened with the pro-Democratic papers' allegations that Republicans had created a "colonization scheme" to force blacks to relocate North in order to sway the vote away.[119]

By the time carloads of whites went to terrorize black neighborhoods on 1 July, the community had gotten prepared. As gunshots rang out, they were answered likewise. Both the Illinois National Guard and the police remained hands off amid random assaults of men, women, and children. When it all was over, more than thirty-nine blacks, most of them unarmed, as well as eight whites had died, some of the latter killed accidentally at the hands of other whites.[120]

In the face of such racial discord, even as the nation was fighting abroad and patriotism was high, Bert shared his views on America. He even revisited his work with Ziegfeld's *Follies*:

> Each time I come back to America this thing they call race prejudice follows me wherever I go. When Mr. Ziegfeld first proposed to engage me for the *Follies* there was a tremendous storm in a teacup. Everybody threatened to leave; they proposed to get up a boycott if he persisted; they said all sorts of things against my personal character. But Mr. Ziegfeld stuck to his guns and was quite undisturbed by everything that was said. Which is one reason why I am with him now, although I could make twice the salary in vaudeville.[121]

Recalling with mild resentment the early incident with the *Follies*, Bert presented himself as being above reproach. Racial prejudice followed him; he constantly had to cope with others' determination to sully his reputation. He had to harden himself against reprisals from those who not only attacked Ziegfeld for his inappropriate selection but also personally attacked him.

Notably, even as he commented on Ziegfeld's admirable bravery, for the first time Bert openly acknowledged his own financial value. The steadfastness he witnessed in Ziegfeld swayed him. Although he knew he could earn twice as much elsewhere, he informed his public and Ziegfeld that dignity was more valuable to him than money. He communicated his own demands to retain his dignity regardless of those with whom he worked. He also recognized his worth despite the unpleasant situations he endured, thereby teaching others a lesson in self-respect.

Bert also spoke about his relationship with others in the company, suggesting that the several years of his participation had been a continual exercise in tact and reserve. It had been a matter of discerning friends from enemies, or at least unsympathetic individuals. Working in the *Follies* necessitated a large degree of self-consciousness and self-reliance as a form of self-protection:

> I always get on perfectly with everybody in the company by being polite and friendly but keeping my distance. Meanwhile I am lucky enough to have real friends, people who are sure enough of themselves not to need to care what their brainless and envious rivals will say if they happen to be seen walking along the street with me. And I have acquired enough philosophy to protect me against the things which would cause me humiliation and grief if I had not learned independence.
>
> It was not people in the company I've since discovered, but outsiders who were making use of that line of talk for petty personal purposes.[122]

A revealing attitude, expressed as self-preservation and -protection from possible humiliation. Carefully avoiding seeming radical or imposing, the actor kept his distance, developed independence, and learned "enough philosophy" to insulate himself against whatever humiliation he might encounter.

Bert fashioned his experience in the company as positive, but the entire description evidenced his self-conscious existence. Polite and friendly, yet always aware that "brainless and envious" people might object to his associates' walking beside him on the street, Bert recognized the limits placed on *him* in connection to others. He remained on the outskirts of the natural exchanges of the company, constantly prepared for moments in which he might be disappointed or humiliated. The philosophy that guarded him provided intellectual distance from deeply painful personal experiences, and perhaps it even supplied the terms in which to articulate the unexpressed disappointments he experienced.[123]

Bert faced the awareness that segregation made people treat him discriminatorily. The societal demand puzzled and angered him, resulting in an even more uncharacteristic venting:

How many times have hotel keepers said to me, "I know you, Williams, and I like you, and I would like nothing better than to have you stay here, but see we have Southern gentlemen in the house and they would object."

Frankly, I can't understand what it is all about. I breathe like other people, eat like them—if you put me at a dinner table you can be reasonably sure that I won't use the ice cream fork for my salad; I think like other people. I guess the whole trouble must be that I don't look like them. They say it is a matter of race prejudice. But if it were prejudice a baby would have it, and you will never find it in a baby. It has to be inculcated on people. For one thing, I have noticed that this "race prejudice" is not to be found in people who are sure enough of their position to be able to defy it.[124]

Racial prejudice is unnatural, he insisted. It is a learned behavior, a trained belief. Some people did not believe in it. Nonetheless, they refused to challenge it because of their own powerlessness or perception of powerlessness, as in the case of the hotel keeper. Insecurity helped maintain the status quo.

Bert's memory of having received better treatment abroad only compounded his aggravation. The knowledge that elsewhere he could still receive better treatment from those in positions of greater influence than the hotel keeper and his patrons undoubtedly caused him anguish. There could be dignity and equality in exchanges between the black man and the white. And for him, the very king of England came to mind:

[T]he kindest, most courteous, most democratic man I ever met was the King of England, the late King Edward VII. I shall never forget how frightened I was before the first time I sang for him. I kept thinking of his position, his dignity, his titles: King of Great Britain and Ireland, Emperor of India, and half a page more of them, and my knees knocked together and the sweat stood out on my forehead. And I found—the easiest, most responsive, most appreciative audience any artist could wish. I was lucky in that he liked my stories and used to send for me . . . to tell some story over that he had taken a liking to, and found he couldn't tell correctly.

He was not the only man in England in whom I found courtesy and kindness.[125]

Using this example to highlight the ridiculousness of the American system, Bert challenged anyone who would defend the racial hierarchy in

America. He criticized the American system and emphasized the hypocrisy of segregation in a democratic society. Moreover, he eloquently illustrated his point regarding the insecurity of those who desperately maintained segregation. If the king of England—who was, after all, *his* king as a Bahamian—could be gracious and egalitarian despite being an imperial monarch, why were Americans not so? Bert expressed a poignant irony, particularly so at a time when Americans entered the national scene to speak of and fight for democracy.

As Bert continued, he answered point-blank a question addressed to him by both whites and blacks. Having chosen, though fair-skinned, to live and perform as a black man rather than attempting to "pass" for white, he would have hardly wanted another identity. Yet, he explained:

> People sometimes ask me if I would not give anything to be white. I answer in the words of the song, most emphatically, "No." How do I know what I might be if I were a white man? I might be a sand-hog, burrowing away and losing my health for eight dollars a day. I might be a street car conductor at twelve or fifteen dollars a week. There is many a white man less fortunate and less well equipped than I am. In truth, I have never been able to discover that there was anything disgraceful in being a colored man. But I have often found it inconvenient—in America.[126]

Bert knew that his life was extraordinary. Sensitive to both racial and class issues, he plainly understood his great fortune and valued his own experience. At the same time, however, he recognized the conditions under which he lived. Indeed, being a "colored man" certainly was "inconvenient."

White colleagues, at a loss for words to express the respectable and admirable traits their friend possessed, had attempted to redefine him racially, as Shoemaker had. Unable to find a manner in which to accept him as both black and talented, black and intelligent, black and generous, they found ways of reading him as "white" so as to include him as part of that group. Without a way to express those exceptional characteristics and acknowledge his race simultaneously, they instead sought to manipulate what he was and whom they saw. Could it be that he referred to the inconvenience of blackness as that which made whites unable to accept him? Was this the inconvenience, not only of the structure of segregated society but also of his marked difference, that made people unable to see and appreciate his humanity regardless of race?

Despite Bert's many struggles with American racism and discrimination, he pronounced, "I have no grievance whatsoever against the world or the people in it; I'm having a grand old time. I am what I am, not because of what I am, but in spite of it."[127] He urged that, in spite of the past and continuing struggles he endured as a black man in theater, he had little reason to complain. His statement about being "what I am" referred to his being a successful comedian and performer in spite of his blackness. He had persevered despite the color line and endeavored to express his talents fully. He had triumphantly surmounted many of the limits placed on him as a black performer. No one handed him anything because of his race, he adjured. If anything, he had actually confronted more trials and more resistance because of it.

Presumably, the fun he enjoyed onstage and in life as a moneyed, well-known comedian countered any possibility of holding grievances with the world. He focused on the "world," however, rather than on America alone. De-emphasizing his reactions to the limitations placed on him in this country, he concentrated on the positive, and thereby he refused to alienate the readership. Instead he expressed hopefulness, regardless of hardship. He spoke of surmounting these obstacles, all the while focusing on his successes "in spite of" what he was. He underlined the fact that being black may have been more than merely "inconvenient": indeed, it was the unfathomable obstacle that barred advancement in society.

In a letter to his friend, Bert expressed his regret at the state of affairs for the race. He exposed his true feelings, the depth of his despair, and the extent of his frustration. Confronting the humiliation of segregation, he sought comfort and reassurance from a friend during a dark moment:

> I was thinking about all the honors that are showered my way at the theatre. How everyone wishes to shake my hand and get an autograph. A real hero, you'd naturally think. However, when I reached my hotel (in downtown Chicago) I am refused permission to ride on a passenger elevator, cannot enter the dining room for my meals and am Jim Crowed (segregated) generally. But . . . I'm not complaining particularly since I know this to be an unbelievable custom. I am just wondering. I'd like to know[,] when ultimate changes come and those persons I meet at the theatre eliminate through education and common decency the kind that run such establishments[,] what will happen. I wonder if the new human beings will believe such persons as I am writing you about actually lived?[128]

Although not normally one to "complain," Bert experienced grievous moments in which his anxieties surfaced. He wondered and asked about the future of the country, hoping there was reason to be optimistic. Unable to contain his disappointment and pain, he still felt he had to rationalize such a need. Discussing segregation as an "unbelievable custom," Bert seemed to believe he was being self-indulgent and that his complaints were useless. At the same time, he appeared powerless to refrain from sharing them.

He further communicated this when he spoke with Lester Walton, who noted that "[i]n one city the leading hotels vie with each other for his patronage; in another where race prejudice is rampant he even finds the second class hostelries closed against him, although any white chorus girl or chorus man may secure accommodations."[129] That whites who were in a lower position in the company received superior treatment than Bert only added to his humiliation. Here he was, a famous professional performer, being made to accept substandard treatment without recourse.

Bert revealed further exasperation when he asked, "Why is it a colored passenger can sleep over or under a white passenger on a Pullman and no color question is raised, but just as soon as a citizen of color applies at a hotel for a room where he could be separated by walls and doors, objection is made to his presence?"[130] He pointed out the paradox of permitting travel in close quarters with whites, while still banning integration of rooming houses and hotels. Throughout his many years of travel, through which he had been exposed to different peoples and cultures, he would never see the logic of this practice and could hardly hide the distress it caused him.

Bert endured discomfort during his travels but also suffered awkwardness in New York, never feeling free to interact with the cast. This, in addition to his struggle for suitable material in the *Follies'* revues, perhaps made him question his position there. As he moved on, he would search for a better way to take up arms in defense of himself and his deeply held ambitions.

11

Dance of Indecision

𝔉or Bert, 22 June 1918 was a day of enormous import. A headline in a New York paper read:

BERT WILLIAMS
NOW A FULL-FLEDGED CITIZEN

Four years before, Bert had applied for citizenship, and now his naturalization papers had finally arrived.[1] Although he had become a citizen, he still faced unresolved concerns about his experiences as a black man in America, both onstage and in society. Perhaps these concerns were even exacerbated by his new status.

One day, Bert dropped by the office of the *New York Age* for a visit and discussed the issue of race. Walton considered him an authority for such a discussion. He explained that Bert "comes in daily contact with more white people than probably any other colored American and is given an excellent opportunity to correctly gauge the attitude of our white fellow Americans towards us."[2]

Bert had become deeply troubled by the realities of American life, particularly following the start of the Great War. He had also become increasingly philosophical. "What is to be the 'ultimate end' of a world in which Germans and Austrians hate Frenchmen and Russians and in which white men despise black men because of a difference in color of the pigment under their skins?" he wondered.[3] He watched as other members of his New York regiment went abroad to serve and observed "the movements of the colored troopers with more interest than is usually displayed by the average civilian." He fervently hoped that their effort "to make the world safe for democracy" would help to "enhance the reputation of the colored warrior for valor."[4] Yet at the same time, Bert continued to experience humiliating discrimination as he traveled the nation.

As much as word of Bert's naturalization was big news—especially in such politically charged times—this story was trumped by another news item related to Bert. The first headline on the front page of the *New York Age* blared:

BERT WILLIAMS
QUITS THE *FOLLIES* IN ATLANTIC CITY.

Citing a "lack of material at hand to make a creditable showing," Bert had decided to withdraw from the show during the tryouts held prior to its New York City opening.[5] His friends claimed "that Ned Wayburn, stage director of the *Follies*, has not shown the proper interest in the comedian's welfare. That the principal fun-maker has not been able to show to best advantage for several seasons, due to poor material and poor 'spots' is common talk in theatrical circles."[6] The *Louisville News* also testified that although "his name was carried to help the show," Bert did not get parts in the revue "commensurate with his ability or reputation." His frustration had come to a head. Although his pay was still as good as ever, particularly in light of the lessening spotlight he received, Bert had decided to leave.[7]

Critics fretted that Bert and Ziegfeld had had a falling out; however, they both assured the press that they were on friendly terms. Bert spoke of Ziegfeld with deep respect, and in meetings with Klaw and Erlanger, they all came to an agreement about his withdrawal. Nonetheless, the fact that Bert withdrew after not having had quality material for several seasons indicated that it had been an escalating concern.

Barely a month after Bert left the *Follies*, however, he resurfaced in Ziegfeld's *Midnight Frolic*. The *Frolic* was a show produced on the New Amsterdam Roof, a secondary stage. It took the same *Follies* audience, a crowd full of the crème de la crème of New York society, like the Rockefeller and Vanderbilt families, and moved them to a theatrical space that was midway between cabaret and theater. Eddie Cantor described it as "a supper club where it cost a person five dollars just to sit down."[8]

Although it was not unusual for entertainers from Ziegfeld's main stage to perform in the *Frolic* in addition to the *Follies*, Bert's choice to perform only in the *Frolic* was extraordinary for someone with his clout. The *Ziegfeld Follies*, more prominent than the *Frolic* as a "prime time" theatrical entertainment, tended to have more seasoned performers as its principals. In 1918, however, the list of comics had lengthened, including Eddie Cantor, W. C. Fields, Frank Carter, Gus Minton, and Harry Kelly, even as the individual slots of time given for their antics had shortened.[9]

Perhaps Bert wanted to try his hand at performance in the more intimate setting of the *Frolic*, where his pacing better suited the environment. He also may have been attracted to the roof—where comics had sway—as opposed to the main stage, where American showgirls dominated. More likely than not, Bert continued with a Ziegfeld production in obeisance to the demands of his contract. Regardless, those in the *Follies* cast whom he left behind sent telegrams with well wishes, including W. C. Fields, Eddie Cantor, and Will Rogers, who had joined the *Follies* in 1917.[10]

The audience cheered Bert as he arrived onstage, giving him "a hearty reception—almost an ovation."[11] His appearance silenced murmurings about his relationship with Ziegfeld, reassuring the public that the two were, indeed, still on good terms. A reviewer announced his use of "new material in every particular—new songs, new jokes, and new dances."[12] Bert "unfolded his quaint monologue in his dry, droll fashion, and gave us some songs which made an instantaneous hit with the capacity audience, earning him a storm of applause which sounded like a barrage and drumfire in one."[13] It appeared to Lester Walton that the *Midnight Frolic* performance was "one of the biggest hits of his career."[14] He reprinted the comments of the *New York Sun*:

> Certainly his popularity is not on the wane, even when it is taken into consideration that sentiment had something to do with his reception. His genially intimate way of talking and his pleasing fashion of singing a song were not tiring in the least. He is a welcome addition to the midnight entertainment, which, it may be said, is as constituted at present, as good if not better than any ever staged on the roof.[15]

When Bert performed on the roof, he found more freedom and attention as there were fewer headlining comedians with whom to share the spotlight. Perhaps he also felt more comfortable in the caberet-style environment.

One of his offerings was "You'll Find Old Dixieland in France." A song that playfully spoke of the absence of "darkies on the Swanee shore," it also recognized the patriotic blacks who "marched away in khaki pants." Bespeaking the reality of black soldiers, albeit with lines that harked back to coon songs, the tune declared, "Instead of pickin' [water]melons off the vine, they're pickin' Germans off the Rhine." Although it retained stereotypical images with its reference to watermelons, the song supplanted them with that of the brave black soldier abroad.

Taking blacks out of the context of dancing and entertainment, the song explained, "They used to play the 'lovin' blues' for ev'ryone/ now they're playin' blues upon a Gatling Gun/ And with Abe Lincoln in their memory/ They've gone to fight for Liberty."[16] Through this performance, Bert had found a way to include blacks as part of the American effort in the Great War. Knowing men from both his New York and Illinois regiments who served abroad, he found a manner of honoring their presence and their contribution to the fight.

While Bert was off from the *Follies*, he invested more time and energy in his work with Columbia, recording new pieces during the late summer and early fall of 1918, one composed by Will Vodery, with whom he maintained a close relationship. "O Death, Where Is Thy Sting?" played on the black preacher's dynamic with his congregation. "When I Return," Will Vodery's composition spoke about reincarnation, which in the song he referred to as "transmigration."[17]

Between February and June of 1919, Bert would return several times to Columbia, recording Prohibition songs following the January 1919 passage of the Volstead Act. The songs "Bring Back Those Wonderful Days" and "Everybody Wants a Key to My Cellar," which became two of his bestsellers, remained in the Columbia catalog for years.[18] He also recorded monologues, which he had not done since his 1913 "lies."

Notably, Bert recorded the Elder Eatmore sermons. Written by Alex Rogers, they featured the relationship between a black preacher and his congregation.[19] Although the sermons might have appeared to be in the coon song vein, they more clearly referenced an in-group of blacks whom Bert mocked through his satirical performance of the "good preacher." For the first time since George had retired from recording years ago, Bert recorded with others. "Elder Eatmore's Sermon on Throwing Stones" and "Elder Eatmore's Sermon on Generosity" included the participation of Alex, Bob Slater, and Mary Straine, who helped set the scene by playing congregation members. These recordings acknowledged a black audience who valued Bert's artistic interpretations and the characters that he fashioned in his performances.[20]

Similar to his story "We Can't Do Nothing Till Martin Gets Here," the Elder Eatmore sermons spoke of the black preacher's travails. In these narratives, however, the preacher turned the tables on his wayward congregations. The first, "Elder Eatmore's Sermon on Generosity," had the shepherd admonishing his flock for their miserly offering. It began with the reading for his sermon:

> I picks my text dis evenin' from de book of 'phesians. De Lawd loveth a cheerful giver! Tonight, my friends, you can omit de "cheerful." De truth is de light! And here is de truth: y'all is way back in my salary! And somethin' has got to be done here dis evenin'. 'Cause if somethin' ain't done, yo' shepherd is gone! Dat's all! Dat is all!

Criticizing his congregation for their neglect of his salary, the preacher admonished them in terms meant to strike fear. Uniting his concern for his wallet with his concern for their immortal souls, he "signified" on them. He cited their insufficient contributions with a revision of the biblical text that applied to their failings. Giving them his truth as their light, he introduced his message. As he continued, he recited the scripture that supported his case: "De Lawd helps them that he'ps theirself!"

For a section of the narrative, the joke turned significantly toward the preacher himself at the same time he implicated others. He described the types of new construction and security measures that made smokehouses and henhouses hard to access:

> Dey's invented locks for 'em, de same as combinations on de Fust National Bank! ["True, True!" a member cries in response] Hmmph! Dat makes it a lot harder fo' all of us! It's pretty nigh ruined me!

Even while the preacher used his message as a means to scold his congregation, he exposed himself as participating in sinful activities. He bemoaned the loss of opportunity for thievery, which most likely necessitated the sermon itself. When he continued he clarified his point:

My friends, I *need*! I need! Tain't no use talkin' 'bout *what* I need: I needs *everything*! From a hat down, and from an overcoat in! No use getting restless brother there now-now-now-now-now, 'cause here is the program. We ain't gwine to pass no plate this evenin'. Y'all is comin' up one at a time and drop your offerings on de table here, whiles I shall look down from the altar here, an eagle eye. We will start with de fust row.

Shamelessly calling on his congregation, Elder Eatmore abolished the practice of a private offering. Instead, he brought all the members forward to obey his command. As they approached, he began to riff on the scripture, so as to emphasize his point. It became a near-challenge to any who would question his words:

Come my lambs! Your shepherd calls unto you sayin': "Give unto me dat I may eat of de bread of life, so dat when dat great day comes, you can meet me in judgment an' shake my hand wit a clearer conscience!"

The preacher then introduced the offering hymn, "We shall build our mansions in the sky by the deeds we sow, de day he come and meet us." The organ began, and in the background, the sounds of jangling tambourines and money being put on a table combined with the congregation of male and female voices. Throughout the offering, the elder called out the names of the congregation, thanking brothers and sisters and complimenting Sister Jenkins: "You lookin' very good this evenin', very good this evenin', yes indeed!" All the while, he cried to his "lambs" that their "shepherd" needed them.

The singing of the hymn continued and Eatmore introduced the next verse:

"And we shall reep our store in de by and by, by what we sow today!" The line created further irony in the narrative. As the preacher urged the members forward to share their resources with him, the congregation's voices swelled in pious sincerity, despite the preacher's demands for more cash.

The hymn progressed for an extended period. In the background, Elder Eatmore more quietly thanked and greeted his now more generous congregation. Then, following the last note of the hymn, he stated in dead seriousness: "Now I'm gon' count it."

In Bert's other monologue, "Elder Eatmore's Sermon on Throwing Stones," the preacher scolded his congregation for criticizing him. Again, he introduced the topic of his sermon with a biblical text:

The elder is in bad humor this mo'nin'. I picks my text from de 11th of the Ecclesiastidese [*sic*]: "He that is amongst you without sin, let 'im throw the fust rock." What it says is, "Let him cast the fust stone," but I ain't takin' no chances on you all misunderstandin' me. Fo' twenty years you all been throwin' rocks at one another, but you wasn't satisfied. You had to commence throwin' 'em at me!

Warming up to his subject, the preacher forewarned the congregation of the lesson yet to be learned. He presented it as a scriptural exegesis rather than a personal complaint. In anticipation and perhaps fear, one female member of the congregation cried, "Uh, uh!" in dismay. But this did not deter the elder:

Uh, uh, nothin'! But I ain't gon' warn y'all no more, but in de language of dat great prophet, Henry Shakespeare: [Said slowly] 'Watch yo' step! Watch yo' step!' What did Nicademus say? I says, what did Nicademus say? He says, 'Wash me, and I shall be whiter than snow.'

Combining erroneous quotations with biblical passages, Elder Eatmore set the tone for the sermon as if to bring forth confession from guilty members. He pursued this even as one shouted "Amen!" as though in agreement with him. Refusing to be fooled by a willing church member when issuing a jeremiad, Eatmore cried in response, "That's all right, too! And there's a lot of you all here this mor'nin' think you been washed. You ain't even been sponged!"

The preacher's resistant congregation seemed unprepared for his speech. One man grunted in disagreement. Despite this, however, the elder told a story leading to his decision to bring a jealous, gossiping party forward for punishment, amid cries of disbelief and disgust:

On night befo' last, Thanksgiving, I think it was long 'bout midnight. Certain brother—he's sittin' right here out there—certain brother was comin' down the road, totin' a bag, and he sees another brother totin' another bag, and gettin' over a fence. Both bags was occupied. Now, neither one of these brothers spoke, but a sound from the bag of de brother on de fence indicated that he had secured the main article for his Thanksgivin' dinner.

Uh, huh! Now, on dat other certain brother had in his sack a member of de same family, but it wasn't exactly de kind of a bird generally used fo' Thanksgivin' dinner!

> And this fills dat certain brothuh's heart so full of jealousy and malice that he goes straight home and tells his wife what he seen and dat does upset her.

The minister proceeded, and a member cried out, "Ain't it de truth!" Thinking that he was being encouraged, the elder shouted, "You know it's de truth! You know it's de truth!" He went on to speak about a chain of rumors resulting in "ev'ry member of dis congregation here . . . whisperin' around that I, me, me [laughs] had stole a turkey!"

Taking advantage of his superior position as minister, Elder Eatmore threatened to start throwing rocks in the future. He then attempted to expose the culprit, demanding, "Now dat certain brother dat I been talkin' 'bout will kindly lead us in prayer." Only too late did Elder Eatmore realize, however, that he had created the perfect opportunity for that member to, in turn, signify on him. The member reversed their roles, calling Eatmore himself the guilty party:

> [partly singing the prayer]
> De scripture says dat who God would let destroy, is who dey fust makes mad. . . . And Elder Eatmore sho' is actin' crazy! [Eatmore: "Now there, there, there, there, there!"] Only Thursday night was it, that I had to almost tote home, that I almost had to carry home bodily! [Eatmore: "No, no, wait a minute! Now wait here!"] Mmm, yes, he was so full of applejack! And who was it, who was it I said, that stole de lodge money? I said who was it, Lawd, dat stole de lodge's money and lost it playin' "five up" down in Sister Mamie Crawford's?

In a tone of embarrassment, the preacher stopped the proceedings, calling "Doxology, doxology, doxology!" The music started in response. He dismissed the congregation with a hurried yell: "Use all the doors! Use all the doors! Use all the doors! We are all leavin' now. All leavin'!"

Throughout these two monologues, Bert spoke to those within the black community as though they were his only audience. The participation of male and female voices, in the form of call and response, added detail and realism to his rendering. He playfully made both the congregation and the minister himself the butt of the joke, their conversation indicative of a much less formal relationship between them than the setting within the church would otherwise suggest.

With such in-group jokes in his recordings, Bert continued to reach a black audience. He spoke in references that communicated well to the audience of blacks who could understand and interpret the comical situations he created. Rather than playing a limited darky defined by minstrelsy, he created a new voice. Furthermore, with evenhanded joke structures that called forth the putatively superior preacher as much as the supposedly subordinate congregation, the monologues amused blacks without simultaneously ridiculing them. Even as he engaged in recordings that served a black public, Bert continued to seek theatrical opportunities that might speak to both his audiences—as well as his professional interests.

Over the years, Bert had added to his store of characters. His nuanced hard-luck Jonah Man had become the quintessence of undeserved misery. With Leon Errol, his methodical porter had got the upper hand opposite the jumpy, loquacious tourist. As a West Indian hallboy, he out-talked his callers and tenants in quick-witted lines through which he had the last word. In his scene with Eddie Cantor, he became the disappointed patriarch facing his immature son. Here, he returned to the black audiences in a new way, creating not only a character but an entire world that reflected their understanding. In the Elder Eatmore sermons, the black audience became priority number one. Interestingly, despite Columbia's knowledge of Bert's success in storytelling onstage, the company waited almost a year before releasing the sermons to the public.

When not recording with Columbia, Bert remained connected to audiences through vaudeville performances. Even as he continued to perform in the *Midnight Frolic*, he also headlined at the Palace and other theaters in the city. He performed in vaudeville two times a day, also keeping the late hours that the *Frolic*'s after-hours show required.[21] At times, dragging himself back home at the end of the night, he would have to hold the railing as he pulled himself up the steps. Chappy, his ever-faithful valet, would walk behind him, there to offer him support.[22]

Critics described vaudeville audiences of mixed races and, especially, crowds of blacks, who filled balconies and galleries.[23] Importantly, they noted his artistry as they mentioned his "far carrying voice. . . . It seemed as if there wasn't a corner of the big playhouse too remote to catch his lowest word."[24] This was no accident. Bert explained his painstaking technique:

> I study carefully the acoustics of each theatre I appear in. There is always one particular spot on the stage from which the voice carries better, more clearly and easily than from any other. I make it my business to find that

spot before the first performance, and once I find it I stick to it like a
postage stamp. People have sometimes observed that I practice unusual
economy of motion and do not move about as much as other singers do.
It is to spare my voice and not my legs that I stand still while delivering a
song. If my voice were stronger I would be as active as anybody, because
it is much easier to put a song over if you can move about.[25]

Bert's description attested to the simplicity of his approach. Even as he
revealed his secrets, he retained his stamp of individuality. Ironically, he
also shored up his individuality when he shared his craft.

In part, Bert's voice made his vaudeville performances inimitable:
"Low, soft, a joy to the ear, yet not losing a bit of its masculinity or firm-
ness. When he talks to you it is as if he has a secret to confide that
concerns just you two."[26] Although he never actually addressed his audiences directly, Bert nonetheless brought them into his confidence,
even in the impersonal space of a large auditorium.

His movement was no less significant, whether that of his body or
his eyes. To Bert, movements continued to be important. At a time
when leading entertainers conformed to one style of exaggerated physicality, Bert brought his own unique interpretation. His use of expression had equal power. A *Chicago Record-Herald* writer explained:

His eyes are no less attractive than his voice for he uses them to emphasize what he is saying. In them is a commingling of pathos, humor and
"dead-earnestness" that charms you and holds your gaze until he is
ready to release your interest. Here is something inexplicably fascinating about such a humanly sympathetic personality, some quality that is
irresistible.[27]

Combining various elements as he played onstage, Bert invented a
magnetic character. He charmed and drew audiences to him—audiences whose thunderous applause stopped only when stage managers
turned off the theater's lights to persuade them that Bert's performance was over.[28]

In spite of Bert's presence and the positive reviews of his performance, no one could be certain what size audience the *Frolic* would
attract to its late-night cabaret setting when the Volstead Act discontinued the distribution and manufacture of alcohol on 1 July. Perhaps attracted to the certain audience as well as the higher potential for

Bert Williams. COURTESY OF THE YALE COLLECTION OF AMERICAN LITER-
ATURE, BEINECKE RARE BOOK AND MANUSCRIPT LIBRARY

visibility in the earlier main stage production, Bert decided to return to
the *Ziegfeld Follies of 1919.*

Before the season began, however, he spoke critically—though playfully—about the challenging Ziegfeld audiences. Asked how he keeps
up with new laughs, he joked, "Is there really a new laugh? Speaking of
new laughs, they are only younger than the old ones, and not quite so
sincere."[29] He joked about old material and new, old audiences and new.
He also discussed the issue of control:

There were times when I was trying out a new song, when I could feel it dying, and I seemed to be hanging on by first one finger, then another, till there was only the little finger left to hold on by.

Yes sir, the new laugh can be awful shy, it can be a timid, tiny little thing that turns against you, and leaves you to perish where you stand, and often does.[30]

Laughter was elusive. He might have thought he controlled the audience, but he soon realized that it controlled him. A comedian could home in on the "laugh" itself, but Bert knew the audience's unpredictability. They could kill the comedian, if the comedian failed to "kill" them, amusing them with his jokes. Who was responsible, Bert asked, if the comedian did his best, but to no avail?

I have often wondered whether an audience does not violate its constitutional rights when it refuses to laugh. When an audience has paid money, including the war tax, to be amused, why isn't it? It has every right to be, and yet sometimes there are actions in the audience that indicate it is not. Sometimes they blame actors, and yet the actor believes he is funny. Is it his fault if the audience is not happy?[31]

His final question concerned transmission. If a good joke—in the comedian's opinion—went out to the audience, but ended up dying, who had failed? It was, after all, the audience, in the end, who determined the performer's success.

In a tongue-in-cheek discussion about the New York audience, Bert created a humorous way of venting his irritation with resistant (white) audience members. He irreverently described them as "a species of half-human-half-stone images, whom I call for short[,] the morbs."

The morbs are born in New York of speedy, but unthrifty parentage. They congregate in places where the lights are glaring. As time rolls over them, they gradually go blind and deaf, acquiring a facial paralysis. They have seen so much, they know so much, and they have so little in return for their wisdom that they have become morbid. Honestly it makes your heart ache to look at their faces. They seem to be spending their money like dead men, as though they didn't care what happened.[32]

These most dissatisfied audience members never expected to be amused, despite their pursuit of entertainment. Perhaps not even knowing how to enjoy themselves, ruined by excessive experience, the morbs were the ultimate immovable audience. Ever-present spectators, nothing impressed them. Privileged, evidently a nouveau riche group—"of speedy but unthrifty parentage"—this crowd's incessant ennui closed them off from comedy.

Bert noted other difficult members of the audience. When an audience member reached "the age just beyond the years of indiscretion, on the edge of innocuous desuetuede [sic]," he became a difficult person for the performer to win over.[33] These analytical spectators, deep in thought, could "make any comedian feel like a strange bug, pinned down under a microscope."[34]

Being a comedian who craved freedom and needed space for his varying performative techniques, Bert felt cornered by such audience members. These "students of the drama," as he termed them, could be young or old, but supposedly loved the theater and followed the careers of actors closely. He imagined an exchange between two such pretentious—and presumptuous—students:

> 1st student of the drama—"As I remember him (of course this is a long time ago, when I was more susceptible to the theatre perhaps, and less exacting in my standards). He had an unction, a *je ne sais quoi*, a mimicry that was truly African."
>
> 2nd student of the drama—"African humor as I recall it in my college days was chiefly delightful, because it had that inimitable banjo flavor. Does he play the banjo?"[35]

Not only professing knowledge regarding the theater generally, but also regarding the performer specifically, students of the drama assessed the actor's value. They examined his act and classified his talent. As they observed the black actor, these critics appreciated only representations consistent with the legacy of minstrelsy. Their pomposity irritated Bert, but their presumptions about the black performer thoroughly infuriated him. They pinned the inventive entertainer down to a single acceptable performance style, which they themselves determined.

Bert's comical impersonation included mockery of his subjects' comments about the actor's private life, as well: "I understand he is a very serious chap outside of his profession. Reads by himself, don't you know, and all that."[36] The condescending spectators respected nothing. Their limited perspectives on black performance extended to their views of the performer's personal life. Bert addressed their ignorance, preferring to deride them rather than believe himself to be subject to their whims.

Arming himself against a contrary crowd that both wanted the new and the performances of the past, Bert explained: "The funnier I try to be the thicker the ice spreads. [This audience member] seems to grow remorseful, on the whole, I am sure he prefers the San Francisco minstrels and he misses the banjo. He takes you seriously, and you wish he wouldn't. There is neither an old laugh nor a new laugh in him."[37]

Bert knew that the audience's retrogressive views, their desire to see the old Negro onstage despite his attempt at innovation, could not likely be conquered. There was no laugh in those audience members. It was as though their feeling of superiority barred them from seeing a joke. The students of drama took Bert seriously, believed that his acts were true. And Bert retaliated with a comical reaction to their rigidity.

Speaking about the particulars of winning over an audience, Bert reminded readers that his material and persona constituted only part of the equation for success as a performer. He also emphasized the audience: "It's not the work one does that gets him [the performer] anywhere; it's keeping everlasting at it until the public knows you. You have to be memorized by that same public. Once they 'film' you in their memory favorably, the picture stays. The public is loyal. If they like one thing you do, you can always get an encore to do that over again."[38] After the performer or comedian did everything in his power to be remembered, the audience then had control. Although a positive result was that they were loyal with long memories, an unfortunate result was that, as the audience desperately desired amusement, it attempted to choose its terms.

Later that month, Bert returned to the *Follies*. He appeared in "He Seldom Misses," a scene about marksmanship, in which he played the unfortunate assistant to a sharpshooter (newcomer George LeMaire) in a shooting gallery. He also took the role of Mr. Bones in the *Follies*' version of a minstrel show. Finally, he sang Prohibition tunes in a skit on the subject. Critic Henry Finck seemed forced to admit that "his song specialty lost effect through the fact that the songs he had to sing were not worth the while of this inimitable artist."[39]

Like Finck, Bert's public remained largely dissatisfied with the offerings. His return to the *Follies* had not improved matters. Furthermore, the material had been disappointing in terms of quality and content. Bert had unbelievably found himself once again playing an endman in a minstrel show.

The Prohibition skit and its related songs did, however, have some strengths. In "When the Moon Shines on the Moonshine," Bert spoke of out-of-business bars and distilleries that lay fallow after Prohibition's enactment on 1 July 1919. He expressed hope only as he recounted in the chorus:

> *But in the mountaintops,*
> *Far from the eyes of cops,*
> *Oh, how the moon shines on the moonshine so merrily,*
> *Oh, oh for once!*[40]

A comical song with echoes of "How Dry I Am," the tune reflected more than the sad state of the soon-to-be-dry nation. It also reflected Bert's own lost chances for socialization. Saloons had remained important to Bert for socialization: they had provided ways in which he could interact with other people in his profession.

In order to have the social interaction he craved, he trolled the saloons at varying times so that he might find and meet with his white colleagues. He explained to his friend Ashton Stevens: "You see, I knew your time for this place, knew Brother [Ring] Lardner's time for that place—I had everybody's schedule, and it required a lot of drinking on my part when you were all on time at your favorite drinking places. . . . I always said I was waiting for somebody . . . even when I was only waiting for anybody. . . . Funny what a man'll do for human companionship!"[41] Desperate to socialize with others in the business, Bert matched his schedule to theirs. When all else failed, he waited around, in a constant search for company.

During Prohibition, Bert would have no shortage of sources for alcohol. The bootleggers found Bert: his reputation had preceded him. The irony is that, although he'd established himself as a drinking man, it had actually been his thirst for company that had kept him in the bars.

*A*lthough Bert was without social company or professional satisfaction, he remained a supporter of colleagues, even during his weak showing in the *Ziegfeld Follies of 1919*. That year Eddie Cantor became famous for his "osteopath scene," during which he got "thumped, thwacked, and twisted into a cruller on the stage." After Cantor's first performance of the scene, the two had begun to amuse themselves. At

Bert's suggestion, they counted each other's laughs when not on-stage. Bert went up first and delivered a hilarious monologue. When it was over, Cantor told him, "Bert, you got twenty-nine laughs."[42]

After Cantor performed his scene and headed to the wings, Bert stood shaking his head. "You got just one laugh," he stated. At Cantor's confusion, he elaborated, "Well, it lasted from the time you got on till the time you came off."[43] Throughout 1919 critics lauded Cantor as "hugely funny."[44]

As the *Follies* comedian entertained New York's toniest crowds over the summer, and black men returned to the States having served abroad in the war, Northern and Southern cities exploded in race riots initiated by whites. The summer of 1919 would become known as "Red Summer" with the three most violent riots occurring in Washington D.C., Chicago, and Elaine, Arkansas.[45] The nation's capital became embroiled in racial violence from the 19th to the 23rd of July, resulting in the deaths of four whites and two blacks.[46] Most widely reported was the Chicago riot, which began on 27 July when white bathers attempted to drive blacks out of their claimed section of the Twenth-ninth Street beach, throwing rocks at interlopers.[47] Tensions escalated when a black boy drowned and police pursued a black man for the arrest rather than the white man involved. For nearly two weeks, the city was in chaos as looting, snipers' gunfire, and arson plagued Chicago. Whites fought, and blacks fought back.[48] In October of that year, Elaine, Arkansas, would be the scene of another violent riot, by the end of which twenty-five blacks and five whites had been killed.[49] Despite Bert's hopes for change after blacks' support of the Great War, the violent outbreaks confirmed the continuing resistance to blacks' participation in society on equal terms.

Even as it appeared to be set at a safe distance from conflict in the country, change would come to Ziegfeld's *Follies*. During the summer, a dispute developed among actors who were members of Actors' Equity Association, an organization in negotiations with theater managers. The Producing Managers' Association (PMA) wished to break the Equity, which demanded not only standard contracts for its members but also union representation for arbitration of grievances.[50] During that summer, the actors decided to strike. Ziegfeld, secretly a member of the PMA, did not expect the members of his revue—as performers in musical comedy, exempt from this decision—to strike as well, but they did. Ziegfeld went so far as to get a court order to prevent his actors from carrying through with the strike, but the actors defied him. On 7 August 1919, the Actors' Equity strike began.[51] By 13 August, led by Eddie Cantor, the members of the *Follies* cast gathered and struck, marching over to the Actors Equity headquarters.[52]

All actors struck—that is, all but Bert. Apparently, he had not been informed of the strike. He later recounted what happened to W. C. Fields, his colleague from the show:

> I went to the theater as usual, made up and dressed. Then I came out of my dressing room and found the big auditorium empty and the strike on. I knew nothing of it: I had not been told. You see, I just didn't belong. So then . . . I went back to my dressing room, washed up and went upon the roof. It all seemed like a nightmare.
>
> There on the roof stood the manager talking with a small group of men. He saw me and said, "Well Bert, are you with us or against us?" I said[,] "Do you want me with you? Then I went home. . . . I went into the library and closed the door. . . .
>
> Then I arranged some chairs in a semi-circle and held a meeting. I started the *Bert Williams Equity*. First I was the president and opened the meeting, and then I was each succeeding officer and I made little speeches—any way [*sic*] I had my own little equity and that is what I called it. I held briefs for both sides, because you see, I don't belong to either side. Nobody really wants me.[53]

Bert felt especially disinclined to take to the streets in protest, or to become part of the organization's struggle. He had no place where he could claim membership: even after nearly ten years, he did not feel fully part of the *Follies*.

As always, Bert found himself caught between worlds, with neither one to claim as his own. Throughout his career, his great leaps in achievement had placed him among leading members of the profession, yet at a distance. While he crossed the color line, he moved farther away from the black public, who at times viewed him with skepticism. It seemed that no matter what action he chose, he was always the outsider.

Eddie Cantor later told of a New Year's Eve that Bert and he had planned to spend together. While out of town, they arranged to have dinner together at the hotel where Bert was "permitted to live provided he used the back elevator." As they headed out the stage door, Cantor reiterated their plan to meet up at the hotel for their meal after he picked up the food. Bert agreed. Then, as they parted, Bert said that he was on his way to the back elevator.[54]

As Cantor listened, he noticed that Bert's voice betrayed the merest trace of bitterness. Speechless, he stopped, and the two stood together "in understanding silence." Then, Bert opened up, just for a moment: "It wouldn't be so bad, Eddie, if I didn't still hear the applause ringing in my years."[55]

Even though he had experienced moments of camaraderie within the company, Bert also had to constantly remind himself of boundaries. A colleague in the *Follies*, Nat M. Willis would say that "Bert Williams is a gentleman," yet would do so referring to the fact that he "minds his own business."[56] The Southerner, who seemed especially entitled to vet the black comedian, assured other whites of Bert's suitable deference. He spoke of Bert's exceptional conduct, his "manliness and tact."[57] Willis's words, while flattering, demonstrated the truth that someone was always watching Bert, examining his behavior, and assessing his comportment.

Although Bert's exclusion from participation in the Actor's Equity strike may not have been the only factor in his subsequent move from the *Follies*, it seemed decisive. The strike emphasized that Bert had nowhere to belong. Perhaps it was the poignancy of Bert's story, though most likely apocryphal, that inspired Fields to say, "Bert Williams was the funniest man I ever saw and the saddest man I ever knew. I often wonder whether other people sensed what I did in him—that deep undercurrent of pathos."[58]

After years of working with members of the cast while being set apart from them, traveling with the *Follies* cast on the road while not being fully free to socialize with them, and starring as a featured player while not having artistic opportunities available to him, Bert could no longer endure the environment. Perhaps he no longer possessed the optimism to try to fit into the *Follies* setting, thereby continuing to face segregation and double standards, especially when on the road. Ironically, when he picked up after leaving Ziegfeld's productions, he pursued a project with some of the former *Follies* members, including Eddie Cantor—who had broken from Ziegfeld—performing in a revue of their own.

12

A Fresh Start

Bert didn't share his reasons for leaving the *Follies* the second time. Between his experience during the actors' strike and his unsatisfactory material, however, he had grounds. Whatever his reasons, he did finally leave and did not return. In 1920, he starred in a revue, *Broadway Brevities*, produced by George LeMaire, his former *Follies* colleague. LeMaire was the man entirely responsible for writing the show, clearly influenced by Ziegfeld's and others' revues. A straightman in the production, he played opposite Bert in two scenes.[1]

Before the show's run, a *Chicago Whip* writer had announced Bert's agreement to appear in *Broadway Brevities* after he completed his engagement with the *Follies*. With the assurance that Bert would be "given much more latitude in the matter of using original comedy than he was allowed in the *Follies*," the journalist awaited the show's eventual arrival in Chicago.[2]

Billed as a star, with "[t]he letters of his name blazed out over the door of the Winter Garden in electric lights," Bert enjoyed a status he had held only when headlining in vaudeville between seasons in the *Follies*. "This was the first time that the particular reward-for-merit, which incandescents symbolize on Broadway, had been his."[3] As opposed to earlier years in which such status had resulted in controversy and the subsequent withdrawal of Bert's deserved privilege, this time audiences and colleagues embraced the honor. LeMaire's great respect for

Bert Williams, the Gentleman. COURTESY OF THE YALE COLLECTION
OF AMERICAN LITERATURE, BEINECKE RARE BOOK AND MANUSCRIPT
LIBRARY

Bert testified to his decision to give the comedian star status: "I admired him as an artist, tremendously because he was a *great artist*. In fact, he was so great that it was impossible for him to do anything he did on the stage, [*sic*] badly."[4] In this project, Bert's fellow cast members were his biggest fans.

Broadway Brevities consisted of twenty-two scenes featuring numerous chorus girls and various comedians. Bert's strongest showings were in the first act, singing in a segment named "That Inimitable Comedian—Bert Williams," and a second act sketch, "The Smart Bootery."

He sang eight pieces in the production, many of which he had performed in the *Ziegfeld Follies of 1919*. Three selections stood out in his new show and would be recorded at Columbia along with three others in the fall of 1920.[5]

His first song, "I Want to Know Where Tosti Went," was a partial parody in first person. The title referred to Italian singer Paolo Tosti's famous piece, "Addio."[6] Spoken in dialect, Bert's song featured a savvy character:

> *Ain't got no ejucation, but I was born with mother wit,*
> *On any kind of subject, can converse a little bit;*
> *You all heared about the elephant's mem'ry,*
> *Well mine is just that way;*
> *Jus' anything that's taught to me,*
> *Right in my brain'll stay;*

Throughout the verse, Bert delivered his lines conversationally. Similarly to the memory of Samuel in "How? Fried," the character's memory was linked to knowledge. Although not formally trained, he was savvy, with "mother wit" that served him well. As he continued the chorus, he provided specifics to substantiate his claim:

> *I know just where Columbus went when he called from sunny Spain,*
> *I know what causes thunder, and I know what causes rain;*
> *My great-granddaddy left to me, a book on ancient history,*
> *I know 'bout Adam and Eve, in the garden of Eden,*
> *'Cause I been reading;*

> *I know 'bout Peter and Paul,*
> *Co'se I don't know it all;*
> *Know all 'bout those planets though, up in the sky. . . .*

Like Uncle Benjamin of "How? Fried," this character had inherited a skill that evidently amounted to more than "mother wit." He read the Bible, the historically central text for the education of many African Americans, yet he also knew ancient history. Not only did this character possess knowledge, he also had curiosity. The joke lay in the character's expression of curiosity *and* Bert's own display of his true singing skills. He first recited then sang:

I can solve most any kind o' mystery,
But there's one thing that's been puzzlin' me,
I want to know where Tosti went when he said,

[singing] "Goodbye, forever, goodbye forever,"
I want to know where Tosti went when he said "Goodbye."

The final lines sung featured Bert's baritone voice in a powerful and stylized rendition of the very chords that Tosti himself sang. Coming after his extensive references to his knowledge, the comparatively insignificant issue of knowing "where Tosti went" emphasized irony.

A witty piece through which Bert used dialect yet illustrated his character's encyclopedic knowledge, the song moved toward an ironic representation of what might have initially seemed to be an ignorant character. The clear contradiction of his lack of education and the quantity of information he knew escalated dramatically in the second verse. He stated that he did not know how to read a note of music, yet cited Wagner and Rubinstein before returning to his final question about the whereabouts of Tosti. Bert had thus expanded his typical Jonah Man character.

"Eve Cost Adam Just One Bone" was Bert's first-person meditation on the relative ease of Adam's life with Eve compared to life in the present day:[7]

Everybody knows the story, how Adam gave his rib for Eve,
Everybody thinks it's awful, the way she caused poor Ad' to grieve;
But I've thought the matta over, and here's the reason why, Yessuh!
I've come to this conclusion that Adam was a lucky guy:

CHORUS
Eve cost Adam just one bone,
Uh, he couldn't get away with that today;
He never had no sealskin coats to buy,
And there was no mill'naire bills to pay;

She gave him trouble, and he never got the blues,
She liked to raise a little Cain, too, that is a fact;
Still she only cost him just one bone,
And you can't expect too doggone much for that;
[spoken as an aside] Can you now, huh? Hah-hah-hah!

Here, the Jonah Man character developed with a different inflection. With an up-tempo tune, the song implicitly referred to the misery of the narrator. The song also retained a vaudevillian critique of married life, a milder version of the often misogynistic jokes of such later performers as Henry (a.k.a. Henny) Youngman ("Take my wife, please!").

> *Eve had several thousand dresses,*
> *All growing on a tree, they say;*
> *And there were lots of woman here now, Yessuh!*
> *Must think that they grow that way today.*

> *Look at all these big fur jackets,*
> *And sealskin coats they wear;*
> *The kind of skin that Eve wore,*
> *Certainly must have been a little bare [or bear?].*

Throughout the chorus with its variation, the narrator continued to argue for the preferable position of Adam. Although he gave his rib, and Eve gave him trouble with her fondness for apples, Adam "owned the earth," which made all the difference. Speaking the song with a light and playful tone, Bert created a differing interpretation for his song of woe, all the while using the singing style that had made him famous.

An instance of Bert's intragroup jokes, "You'll Never Need a Doctor No More" told the story of the sick Deacon Jones who visited with Dr. Bones, a doctor who gave him a cure likely to make him so sick he'll "never need a doctor no more." A multiverse tale about black characters, "You'll Never Need a Doctor No More" featured Deacon Jones, who was unaware of why the doctor should wish him ill, and Matilda Jenkins, who admonished the deacon. Despite being in a different vein from the Elder Eatmore sermons, which were spoken rather than sung, "You'll Never Need a Doctor No More" paralleled them with its creation of an entirely black world:

> *You a fool to send for Dr. Bones,*
> *Don't you know the doctor's sore on you;*
> *Sho' he loved dat Widow Brown,*
> *You was kinda likin' her too;*

> *Don't you remember how peculia' it was how her husband died,*
> *Why he, the way dat man suffered, the neighbors all cried;*

His chance for life was so slim,
And here's what Dr. Bones prescribed for him. . . .

Weaving a tale about an incident within the black community, Bert painted a picture. He made the spoken song function as a monologue in the way his narratives without music did. Bert continued as Matilda Jenkins, citing the lethal "cure" that ended Mr. Brown's life:

A watermelon, and peach ice cream,
Sour milk, apple sauce, and spinach greens;
Puddin', prunes and rice, a half-cooked shad,
Dozen eggs, and half the eggs bad;

Some corned beef and cabbage, some lima beans,
Oh my! It was an awful cure, 'deed it was!
And don't you know Brother Brown went and ate
everything he was told to eat?
You see the reason he don't need a doctor no mo'?

Partly warning, partly gossip, the piece echoed the natural exchange between friends. The only exaggeration in their discourse came during the lines about the jealous Dr. Bones's retaliatory cure. A doctor who warped his healing powers in order to punish foes, a man more likely to usher his patients into the grave than into wellness, the nefarious Dr. Bones's reputation preceded him, indicated by his very name. In the character of the sincere and all-knowing keeper of truth, Matilda Jenkins, the goodly Deacon Jones—a man of the church—gained protection. With the dark joke focusing on Dr. Bones and his contemptible acts, the song avoided collapsing all the characters into stereotype.

Another scene titled "The Smart Bootery" had developed during an exchange between George LeMaire and Bert. Both tall men with large feet, the two commiserated one day about the suffering they endured when buying and keeping shoes. So difficult was it to find a pair of comfortable and reliable shoes that they would wear the same ones day after day, rather than "break in" a new pair. Bert explained that although he had a closet of shoes all in a row, he would merely look at them occasionally, subsequently returning to wear the same old pair.[8]

For Bert, his problem was more than merely a bother. It indicated the circulation problems that continued to plague him. Nonetheless, he determined to make it fodder for a sketch. In the scene, Bert arrives at George's store. A pained and nervous would-be customer, he desperately needs shoes. Several times, Bert attempts to enter the store but ducks away until the clerk finally addresses him: "What can I do for you?" To that, Bert responds, "I'd like a pair of yalla shoes." He selects the shoes, a size fifteen, tries them on in front of a mirror, and finally buys them, satisfied. He then tosses his old ones away and leaves the store.

Following the exchange between clerk and customer, numerous chorus girls enter dancing. The interval signals the passage of time and the gaiety that transpires as the customer is elsewhere, presumably enjoying his shoes. After that interlude, however, Bert returns, hobbling. He digs in the garbage can to find his old shoes and clutches them in his arms after discarding the new "yalla" ones in disgust. He sings a closing piece, "Cruel and Brutal," then exits shoeless.[9]

Despite being tailored to the shoe-buying fiasco, Bert's song was a typical Bert Williams tune. This time, however, rather than being overlooked by family and friends, the unfortunate Jonah Man's very own feet tormented him:

> *The only trouble with my feet is that they hurt; that's all,*
> *They constantly remind me every time they rise and fall;*
> *Because they do not hurt the same,*
> *I call them each by a different name;*
> *Cruel, is the left one here, and Brutal is the other's name.*

Bert recounted a sad and silly story of owning "cruel and brutal" feet, yet the scene preceding set the tone for the audience's empathy. Having seen the character's suffering prior to the song, the audience could better commiserate:

> *Cruel, Brutal, they know not what they do to me,*
> *There ain't a thing about the weather they don't know;*
> *When that big front toe on Brutal starts its own peculiar pain,*
> *I don't need to read no paper, man, I know it's going to rain;*

> *And Cruel has a power to predict a thunder shower,*
> *By swelling till with pain my brain has reeled;*

On the callouses and other things
that bud and blossom every spring,
'Way down yonder in my cornfield!'[10]

Specifying his aches and pains, the Jonah Man cried for mercy while knowing that his pain was ceaseless. Like the stories of "Nobody" and "Constantly," he knew he would find no relief.

On opening night a "large and friendly" audience showed up to see Bert, LeMaire, and Eddie Cantor, all being popular comedians.[11] Some reviewers, excited, declared the production a hit, but the show would close after a mere thirteen weeks. A charitable reviewer from the *New York Evening Post* acknowledged its combination of good and bad acts, a truth of any vaudeville show, but insisted that rewrites would be necessary. Prescient, the writer stated that "some speed will have to be used in the process of elimination or it may be too late."[12]

In general, the revue appeared derivative to its critics, inviting statements about its status as a lesser *Follies*. It featured a series of chorus girls, whose glamour impressed but could hardly compare with the *sui generis* Glorified girls of the *Follies*. Furthermore, some of the scenes, such as that in which Eddie Cantor got twisted and turned by a dentist, were obvious variations on sketches done in the original *Follies* to great acclaim. The most optimistic of the critics depended on the show's clear relationship to the *Follies* as a sign that it could survive as an annual.[13]

Even Bert bore some of the criticism. One reviewer stated: "Bert Williams was amusing in spots. [H]is songs were poor and sometimes in bad taste."[14] Although the writer did not specify which songs, it is possible that "Eve Cost Adam Just One Bone" and "You'll Never Need a Doctor No More" were the culprits. Bert's playful manner of commenting on the biblical couple might have been considered too risqué, and the notion that a doctor would kill his own patients perhaps seemed outré to the critic. In this instance, it seemed that Bert's choice of material did not quite pass the "cleanness" test against which he continually had to measure himself.

As Bert sought other roles and prepared to delve himself into another production, the rave reviews of Eugene O'Neill's *The Emperor Jones* reached him. The show had opened off Broadway on 1 November 1920, a production by the Provincetown Players performed at the Playwright's Theatre on McDougal Street in Greenwich Village.[15] Within a month, it would move to Broadway.

Charles Gilpin, a former Williams and Walker Company member, played the title role. As one proud writer expressed, "the credit given Charley is of the sort that makes the world sit up and look when the critics involved are concerned."[16] Heywood Broun praised his performance at length:

> He sustains the succession of scenes in monologue not only because his voice is one of a gorgeous natural quality, but because he knows just what to do with it. All the notes are there and he has also an extraordinary facility for being in the right place at the right time. . . . One performance is not enough to entitle a player to the word great, even from a not too careful critic, but there can be no question whatever that in *The Emperor Jones* Gilpin is great. It is a performance of a heroic stature.[17]

The Emperor Jones was, in James Weldon Johnson's words, "another important page in the history of the Negro in the theatre. . . . By his work in *The Emperor Jones* Gilpin reached the highest point of achievement on the legitimate stage that had yet been achieved by a Negro in America."[18] Unlike David Belasco, O'Neill had dared to write a dramatic role for a black man. Gilpin had triumphed in the part. In later periods, blacks would denounce O'Neill's characterization of Brutus Jones as an archetypal savage, noble at best. During its time, however, many would congratulate Gilpin on his success and O'Neill on his audacity.

White critics would affirm the appeal of the play as the "tragedy of fear of a Negro porter and ex-convict, turned primitive man again, unfolds itself before the fascinated imagination."[19] *The Emperor Jones* tells of Brutus Jones, a hubristic, murderous Pullman Porter who becomes dictator of an unnamed West Indian island and is later dogged by the rebellious subjects who demand his ousting. The play included long monologues, which gave its leading actor room to develop the hero/villain he played. It was, in fact, a coup for Gilpin to have secured the substantive role.

Some would claim that Bert enjoyed Gilpin's performance in the production, proud of his achievement.[20] Others, like friend Tom Fletcher, would speak of the sadness Bert felt that Gilpin received this extraordinary break: "One of the things Bert couldn't understand, and it worried him slightly, was about Charles becoming a star before him. Charley, he would point out, was just a chorus boy in one of the Williams and Walker shows, and now he had stardom."[21]

Bert had his own idea of what stardom was, and while he was famous, he did not see himself as a star. Yes, he had starred in history-making black musical theater productions with Williams and Walker. It was true that he had gone on to big-time vaudeville, crossing the color line. It was also a fact that he had done so again when he became the first black actor in Ziegfeld's *Follies*, and then topped that achievement by becoming the highest-paid principal.

To all of those folks who crowded the audience each night, Bert was already a star. Bert's idea of stardom, however, was specific and particular:

> When you are the star of the show and unable to appear, the company closes until the star can appear. If you can't come back, then the company stays closed. When Gilpin was unable to appear, the show would close.[22]

To Bert, his own status in the *Follies* as one principal among many had made him less than a star. Moreover, the rejection he experienced toward the end of his tenure in the annual revue left him even more doubtful than ever about his clout. Watching his former company member play a dramatic role that Bert himself likely coveted, as well as receive star treatment in a Broadway show, which Bert felt entitled to but never received, Bert became pained and saddened.

Despite Bert's perhaps understandable feelings about Gilpin's qualifications, the actor had been establishing himself in the profession for years. Although he had starred as a member of the Williams and Walker Company, Gilpin had distinguished himself as a performer. Claiming that he had always wished to do "real" acting, "not the comical kind," he had quickly set his sights on such work. During the term of exile, he abandoned Broadway aspirations to perform in the Pekin Players in Chicago. Looking back, he would say about his foray into dramatic theater, "The people came down to laugh at us . . . but when we gave them sure enough drama, they didn't laugh. They liked it better than when we were just naturally acting funny."[23]

In 1913, when the "Negro Players" opened in Philadelphia, Gilpin had caught the eye of Lester Walton as "an actor of some parts." When the production moved to the Lafayette Theatre, Gilpin had success in legitimate roles in addition to his singing.[24] Through *The Emperor Jones*, Gilpin stepped forward as the leading black dramatic actor of his time.

*E*ven as Gilpin starred in the history-making production, another groundbreaking show waited in the wings, readying to make its appearance. On 23 May 1921, *Shuffle Along*, "a record-breaking, epoch-making musical comedy," would herald the return of all-black musical theater.[25]

Although the production did not boast the participation of former Williams and Walker Company members, its creators certainly shaped their work under the influence of the black musicals of the preceding generation. Flournoy Miller and Aubrey Lyles, Bert's friend Nobel Sissle, and Eubie Blake led the charge to bring the production into being.[26]

They organized the show in New York and took it out of town for a run in Washington, D.C., at a black theater, the Howard. Nonetheless, the show's producers aimed for Broadway. After success in the nation's capital, they went on to Philadelphia's Dunbar, another black theater. When they made it to New York, they mounted the production on a "shoe-string" at the Sixty-third Street Theatre, which had long been dark. Within weeks, however, the show "made the Sixty-third Street Theatre one of the best-known houses in town and made it necessary for the Traffic Department to declare Sixty-third Street a one-way thoroughfare."[27] *Shuffle Along* would run "for over five hundred performances, grossing close to eight million dollars before closing in 1923."[28]

Even as opportunities for black musical theater on Broadway again opened up—the first time since Williams and Walker's all-black spectacles—Bert moved farther away from working within the black theatrical community. He would not create an all-black production, nor would he pursue work with a black company. Rather, he would strive to achieve a dream: to star in legitimate theater—on Broadway.

13

A "Legitimate" Star

$\mathcal{A}$s Bert was on the road with *Broadway Brevities*, an 11 February article in the *Afro-American* announced his plans to star in a "musical play" titled *The Pink Slip*. Furthermore, according to the article, Bert had signed a three-year contract with the show's producer, Albert H. Woods.[1] A well-connected, successful producer and manager, Albert Herman Woods had been playing Broadway theaters for years, mainly financing melodramas and farces. He owned the Eltinge Theater, named after Julian Eltinge, the female impersonator whom he had signed to an exclusive contract, which made Woods rich.[2] Creating a connection with Woods, Bert meant to ensure that the production would play Broadway, featuring a new type of character. John Nail later said, "He wanted New York, that knew him only in the *Follies* and in vaudeville and the music hall, to see him in that new light." Bert was single-minded in his aim: to fulfill his long-held ambition.

When Bert signed his contract with Woods, he secured all the details like a veteran performer. First, he insisted that the production would be presented "in a first-class manner by a first-class company in one or more first-class theatres," making certain that the bookings would be up to his standard. Next, confident of his value as top performer, he negotiated terms that not only guaranteed him a salary of $1,250 per week regardless of how the production fared but also ensured that he would receive a sum equal to 10 percent of the gross weekly box office receipts.

Perhaps recalling his ordeal with Comstock, he also made sure that his contract included that all box office receipts be submitted to him on a weekly basis.[3]

As "actor-manager," Bert also took responsibility for the production. He selected the show's composer, handpicking his former colleague, Will Vodery. Bert alone had the power to choose and hire the show's manager, as well as the set designer and costumer. In a manner he hadn't done since *Mr. Lode of Koal*, Bert headed up the company.[4] He threw himself fully into this venture, with absolute vigor.

Ashton Stevens, dramatic critic and friend, spoke with Bert about the new show while Bert was performing in *Broadway Brevities*. Bert told him that he had asked Woods to write the bill as "*The Pink Slip* with Bert Williams" so as not to overemphasize his role, although he had the leading part. Perhaps concerned about having top billing after his history of controversy, he underplayed his participation in the production.

The Pink Slip takes place at a hotel on Catalina Island, California, following the death of a millionaire named Coglan. Before his death, Coglan claimed to have buried treasure on the island. Subsequently, the owner of the hotel posts notices stating that there are known to be six pieces of pink paper that, combined, reveal the treasure's location. Each may be found in one of Coglan's favorite spots on the island.

Numerous characters arrive at the hotel, including a clairvoyant, a millionaire hotelier and his daughters, a detective, and the island hotel owner's son. Bert plays Ananias Washington, a hotel employee who is as eager a treasure seeker as any. The plot revolves around Washington's plan to place his own pink slips in various locations that he claims to be Coglan's favorites, while inveigling the guests into paying him for the clues.[5] Amidst his wheeling and dealing, a romance develops between two other characters, and the players sing and dance several numbers.

Although Bert's starring role seemed to signal a change, that the production's romance would play out around him—rather than involve him—indicated the limits of his public's expectations of him. Musical comedies still, as ever, incorporated romance. Although Bert finally could be the leading actor—or comic—he could not and would not be the leading man.

In an additional irony, Bert *would* grace the stage time and again among numerous white women. The old prohibition against his presence with them onstage had long been laid to rest. This, at least, suggested the possibility of Bert's new representation in *The Pink Slip*.

Bert with Members of the Under the Bamboo Tree *Cast.* COURTESY OF THE SHUBERT
ARCHIVE

Bert with Twelve Female Cast Members of Under the Bamboo Tree. COURTESY OF
THE SHUBERT ARCHIVE

He explained the role's importance to his future as an actor:

I'm a porter in the hotel at Catalina Island; an awful liar; but a *character*. And I've got a song coming along that ought to have character in it, too. I sing with a dog; with a gangling-legged outcast dog. A lady had given me a dollar to take this dog out and feed him, and her husband has given me five dollars to take the dog out and drown him. There ought to be some character in that song, not to say problem. I'm working it out—slow—the way I do everything, Brother Stevens. But I think I ought to be able to understand the way that old black porter feels. Yes . . . and I think I ought to be able to understand how the dog feels, too.[6]

Having played the Jonah Man countless times before, Bert recognized comedy and tragedy in both the porter's and the dog's roles. Outcasts in the hotel and within the play, they are not necessarily welcome but, nonetheless, remain. Ananias Washington, integral to the hotel's operations, has no true friends or colleagues within the play. Bert could indeed empathize with the character, having played an integral part in the *Follies*, yet never felt fully accepted or included by others. Regarding the dog, one would-be owner rejects him, the other accepts him nominally, yet distances herself by paying off the porter to take care of him. Bert knew these all-too-familiar dynamics. His idea that the porter should sing, speaking to both the dog's and the man's problems, underscored his belief that abject characters—like the Jonah Man—deserved to have their stories heard.[7]

The show played Atlantic City and Asbury Park, outlying New Jersey seaside towns, in August of 1921, in preparation for a later move to New York. Bert was clearly, as the *Morning Telegraph* critic noted, the "principal star." The *Union* recognized that the support of a cast "aids Bert in his mirth manufacturing."[8] As usual, Bert delivered a wholehearted performance for his audience. The writer testified, "Bert squeezed every atom of expression possible from the opportunities offered him."[9] As the porter, Bert provided "dry, deliberate, infectious humor" and "held the center of attraction and approval throughout the whole performance."[10] Nonetheless, the writer saw need of revisions in order to strengthen the show. Making plain the suggestion of the *Morn-*

ing Telegraph, Variety complained that Bert's role was still too small and that the current script "fails to give him as great an opportunity as his talent deserves."[11]

The Pink Slip's run in New Jersey was lucrative enough for Woods to declare Bert "the best drawing card in the business."[12] Although a promising play, *The Pink Slip* was not yet polished, however. It lacked that "spontaneity and snappiness of action that goes to make a musical comedy a sure-fire success."[13] The producer undertook to revamp it. With Shubert brothers J. J. and Lee sharing in his investment, they added scenery and new costumes.[14] Furthermore, they set writer Walter de Leon to the task of pruning and sharpening the script.

Although Bert might have wanted to take the production to New York, the play, once revised, revamped, and renamed *Under the Bamboo Tree*, headed to Cincinnati for its premiere. It would go from there to Chicago and later to Detroit with the hope of returning home to a Broadway opening. In addition to providing the opportunity of a tryout before shooting for the Great White Way, an opening out of town permitted a larger theater capacity for the more expensive production, which cost at least $6,000 per week. Not only did the show need to play in the Shuberts' first-class theaters, it would also need to play in houses that were large enough to ensure that its investors could clear their expenses and make a profit.[15]

On opening night in Cincinnati, 4 December 1922, J. J. Shubert himself attended, taking copious notes throughout. It couldn't have been a secret to anyone—especially as seasoned a performer as Bert—how much was riding on this production. Not just for himself but for others as well. Good news came in the reviews, as an *Enquirer* reviewer exclaimed that Bert's role "fits him like a glove." Attuned to his audience, Bert smoothed out some rough spots in the new production and delivered his songs skillfully: "[P]eople will go to the theater to hear him sing them," the reviewer affirmed. "No one else could do it quite as he does." Again, the show succeeded, and it was sure to become even stronger as the writers and performers continued to work on it before it finally opened in New York.[16]

As he had in *The Pink Slip*, Bert sang "Puppy Dog" in *Under the Bamboo Tree*. It had the familiar Jonah Man mournfulness, but this song was unique. The singer shared his pain, and the rejected pet to which Ananias sang was as pitiful and plaintive as he:

When folks look at you,
The first thing they do is to laugh;
You ain't comical but,
You is such a mutt, they just laugh.

Your earses and your pawses, too,
Don't look like they was meant for you;
The reason I like you's because
You remind me of me; I'm telling true.

Bert's comment regarding being able to relate to both porter and dog added layers of meaning to the song. Assumed to be naturally comical, Bert had made his audiences laugh. A mixed "mutt," the dog seemed similar not only to the misplaced porter but also to Bert himself. Fodder for others' laughter, porter, dog, and Bert felt the pain of exclusion and rejection:

You're so mournful and blue,
Dog-gone blue, dry-bone blue, puppy dog;
And your eyes is so sad,
Like you had, news that's bad, puppy dog.

All you life old Misery has hounded you,
When you was born, folks should have took and drowned you;
Ain't much difference betwixt me and you,
I'm telling true, puppy dog.[17]

The porter sang of misery plaguing the dog—and himself—all his life, up to and including the present moment. In the final segment of the song, Ananias's comparison of the dog's life to himself became even closer, as he continued:

A gunny sack and the ocean blue
Would certainly be a favor to you,
'Cause you're only a joke
To educated folk, just like me;
I'm telling true. . . .

> *You ain't got no wife or friends to grieve or care*
> *You got no home on earth, in Heaven or anywhere;*
> *And when you go away, far away,*
> *They'll just say, "Puppy's gone."*[18]

"Puppy Dog" became the means by which the porter could express his own frustration when he was used as entertainment by "educated" folks. The song dramatized his utter isolation and hopelessness. As he noted the dog's lack of spouse or friends or any place to call home, he completed the picture of desolation. The song, rather than a comic Jonah Man tune, became a dramatic tale.

Critic Amy Leslie acknowledged the drama of the plaintive song, stating that "Williams touches the heart of heart." She undermined the dramatic element, however, when she subsequently wrote that his "voice is kept in [*sic*] background while [his] feet tell all sorts of stories buoyantly."[19] The dramatic moment that seemed possible while Bert sang the doleful tune lost its power once he began to move. It appeared that the comedian's physical movements countered the potential for pathos. His actions obliterated the opportunity for his audience to recognize the drama occurring within the scene, pulling the critic's focus away from the dramatic and toward the comical. This became more apparent when she described Bert as having provided the "'coon essence' of another era of black joy in shuffle and wing."[20]

Even though the critic underemphasized the dramatic moment in the scene, she declared Bert "a splendid actor and a singularly original and quaint provider of fun."[21] As a talented performer, Bert was somehow contradictory: both an original and an old-fashioned relic. He transcended the typical role of the black performer while he also reified that same role. Even after all his years in theater, the traditional expectations of his white audience still influenced the interpretation of his performance.

Proceeding to enumerate Bert's various attributes, Leslie noted the depth of "uncanny eyes," and "white teeth and catching smile."[22] Always a strength, Bert's physical presence drew in his audience and distinguished him as a performer. The critic also saw "a little pathos in his long simian arms and splay feet" as he moved across the stage. In her loaded statement, Leslie envisioned Bert's bodily movements as communicating more powerfully than his voice. Moreover, they communicated in ways that rendered the actor more monkey-like than human.

For Leslie, Bert's bodily action became his dominant means of expression. Ultimately, whether embodying the "coon" of days gone by or a pathetically simian (black) man, Bert's actions trumped the voice that was meant to define his new role onstage. His body, marked as black through his continuing use of blackface and traditional role as porter, foretold and controlled the meanings his performance could have. Such critics declared Bert an eternal mimic. A natural actor. Although Bert moved, spoke, and sang, it was his body that communicated most expressively, ruling out other interpretations of his performance. It seemed that, as James Weldon Johnson had stated about black dialect, rather than possessing the full range of human emotion and expression Bert desired, his performance would have only the two stops: humor and pathos.

As actor-manager of the show, Bert felt the need not only to perform well, but also to manage the production well, despite having hired an able manager in Robert Evans. To his dismay, however, *Under the Bamboo Tree* sank under the weight of its expenses. The show moved on from Cincinnati to Chicago to play for twelve weeks. During half its run in the Windy City, the show lost money.[23] Furthermore, while Bert labored to make the show a success, he became sick.

As the weeks passed, what had seemed like an innocuous cold worsened severely and rapidly. When Bert's lawyer visited him in mid-February, he found Bert lying on the couch in his dressing room. Bert made light of his illness, claiming a "bad" stomach, but admitted, "[T]hat's the way I am, feeling fine one day and not so good the next." Then he changed the subject.[24]

Regardless of Bert's seeming nonchalance toward his illness, his lawyer later returned to discuss it. He suggested to Bert that he close the show after the Chicago run in order to take a rest. The proud Bert, unwilling to quit the show and determined to persevere, refused. "Throw a lot of people out of work? Never. I feel a lot better to-day." In spite of his light tone, however, that same day he spoke of drawing up his will.[25]

The desperate desire to save his show and make it a hit became Bert's reasons to press on. But the stress of that burden, along with his sickness, broke him down even further. By the time he left Chicago for the show's next stop in Detroit, he had become all but confined to his bed. Moreover, he was dependent on manager Evans and his valet Chappy. Few people knew that they had to dress and undress him "like a baby," and that between scenes he reclined on a couch in his dressing room, attempting to conserve his draining energy.[26]

Some people, like Bert's friend John Nail, would later say that Bert's extraordinary drive and overwork pushed him over the edge. In the weeks preceding his last performance, he was once again advised not to perform. Upon hearing that the theater held a capacity audience, however, Bert rallied, giving a performance on 26 February at the illustrious Garrick Theater.[27]

Despite his weakened condition, Bert performed well that night. Critic Al Weeks praised him for finally having a show of his own. Although he admitted that audiences might still cry for more of the comedian, Weeks seemed satisfied that Bert had a good opportunity to display his considerable skills. He commended Bert for his "Puppy Dog" song above all, recognizing it as "a gem of artful acting that inspires much laughter and that at the same time brings the listener close to tears."[28] To Weeks, Bert did balance comedy and drama, pleasing his audience and testifying to his undiminished talent as an actor as well as a comedian. Perhaps this promising type of review drove Bert, who determined to finish his run and eventually continue on to a New York opening.

On 27 February, Bert suffered one of his bad days, but he resolved to perform, nonetheless. Donning the black cork to become Ananias Washington, he imagined the full house of fans who awaited him. In the past, under all circumstances he drove himself to deliver his finest performance. Tonight would be no different. Despite his ill health, his hope for the future helped him to go on.

His scene was with Sammy White. And soon after he began to perform, he faltered. As White recalled, when Bert delivered his lines "there was the most terrible sound in his voice that I've ever heard . . . Williams gamely went along with his lines, but each time, it was a terrible effort. His voice had a curious croak in it, and at the sound of this old voice, the hysteria of the audience mounted."[29]

All the while, Bert struggled to stay in character and perform. But he began perspiring so much that he mopped his brow, removing some of his makeup. The unknowing audience, thinking that it was part of the show, began to laugh uproariously.[30]

As if echoing his first embarrassing performance in blackface, Bert's makeup streaked as the audience howled. Now, however, it was not mortification that threatened to cow him. Against all odds, Bert finished the scene, barely making it to the wings before he collapsed. Stage-hands quickly moved him to his dressing room and called a doctor. In the meantime, flustered, they put on a filler act of dance and stories. They sought the manager of the house, someone to advise them about what to do. Bert, weak, could hardly move. And the packed house waited, first in anticipation, then, as time passed, in confusion.[31]

Finally, they announced to the audience that Bert could not perform and prepared to send in an understudy to cover him. But Bert's public would not have it. Irate, the audience rose, "like one man," seemingly every member seeking the box office to demand a refund.[32] How ironic that, after Bert's envy of Charles Gilpin, and his belief that his shows could always go on without him, Bert hardly had the opportunity to note the audience's devastation at his absence.

By the next night, Bert was transported by train to New York, where Lottie, who no longer traveled with him on tours, met him on arrival. Two doctors examined him, and they determined that the cold that Bert had caught in Chicago had developed into pneumonia. Further-more, he suffered a heart condition, just as his father had, and this heart ailment further weakened him.[33]

By 4 March, his condition declined more drastically, necessitating a blood transfusion. Bert's protégé, Will Vodery, offered, eager to do his part in trying to save the life of his friend. After the procedure, in an-swer to a doctor's question, "How do you feel?" Bert answered, "80% better." But he also had his will drawn up, thereby ensuring that Lottie and the girls would be well provided for. Hopeful, they all awaited his body's response to the transfusion, believing that it would save his life.[34]

The transfusion did little to improve his condition, however. Before midnight, the great comedian passed away.[35]

A bereaved Lottie, supported bravely by her three adopted daugh-ters, held three funeral services for her fallen husband: one for family alone, a second Masonic service for the public, and a third pri-vate Masonic service.[36] On 7 March, the public viewed the body at St. Phillips Episcopal Church in Harlem. Reportedly, 5,000 people were in attendance, and thousands more lined the streets, wishing to be near Bert, although they could not hope to gain access to the church.[37] Lester Walton noted that "people in every walk of life, irrespective of race, creed or color, paid homage to one who, during life, helped to drive away dull care and worry with his original, quaint humor, always clean and at no time suggestive of ridicule."[38]

The obituaries of Bert were quite different from those published when George died. When George died, members of the black public had affirmed and praised his role as a race man and a performer. They made their proclamations with certainty. Eulogies and memorials of Bert attempted to determine the performer's contributions along racial and artistic lines, however. At his death, his public sought to assess his role as a black man as well as his influence as a performer. All who remembered Bert seemed concerned with taking a step back to contemplate his legacy.

Members of the white press as well as Bert's colleagues concerned themselves with the question of how to remember and appreciate his contributions. The *New York Tribune* quoted words written a dozen years before by the late Booker T. Washington:

> Bert Williams is a tremendous asset of the negro race. The fact of his success aids the negro many times more than he could have helped the race by merely contenting himself to whine about racial difficulties. The fact is the American people are ready to honor any man who does something worth while [*sic*], irrespective of his color.[39]

Washington's words proclaimed Bert not only a successful artist but also a man worthy of appreciation for his willingness to take personal responsibility. Framing Bert's contribution in terms used by the accommodationist leader, the *Tribune* writer affirmed Bert's propriety and dignity, rather than focusing on his artistic talent.

When speaking of Bert and his art, the author described him as "one of the best known actors of the American stage, but in the opinion of critics at home and abroad a creator of comedy character possessing originality that amounted to genius."[40] To illustrate his point, he quoted Washington again on the performer's particular gift in characterization: "Williams put into his quaint songs and humorous sayings the quality and philosophy of the negro race. He did for one side of negro life and character just what the plantation negroes did for another. He gave expression to and put into form easily understood and appreciated something of the inner life and peculiar talent of the negro."[41]

In a general description of Bert's talent, the writer reminded readers of Bert's representations of a different side of the Negro. He illustrated not merely the nature of blacks through their actions but also their inner, philosophical life. The critic supported the view that the actor merely performed realistically, focusing on verisimilitude rather than innovation. Such an assumption might have been Bert's fault as much as his critic's. The emphasis that the performer himself had placed on study when discussing his work suggested that he had intended to embody a "true" type.

The *New York Times* summed up Bert's work just as the writer eulogized him. He "had a comedy method of his own. The slow, shambling gait, the balanced intonation, the slow diction, the skillful pauses, are familiar to most theater-goers of this generation. Although not really a great singer, he could 'put over' with real effect a song that was a really funny story told to music."[42] Focusing on Bert's artistry, the journalist assessed his skills in terms of his unique approach. He concluded that Bert stood out, not so much for having been the most skilled comedian, but rather for having created an extraordinary style.

New York Evening Post writer Percy Hammond addressed Bert's limitations as an effect of race, discussing the reality of racial prejudice in terms more thorough than he had years before. In a manner never fully undertaken during Bert's life, Hammond both extolled the actor's gifts and stated that "the doors of advancement [were] closed against him, as they were not for Mr. Warfield and others."[43] It seemed that the statements Bert himself had made about his aspirations, desiring the chance that David Warfield had had to move from comedy to drama, had not been forgotten.

Referring again as before to Bert's "thwarted aesthetic yearnings," Hammond openly cited the "descriptive phraseology of the press agent, a 'distinguished colored comedian.'"[44] He noted the limitations placed on the actor, quoting the words that were used to qualify the superlatives that described his talent. Hammond spoke on Bert's behalf, bemoaning that he seemed fated to be assessed in terms of his racial identity. Although Hammond refrained from criticizing the theatrical world or the general society that judged Bert by his race, he fully acknowledged the obstacles the comedian faced, and he discussed them frankly.

Critic Heywood Broun wrote even more openly. For him, Bert's talents "were largely wasted." Bert's life was tragic, for he never achieved all he should have. After years of observing and reviewing Bert's work, Broun believed that the comedian suffered. Counting racial prejudice as one of the causes of Bert's "downfall," Broun complained that writers typecast the comedian as a result of being a Negro. For the first time, he addressed the issue and influence of the racialized society on Bert's professional prospects.[45]

In a revealing aside regarding Bert's race, however, Broun puzzled that, although Bert possessed "more white blood than black"—a reference to his mixed-race background—the public considered him a Negro. It seemed to Broun that "some illogical process has decided that any discernible strain, however slight, of negro blood extraction outweighs all other lines."[46] Such words revealed that, rather than questioning the societal structure, certain critics described the comedian as an exception. Bert's fair skin and his background excluded him unnecessarily from the white society. Even in death, this theme, which had once frustrated Bert to the extent that he decried the importance or value of so-called "white" blood, resurfaced again. It seemed infuriating to Broun that Bert's trace of black blood barred him from society, being so nearly white, rather than disturbing to Broun that society discriminated against blacks generally. Broun separated Bert from the others of his race and considered him to be worthy of greater access and freedom than others had.

Broun proceeded to comment that the audience did not appear to discriminate against Bert with regard to applause, for they "applauded him generously and laughed hard from the moment he came before the footlights." As a result, he concluded that "[s]omehow or other laughing at Bert Williams came to be tied up in people's minds with liberalism, charity and the Thirteenth Amendment."[47] Eager to relieve their white man's burden, the audience had connected their acceptance of the comedian and his performance with their acceptance of the black community. As proof of their willingness to accept the very people that, as Bert himself once declared, were "unamalgamated," the audience applauded him. Their applause thereby released their feelings of guilt. In effect, Bert served as a vehicle for their own catharsis.

Although such positive audience response might have been charitable, Bert faced the challenge to "be funny," Broun stated, which is what resulted in his failure. "He did his best to comply with this request, but in his later years determination came to be written all over his work. The burnt cork weighed him down. It smothered what may have been genius."[48] Forced to be a comedian, Bert responded to the requirements of producers who wanted him to remain consistently comical.

Broun saw that Bert had been underestimated by audience members and producers alike.

As Broun continued, he moved away from understanding Bert's loss as "peculiar to the Negro." Rather, he thought it was a result of being in the community of performers who "are doing their best to obey the cruel command, 'Be funny.'"[49] Shifting the subject to address a comic performer's obligation to his audience, and thus turning away from the issue of racism in the society, Broun revealed his anxiety about grappling with the real consequences of racist thought and minstrelsy's legacy. As had others before him, while he acknowledged Williams's race, he still distanced himself from directly addressing it.

Another critic considered the comedian's racial biography alongside his skill: "The most successful of negro comedians is dead. Born in the West Indies and reared in San Francisco, Bert Williams had more white blood than black, but the strain of the negro in his veins determined his race and he accepted it and earned for himself an [*sic*] unique place on the American stage."[50] Commending the actor for his choice to embrace his black identity, which thereby allied him with the Negro community, the author also underscored Bert's tenuous relationship to that same community. His West Indian ethnicity distanced him from the group of which he was to be considered a member, yet his choice to identify with blacks made him extraordinary.

Ultimately, the writer homed in on Bert's virtuosity as a comedian. "In spite of his lack of first-hand acquaintance with the life and dialect of the southern negro he won his great following as a negro entertainer."[51] Bert had chosen not only to accept his blackness but also to enact it on stage. The critic utilized Bert's ethnic difference as a means to compliment him. Bert's apparent distance from quotidian involvement with black American life paradoxically enabled a deeper appreciation and recognition of his talents—significantly—by nonblacks.

Composer Ring Lardner, who had once written a song for the comedian when he was in the *Follies*, sought to reframe appreciation of Bert's skills. In Lardner's opinion, Bert did his best work in the Williams and Walker shows. He aimed to correct misinterpretations of the actor's career and talent by reminding readers of his earlier accomplishments: "The people who wrote the Williams and Walker shows knew how to write for Bert. The *Follies* people didn't, and he lacked energy to write for himself. Besides, he was under the impression, the delusion, that *Follies* audiences were drawn by scenery and legs[,] and didn't want to laugh. He used to say, 'I'm out there to give the gals time to change.'"[52] Resisting even Bert's own reading of his role and importance in the *Follies*, Lardner introduced a new way for the audience to recall his career. He lauded Bert's strengths as a performer, recounting the regrettable fact that Bert's writers hardly understood his particular talents when he was alive.

Furthering his point about Bert's vast range, Lardner elaborated:

> [I]f you'd seen him just dance in the old days you'd have pronounced him both comedian and clown as well as the champion eccentric "hoofer" of all time. In my record book he leads the league as a comedian and can be given no worse than a tie for first place as a clown, pantomimist, story teller, eccentric dancer and singer of a certain type of songs. Otherwise he was a flop.[53]

At the same time that Lardner created an image of Bert as a legend, he detailed the extensive parameters of Bert's domain as an artist.

Lardner's endorsement prompted a reevaluation of Bert. In response to Lardner, another critic wrote: "We saw him once with Walker in a musical comedy called 'Abyssinia' and he was then a different person."[54] Recalling that Bert represented himself differently in his black shows, the writer created a second view of the performer rather than unifying or reconciling the later Bert Williams with the earlier Bert Williams. He then redefined the ideal setting in which Bert shone, positing, "Perhaps it was the scenery of the more ornate Ziegfeld shows which squeezed most of the fun out of him. As a purveyor of attraction for the eyes Ziegfeld leads America and, for all we know, the world, but he has never quite learned the trick of making humor hold up its head under the burden of so much magnificence."[55] The burden of representing the talented performer rested on the head of Ziegfeld himself, a misdirected man whose interest in show design did not necessarily include highlighting his comedians. Rather than blame this deficiency on Bert, the writer shifted the focus to Ziegfeld.

Stating his newfound appreciation of Bert's achievement, the critic then compared him to other comedians who succeeded in Ziegfeld's ornate environments, yet were not necessarily more talented than he:

> One or two people have managed to slash their way through the lush Urban jungles [Joseph Urban, Ziegfeld's set designer]. Eddie Cantor did

it in his scene in the osteopath's office, but Cantor's style of comedy has none of the subtlety which belonged to Williams at his best. The secret of Cantor's appeal lies almost wholly in pace. He goes after a joke as if he were a substitute guard tackling a dummy for the benefit of the head coach. He will leave his feet at any time for a laugh and not even the heaviest scenery in the world can block him off.

   ... The old Bert Williams gave you more quiet and consolidation.[56]

Throughout this segment, the writer established the distinction between Bert and the other great comedians of his time. In Joseph Urban's landscapes, comedians had to play their comedy large, in order to speak more loudly—both literally and figuratively—than the setting that threatened to eclipse them. Urban's famous sets were lavish and extremely decorous. Any successful comedian would have been expected to find some manner of counterbalancing the larger-than-life sets.

That Bert's particular talents could so nearly go unrecognized or, at least, underrecognized, reveals audiences' expectations of comedians during the period. Audiences sought physical comedy that Bert's nuanced performances did not allow for onstage. If less than perceptive, an audience might miss his quiet jokes. The critic thus reconsidered Bert, choosing instead to honor him for his talent. He was an underappreciated actor, a uniquely skilled comedian, a frustrated genius. Whether or not writers turned their attention to his race, they attempted to reevaluate the comedian's life work.

Eddie Cantor eulogized Bert in terms that straddled the issues of race and artistic appreciation. Acknowledging him immediately as having the "advantage" of being of the race that blackface performers imitate when donning burnt cork, Cantor credited him with analyzing the group he strove to portray. Despite recognition that both he and Bert *created* their characters, Cantor, compelled to associate Bert's blackness with privileged access to the role he played, understated the actor's talents. He seemed to suggest that Bert's talents were an extension of his race, even as he praised the comedian's skills.

Later, in his eagerness to find suitable terms to communicate his respect for Bert, Cantor borrowed the words of J. J. Shubert, describing Bert as "one of the whitest actors I have ever known."[57] Echoing Jack Shoemaker's comment ten years before, Cantor offered the phrase as shorthand for: "Williams had a splendid regard for every little feeling or emotion of his fellow man."[58] He stated that Bert "dipped into the great realm of the fundamental art of acting and gave us emotion or comedy which was as universal in its appeal as the very writings of Shakespeare himself."[59] In this way, Bert's talents seemed to confer upon him a distinction that metaphorically whitened him, making him "more than" his race, perhaps "more than" a blackface comedian. Intending "whiteness" to function as a compliment, Cantor juxtaposed it with his remarks that although Bert was a "natural" actor, he also "cultivated industriously" those talents, resulting in compelling characterization.

As evidenced by Cantor's comments, even in death Bert's qualities were used to distinguish him from his race. These efforts to define Bert's talents and extol his particular abilities continued to result in a language of exceptionalism that bracketed him from other blacks. If he suffered because of his race, then he also benefited because of his "natural" advantage. Critics' inability to cheer his achievement while also seeing the racialized context in which he had to perform ultimately left them conflicted as to how to present him and his life's work.

*M*eanwhile, black writers' comments ranged from hagiography to sharp criticism, as various people grappled with the contradictory representations of the comedian. In the *Crisis*, the organ of the National Association for the Advancement of Colored People, a phonograph company praised Bert as "the greatest entertainer the world has ever known."[60] Indeed, "many men learned to laugh because of him." Perhaps in an effort to cope with the limitations that Bert had evidently faced, the announcement declared, "He might have been known as a great tragedian had he been white. But the world for a long time now has refused to take black men seriously. So the white world made Bert Williams the world's greatest comedian."[61]

Although an advertisement rather than a eulogy, the ad spoke of Bert's struggles and charity. Revealing that although Bert had a contract with a white company, Columbia Records, he had promised to record with black company Black Swan, the advertiser exalted him. Moreover, they wrote about him as though he were their champion: "He put thousands of dollars into the making of Black Swan Records." In the opinion of the company, Bert combined art and activism.

A disapproving critic, however, wrote a censorious piece on the comedian. Bert was a debit to the race for having "played in theaters that either barred or Jim-Crowed Negroes—a policy born of the conception that all men of color are inherently inferior to white men—and by a strange irony of fate, Bert Williams himself was a facile instrument of this insidious cult."[62] By performing in such theaters, Bert had done a disservice to the race by upholding a deleterious policy.

Despite such harsh judgment, the writer took heart at the thought that Bert was one of the "few Negro stage folk who smart under the cork and struggle to rend the veil even though but a few succeed; for this is our only hope."[63] Introducing an intriguing paradox, the critic explained, "[H]e lamented his failure to be considered and acclaimed as a *whole, full-orbed man* on the American stage and yet his life's work rendered it possible for the Negro actor to be received as a *half-man only*."[64] Guilty for having contributed to his own unfortunate position, Bert had accepted roles through which he could have never achieved his dream of showing the many sides of the Negro. The journalist believed that Bert's life provided proof that "the oppressed have always acquiesced in and defended their own oppression."[65] Dissatisfied with Bert's passivity, the writer criticized him as complicit in his own subjugation, for which he could not be pitied.

In the critic's view, there was no intelligence in Bert's work, for "[h]is was the ignoble lot of dragging his people through the flotsam and jetsam of art to the derisive and vulgar hand-clapping of race prejudiced America. His funmaking, of course, was what they wanted, the lowest form of intellection."[66] Despite Bert's professed desire to make audiences think and to give them philosophy, the commentator saw instead his role as the court jester, one "content to make the world *laugh* . . . not concerned about making it *think*."[67] Bert played a part not only in his own capitalist exploitation but through his work supported the race's continued degradation, thereby damaging everyone. His presumed art did not transcend but, conversely, reified the position of blacks.

Perhaps the most intriguing of African Americans' assessments was that of author and critic Jessie Fauset. Speaking of Bert's "symbolism," Faucet confronted and exposed a dilemma that black performers faced: the criticism of those within the race for their representations of the race. With respect for Bert's talents, she spoke of his considerable attention to craft and his serious and deliberate intent. Speaking an artistic truth, Bert had embodied an actual racial type. As Fauset wrote: "He was so real, so simple, so credulous. His colored auditors laughed but often with a touch of rue—this characterization was too near to us; his hardluck was our own universal fate."[68] Bert's work was profound, touching upon deep concerns, expressing the humanity of blacks.

Even as Fauset focused on Bert's talents, she recognized the vexing limitations placed on him and that "[i]n spite of his greatness he was unusually modest. He did not push himself, he was tolerant in the presence of intolerance."[69] The tact and humility that Bert displayed with regard to racial discrimination proved his respectability. She queried, "Why should he and we obscure our talents forever under the bushel of prejudice, jealousy, stupidity—whatever it is that makes the white world say: 'No genuine colored artists; coons, clowns, end-men, claptrap, but no undisguisedly beautiful presentation of Negro ability'?"[70] She drove at the notion that, as Bert strove to excel, so did the race. As the prospects of his unfortunate character rose and fell, so did those of the race. His desire to persevere and remain impervious to heartbreak paralleled what the race endured. As Fauset praised Bert, she also held him as an example: in art and in life, he faced challenges to his triumphs, yet persisted. It was the duty of the race to do the same, hoping and striving for freedom.

(W)hat about Bert himself? His own views, hopes, and beliefs? He had struggled throughout his career to define himself and his work in his own terms, yet experienced the frustration of misunderstanding. He had lived to perform, hoping to use blackface makeup as a vehicle to ultimately realize his deepest ambitions. Yet all this was to no avail.

Eric Walrond, a fellow West Indian who would later come to fame as a writer of the Harlem Renaissance, voiced the contradictory viewpoints that Bert himself held. He explained, "Although it was his business to make people laugh, there were times when he would go into his shell-like cave of a mind and reflect—and fight it out."

> "Is it worth it?" One side of him would ask. "Is it worth it, the applause, the financial rewards, the fame? Is it really worth it—lynching one's soul in blackface twaddle?"
>
> "But it is the only way you can break in," protests the other side of the man. "It is the only way. That is what the white man expects of you—comedy—blackface comedy. In time you know, they'll learn to expect serious things from you. In time."[71]

Although Walrond perhaps did not have such access to Bert's inner self, he seemed to know quite well Bert's sufferings.

The truth that Bert did have "thwarted aesthetic yearnings" is clear from the words of John Nail. Nail spoke of Bert's plans for the following year, stating that "his heart was set on . . . going to London to open in a serious play. He chose London because he was afraid that at first New York wouldn't be able to dissociate him from his old type of work."[72] Remembering that his audience "filmed" him a certain way, Bert had planned to strike out in a brave new fashion.

As one who saw his yearnings and desires more than anyone, Bert's wife Lottie deeply lamented the confined role her husband had been forced to accept. Lottie, Bert's partner on his journey through the world of show business, had witnessed his pains. She knew all of his disappointments.

It was sad that Bert never realized his ambition to play a dramatic role. But what was particularly tragic was that he had held in his very hands a dramatic play in which he had so fervently wished to star. Lottie explained that it had been Bert's "inseparable comrade" for months. She called it

> his Bible. . . . He had hoped that it might do for him what "The Emperor Jones" did for Mr. Gilpin. They were very good friends, and my husband knew what a fight Mr. Gilpin had had—and how much courage the producers needed. This piece that he hung his hope on was very somber. There was a voodoo theme: a jealous husband, a half-caste, tortures his wife's child inside a charmed circle that she cannot cross, and she dies of horror. The part of the husband might seem the opposite of any one would choose for Bert . . . but that may have been just the reason he wanted to play it. He worshipped that manuscript.[73]

Determined to stretch himself, desperate to pursue his long-held dream, Bert cherished the vision, which he never had the chance to realize. That fact hurt his loving wife nearly as much as it hurt Bert himself.

Despite Bert's greater interest in his art and his artistic development, both his publics sought to reframe him. They took his race as a central concern, whether they aimed to laud him as exceptional and therefore unlike other blacks, to lambaste him for playing into racists' hands, or to lend him as a representative example of the sufferings of the race.

Although at certain moments, these audiences remembered his art and praised him for the work he did onstage, ultimately they also turned and twisted his image in directions they thought best to interpret him. The influence of the prevailing legacies of minstrelsy and representation could be seen as writers did not speak specifically about Bert's life so much as place him within their existing debates and discussions. He was a certain kind of entertainment for anxious guilty whites and a symbol of the continuing travails of hopeful blacks.

In his quiet, methodical way, Bert had worked with and against stereotypical representation. Onstage, he had transcended the minstrel stereotype by offering new inflections of the darky voice. His Jonah Man became a nuanced character with depth, who dared to tell the world about the injustice of his misfortune. Performing alone or with others, he had made the classic character new through various performative approaches that spoke to audiences both black and white.

His work had not stopped there, however, as he posited blackness as a different presence when he was offstage. He had emphasized his connection to the black community as well as his own distinct individualism. He had underscored his dedication to his art as well as his diplomacy and tact when facing issues of racial discrimination. Neither his white nor his black audiences consistently responded to these efforts, but, nonetheless, their many approaches to assess him spoke to the complexity of his performances.

In life, activist or not, Bert had been a trailblazer. With George, he had created new opportunities for blacks in musical theater. On his own, headlining in vaudeville and starring in the *Follies*, he had crossed the color line while remaining acclaimed by the public. It is remarkable that, even during his final appearance in funeral services held on 8 March 1922 at the Masonic lodge in Manhattan, this tradition of understated groundbreaking continued. The reserved comedian was the first Negro to have his service at the all-white Grand Lodge. The *New York Age* recorded that this was "the first time in history that the memory of a Negro had been so revered by white Masons of New York City."[74]

During the private service, fellow Masons placed sprigs of acacia and the lambskin given him by the members of his Scottish lodge in his coffin, both being "symbols of the Mason's faith in the immortality of the soul."[75] For the public service, they opened their doors to nearly 2,000 friends, fans, and colleagues. Black and white alike gathered together, standing side by side in the crowded Grand Lodge room. They had all come to honor the life and career of the "inimitable" Bert Williams.

Epilogue

> . . . THE MASK WHICH THE ACTOR WEARS
> IS APT TO BECOME HIS FACE.
>
> —PLATO

On the years following Williams's death, fans would struggle to keep his memory—and his legacy—alive. Some commemorations came soon after his death, such as a 7 April 1922 article that declared, "All 135th Street is Missing Bert Williams." Recounting the innumerable neighborhood children who missed seeing their world-renowned and lovable fellow Harlemite, the *New York Evening Post* journalist reminded readers of the humanity of the actor, his gentle side, and his groundbreaking work. In a 1923 book of essay tributes collected by Mabel Rowland, writers memorialized Williams and reminded the public of the character he played: one very distinct from himself. Before the end of the decade, cartoonist A. W. Rennegarbe and writer Ben Davis, Jr., penned a series of strips on the life and trials of Williams published in the *Afro-American*. The *Chicago Defender*, another black periodical, honored his memory with a 1930 résumé of his success and a discussion of his contributions to theater.[1]

Although over time, memorials to Williams came with less frequency, references to him and his work persisted in letters to the editor, articles enumerating the "great comics" of all time, and lists of "Notable Negroes." These references appeared not only in African American periodicals but also in the white press. The writers and critics shared a common desire to declare to the public that "few made so many people laugh" the way Williams did.[2] They also debated his greatest theatrical contributions: were they when he performed with Walker in musicals, starred in the *Follies* revue, or headlined in vaudeville?

Mentions of Williams came with greater frequency for a short while when vaudeville was pronounced "dead" and its mourners wished to recall the best and brightest from that golden era.[3] The desire to hold on to this legendary figure, to place him somewhere in history so he would not be lost to later generations, seemed to motivate the varying discussions about his work even as much as ten and twenty years after his own death.

As the time since Williams's death lengthened further, however, the mask he wore began to endanger his place in history. Following the efforts of the Civil Rights Movement as well as the Black Arts Movement's drive to seek positive and, more importantly, politically proactive role models, more than ever Williams became displaced. Blackface, a disturbing image, became a reminder of a shameful past that whites and blacks alike wished to forget. Increasingly, Williams's genius as he worked *against* the mask got lost as the public only saw his work *within* it. The artistry of his work—and the manner in which he had taken a stereotype and transformed it—took a backseat to the means by which he was compelled to present it. The mask that had been both freedom and fixity in his own lifetime threatened to imprison him eternally.

Even as Williams risked fading into obscurity, a 1981 tribute created a "storm of controversy." It demonstrated just what was at stake in honoring Williams. Tony Award–winning African American performer, Ben Vereen, brought Williams back to the stage at the inaugural gala of president-elect Ronald Reagan.[4]

Vereen had discovered Williams as he himself had taken the Broadway stage in the 1972 *Pippin* as leading player. He had learned of the pain and humiliation Williams had suffered, the burden of wearing blackface every time he crossed the stage. He read voraciously in order to get inside the actor, to understand what it would have been like to be Bert Williams. To *have* to perform in blackface. Vereen's 1976 one-man show had been an effort to render that experience with respect and dignity, but audiences had rejected it. Vereen felt that he had been misunderstood.

Seeing the performance at the inauguration as an opportunity to present Williams again, Vereen took the chance. His appearance, which would be aired before a national television audience, included an intro-duction that provided context for Vereen's later performance of "No-body." In a sketch that described Williams's struggles, Vereen depicted the humiliation the actor had endured and the sacrifices he had made in order to be on the stage. He literally shone a spotlight on the makeup that weighed Williams down, threatening to make him seem less than the man he was.

When the performance aired, to Vereen's dismay, the introduction had been cut. The appearance included only an image of Ben Vereen, a black man, seemingly shuffling and dancing in blackface. That image upset and confused audiences—African Americans in particular—be-cause "Ben was such a major entertainer, and they just couldn't under-stand where he was coming from and why [he would choose to perform the role]." Later, Vereen himself recalled one black person who had menacingly said, "We're going to watch your show from behind a rifle."

For Vereen, Bert Williams was an important historical figure. He took Williams seriously, believing Williams to be a black hero who had paved the way for others. Through his performance, Vereen had in-tended to make a statement because he understood that Williams's ex-perience was worth telling. As a result, he refused to "stand down" in the face of criticism and controversy. Urged by a friend to apologize for his performance, Vereen responded, "I can't. My people went through this. My people, they bled through this. I can't." Vereen had aimed to tell the history of blacks in America through Williams. He had meant to unveil the reality of the black entertainer's challenges. To him, Williams's story was one worth defending.

The critique Vereen had intended was missed by the 1981 viewing audience, just as Williams himself continued to be misunderstood by later audiences. A performance intended to open up discussion ironi-cally shut it down. And later generations refused to face, accept, or ac-knowledge Williams's choice.

In recent years, there has been a consideration of the injurious im-ages of minstrelsy and vaudeville as well as a reconsideration of its black performers. Marlon Riggs's documentary, *Ethnic Notions*, exam-ined the legacy of stereotypes from minstrelsy, vaudeville, and beyond that powered antiblack racist thought from before the Civil War into the late twentieth century. Within the narrative of the perpetuation of stereotypes and the damaging effect of those images, Riggs touched on Williams's story. Although Riggs discussed the performer's evident dignity, the misfortune of his existence because of minstrelsy's legacy figured prominently, perhaps even more so than his unparalleled artistry.

Theatrical productions, such as Loften Mitchell's *Star of the Morning* and a two-man show entitled *Williams and Walker*, cast and recast Williams's torment and loss alongside his success. These endeavors continually placed him in the wretched position of the black entertainer forced to accept his role. When filmmaker Spike Lee's 2000 release *Bamboozled* addressed Williams and minstrelsy, it critiqued the history of the black image in American entertainment, yet refused a deep discussion of the realities of black life that would address both the limitations and inroads blacks at that time had made.

The black public may not have utterly lost sight of Williams as one among many who opened doors for other black entertainers, but the tireless work of further examination of such historical black performers must continue. Looking beyond the damaging legacy of minstrelsy to those who attempted to work against it, recognizing the specific efforts of those who courageously sought self-definition in the face of disparate and demanding audiences, embracing the artists on their terms even while we desire to make meaning of them in our own, we must engage with the many sides of the individuals whom we encounter. Although we may never uncover the "whole truth" of who Bert Williams was—both clown and melancholy man, ignorant buffoon and learned philosopher—we must accept his many facets instead of choosing to pin him down. Journeying with him on his rocky paths through medicine shows and minstrelsy, musical theater and motion pictures, we learn that he was, indeed, during his lifetime "The Greatest Comedian on the American Stage."

Acknowledgments

*I*nnumerable people have supported this project in my journey to transform it from a dissertation in the Program of American Civilization at Harvard University to a monograph. Many thanks to members of my dissertation committee, Werner Sollors, Doris Sommer, and Henry Louis Gates, Jr., who guided me as I developed an earlier incarnation of the project during my graduate studies.

I especially owe gratitude to Henry Louis Gates, Jr., for sharing with me Tina Bennett, the most brilliant, capable agent I could have ever wished for. My heartfelt appreciation goes to Tina. She believed in this project, guiding me as I prepared the book proposal, cheering me as we forged ahead to find the perfect publisher.

Thanks to the staff at Basic Civitas, who shared their enthusiasm for this project with me. Liz Maguire, who had faith in the possibilities of this project right from the start, was a gentle and inspirational editor whose loss I have felt keenly. Jo Ann Miller stepped in to guide me, and the spirited Chris Greenberg saw this work through to the end.

Various institutions and individuals welcomed my repeated trips to their archives. I express my thanks to the staff at the Recorded Sound Reference Center of the Library of Congress (David Sager); the Shubert Archives (Maryann Chach); the Museum of the City of New York (Marty Jacobs); the Academy Film Archive (Snowden Beckert and Brian Meacham); the Harvard Theatre Collection; the University of Iowa; the Harry Ransom Humanities Center at the University of Texas at Austin; and the Theatre Museum in Covent Garden.

For providing invaluable research funds and time off from teaching, I thank the UCSD Center for the Humanities, the UCSD Faculty Career Development Program, and the Hellman Fellowship. For publishing a portion of this research in *Theatre Journal*, I am grateful to Harry J. Elam, Jr., who supported the work.

I have been blessed with wonderful friends and colleagues at the University of California, San Diego. Deepest thanks to Rebecca Plant and Lisa Lampert-Weissig for their terrifically important encouragement and words of wisdom, and to colleagues Rosemary George, Stephanie Jed, Eileen Myles, Kathryn Shevelow, and Anna Joy Springer for the guidance and excellent feedback they offered in discussions about this project.

Many people buoyed me throughout the process of researching and writing. Thanks to Krie Alden, Annalisa Berns, Kathy Case, Brian Jonas, Carolyn King, Kate McCarthy, Anne-Marie Mulagha, Andrelle Quammie, Tina Royster, Debbie Smith, Allicia Salomon, and Melissa Watson. The Netty family (Marilena, Pierre, Alexa, and Don Camillo) and Marina Anagnostou opened their lovely homes to a weary researcher, for which I will be eternally grateful. Esther Vanderpot, a brilliant photographer and consummate professional, made a photo shoot fun despite her reluctant subject.

Ghada Osman, miraculous sister-friend in my life, you always fed me with comforting words and gracious actions. You were among my biggest champions with this project, and I look forward to returning the favor. Gerald Vanderpot, my quiet yet solid supporter, your certainty about my abilities gave me one more reason to love you.

Hazel and Rawle Quammie, I am deeply grateful for your continuing unshakable faith in me. Homero and Lejmarc, strong yet sensitive young men, your courage has made me proud. Carol, Cheryl, Darlene, and Tony, you are my models; you remain shining examples of how to be and remain dedicated to a dream. To Tamar and Keith Forbes, I give my deepest love. Your assurances have comforted me; your unerring love has strengthened me. Finally, I thank God for countless blessings, willing me to achieve what I'd hoped for, and granting me the love and support of people who always believed I could make it happen.

Notes

ABBREVIATIONS

BRTC	Billy Rose Theatre Collection
BU	John Hay Library, Brown University
HR	Harry Ransom Humanities Research Center
HTC	Harvard Theatre Collection
MCNY	Museum of the City of New York
NYMA	New York Municipal Archives
NYPL	New York Public Library for the Performing Arts
SC	Schomburg Center for Research in Black Culture
SA	Shubert Archives
KA	University of Iowa, Special Collections, Keith/Albee Collection

CHAPTER 1

1. Lloyd Lewis, *It Takes All Kinds* (New York: Harcourt, Brace, 1928), 232.

2. Michael Craton, *A History of the Bahamas* (London: Collins, 1962), 246.

3. W. W. Robinson, *The Story of Riverside County* (Los Angeles: Pioneer Title Insurance Company, 1957), 25, 29–30; *Southern California, Comprising the Counties of Imperial, Los Angeles, Orange, Riverside, San Bernardino, San Diego, Ventura* (Southern California Panama Expositions Commission, 1914), 132.

4. Eric Ledell Smith, *Bert Williams: A Biography of the Pioneer Black Comedian* (Jefferson, NC: McFarland, 1992), 6.

5. Ann Anderson, *Snake Oil, Hustlers and Hambones: The American Medicine Show* (Jefferson, NC and London: McFarland, 2000), 3. Anderson takes us even farther back in history, discussing the medieval origins of the medicine show and connecting it to the historical scorn of both performance and performers themselves. She suggests that the medicine show began sometime during the Middle Ages (600–1350 C.E.).

6. Brooks McNamara, *Step Right Up* (Jackson: University Press of Mississippi; revised edition, 1995), 3–4.

7. Ibid., 19.

8. Ibid., 21.

9. Ibid., 20.

10. Ibid., 23.

11. Ibid., 44, 47.

12. Ibid., 46.

13. Ibid.

14. Ibid., 20.

15. Robert M. Lewis, ed., *From Traveling Show to Vaudeville: Theatrical Spectacle in America, 1830–1910* (Baltimore and London: Johns Hopkins University Press, 2003), 5.

16. McNamara, *Step Right Up,* 18.

17. Anderson, *Snake Oil,* 173; and The Public Health Museum, "Patent Medicine," http:www.publichealthmuseum.org/exhibits-patentmed.html (accessed 10 April 2007).

18. Robert Lewis, *Traveling Show,* 2.

19. McNamara, *Step Right Up,* 53.

20. "Tonguesters of the Midway," *San Francisco Examiner,* 11 March 1894, 1.

21. Lloyd Lewis, *It Takes All Kinds,* 232.

22. Anderson, *Snake Oil,* 5.

23. Ibid., 1.

24. Lloyd Lewis, *It Takes All Kinds,* 232.

25. Mabel Rowland, ed., *Bert Williams* (New York: English Crafters, 1923), 9.

26. Anderson, *Snake Oil,* 41.

27. McNamara, *Step Right Up,* 12–13.

28. Ibid., 13.

29. Ibid., 59.

30. Howard Johnson, "Bahamian Labor Migration to Florida in the Late Nineteenth and Early Twentieth Centuries," *International Migration Review* 22, no. 1 (1988): 85. In 1885, Governor Henry Blake noted blacks' migration from Nassau in order to work in cigar manufacturing, sponging operations, and the pineapple industries. Such opportunities had proven so promising that Bahamians often chose not to return. Johnson, "Bahamian Labor Migration to Florida," 86.

31. "Bert Williams: Boy-Gentleman-Comedian," *Chicago Record-Herald,* 25 September 1910, 7.

32. Ibid.

33. Ibid.

34. Ibid.

35. Lloyd Lewis, *It Takes All Kinds,* 232.

36. "Bert Williams: Boy-Gentleman-Comedian," 7.

37. Rowland, *Bert Williams,* 8.

38. "Bert Williams: Boy-Gentleman-Comedian," 7.

39. Rowland, *Bert Williams,* 9.

40. Ibid.

41. Ibid., 2.

42. Ibid., 3.

43. Ibid., 3–4.

44. Ibid., 5.

45. Robert Lewis, *Traveling Show,* 5.

46. McNamara, *Step Right Up,* 53.

47. Ibid., 54.

48. Anderson, *Snake Oil,* 1.

49. McNamara, *Step Right Up,* 131–2.

50. Ibid., 120–1.

51. Ibid., 127.

52. Ibid., 137; Anderson, *Snake Oil,* 51.

53. McNamara, *Step Right Up,* 135.

54. Ibid., 128–29.

55. Ibid., 127.

56. Ibid., 24.

57. Ibid., 133, 135.

58. Anderson, *Snake Oil,* 120.

59. Ibid., 124.

60. McNamara, *Step Right Up*, 62.

61. Ibid.

62. Ibid., 62.

63. Ibid., 64. Some of the primary ingredients in Hamlin's famous Wizard Oil.

64. Anderson, *Snake Oil,* 88, quoting Violet McNeal, *Four White Horses and a Brass Band* (Garden City, NY: Doubleday and Company, 1947), 75.

65. Anderson, *Snake Oil,* 88.

66. McNamara, *Step Right Up*, 128.

67. Ibid., 54.

68. Ibid.

69. Ibid., 128, 141.

70. Ibid., 5.

71. Ibid., 142.

72. U. S. Bureau of the Census, *Statistics of the Population of the United States, 1880,* prepared by the Department of the Interior, Bureau of the Census (Washington, DC, 1880), 66D.

73. George W. Walker, "The Negro on the American Stage," *Colored American Magazine*, October 1906, 243.

74. Ibid.

75. Ibid.

76. Smith, *Bert Williams*, 229.

77. Walker, "The Negro on the American Stage," 243.

78. Walker, "The Negro on the American Stage," 243; Isaac Goldberg, *Tin Pan Alley: A Chronicle of American Popular Music* (New York: Frederick Ungar, 1961), 53.

79. Walker, "The Negro on the American Stage," 243.

80. McNamara, *Step Right Up*, 143–4.

CHAPTER 2

1. Smith, *Bert Williams,* 8.

2. City of Riverside, CA, "Frank Miller: Myths, Mission Inn, and the Making of Riverside," http:www.riversideca.gov/rlhrc/historydiv/Miller%20Exhibit.htm. (accessed 23 April 2007); Anonymous, *An Illustrated History of Southern California* (Chicago: Lewis Publishing, 1890), 468; Mission Inn Hotel and Spa, *Explore Our History of the Hotel,* http:www.missioninn.com/hotel-history.php (accessed 23 April 2007).

3. Edmond Gagey, *The San Francisco Stage: A History* (New York: Columbia University Press, 1950; reprint, 1970), 6–7, 13.

4. Ibid., 177.

5. Ibid., 172.

6. Ibid., 179.

7. Smith, *Bert Williams*, 8.

8. Ann Charters, *Nobody: The Story of Bert Williams* (New York: Macmillan, 1970), 17.

9. Bert Williams, "The Comic Side of Trouble," *American Magazine* 85 (January 1918), 34.

10. Rowland, *Bert Williams*, 11–12.

11. Bert Williams, "Bert Williams Tells of Walker," *Indianapolis Freeman*, 14 January 1911, 5.

12. Robert C. Toll, *Blacking Up: The Minstrel Show in Nineteenth-Century America* (London and New York: Oxford University Press, 1974), 4–5.

13. Ibid., 11–12.

14. Toll, *Blacking Up*, 13–14; Richard M. Dorson, "The Yankee on the Stage—a Folk Hero of American Drama," *New England Quarterly* 13, no. 3 (1940); James Atkins Shackford, *David Crockett: The Man and the Legend* (Lincoln: University of Nebraska Press, 1956; reprint, 1994).

15. Toll, *Blacking Up*, 28.

16. Ibid. Although most historians cite 1828 as the landmark date, Dale Cockrell argues that Rice likely performed first in 1830 before thrilling Philadelphia crowds in 1832. See Dale Cockrell, *Demons of Disorder: Early Blackface Performers and Their World,* ed. Don B. Wilmeth, 10 vols., Vol. 8 (Cambridge: Cambridge University Press, 1997), 63–65. Eric Lott recognizes this story as a possible legend of origination, never to be fully confirmed or refuted. See Eric Lott, *Love and Theft: Blackface Minstrelsy and the American Working Class* (New York and Oxford: Oxford University Press, 1993), 51–52. W. T. Lhamon, Jr., however, patently rejects acceptance of the story. Furthermore, he criticizes scholars' validation of such originative tales as an acceptance of contemporaneous journalists' "patronizingly reconstructed" stories meant to belittle the extant "integrative protocols" among blackface minstrelsy's publics and performers. See W. T. Lhamon, Jr., *Raising Cain: Blackface Performance from Jim Crow to Hip Hop* (Cambridge and London: Harvard University Press, 1998), 55, 153.

17. Williams J. Mahar, *Behind the Burnt Cork Mask: Early Blackface Minstrelsy and Antebellum American Popular Culture* (Urbana and Chicago: University of Illinois Press, 1999), 1.

18. Toll, *Blacking Up*, 66.

19. Cockrell, *Demons of Disorder*, 99.

20. Toll, *Blacking Up*, 68. Stanley J. Lemons, "Black Stereotypes as Reflected in Popular Culture, 1880–1920," *American Quarterly* 29 (Spring 1977): 102.

21. *Oxford English Dictionary*, "Ethiopian," http:dictionary.oed.com/cgi/entry/50078488? (accessed 23 April 2007).

22. Lott, *Love and Theft*, 20.

23. Toll, *Blacking Up*, 30–2.

24. Goldberg, *Tin Pan Alley*, 40–1.

25. Ibid., 41.

26. Ibid., 42.

27. Toll, *Blacking Up*, 52, 55, 56.

28. Alexander Saxton, "Blackface Minstrelsy," in *Inside the Minstrel Mask: Readings in Nineteenth-Century Blackface Minstrelsy*, ed., Annemarie Bean, James V. Hatch, and Brooks McNamara (Hanover and London: Wesleyan University Press, 1996), 75.

29. Toll, *Blacking Up*, 67.

30. Mel Watkins, *On the Real Side: Laughing, Lying and Signifying—The Underground Tradition of African-American Humor* (New York: Simon and Schuster, 1994), 109.

31. Toll, *Blacking Up*, 196.

32. Terry Ramsaye, *A Million and One Nights: A History of the Motion Picture* (New York: Simon and Schuster, 1964), 303–4.

33. Ibid.

34. "Colored Actor," *Toledo Bee*, n.p., in Robinson Locke Collection (Envelope 2461), Williams and Walker, Walker: Aida Overton, BRTC.

35. Walker, "The Negro on the American Stage," 243–4.

36. Williams, "Bert Williams Tells of Walker," 5.

37. Ibid.

38. Gagey, *The San Francisco Stage*, 198.

39. Julie Rose, *The World's Columbian Exposition: Idea, Experience, Aftermath*, http:xroads.virginia.edu/~MA96/WCE/title.html 1996 (accessed 23 April 2007).

40. David Whitten, "Depression of 1893," EH.Net Encyclopedia, edited by Robert Whaples, 15 August 2001, http:eh.net/encyclopedia/article/whitten.panic.1893.

41. "Thousands at the Fair," *San Francisco Examiner*, 2 January 1894, 1.

42. "Glimpses of the Throng," *San Francisco Examiner*, 28 January 1894, 8.

43. "The Fair's Closing Month," *San Francisco Examiner*, 2 June 1894, 8.

44. "From the South," *San Francisco Examiner*, 2 January 1894, 10.

45. "Tonguesters of the Midway," *San Francisco Examiner*, 11 March 1894, 1.

46. Anderson, *Snake Oil*, 16–17, 49–51.

47. "Queer People at the Fair," *San Francisco Examiner*, 8 May 1894, 14.

48. Ibid.

49. "Sunday at the Exposition," *San Francisco Examiner*, 15 January 1894, 5.

50. "The French in Dahomey," *New York Times*, 9 March 1890, 5; "Prisoners in Dahomey: A Number of Europeans in the Hands of King Behanzin," *New York Times*, 15 April 1892, 6; "Work for French Armies," *New York Times*, 10 October 1892, 6; Thomas L. Riis, ed., *The Music and Scripts of "In Dahomey"* (Madison, WI: A-R Editions for the American Musicological Society, 1996), xix.

51. Thomas L. Riis, *The Music and Scripts of "In Dahomey,"* xix.

52. "Prisoners in Dahomey: A Number of Europeans in the Hands of King Behanzin," 6.

53. "Fire in Little Dahomey," *San Francisco Examiner*, 20 June 1894, 6; Walker, "The Negro on the American Stage," 248.

54. "Two Parades at the Fair," *San Francisco Examiner*, 30 May 1894, 4.

55. Ibid.

56. "Strange Sports of Strange People," *San Francisco Examiner*, 9 June 1894, 10.

57. Ibid.

58. Ibid.

59. Ibid.

60. Walker, "The Negro on the American Stage," 248.

61. Ibid., 247–8.

62. Williams, "Bert Williams Tells of Walker," 5.

63. Ibid.

64. Smith, *Bert Williams*, 17.

65. Thomas L. Riis, *Just before Jazz: Black Musical Theater in New York, 1890–1915* (Washington, DC, and London: Smithsonian Institution Press, 1989), 20; Kellee Rene Van Aken, "Race and Gender in the Broadway Chorus" (Ph.D. diss., University of Pittsburgh, 2006), 164–5.

66. *New York Dramatic Mirror*, 19 June 1895, 11.

67. Thomas L. Riis, *Just before Jazz*, 26, 28.

68. Williams, "The Comic Side of Trouble," 60.

69. Ibid.

70. Bert Williams, "Oh! I Don't Know, You're Not So Warm!" sheet music (London: Charles Sheard, 1896), 2–4.

71. Williams, "The Comic Side of Trouble," 60.

72. "Bert Williams a Real Optimist," in Bert Williams File, HTC.

73. Ibid.

74. Lester A. Walton, "Bert Williams, Philosopher," *New York Age*, 29 December 1917, 6.

75. Ibid.

CHAPTER 3

1. Ric Burns and James Sanders, *New York: An Illustrated History*, exp. ed. (New York: Alfred A. Knopf, 2003), 183, 192.

2. The book was released in 1890.

3. David Leviatin, introduction to Jacob A. Riis, *How the Other Half Lives: Studies among the Tenements of New York*, ed. David Leviatin (Boston and New York: Bedford Books of St. Martin's Press, 1996), 3–4, 7.

4. David Leviatin, introduction to *How the Other Half Lives*, 10.

5. Burns and Sanders, *New York*, 221–2.

6. Edwin G. Burrows and Mike Wallace, *Gotham: A History of New York City to 1898* (New York and Oxford: Oxford University Press, 1999), 1234–5; Mary C. Henderson, *The City and the Theatre*, rev. and exp. ed. (New York: Back Stage Books, 2004), 152.

7. Henderson, *The City and the Theatre*, 170.

8. Ibid., 116–7.

9. Burns, *New York*, 294.

10. Henderson, *The City and the Theatre*, 170.

11. Ibid., 145.

12. Ibid., 170.

13. Ibid., 171.

14. Burns and Sanders, *New York*, 295.

15. Henderson, *The City and the Theatre*, 203; Smith, *Bert Williams*, 20.

16. Smith, *Bert Williams*, 20.

17. "George Lederer Interview," *Variety*, 17 March 1922, 14.

18. Smith, *Bert Williams*, 21.

19. "George Lederer Interview," 14.

20. Edward A. Berlin, *Reflections and Research on Ragtime*, vol. 24, *I.S.A.M. Monographs* (Brooklyn, NY: Institute for Studies in American Music, Conservatory of Music, Brooklyn College, 1987), 1.

21. Ibid., 2.

22. Ibid., 3.

23. Terry Waldo, *This Is Ragtime* (New York: Hawthorn Books, 1976), 49.

24. Ibid., 57–8.

25. Karen Sotiropoulos, *Staging Race: Black Performers in Turn of the Century America* (Cambridge, MA, and London: Harvard University Press, 2006), 93.

26. Waldo, *This Is Ragtime*, 86.

27. Ibid., 4.

28. Ibid., 5–6.

29. James H. Dormon, "Shaping the Popular Image of Post-Reconstruction American Blacks: The 'Coon Song' Phenomenon of the Gilded Age," *American Quarterly* 40 (December 1988), 450.

30. Sotiropoulos, *Staging Race*, 92.

31. Ibid., 90.

32. Ernest Hogan, "All Coons Look Alike to Me: A Darkey Misunderstanding," sheet music (New York: M. Witmark and Sons, 1896).

33. *Oxford English Dictionary Online*, "Coon," 1989, http:dictionary.oed. com/cgi/entry/50049496?query_type=word&queryword=coon&first=1&max_to_show= 10&sort_type=alpha&result_place=1&search_id=DsEO-r5h9tR-14665&hilite=50049496 (accessed 23 April 2007).

34. *Encyclopedia Brittanica Online*, "Whig Party," 2007, http:concise. britannica.com/ebc/article-9382609/Whig-Party (accessed 23 April 2007).

35. Sotiropoulos, *Staging Race*, 91.

36. See Rayford W. Logan, *The Betrayal of the Negro: From Rutherford B. Hayes to Woodrow Wilson*, new and enl. ed. (London: Collier Books, 1965; reprint, 1969).

37. Saidiya V. Hartman, *Scenes of Subjection: Terror, Slavery and Self-Making in Nineteenth-Century America* (New York and Oxford: Oxford University Press, 1997), 193–4.

38. Ibid., 195–6.

39. Ibid., 197, 202.

40. C. Vann Woodward, *The Strange Career of Jim Crow*, 2nd rev. ed. (New York and London: Oxford University Press, 1955; reprint, 1966), 97–102.

41. Ibid., 83–6.

42. Lemons, "Black Stereotypes," 106.

43. Joseph Boskin, *Sambo: The Rise and Demise of an American Jester* (New York and Oxford: Oxford University Press, 1986), 79, 108.

44. Logan, *The Betrayal of the Negro*, 371.

45. George M. Fredrickson, *The Black Image in the White Mind: The Debate on Afro-American Character and Destiny, 1817–1914* (Hanover, NH: Wesley University Press, 1971), 230.

46. Fredrickson, *The Black Image*, 236. For historical studies on black extinction, see Thomas H. Huxley, "Emancipation—Black and White [1865]," in *Science and Education* (London: Macmillan, 1893); John Richard Dennett, *The South As It Is, 1865–1866*, ed., Henry Christman (Athens: University of Georgia Press, 1986). On the census, Fredrickson, *The Black Image*, 239–40.

47. Fredrickson, *The Black Image*, 249.

48. Ibid., 253. Various writers espousing racist views published works that sought to combine statistical material with Darwinism. See Charles L. Brace, *The Races of the Old World: A Manual of Ethnology* (New York: Charles Scribner, 1870); Philip A. Bruce, *The Plantation Negro as a Freeman* (New York: G. P. Putnam's Sons, 1889); Charles Carroll, *The Negro as Beast* (St. Louis, MO: American Books and Bible House, 1900); Thomas Nelson Page, *The Negro: The Southerner's Problem* (New York: Charles Scribner's Sons, 1904); Alfred P. Schultz, *Race or Mongrel* (Boston: L. C. Page and Co., 1908); Williams P. Pickett, *The Negro Problem* (New York: G. P. Putnam's Sons, 1909).

49. Fredrickson, *The Black Image*, 250, 252.

50. Dormon, "Shaping the Popular Image," 453.

51. Bert Williams, "Oh! I Don't Know, You're Not So Warm!" sheet music. Italics in original.

52. Tom Logan, "The Coon's Trade-Mark" sheet music (New York: Jos. W. Stern, 1898).

53. Lemons, "Black Stereotypes," 111.

54. Berlin, *Reflections*, 45.

55. Ibid., 46.

56. Goldberg, *Tin Pan Alley*, 202–4.

57. Waldo, *This Is Ragtime*, 80.

58. Lemons, "Black Stereotypes," 103.

59. Ibid., 104.

60. Smith, *Bert Williams*, 22–3.

61. George W. Walker, "Bert and Me and Them," *New York Age*, 24 December 1908, 4.

62. Robert W. Snyder, *The Voice of the City: Vaudeville and Popular Culture in New York* (New York: Oxford University Press, 1989; reprint, 2000), 12–13. The origins of vaudeville are complicated; the term is said to refer either to "pastoral ballads from the valley of the River Vire [in Normandy, France] or urban folksongs: *voix de ville*, or 'voice of the city.'" DiMeglio writes that "vaudeville" might also "refer to the valley of the Vire River, where Val de Vire was often pronounced Vau de Vire." John E. DiMeglio, *Vaudeville U.S.A.* (Bowling Green, OH: Bowling Green University Popular Press, 1973), 19.

63. Snyder, *The Voice of the City*, 12. For more on Pastor, see Susan Kattwinkel, *Tony Pastor Presents: Afterpieces from the Vaudeville Stage* (Westport, CT: Greenwood Press, 1998).

64. Burns, *New York*, 213; Snyder, *The Voice of the City*, 3–4.

65. James Traub, *The Devil's Playground: A Century of Pleasure and Profit in Times Square* (New York: Random House, 2004), 9.

66. David Nasaw, *Going Out: The Rise and Fall of Public Amusements* (Cambridge, MA: Harvard University Press, 1999), 26.

67. Traub, *Devil's Playground*, 10.

68. Snyder, *The Voice of the City*, xiii.

69. Dormon, "Shaping the Popular Image," 454.

70. M. Alison Kibler, *Rank Ladies: Gender and Cultural Hierarchy in American Vaudeville* (Chapel Hill: University of North Carolina Press, 1999), 15.

71. Albert F. McLean, Jr., "Genesis of Vaudeville: Two Letters from B. F. Keith," *Theater Survey* 1 (1960), 86.

72. Nasaw, *Going Out*, 13.

73. Ibid., 21, 36–7.

74. Charles and Louise Samuels, *Once Upon a Stage: The Merry World of Vaudeville* (New York: Dodd, Mead, 1974), 41; Watkins, *On the Real Side*, 155.

75. Snyder, *The Voice of the City*, 158.

76. Edwin Milton Royle, "The Vaudeville Theatre," *Scribner's Magazine* 26 (October 1899), 487.

77. Watkins, *On the Real Side*, 155, quoting Hartley Davis, *Everybody's Magazine* 13 (August 1905), 231–40.

78. Anthony Slide, ed., *Selected Vaudeville Criticism* (Metuchen, NJ: Scarecrow Press, 1988), 206.

79. Kibler, *Rank Ladies*, 25.

80. Nasaw, *Going Out*, 11.

81. Ibid., 11, 31.

82. Chicago Commission on Race Relations, *The Negro in Chicago: A Study of Race Relations and a Race Riot* (Chicago: 1922), 317–18. Quoted in Nasaw, *Going Out*, 49.

83. Lemons, "Black Stereotypes," 104.

84. Nasaw, *Going Out*, 57.

85. Ibid.

86. Ibid., 31, 59.

87. Henderson, *The City and the Theatre*, 126.

88. Ibid., 138.

89. Ibid.

90. Walker, "The Negro on the American Stage," 246.

91. For more on this strategy of "reinscription," see David Krasner, *Resistance, Parody, and Double Consciousness in African American Theatre, 1895–1910* (New York: St. Martin's Press, 1997), 26. "Natural black" was Walker's expression to describe those performers whose racial identification was Negro.

92. "Vaudeville Stage—Koster and Bial's," *New York Dramatic Mirror*, 31 October 1896, 19.

93. "Vaudeville Stage—Last Week's Bills: Koster and Bial's," *New York Dramatic Mirror*, 9 January 1897, 17.

94. Yiddish vaudeville comedians Weber and Fields performed as an ethnic duo, although interestingly, they chose to perform as "Germans" rather than their actual ethnic group.

95. Douglas Gilbert, *American Vaudeville: Its Life and Times* (New York: Whittlesey House, 1940), 285–6.

96. Christie Davies, *Ethnic Humor around the World* (Bloomington and Indianapolis: Indiana University Press, 1990), 19.

97. Toll, *Blacking Up*, 262–3; Krasner, *Resistance, Parody, and Double Consciousness*, 22.

98. Barbara L. Webb, "Authentic Possibilities: Plantation Performance of the 1890s," *Theatre Journal* 56 (2004): 74–5.

99. *New York Times*, 26 May 1895, quoted in Riis, *Just before Jazz*, 23.

100. Lemons, "Black Stereotypes," 102–3.

101. William Foster, "Memoirs of William Foster: Pioneers of the Stage," in *The Official Theatrical World of Colored Artists*, ed. Theophilus Lewis (New York: Theatrical World Publishing, 1928), 47.

102. Ibid.

103. Ibid.

104. David Krasner notes that Ada's name did not become official until 1906, but as early as 1902 her name would begin to appear as "Aida." Krasner, *Resistance, Parody, and Double Consciousness*, 171, f4.

105. Marshall and Jean Stearns, *Jazz Dance: The Story of American Vernacular Dance* (New York: Schirmer, 1979), 123.

106. Lawrence W. Levine, *Black Culture and Black Consciousness: Afro-American Folk Thought from Slavery to Freedom* (New York and Oxford: Oxford University Press, 1977), 16.

107. Lynne Fauley Emery, *Black Dance in the United States from 1619 to 1970* (Palo Alto, CA: National Press Books, 1972), 91.

108. Toll, *Blacking Up*, 263.

109. Waldo, *This Is Ragtime*, 25.

110. Emery, *Black Dance in the United States*, 208.

111. Krasner, *Resistance, Parody, and Double Consciousness*, 75.

112. Carl Van Vechten, *In the Garrett* (New York: Alfred A. Knopf, 1920), 313–4.

113. Marshall and Jean Stearns, *Jazz Dance*, 117, quoting *Boston Traveller*, 13 May 1909, n.p.

114. Thomas DeFrantz, "Simmering Passivity: The Black Male Body in Concert Dance," in *Moving Words: Re-Writing Dance*, ed. Gay Morris (London and New York: Routledge, 1996), 108.

115. Emery, *Black Dance in the United States*, 212.

116. "Vaudeville Stage—Koster and Bial's," *New York Dramatic Mirror*, 16 January 1897, 19; "Vaudeville Stage—Koster and Bial's," *New York Dramatic Mirror*, 20 February 1897, 17.

117. "Vaudeville Stage—Last Week's Bills: Koster and Bial's," *New York Dramatic Mirror*, 27 February 1897, 17.

118. Ibid.; "Vaudeville Stage—Last Week's Bills: Koster and Bial's," *New York Dramatic Mirror*, 13 March 1897, 18.

119. "Vaudeville Correspondence—Chicago, Ill.," *New York Dramatic Mirror*, 18 June 1898, 18; "Vaudeville Correspondence—San Francisco, Cal.," *New York Dramatic Mirror*, 30 April 1898, 18; "Vaudeville Correspondences," *New York Dramatic Mirror*, 27 March 1897, 20.

120. Williams, "The Comic Side of Trouble," 60.

121. "Vaudeville Stage—Last Week's Bills: Keith's Union Square," *New York Dramatic Mirror*, 17 April 1897, 17.

122. Ethel Barrymore, *Memories: An Autobiography* (New York: Harper and Brothers, 1955), 178. Although Ethel Barrymore attributes the story to her brother Lionel, it is apparent from the reviews of the time that it was her father, Maurice, with whom Williams and Walker actually appeared in vaudeville.

123. "Vaudeville Stage—Last Week's Bills: Keith's Union Square," 17; "Vaudeville Stage: Proctor's," *New York Dramatic Mirror*, 1 January 1898, 16.

124. James Weldon Johnson, *Black Manhattan* (New York: Alfred A. Knopf, 1930), 105.

125. *Indianapolis Freeman*, 2 February 1898, 4.

126. *Indianapolis Freeman*, 9 September 1899, 1.

CHAPTER 4

1. Walker, "The Negro on the American Stage," 247.

2. Ibid.

3. Ibid.

4. Joanne M. Braxton, ed., *The Collected Poetry of Paul Laurence Dunbar* (Charlottesville and London: University Press of Virginia, 1993), ix.

5. Seth M. Scheiner, *Negro Mecca: A History of the Negro in New York City, 1865–1920* (New York: New York University Press, 1965), 6.

6. Gilbert Osofsky, *Harlem: The Making of a Ghetto, New York, 1890–1930*, 2nd ed. (New York: Harper and Row, 1963; reprint, 1971), 3; Scheiner, *Negro Mecca*, 7, 10.

7. Scheiner, *Negro Mecca*, 16.

8. Osofsky, *Harlem*, 9.

9. Jacob A. Riis, *How the Other Half Lives*, 157.

10. Osofsky, *Harlem*, 13.

11. Jacob A. Riis, *How the Other Half Lives*, 157.

12. Marcy S. Sacks, *Before Harlem: The Black Experience in New York City before World War I* (Philadelphia: University of Pennsylvania Press, 2006), 5.

13. Berlin, *Reflections*, 45.

14. Osofsky, *Harlem*, 12.

15. Ibid., 13.

16. Ibid., 4–5.

17. Ransom quoted in Ibid., 15.

18. Sotiropoulos, *Staging Race*, 53.

19. Ibid.; Berlin, *Reflections*, 60–1.

20. Quoted in Sacks, *Before Harlem*, 188.

21. Ibid., 188–9.

22. Ibid., 189.

23. James Weldon Johnson, *Along This Way: The Autobiography of James Weldon Johnson* (New York: Viking, 1934), 171.

24. Berlin, *Reflections*, 62–3.

25. Waldo, *This Is Ragtime*, 19.

26. Stanley Appelbaum, *The Chicago World's Fair of 1893: A Photographic Record* (New York: Dover, 1980), 103.

27. Sotiropoulos, *Staging Race*, 27, 28.

28. Braxton, *The Collected Poetry of Paul Laurence Dunbar*, xiii.

29. Ibid.

30. Thomas L. Riis, *Just before Jazz*, 40–1.

31. St. Clair Drake and Horace R. Cayton, *Black Metropolis: A Study of Negro Life in a Northern City*, Rev. and enl. ed. (Chicago: University of Chicago Press, 1993), 51–2.

32. Sotiropoulos, *Staging Race*, 29.

33. Ibid., 27–28, 32–33.

34. Quoted in Sotiropoulos, 34.

35. Braxton, *The Collected Poetry of Paul Laurence Dunbar*, 71.

36. Sotiropoulos, *Staging Race*, 59; Thomas L. Riis, *Just before Jazz*, 41.

37. Thomas L. Riis, *Just before Jazz*, 42–3.

38. Krasner, *Resistance, Parody, and Double Consciousness*, 25.

39. Will Marion Cook, "Clorindy, the Origin of the Cakewalk," *Theatre Arts* 31, no. 9 (1947), 61. Emphasis in original.

40. Ibid., 61–2.

41. Ibid., 62.

42. "Will Marion Cook File," Helen Armstead-Johnson Collection, SC.

43. Cook, "Clorindy," 64.

44. James Weldon Johnson, *Along This Way*, 160.

45. Thomas L. Riis, *Just before Jazz*, 49.

46. Tim Brooks, *Lost Sounds: Blacks and the Birth of the Recording Industry, 1890–1919* (Urbana and Chicago: University of Illinois Press, 2004), 108.

47. Smith, *Bert Williams*, 34.

48. "The Theaters," *Cincinnati Enquirer*, 20 September 1898, 3.

49. "*Senegambian Carnival*," *Boston Globe*, 2 September 1898, 2.

50. Smith, *Bert Williams*, 34.

51. Tim Brooks, *Lost Sounds*, 108.

52. Thomas L. Riis, *Just before Jazz*, 51.

53. Ibid., 62.

54. "Williams and Walker's *Senegambian Carnival* at the Academy," *Washington Post*, 11 October 1898, 7.

55. Lloyd Lewis, *It Takes All Kinds*, 236–7.

56. Marriage Certificate, *Vital Records*, NYMA.

57. James Weldon Johnson, *Along This Way*, 176–7.

58. Smith, *Bert Williams*, 36.

59. Tim Brooks, *Lost Sounds*, 108.

60. Krasner, *Resistance, Parody, and Double Consciousness*, 27.

61. Description in "The Gayety," *Brooklyn Eagle*, 17 January 1898, 5.

62. "Williams and Walker in *A Lucky Coon* at the Academy," *Washington Post*, 9 May 1898, 7.

63. Smith, *Bert Williams*, 39.

64. Thomas L. Riis, *Just before Jazz*, 51–2.

65. Smith, *Bert Williams*, 40.

66. Tim Brooks, *Lost Sounds*, 108.

67. *Boston Globe*, 13 March 1900, 9.

68. Unidentified newspaper clipping in (Bert) Williams and (George) Walker (Comedy Team) Clipping File, BRTC.

69. "Lyceum—Williams and Walker," *Detroit Free Press*, 19 December 1899, n.p., in Bert Williams File, HTC. In 2006, such a sum would be roughly equivalent to $11,680. See S. Morgan Friedman, "The Inflation Calculator," http:www.westegg.com/inflation (accessed 23 April 2007).

70. Osofsky, *Harlem*, 46–7.

71. Ibid., 47–8.

72. Tim Brooks, *Lost Sounds*, 108.

73. James Weldon Johnson, *Black Manhattan*, 127.

74. Sotiropoulos, *Staging Race*, 42–3.

75. Ibid., 43.

76. Tim Brooks, *Lost Sounds*, 109.

77. Cecil Mack (Richard C. McPherson, music) and Thomas Lemonier (lyrics), "Miss Hannah from Savannah," sheet music (J. W. Stern & Co., 1901). Music Division, Library of Congress.

78. Willard B. Gatewood, *Aristocrats of Color: The Black Elite, 1880–1920* (Fayetteville: University of Arkansas Press, 1991; reprint, 2000), ix, x, 7–8.

79. "The Sons of Ham," *Denver Post*, 25 May 1901, 1.

80. "Star—*Sons of Ham*," *New York Dramatic Mirror*, 20 October 1900, 17.

81. Smith, *Bert Williams*, 44.

82. "Park—Williams and Walker," 7 May 1901, n.p., in *Sons of Ham* Clipping File, HTC.

83. *Brooklyn Eagle*, 1 October 1901, 6.

84. Tim Brooks, *Lost Sounds*, 109.

85. Ibid., 2.

86. Ibid., 4.

87. Ibid., 2.

88. Ibid., 6.

89. Benjamin L. Aldridge, "The Victor Talking Machine Company" (R.C.A. Victor, 1964), 6. Online at http:www.davidsarnoff.org/vtm-chapter2.html.

90. Tim Brooks, *Lost Sounds*, 2.

91. Jim Walsh, "Favorite Pioneer Recording Artists: Bert Williams, a Thwarted Genius," *Hobbies*, September 1950, 25. Emphasis added.

92. James Weldon Johnson, "The Dilemma of the Negro Author," *The American Mercury* 15.60 (December 1928), 477.

93. See Leon F. Litwack, *Been in the Storm So Long: The Aftermath of Slavery* (New York: Vintage, 1979), for a discussion of the endeavor of blacks and whites to adapt after slavery's end.

94. August Meier, *Negro Thought in America, 1880–1915: Racial Ideologies in the Age of Booker T. Washington* (Ann Arbor: University of Michigan Press, 1969), 15.

95. Henry Louis Gates, Jr., "The Trope of a New Negro and the Reconstruction of the Image of the Black," *Representations* 24 (Autumn 1988), 129–55.

96. Ibid., 129.

97. Ibid., 131.

98. Gates, "The Trope of a New Negro," 129, 132; Frank M. Kirkland, "Modernity and Intellectual Life in Black," *The Philosophical Forum* 24.1–3 (Fall–Spring 1992), 136–65.

99. Evelyn Brooks Higginbotham, *Righteous Discontent: The Women's Movement in the Black Baptist Church* (Cambridge, MA: Harvard University Press, 1993), 185–229.

100. Alexander Crummell, *Africa and America: Addresses and Discourses* (Miami: Mnemosyne Publishing, 1969), 13–9.

101. Although Washington's and Du Bois's roles were quite prominent during the period, my exclusive attention to them by no means suggests that they embody the totality of Negro leadership and thought during the period.

102. Booker T. Washington, *Up from Slavery* (New York: Doubleday, 1998); W. E. Burghardt Du Bois, *The Souls of Black Folk*, 5th ed. (Chicago: A.C. McClurg, 1904); Cary D. Wintz, *Black Culture and the Harlem Renaissance* (Houston, TX: Rice University Press, 1988), 42–4.

103. The bibliographies of Washington and Du Bois are extensive. Studies include comparative works such as: Manning Marable, *Black Leadership: Four Great American Leaders and the Struggle for Civil Rights* (New York: Penguin, 1999); Cary D. Wintz, ed., *African American Political Thought, 1890–1930* (Armonk, NY: M. E. Sharpe, 1996). On Booker T. Washington: Louis R. Harlan, *Booker T. Washington: The Wizard of Tuskegee, 1901–1915* (New York: Oxford University Press, 1983); Louis R. Harlan, *Booker T. Washington: The Making of a Black Leader, 1856–1901* (New York: Oxford University Press, 1972). On W. E. B. Du Bois: Bernard Bell, Emily Grosholz, and James Stewart, eds., *W. E. B. Du Bois on Race and Culture: Philosophy, Politics, and Poetics* (New York: Routledge, 1996); Shamoon Zamir, *Dark Voices: W. E. B. Du Bois and American Thought, 1888–1903* (Chicago: University of Chicago Press, 1995); David L. Lewis, *W. E. B. Du Bois—Biography of a Race, 1868–1919* (New York: H. Holt, 1993).

104. W. E. Burghardt Du Bois, *The Gift of Black Folk: The Negroes in the Making of America* (Boston: Stratford Company, 1924; reprint, 1968); Booker T. Washington, *The Story of the Negro: The Rise of the Race from Slavery*, vol. 2 (New York: Doubleday, Page, 1909).

105. Washington, *The Story of the Negro*, 280–1.

106. Du Bois, *The Gift of Black Folk*, 310.

107. Ibid., 310.

108. Louis R. Harlan and Raymond W. Smock, eds., *The Booker T. Washington Papers*, vol. 10 (Urbana and Chicago: University of Illinois Press, 1977), 389. From a September 1910 article in *American Magazine*.

109. Ibid., 389.

110. Ibid., 391.

111. My thanks to Adam Biggs for suggesting this phrase.

112. Peggy Phelan refers to this as "representational visibility." Peggy Phelan, *Unmarked: The Politics of Performance* (London and New York: Routledge, 1993), 1, 7.

113. Ibid., 7.

114. *Bandanna Land* was also written as *Bandana Land* in various reviews of the period. Both are used here, accordingly.

115. Thomas L. Riis, *Just before Jazz*, 43.

CHAPTER 5

1. Thomas L. Riis, *The Music and Scripts of "In Dahomey,"* xxi–xxii, xxiii.

2. Krasner, *Resistance, Parody, and Double Consciousness*, 63, 42.

3. Gerald Bordman, *American Musical Theatre: A Chronicle*, exp. ed. (Oxford and London: Oxford University Press, 1986), 190; Charters, *Nobody*, 69.

4. Smith, *Bert Williams*, 50.

5. Rowland, *Bert Williams*, 182.

6. Sarah L. C. Clapp, "The Subscription Enterprises of John Ogilby and Richard Blome," *Modern Philology* 30, no. 4 (1933), 366; *Encyclopedia Britannica Online*, "Ogilby, John," 2007, http:www.britannica.com/eb/article-9056830 (accessed 6 June 2007).

7. Nicholas Hudson, "From 'Nation' to 'Race': The Origin of Racial Classification in Eighteenth-Century Thought," *Eighteenth-Century Studies* 29, no. 3 (1996): 249.

8. Ibid.

9. John Ogilby, *Africa: Being an Accurate Description of the Regions of Egypt, Barbary, Lybia, and Billedulgerid, the Land of Negroes, Guinee, Ethiopia and the Abyssines.* (London: Printed by Tho. Johnson for the author, 1670), 643, 644.

10. Ibid., 321.

11. Rowland, *Bert Williams*, 183.

12. "Rebellion in Dahomey Feared," *New York Times*, 17 January 1901, 7; "Behanzin, Deposed King of Dahomey, Probably Perished," *New York Times*, 1 June 1902, 24.

13. Krasner, *Resistance, Parody and Double Consciousness*, 43.

14. David Krasner writes that *In Dahomey* is the third and final version of two earlier, more challengingly critical, satirical, and parodic musicals, *Jes Lak White Fo'ks* and *The Cannibal King*. In effect, *In Dahomey* is itself a product of the need for the musical's black creators to respond to the demands of time, and an indication of the limits placed on African American theater. See Ibid., 55–75.

15. Ibid., 54.

16. Walker, "The Negro on the American Stage," 248.

17. Krasner, *Resistance, Parody, and Double Consciousness*, 67.

18. *Encyclopedia Britannica Online*, "Conan Doyle, Sir Arthur," http:www. britannica.com/eb/article-9031102 (accessed 10 June 2007); *Encyclopedia Britannica Online*, "Pinkerton, Allan," http:www.britannica.com/eb/article-9060099 (accessed 10 June 2007). For more on the nineteenth-century audience's relationship to Shakespeare, see Lawrence W. Levine, *Highbrow/Lowbrow: The Emergence of Cultural Hierarchy in America* (Cambridge, MA, and London: Harvard University Press, 1990).

19. *Encyclopedia Britannica Online*, "Newspaper Syndicate," http:www. britannica.com/eb/article-9055610 (accessed 12 June 2007); Thomas L. Riis, *The Music and Scripts of "In Dahomey,"* xxv.

20. Ibid., xxv, xxviii.

21. Ibid., xxv, lxvii. Charters details a quite distinct plot line, no doubt a different version of the play performed during its run from September 1902 to June of 1905. See Charters, *Nobody*.

22. Charters stated that the show made $64,000. Charters, *Nobody*, 77.

23. "Dahomey on Broadway," *New York Times*, 19 February 1903, 9.

24. Krasner, *Resistance, Parody, and Double Consciousness*, 67.

25. A "pigs in clover" puzzle is a dexterity game using a rolling ball, designed in 1889 by Charles Crandall. The aim was to be the first to get one's marble, "a pig"—each of which represented a politician of the time—into the "pig pen," the White House, at the center of the board.

26. "We are Now Broadway Stars," in (Bert) Williams and (George) Walker (Comedy Team) Clipping File, BRTC.

27. Ibid.

28. Ibid.

29. Ibid.

30. "Dahomey on Broadway," 9.

31. Ibid.

32. Thomas L. Riis, *The Music and Scripts of "In Dahomey,"* xvi.

33. Ibid., xxiv.

34. Krasner, *Resistance, Parody, and Double Consciousness*, 73.

35. "Dahomey on Broadway," 9.

36. Thomas L. Riis, *The Music and Scripts of "In Dahomey,"* 156.

37. Ibid., 155, 158.

38. Krasner, *Resistance, Parody, and Double Consciousness*, 71.

39. Ibid., 72.

40. Thomas L. Riis, *The Music and Scripts of "In Dahomey,"* 142.

41. Ibid., 142–3.

42. Ibid., 146.

43. Ibid., xxxv, 154.

44. Ibid., 86.

45. James Weldon Johnson, *The Book of American Negro Poetry* (New York: Harcourt, 1931), 4.

46. Thomas L. Riis, *The Music and Scripts of "In Dahomey,"* lxi.

47. Ibid.

48. Ibid.

49. Ibid.

50. Ibid., lxi–lxii.

51. Ibid., lxii.

52. Ibid.

53. Irene Mawer, *The Art of Mime: Its History and Technique in Education and the Theatre* (London: Methuen, 1932), 125.

54. Ibid., 127.

55. Unidentified newspaper article in *In Dahomey* Clipping File, BRTC.

56. Rowland, *Bert Williams*, 42.

57. Lester Walton, "Bert Williams, Philosopher," *New York Age*, 29 December 1917, 6.

58. J. B., "Bert Williams," *The Soil: A Magazine of Art*, December 1916, 19.

59. Ibid. Emphasis in original.

60. Ibid.

61. Walton, "Bert Williams, Philosopher," 6.

62. "Dahomey on Broadway," 9.

63. *New York World*, 19 February 1903, 3.

64. *New York Clipper*, 28 February 1903, 6.

65. "Dahomey on Broadway," 9. Emphasis added.

66. Lester A. Walton, "The Future of the Negro on the Stage," *Colored American Magazine*, May and June 1903, 440.

67. Ibid., 442.

68. Ibid.

69. "Darktown is Desolate," 29 April 1903 article in Robinson Locke Collection, Robinson Locke Collection (Envelope 2461), Williams and Walker, Walker: Aida Overton, BRTC.

70. Bert Williams, "Fun in the Land of J. Bull," *The Green Book Album*, July 1909, 73.

71. "Darktown is Desolate," 29 April 1903 article in Robinson Locke Collection (Envelope 2461), Williams and Walker, Walker: Aida Overton, BRTC.

72. Ibid.

73. Williams, "Fun in the Land of J. Bull," 72.

74. "From 'Dahomey' to Buckingham Palace," *The (London) Era*, 27 June 1903, 13.

75. *"In Dahomey:* At the Shaftesbury Theatre," *(London) Playgoer*, 465. In *In Dahomey* Clipping File, SC.

76. Ibid.

77. Raymond Mander and Joe Mitchenson, *The Lost Theatres of London* (London: Rupert Hart-Davis, 1968), 492, 493.

78. Williams, "Fun in the Land of J. Bull," 75.

79. Ibid., 75–6.

80. Rowland, *Bert Williams*, 53.

81. *"In Dahomey.* Amusing Production at the Shaftesbury Theatre," *Daily Mail (London)*, 18 May 1903, 3.

82. Emphasis added. P. C., "Shaftesbury Theatre. *In Dahomey*," *Daily News (London)*, 18 May 1903, 12.

83. Ibid; *"In Dahomey* at the Shaftesbury," *Sphere (London)*, 23 May 1903, 162.

84. Unidentified article in *In Dahomey* Clipping File, BRTC.

85. Ibid.

86. Daphne A. Brooks, *Bodies in Dissent: Spectacular Performances of Race and Freedom, 1850–1910* (Durham, NC and London: Duke University Press, 2006), 207–8.

87. Ibid., 209.

88. "Shaftesbury Theatre," 18 May 1903, n.p., in *In Dahomey* Clipping File, BRTC.

89. P. C., "Shaftesbury Theatre. *In Dahomey*," 12.

90. *The (London) Era*, 23 May 1903, 14, quoted in Jeffrey Green, "*In Dahomey* in London in 1903," *The Black Perspective in Music,* Vol. 11, no. 1 (1983), 35.

91. "*In Dahomey:* At the Shaftesbury Theatre," *The (London) Playgoer*, 465, in *In Dahomey* Clipping File, SC.

92. "Black but Comely," *The (London) Star*, 16 May 1903, 3.

93. "*In Dahomey,*" *The (London) Era*, 16.

94. "The Shaftesbury," *The (London) Stage*, 21 May 1903, 14.

95. Ibid.

96. Ibid.; "*In Dahomey,*" *The (London) Era*, 16.

97. "*In Dahomey,*" *The (London) Era* 16.

98. "Plays and Players," *Weekly Dispatch*, 24 May 1903, 8.

99. "Prince Edward's Birthday Party," *St. James's Gazette (London)*, 24 June 1903, 7.

100. Rowland, *Bert Williams*, 54.

101. Ibid., 55.

102. Ibid., 57.

103. John H. Cook (music), Paul Laurence Dunbar and E. P. Moran (lyrics), "Evah Dahkey is a King," sheet music (Chicago: Harry Von Tilzer Music Publishing, 1902). In Charles M. Templeton, Sr., Sheet Music Collection, Mississippi State University.

104. Ibid.

105. *New York World,* 27 June 1903, n.p., in Robinson Locke Collection (Envelope 2461), Williams and Walker, Walker: Aida Overton, BRTC.

106. "Nobility Learns the Cakewalk," *London Notes*, 4 July 1903, n.p., in Robinson Locke Collection (Envelope 2461), Williams and Walker, Walker: Aida Overton, BRTC.

107. Unidentified 29 March 1903 article in Robinson Locke Collection (Envelope 2461), Williams and Walker, Walker: Aida Overton, BRTC.

108. Constance Beerbohm, "The 'Cake-Walk' and How to Dance It," *The (London) Tatler*, 1 July 1903, 13.

109. Unidentified 29 March 1903 article in Robinson Locke Collection (Envelope 2461), Williams and Walker, Walker: Aida Overton, BRTC.

110. Beerbohm, "The 'Cake-Walk' and How to Dance It," 13.

111. Ibid.

112. *New York World,* 27 June 1903 n.p., in Robinson Locke Collection (Envelope 2461), Williams and Walker, Walker: Aida Overton, BRTC.

113. Michael Craton and Gail Saunders, *Islanders in the Stream: A History of the Bahamian People*, vol. 2 (Athens and London: University of Georgia Press, 1998), 217–9.

114. Henry Sampson, *The Ghost Walks: A Chronological History of Blacks in Show Business, 1865–1910* (Metuchen, NJ, and London: Scarecrow Press, 1988), 80.

115. "The Alexandra, N.," *The (London) Stage*, 11 February 1904, 15.

116. "The Marlborough," *The (London) Stage*, 25 February 1904, 17.

117. Clipping from *Royal Magazine*, September 1903, 387, in *Footlight Notes*, 1994, "Press Clippings for the Week Ending Saturday, 15 February 1903," http:www.gabrielleray.150m.com/ArchivePressText2003/20030215.html (accessed 15 June 2007).

118. "The Alexandra, N.," 15.

119. "Globe Theatre: *In Dahomey*," *Boston Transcript*, 21 March 1905, n.p., in *In Dahomey* Clipping File, BRTC.

120. "Globe Theatre," *Boston Post*, 21 March 1905, n.p., in *In Dahomey* Clipping File, BRTC.

121. R. C. Murray, "Williams and Walker," *Colored American Magazine*, September 1905, 496.

CHAPTER 6

1. "People Who Amuse Us," *New York Globe and Commercial*, 27 October 1905, n.p., in Robinson Locke Collection (Envelope 2461), Williams and Walker, Walker: Aida Overton, BRTC.

2. Thomas L. Riis, *Just before Jazz*, 35, 39, 46.

3. Wayne D. Shirley, "The House of Melody: A List of Publications of the Gotham-Attucks Music Company at the Library of Congress," *The Black Perspective in Music* 15, no. 1 (1987), 90; Thomas L. Riis, *The Music and Scripts of "In Dahomey,"* xxii.

4. Shirley, "The House of Melody," 80. The company would become Gotham-Attucks following a merger in 1905. Ibid., 79.

5. Ibid., 90.

6. "Washington, Williams and Walker," *New York Age*, 3 August 1905, 7.

7. Ibid.

8. Ibid.

9. Thomas L. Riis, *Just Before Jazz*, 113.

10. Rowland, *Bert Williams*, 68.

11. Charters, *Nobody*, 83.

12. Benjamin H. Hurtig, *Jules Hurtig and Harry J. Seamon vs. Bert A. Williams and George W. Walker,* 19 June 1905, 5, NYMA.

13. Ibid.

14. Ibid.

15. Ibid.

16. "Abyssinia in Receiver's Hands," *New York Telegraph*, n.p., in Robinson Locke Collection (Envelope 2461), Williams and Walker, Walker: Aida Overton, BRTC. This sum would be equivalent to roughly $865,500 in 2006. S. Morgan Friedman, "The Inflation Calculator," http:www.westegg.com/inflation/ (accessed 6 June 2007).

17. *Encyclopedia Britannica Online*, "Niagara Movement," http:www.britannica.com/eb/article-9055675 (accessed 6 June 2007).

18. "To Pension President," *New York Times*, 7 January 1905, 1; "Burnett to Lose His Fees," *New York Times*, 3 March 1905, 1.

19. Mary C. Henderson, "*The Voice of the City: Vaudeville and Popular Culture in New York* (Review)," *Theatre Journal* 53, no. 2 (2001), 350.

20. Snyder, *The Voice of the City*, 95; DiMeglio, *Vaudeville U.S.A.*, 20.

21. Snyder, *The Voice of the City*, 84. In small-time vaudeville, the leading owner was Marcus Loew, who started in New York in 1905, spreading his chain through the boroughs of Brooklyn, Manhattan, and the Bronx. By 1918, it had expanded to 112 theaters between the United States and Canada. Snyder, *The Voice of the City*, 76.

22. *Indianapolis Freeman*, 9 December 1905, n.p., in (Bert) Williams and (George) Walker (Comedy Team) Clipping File, BRTC. See also Henry Sampson, *The Ghost Walks: A Chronological History of Blacks in Show Business, 1865–1910*, 353.

23. Rowland, *Son of Laughter*, 21–2.

24. R. C. Murray, "Williams and Walker," 502.

25. "Only Afro-American Theatre in World," *New York Age*, 18 October 1906, 5.

26. Ibid.

27. "Colored Actor," *Toledo Bee*, n.p., in Robinson Locke Collection (Envelope 2461), Williams and Walker, Walker: Aida Overton, BRTC.

28. Charters, *Nobody*, 88.

29. Ibid.

30. Ibid.

31. Tom Fletcher, *100 Years of the Negro in Show Business* (New York: Burdge, 1954), 239, 241–2.

32. James Weldon Johnson, *Along This Way*, 176.

33. "People Who Amuse Us," *New York Globe and Commercial*, 27 October 2005, n.p., in Robinson Locke Collection (Envelope 2461), Williams and Walker, Walker: Aida Overton, BRTC.

34. Ibid.

35. Ibid.

36. *New York Globe,* 27 October 1905, n.p., in Robinson Locke Collection (Envelope 2461), Williams and Walker, Walker: Aida Overton, BRTC.

37. Great Northern Theatre program, in *Abyssinia* Clipping File, SC.

38. Sotiropoulos, *Staging Race*, 149.

39. Ibid.

40. Ibid.

41. Ibid., 150.

42. *Abyssinia* script, SC; Krasner, *Resistance, Parody, and Double Consciousness*, 101; Sotiropoulos, *Staging Race*, 151. As with *In Dahomey*, differences in summaries of the plot indicate the scripts' evolutionary nature.

43. Allen Woll, *Dictionary of Black Theatre* (Westport, CT: Greenwood Press, 1983), 3.

44. Gerald Bordman, *American Musical Theatre: A Chronicle*, exp. ed. (Oxford and London: Oxford University Press, 1986), 219.

45. Loften Mitchell, *Black Drama: The Story of the American Negro in the Theatre* (New York: Hawthorn, 1967), 49.

46. "The Color Line in Musical Comedy," *Chicago Herald*, n.p., in Robinson Locke Collection (Envelope 2461), Williams and Walker, Walker: Aida Overton, BRTC.

47. Ibid.

48. Krasner, *Resistance, Parody, and Double Consciousness*, 107.

49. Ibid., 107–8.

50. Unidentified article in Robinson Locke Collection (Envelope 2461), Williams and Walker, Walker: Aida Overton, BRTC.

51. *"Abyssinia:* Williams and Walker Make a Hit with a New Comedy," *New York Age*, 22 February 1906, 1.

52. *"Abyssinia* at the Park," *Philadelphia Inquirer*, 10 April 1906, 4.

53. *"Abyssinia,"* New York Evening Post, 21 February 1906, 7.

54. Unidentified article in Bert Williams File, HTC.

55. "Williams and Walker's Fine Show," *Toledo Blade*, 28 January 1907, n.p., in Robinson Locke Collection (Envelope 2461), Williams and Walker, Walker: Aida Overton, BRTC.

56. Unidentified clipping in Robinson Locke Collection (Envelope 2461), Williams and Walker, Walker: Aida Overton, BRTC.

57. Rowland, *Bert Williams*, 77.

58. *Chicago Tribune*, 29 May 1906, 6.

59. *Chicago News* article in Robinson Locke Collection (Envelope 2461), Williams and Walker, Walker: Aida Overton, BRTC.

60. Mitchell, *Black Drama*, 51.

61. *"Abyssinia* Opens at the Lyceum," in Robinson Locke Collection (Envelope 2461), Williams and Walker, Walker: Aida Overton, BRTC.

62. Carle Browne Cooke, *New York Telegraph*, 22 February 1906, n.p., in Robinson Locke Collection (Envelope 2461), Williams and Walker, Walker: Aida Overton, BRTC.

63. Unidentified Boston newspaper, in *Abyssinia* Clipping File, HTC.

64. *"Abyssinia,"* 7.

65. Ibid.

66. *Chicago Tribune* article, in *Abyssinia* Clipping File, HTC.

67. Carle Browne Cooke, *New York Telegraph*, 22 February 1906, n.p., in Robinson Locke Collection (Envelope 2461), Williams and Walker, Walker: Aida Overton, BRTC.

68. "Colored Actor," *Toledo Bee*, n.p., in Robinson Locke Collection (Envelope 2461), Williams and Walker, Walker: Aida Overton, BRTC.

69. Ibid.

70. *New York Globe*, 27 October 1905 article in Robinson Locke Collection (Envelope 2461), Williams and Walker, Walker: Aida Overton, BRTC.

71. Tim Brooks, *Lost Sounds*, 115.

72. Ibid., 116.

73. See Chapter 8, "Vaudeville as a Single," for a discussion of Bert's onstage performance of the song.

74. Alex Rogers, "Nobody" (1905), *The Complete Bert Williams, Vol.1 The Early Years* (compilation), Archeophone Records, CD edition 5004. Author's transcription includes Williams's embellishments to the lyrics, as performed on the recording.

75. Tim Brooks, *Lost Sounds*, 117, 118, 119.

76. "Ada O. Walker Taking a Rest," in Robinson Locke Collection (Envelope 2461), Williams and Walker, Walker: Aida Overton, BRTC.

77. Charters, *Nobody*, 89.

78. "Williams and Walker are Unhappy," and "Williams and Walker Say They're Happy," in Robinson Locke Collection (Envelope 2461), Williams and Walker, Walker: Aida Overton, BRTC.

79. *New York Telegraph* article in Robinson Locke Collection (Envelope 2461), Williams and Walker, Walker: Aida Overton, BRTC.

80. "George Walker's Flashy Clothes," *Toledo Courier*, 20 December 1907, n.p., in Robinson Locke Collection (Envelope 2593), Williams and Walker, BRTC.

81. Ibid.

82. The exchange was reprinted in *Variety*. "The Stage Negro," *Variety*, 14 December 1907, 30.

83. Ibid.

84. Ibid.

85. Walker, "The Negro on the American Stage," 246.

86. Ibid., 248.

87. Ibid.

88. Ibid.

89. Ibid.

90. Theatrical contract, F. Ray Comstock, Egbert A. Williams, and George W. Walker, 1 March 1907, NYMA.

91. *Encyclopedia Britannica Online,* "Shubert Brothers," http:www.britannica.com/eb/article-9067557 (accessed 1 June 2007).

92. Lester A. Walton, "The Coming Season," *New York Age*, 30 July 1908, 6.

93. "First Class Theater," *Virginia Law Register* 13, no. 10 (1908), 819.

94. Lester A. Walton, "In First-Class Theatres," *New York Age*, 26 November 1908, 6.

95. "Shuberts Want Williams and Walker," in Robinson Locke Collection (Envelope 2461), Williams and Walker, Walker: Aida Overton, BRTC.

96. Walton, "In First-Class Theatres," 6.

97. "Anniversary Celebration of Williams and Walker a Gala Event," *New York Age*, 2 April 1908, 6.

98. Ibid.

99. Krasner, *Resistance, Parody, and Double Consciousness*, 151.

100. "'Art Knows No Color Line,' Says Brooklyn Eagle," *New York Age*, 30 April 1908, 6.

101. "Majestic—*Bandanna Land*," *New York Dramatic Mirror*, 15 February 1908, 3.

102. Ibid.

103. Lester A. Walton, "A Memorable Event," *New York Age*, 5 March 1908, 6.

104. "Mrs. Lottie Williams Convalesces," *New York Age*, 7 May 1908, 6.

105. Rennold Wolf, "The Greatest Comedian on the American Stage," *Green Book*, June 1912, 1177.

106. "Bert Williams Buys Property in New York City," *New York Age*, 7 May 1908, 6.

107. Rowland, *Bert Williams*, 167.

108. Sotiropoulos, *Staging Race*, 198.

109. Burns and Sanders, *New York*, 324.

110. Sotiropoulos, *Staging Race*, 200.

111. Burns and Sanders, *New York*, 324.

112. James Weldon Johnson, *Black Manhattan*, 148.

113. *New York Age*, 5 January 1911, 2.

114. James Weldon Johnson, *Black Manhattan*, 149.

115. Gilbert, *American Vaudeville*, 286; Greg Palmer, "Vaudeville: An *American Masters* Special," in *American Masters* (Seattle: Thirteen/WNET, KCTS/Seattle, 1997).

116. Alex Rogers (lyrics) and Will Marion Cook (music), "Bon Bon Buddy," sheet music (New York: Gotham-Attucks Music Publishing, 1907), BU.

117. David Krasner, *A Beautiful Pageant: African American Theatre, Drama, and Performance in the Harlem Renaissance, 1910–1927* (New York: Palgrave Macmillan, 2002), 64. See Chapter 3, "Exoticism, Dance, and Racial Myths: Modern Dance and the Class Divide in the Choreography of Aida Overton Walker and Ethel Waters," for further discussion of Aida Overton Walker's interpretation of *Salome*.

118. Sotiropoulos, *Staging Race*, 176.

119. Ibid.

120. "Orpheum Theatre Reopens," in *Bandanna Land* Clipping File, HTC.

121. Ibid.

122. "Bandanna Land," unidentified newspaper in *Bandanna Land* Clipping File, HTC.

123. *Boston Transcript* article in *Bandanna Land* Clipping File, HTC.

124. "Dr. Washington Stops Show," *New York Age*, 13 February 1908, 6.

125. Lester A. Walton, *"Bandanna Land," New York Age*, 6 February 1908, 6.

126. Ibid.

127. "Art Knows No Color Line," 6.

128. *"Bandanna Land* at the Majestic," unidentified newspaper in *Bandanna Land* Clipping File, HTC.

129. Walker, "Bert and Me and Them," 4.

130. Ibid.

131. "The Secret of Williams and Walker's Success," *New York Age*, 27 February 1908, 6.

132. "People Who Amuse Us," *New York Globe and Commercial*, 27 October 1905, n.p., in Robinson Locke Collection (Envelope 2461), Williams and Walker, Walker: Aida Overton, BRTC.

133. Ibid.

134. Lester A. Walton, "W. and W. In Vaudeville," *New York Age*, 4 June 1908, 6.

135. "Negro Actors to Have a Society, *New York Telegraph*, 25 January 1906, n.p., in Robinson Locke Collection(Envelope 2461), Williams and Walker, Walker: Aida Overton, BRTC.

136. "Introductory Note," in Aristophanes, *The Frogs*, ed. Charles Eliot, trans. B. B. Rogers, vol. 8, part 9, of 51, *The Harvard Classics* (New York: P. F. Collier, 1909–14); Bartleby.com, 2007, http:www.bartleby.com/8/9/1001.html (accessed 1 June 2007).

137. Smith, *Bert Williams*, 107.

138. "General Correspondence, Box 30, Folder Fir-Fiz 1908–1909," 11 September 1908, SA.

139. "General Correspondence, Box 30, Folder Fir-Fiz 1908–1909," 14 September 1908, SA.

140. "Retirement of Lottie Williams," *New York Age*, 24 December 1908, 6.

141. Mitchell, *Black Drama*, 53.

142. Division of STD Prevention, "Syphilis—Fact Sheet," Centers for Disease Control and Prevention, http:www.cdc.gov/std/syphilis/STDFact-Syphilis.htm#hatIs (accessed 1 June 2007).

143. Excerpt from an interview with "Chappy," Williams's valet. *New York Herald Tribune* article, in Bert Williams Clipping File, HTC.

144. "Williams and Walker Mystery is Deeper," *New York Telegraph*, in Robinson Locke Collection (Envelope 2593), Williams and Walker, BRTC.

145. Walker, "Bert and Me and Them," 4.

CHAPTER 7

1. For this discussion, I am indebted to Joseph Roach's concept of surrogation. See Joseph Roach, *Cities of the Dead: Circum-Atlantic Performance* (New York: Columbia University Press, 1996).

2. Veronica Adams, "The Dramatic Stage as an Upbuilder of the Races," *Chicago Inter Ocean*, 17 January 1909, 2.

3. Ibid.

4. Ibid.

5. Ibid.

6. Ibid.

7. Ibid.

8. James Weldon Johnson, *Black Manhattan*, 109.

9. "Negro on the Stage," *New York Age*, 24 November 1910, 6.

10. Adams, "The Dramatic Stage as an Upbuilder of the Races," 2.

11. Ibid.

12. Ibid.

13. Ibid.

14. "Two Noted Negroes Meet," *Kansas City Times*, 21 September 1909, 5.

15. "Star Sees Humor in Being Socially Aloof," *Minneapolis Journal*, 30 April 1911, n.p., in Robinson Locke Collection (Envelope 2593), Williams and Walker, BRTC.

16. Adams, "The Dramatic Stage as Upbuilder," 2.

17. Ibid.

18. Levine, *Highbrow/Lowbrow*, 23–4, 36.

19. Ibid., 14–6.

20. Ibid., 72.

21. Rowland, *Bert Williams*, 79.

22. "Williams Alone Next Year," *Variety*, 22 May 1909, 5.

23. Smith, *Bert Williams*, 112.

24. Gilbert, *American Vaudeville*, 286. Many writers and critics agreed that Williams's work in vaudeville was the highlight of his career. Walter Monfried, "Bert Williams: The Modern Pagliaccio," *Negro Digest*, November 1961, 28–32; Joe Laurie, Jr., *Vaudeville: From the Honky-Tonks to the Palace* (New York: Henry Holt, 1953), 174; Samuels, *Once Upon a Stage*, 186; DiMeglio, *Vaudeville U.S.A.*, 34.

25. Samuels and Samuels, *Once Upon a Stage*, 6.

26. Quoted in Kibler, *Rank Ladies*, 174.

27. Max Gordon, with Lewis Funke, *Max Gordon Presents* (New York: Bernard Geis, 1963), 38–9.

28. Although vaudeville bills consisted of a vast array of acts, comedy reigned supreme.

29. Walton, "Bert Williams, Philosopher," 6.

30. Ibid.

31. J. B., "Bert Williams," 21–2.

32. DiMeglio, *Vaudeville, U.S.A.*, 55. Various performers have written autobiographies and articles that incorporate this as a theme of the vaudeville experience. June Havoc, "Old Vaudevillians, Where Are You Now?," *Horizon*, July 1959; Charles Bickford, *Bulls, Balls, Bicycles and Actors* (New York: Paul S. Eriksson, 1965); Buster Keaton with Charles Samuels, *My Wonderful World of Slapstick* (New York: Doubleday, 1960).

33. African American entertainers who did not perform in big-time often traveled and worked together on the circuit of the Theatre Owners Booking Association (TOBA), also dubbed "the Chitlin' Circuit," founded in 1907 by F. A. Barasso. Another smaller theatrical circuit was that started by Sherman H. Dudley, a black comedian, in 1913.

These circuits catered almost exclusively to black performers and audiences, except in some areas where a section of the seating might be reserved for whites. For more on the TOBA, see Watkins, *On the Real Side*.

34. *Encyclopedia Britannica Online*, "Volstead Act," http:www.britannica.com/eb/article-9075697 (accessed 1 June 2007).

35. Ashton Stevens, "Bert Williams's Last Interview," in *Actorviews*, 227–31 (Chicago: Covici-McGee, 1923), 229.

36. Ibid., 230.

37. Keaton, *My Wonderful World of Slapstick*, 78.

38. Ibid., 78–9.

39. Snyder, *The Voice of the City*, 38, 39. Snyder claims that the name derived from a British musical hall organization (the Water Rats) and a joke about one vaudevillian's white hair.

40. Kilber, *Rank Ladies*, 171–2.

41. Ibid., 172.

42. "The White Rats of America," *New York Dramatic Mirror*, 21 July 1900, 7.

43. "Bert Williams in Vaudeville," *New York Age*, 20 May 1909, 6.

44. *New York Herald Tribune*, 8 September 1935, n.p., in Bert Williams File, HTC.

45. Ibid.

46. *New York Age*, 13 May 1909, 6.

47. Alex Rogers collected Bert's jokes and observations, terming the collection "Bert Williams Jokebooks." The jokes in these collections are examples of the "lies" he told prior to those of more substantial length, which he would record for Columbia and perform on the stage in later years.

48. "Bert Williams Jokebooks," Second Volume, 20, SC.

49. Ibid., 32, SC.

50. *New York Age*, 13 May 1909, 6.

51. Stearns, *Jazz Dance*, 117.

52. J. B., "Bert Williams," 21.

53. Ibid., 23.

54. Stearns, *Jazz Dance*, 54.

55. "Bert Williams in Vaudeville," 20 May 1909, 6.

56. *Indianapolis Freeman*, 3 July 1909, 5.

57. "The Passing of a Mind," *New York Star*, 9 June 1909, n.p., in Robinson Locke Collection (Envelope 2593), Williams and Walker, BRTC.

58. *New York Age*, 21 October 1909, 7.

59. Unidentified article in Robinson Locke Collection (Envelope 2461), Williams and Walker, Walker: Aida Overton, BRTC.

60. Lester A. Walton, "Have Williams and Walker Separated?," *New York Age*, 27 January 1910, 6.

61. Fiddler and Shelton, "A Day with the Bert A. Williams Company," *Indianapolis Freeman*, 9 October 1909, 5; "Bert Williams' [sic] Team Loses, *Indianapolis Freeman*, 2 October 1909, 4; Fletcher, *100 Years of the Negro in Show Business*, 249.

62. There is no known extant book for the musical, although there is a song album, in which these two selections Williams performed are included.

63. Charters, *Nobody*, 108.

64. Smith, *Bert Williams*, 117–8.

65. Unidentified 13 November 1909 newspaper in *Mr. Lode of Koal* File, HTC.

66. Thomas L. Riis, *Just Before Jazz*, 123.

67. Mitchell, *Black Drama*, 53.

68. "Bert Williams at the Shubert," *Kansas City Times*, 20 September 1909, 5.

69. Jesse Shipp and Alex Rogers, "*Mr. Lode of Koal* Song Album," in Music Collection, NYPL.

70. Reprinted in Lester A. Walton, "Theatrical Comment," *New York Age*, 9 September 1909, 6; unidentified New York newspaper in *Mr. Lode of Koal* File, HTC. Emphasis added.

71. Reprinted in "Bert Williams Scores in Chicago," *New York Age*, 7 October 1909, 6.

72. "*Mr. Lode of Koal*," *Boston Globe*, 25 January 1910, n.p., in *Mr. Lode of Koal* File, HTC.

73. Unidentified Boston newspaper, 25 January 1910, in *Mr. Lode of Koal* File, HTC.

74. Krasner, *Resistance, Parody, and Double Consciousness*, 142. Importantly, Krasner notes that while the production "avoided stereotyping African Americans, it was not so generous to Native Americans."

75. Thomas Wallace Swann, "Bert Williams Wins West," *Indianapolis Freeman*, 9 November 1909, 6.

76. Ibid.

77. Ibid.

78. Ibid.

79. Ibid.

80. J. D. Howard, "*Mr. Lode of Koal*," *Indianapolis Freeman*, 6 November 1909, 5.

81. Ibid.

82. Lester A. Walton, "Theatrical Comment," *New York Age*, 30 September 1909, 6.

83. Ibid.

84. "Closing of *Mr. Lode of Koal Co.*," *New York Age*, 24 February 1910, 6.

85. Ibid.

86. "Bert Williams in Vaudeville," *New York Age*, 21 April 1910, 6.

87. Ibid. The actress utilized both "Maud" and "Maude" as spellings of her name.

88. Ibid.

89. Quoted in Ibid.

90. Ibid.

91. Ibid.

CHAPTER 8

1. Lester A. Walton, "Theatrical Comment," *New York Age*, 10 March 1910, 6. Walton paraphrased Williams in the article.

2. Ibid.

3. Lester A. Walton, "Death of George W. Walker," *New York Age*, 12 January 1911, 6.

4. "Clubs Elect Officers," *New York Age*, 26 May 1910, 6.

5. Lester A. Walton, "Theatrical Comment," 6.

6. Gerald Bordman, *American Musical Revue: From "The Passing Show" to "Sugar Babies"* (New York and Oxford: Oxford University Press, 1985), 36–7.

7. Ziegfeld did not create the catchphrase "Glorifying the American Girl" until 1922, but his show's emphasis on American beauties was evident from the start. See Bordman, *American Musical Revue*, 36.

8. "Would Enjoin Bert Williams," *New York Times*, 13 May 1910, 9.

9. Smith, *Bert Williams*, 127. All subsequent references are from Smith's text. The materials from *Comstock v. Williams*, New York Supreme Court, May 1910, archived at the New York Municipal Archives, have been lost.

10. Ibid., 127, 129.

11. Ibid., 128–30.

12. Ibid., 130.

13. Ibid., 130.

14. Ibid., 130–1.

15. Ibid., 131.

16. Randolph Carter, *The World of Flo Ziegfeld* (New York: Praeger, 1974), 9.

17. Eddie Cantor and David Freedman write that Held captivated a generation, touring the United States "like a conqueror" between 1896 and 1910. Eddie Cantor and David Freedman, *Ziegfeld, the Great Glorifier* (New York: Alfred H. King, 1934), 33. For more on the "little French invader," see Eve Golden, *Anna Held and the Birth of Ziegfeld's Broadway* (Lexington: University Press of Kentucky, 2000).

18. Carter, *The World of Flo Ziegfeld*, 20; Linda Mizejewski, *Ziegfeld Girl: Image and Icon in Culture and Cinema* (Durham, NC, and London: Duke University Press, 1999), 41.

19. Mizejewski, *Ziegfeld Girl*, 13, quoting Rennold Wolf, "The P. T. Barnum of the Theatre," *Green Book*, June 1914, 933–46.

20. Golden, *Anna Held*, 17–8.

21. Cantor, *Ziegfeld*, 41; Golden, *Anna Held*, 111; Richard Ziegfeld and Paulette Ziegfeld, *The Ziegfeld Touch: The Life and Times of Florenz Ziegfeld, Jr.* (New York: Harry N. Abrams, 1993), 41. There is a slight variation on Held's words cited in Carter, *The World of Flo Ziegfeld*, 27. Charles Higham downplays Held's influence in his account of the *Follies'* beginnings, see Charles Higham, *Ziegfeld* (Chicago: Henry Regnery, 1972), 63.

22. Golden, *Anna Held*, 111.

23. "The Ziegfeld touch" had little to do with business acumen. Ziegfeld frequently went in and out of debt as a result of his practices. Rather, it had to do with Ziegfeld's apparent gift for creating a magical mystique around his productions through his effective use of publicity and consistent use of lavish staging and elaborate costumes.

24. Stephen Burge Johnson, *The Roof Gardens of Broadway Theatres, 1883–1942*, ed. Oscar G. Brockett, vol. 31, *Theater and Dramatic Studies* (Ann Arbor: University of Michigan Research Press, 1985), 120.

25. Higham, *Ziegfeld*, 63, 64.

26. Ziegfeld and Ziegfeld, *The Ziegfeld Touch*, 41.

27. Bordman, *American Musical Revue*, 36.

28. Stephen Burge Johnson, *The Roof Gardens*, 121.

29. Ibid., 121.

30. Ibid., 121.

31. "Ziegfeld's Actors Draw the Color Line," *Cincinnati Commercial*, 5 June 1910, n.p., in Robinson Locke Collection (Envelope 2593), Williams and Walker, BRTC.

32. James Weldon Johnson, *Along This Way*, 180–1.

33. Ibid., 181.

34. Lester A. Walton, "Responsibility of Theatre-Goers," *New York Age*, 26 August 1909, 6.

35. Ibid.

36. "A Unique Situation," *New York Age*, 5 January 1911, 6.

37. James Weldon Johnson, *Black Manhattan*, 109.

38. James Weldon Johnson's term, in *Black Manhattan*, 170. Allen Woll, *Black Musical Theatre: From Coontown to Dreamgirls* (Baton Rouge and London: Louisiana State University Press, 1989), 51.

39. Ibid., 50–3.

40. Ibid., 54–5.

41. Walton, "Bert Williams Turns Philosopher," 6.

42. Watkins, *On the Real Side*, 177.

43. Fletcher, *100 Years of the Negro in Show Business*, 243.

44. Ziegfeld and Ziegfeld, *The Ziegfeld Touch*, 46–7.

45. "Tremont Theatre: *Follies of 1910*," unidentified Boston newspaper, 10 January 1911 in *Follies of 1910* File, HTC.

46. Mizejewski, *Ziegfeld Girl*, 6.

47. "Ziegfeld's Actors Draw the Color Line," *Cincinnati Commercial*, 5 June 1910, n.p., in Robinson Locke Collection (Envelope 2593), Williams and Walker, BRTC.

48. Gilbert, *Vaudeville*, 284-5.

49. *"Follies of 1910," New York Tribune*, 21 June 1910, 7.

50. "Bert Williams Feature of *Follies of 1910*," *New York Age*, 23 June 1910, 6.

51. *"Follies of 1910* Arrives," *New York Sun*, 21 June 1910, 9.

52. "Chicago Critics on Bert Williams," *New York Age*, 15 September 1910, 6.

53. Ralph E. Renaud, "Ziegfeld Offers Big Attraction," *San Francisco Chronicle*, 17 April 1911, 2.

54. *"Follies of 1910," New York Evening Post,* 21 June 1910, 9.

55. "Chicago Critics on Bert Williams," 6.

56. Ibid.

57. Harry B. Smith, James Henry Burris, and Bert Williams, "Constantly" (recorded pre-November 1910), *The Complete Bert Williams, Vol. 2, Bert Williams: The Middle Years, 1910–1918* (compilation), Archeophone Records CD edition 5003. Transcribed by author.

58. "Chicago Critics on Bert Williams," 6.

59. Ibid.

60. Smith, *Bert Williams,* 142. Punctuation added.

61. Ibid.

62. "Chicago Critics on Bert Williams," 6.

63. "The Follies of 1910," article in *Follies of 1910* File, HTC; "Johnson Wins in 15 Rounds; Jeffries Weak," *New York Times,* 6 July 1910, 1.

64. "Crowd Is Saddened When Johnson Wins," *New York Times,* 5 July 1910, 4.

65. "Bar Fight Pictures to Avoid Race Riots," *New York Times,* 6 July 1910, 3; "Eight Killed in Fight Riots," *New York Times,* 6 July 1910, 1, 4.

66. "Chicago Critics on Bert Williams," 6.

67. Ibid.

68. Sylvester Russell, "Bert Williams in a White Show Makes a Big Hit at the Colonial," *Indianapolis Freeman,* 10 September 1910, 7.

69. Sylvester Russell, "The Bert Williams Interview and Its Value and Importance," *Indianapolis Freeman,* 8 October 1910, 2.

70. Walton, "Bert Williams Turns Philosopher," 6.

71. Russell, "The Bert Williams Interview and Its Value and Importance," 2.

72. "George Walker Dead," *New York Times,* 8 January 1911, 13.

73. Russell, "The Bert Williams Interview and Its Value and Importance," 2.

74. "Burt [sic] Williams," *Indianapolis Freeman,* 1 October 1910, 5.

75. "Actors' Field Day Brings Great Crowd," *New York Times,* 20 August 1910, 7.

76. Tim Brooks, *Lost Sounds,* 124.

77. Ibid., quoting "Bert Williams the World Famous Comedian Now Makes Records Exclusively for the Columbia," *Columbia Records Supplement,* November 1910, 6.

78. Ibid.

79. Ibid.

80. Ibid.

81. Tim Brooks, *Lost Sounds,* 125.

82. Ibid.

83. Percy A. Scholes, ed., *The Oxford Companion to Music* (London: Oxford University Press, 1938), 77, quoted in Lynn Abbott, "'Play That Barber Shop Chord': A Case for the African-American Origins of Barbershop Harmony," *American Music* 10, no. 3 (1992), 296.

84. Abbott, "'Play That Barber Shop Chord,'" 312; C. T. "Deac" Martin, "The Evolution of Barbershop Harmony," *Music Journal Annual* 34 (1965), 41, 106.

85. Ballard MacDonald, William Tracey, and Lewis F. Muir, "Play That Barber Shop Chord," (pre-December 1910), *The Complete Bert Williams, Vol. 2, The Middle Years, 1910–1918,* (compilation), Archeophone Records CD edition 5003. Transcribed by author.

86. Walton, "Bert Williams Turns Philosopher," 6.

87. Ibid.

88. Ibid.

89. Ibid.

90. Ibid.

91. Ibid. Years later, Williams declared that there actually had been no written contract; rather, theirs had been a "gentleman's agreement."

92. Ibid.

93. "A Unique Situation," 6.

94. Ibid.

95. Sylvester Russell, "George Williams [*sic*] Walker, of Williams and Walker," *Indianapolis Freeman*, 14 January 1911, 5.

96. Williams, "Bert Williams Tells of Walker," 5.

97. Walton, "Death of George W. Walker," 6.

98. Ibid.

99. Russell, "George Williams [*sic*] Walker, of Williams and Walker," 5.

100. "George W. Walker," *New York Age*, 12 January 1911, 4.

101. Walton, "Death of George W. Walker," 6.

102. R. W. Thompson, "Theatrical Chit-Chat of Washington," 5.

103. "Bert Williams in Demand," *New York Age*, 25 May 1911 in Tuskegee Institute, Division of Behavioral Science Research, Carver Research Foundation, *Tuskegee Institute News Clippings File* (Sanford, NC: Microfilming Corp. of America, 1981), Series II, Reel 241, Frame 2.

104. *"Follies of 1911* Here," *New York Tribune*, 27 June 1911, 8.

105. Quoted in Lester A. Walton, "The Star among Stars," *New York Age*, 6 July 1911, 6.

106. Smith, *Bert Williams*, 152.

107. Lester A. Walton, "More Praise for Comedian," *New York Age*, 14 September 1911, 6.

108. Walton, "The Star among Stars," 6.

109. Wolf, "The Greatest Comedian on the American Stage," 1184.

110. *"Follies of 1911,"* *New York Herald*, 27 June 1911, 10.

111. *"Follies of 1911,"* *New York Evening Post*, 27 June 1911, 9.

112. Charters, *Nobody*, 118.

113. Walton, "The Star among Stars," 6.

114. Walton, "More Praise for Comedian," 6.

115. Walton, "More Praise for Comedian," 6; Walton, "The Star among Stars," 6.

116. Charters, *Nobody*, 118.

117. Charters's work does not detail any archives from which she might have gleaned her information on the sketch. It is likely she gathered this material during the personal interviews she conducted.

118. Charters, *Nobody*, 118.

119. Ibid., 118–9.

120. Ibid., 119.

121. Ibid., 119.

122. Ann Douglas, *Terrible Honesty: Mongrel Manhattan in the 1920s* (New York: Farrar, Straus and Giroux, 1995), 329.

123. Wolf, "The Greatest Comedian on the American Stage," 1184.

124. Charters, *Nobody*, 120.

125. "The Follies Again," unidentified Boston newspaper clipping, 9 January 1912 in *Ziegfeld Follies of 1911* File, HTC.

126. Walton, "More Praise for Comedian," 6.

127. Unidentified Boston newspaper clipping, 9 January 1912 in *Ziegfeld Follies of 1911* File, HTC.

128. Walton, "The Star among Stars," 6.

129. *"Follies of 1911,"* *New York Evening Post*, 27 June 1911, 9.

130. Walton, "The Star among Stars," 6.

131. Ibid.

132. Ibid.

133. "Tells About Larkins' [*sic*] Company," *New York Age*, 6 July 1911, 6.

134. "Pekin Stock Co.," *New York Age*, 1 December 1910, 6.

135. Walton, "The Star among Stars," 6. Emphasis added.

136. Ibid.

137. Lester A. Walton, "Broadway Individual Success," *New York Age*, 31 August 1911, 6.

138. Ibid.

139. Ibid.

140. Ibid.

CHAPTER 9

1. "Bert Williams Signs Contract," *New York Age*, in *Tuskegee Institute News Clipping File*, Series 2, Reel 241, Frame 29; Wolf, "The Greatest Comedian on the American Stage," 1174. "Bert Williams? He Was Greatest, Most Imitated Comic in U.S.," *Jet*, 12 February 1981, 60. Williams's salary of $62,400 is roughly equivalent to $1,350,696 in 2006. See S. Morgan Friedman, "The Inflation Calculator," 2006, http:www.westegg.com/inflation/ (accessed 1 June 2007).

2. Certificate of Death, NYMA. *Medline Plus Online*, "Endocarditis," http:www.nlm.nih.gov/medlineplus/ency/article/001098.htm (accessed 1 June 2007).

3. Smith posits that Belasco pursued Williams at the start of his work in the *Follies* in 1910. The dates of announcements regarding Williams's three-year contract (January 1912 in the *New York Age*), and references to Belasco's offer in the June 1912 issue of *Green Book,* and the 16 June 1912 edition of the *Indianapolis Freeman* make a compelling case for this later date, however.

4. *Encyclopedia Britannica Online*, "Belasco, David," http:www.britannica.com/eb/article-9015177 (accessed 1 June 2007).

5. *Encyclopedia Britannica Online*, "Carter, Mrs. Leslie," http:www.britannica.com/eb/article-9002177 (accessed 1 June 2007).

6. *Encyclopedia Britannica Online*, "Belasco, David."

7. Unidentified article in Robinson Locke Collection (Envelope 2593), Williams and Walker, BRTC.

8. Wolf, "The Greatest Comedian on the American Stage," 1180; Andrew Burstein, *The Original Knickerbocker: The Life of Washington Irving* (New York: Basic, 2007), 337–8.

9. Rowland, *Bert Williams*, 106.

10. Ibid., 111.

11. "Bert Williams a Real Optimist," in Bert Williams File, HTC.

12. Ibid.

13. Thomas S. Hischak and Gerald Bordman, eds., *The Oxford Companion to American Theatre*, 3rd ed. (New York and Oxford: Oxford University Press, 2004), 45.

14. "Bert Williams a Real Optimist," in Bert Williams File, HTC.

15. Rowland, *Bert Williams*, xii.

16. Ibid.

17. Ibid., 107–8.

18. Ibid., 108–9.

19. Ibid., xiii.

20. "White Is as White Does," *New York Age*, 25 July 1912, 6.

21. *Variety*, 22 July 1911, article in Robinson Locke Collection (Envelope 2461), Williams and Walker, Walker: Aida Overton, BRTC.

22. Aida Overton Walker, "Respect Memory of the Dead," *New York Age*, 1 August 1912, in *Tuskegee Institute News Clippings File*, Series 2, Reel 241, Frame 39.

23. Unidentified newspaper clipping in *Ziegfeld Follies of 1912* File, HTC.

24. Sime Silverman, "*Ziegfeld Follies*," *Variety*, 25 October 1912, 22.

25. *"Follies of 1912," New York Tribune*, 22 October 1912, 9.

26. Charters, *Nobody*, 119.

27. Ibid.

28. Ibid., 119–20.

29. Ibid., 120.

30. "Broadway Belated Night of Follies," *New York World*, 22 October 1912, 5.

31. That Walton wrote in language suggesting that he saw the *Follies of 1912* raises the question of his possible access to the production. There was no known general house policy change at that time or when the *Follies* later moved to the New Amsterdam

Theatre (see Chapter 11 for Walton's discussion of the *Midnight Frolic*). The question of theater policies versus practices during this period merits further investigations.

32. Sotiropoulos, *Staging Race*, 207.

33. Jean Havez and Bert Williams, "Borrow from Me" (13 January 1913), *The Complete Bert Williams, Vol. 2. The Middle Years: 1910–1918* (compilation), Archeophone Records CD edition 5003. Transcribed by author.

34. "Two Noted Negroes Meet," 5.

35. Ibid.

36. Lester A. Walton, *"The Follies of 1912," New York Age*, 24 October 1912, 6. These are Walton's words.

37. Ibid.

38. Wolf, "The Greatest Comedian on the American Stage," 1174.

39. "Klaw and Erlanger's New Productions," *New York Times*, 19 July 1913, 7; "Bert Williams to Star," *New York Times*, 8 November 1913, 13.

40. Lloyd Lewis, *It Takes All Kinds*, 231–2. Marian Storm, "All 135th Street Is Missing Bert Williams," *New York Evening Post*, 7 April 1922, 16.

41. Ibid., 232.

42. Wolf, "The Greatest Comedian on the American Stage," 1177.

43. Ibid.

44. Lloyd Lewis, *It Takes All Kinds*, 234.

45. Smith, *Bert Williams*, 157.

46. Lester A. Walton, "A Big Undertaking," *New York Age*, 21 August 1913, 6; Lester A. Walton, "Monster Show Planned," *New York Age*, 24 July 1913, 6.

47. Walton, "A Big Undertaking," 6; Walton, "Monster Show Planned," 6.

48. Lester A. Walton, "Historic Pilgrimage," *New York Age*, 7 August 1913, 6.

49. Walton, "A Big Undertaking," 6; Walton, "Monster Show Planned," 6.

50. Lester A. Walton, "An Unusual Bill," *New York Age*, 14 August 1913, 6.

51. Lester A. Walton, "Theatrical Comment," *New York Age*, 18 December 1913, 6.

52. Rush, "New Acts," *Variety*, 26 December 1913, 17; "Palace," *Variety*, 26 December 1913, 18.

53. Ibid.

54. Snyder, *The Voice of the City*, 60.

55. Samuels and Samuels, *Once Upon a Stage*, 260; Snyder, *The Voice of the City*, 88.

56. Samuel and Samuels, *Once Upon a Stage*, 261–2.

57. Snyder, *The Voice of the City*, 88; Samuels and Samuels, *Once Upon a Stage*, 258.

58. DiMeglio, *Vaudeville U.S.A.*, 119.

59. Snyder, *Voice of the City*, 88; Laurie, *Vaudeville*, 248.

60. DiMeglio, *Vaudeville U.S.A.*, 120.

61. Laurie, *Vaudeville*, 498.

62. Samuels and Samuels, *Once Upon a Stage*, 262.

63. DiMeglio, *Vaudeville U.S.A.*, 122.

64. Brett Page, *Writing for Vaudeville* (Springfield, MA: Home Correspondence School, 1915), 11.

65. Page, *Writing for Vaudeville*, 7; "Palace," *Variety*, 26 December 1913, 18.

66. Page, *Writing for Vaudeville*, 8.

67. Rush, "New Acts," *Variety*, 26 December 1913, 17.

68. "Palace," *Variety*, 26 December 1913, 18.

69. Page, *Writing for Vaudeville*, 8.

70. "Palace," *Variety*, 26 December 1913, 18. Most likely, Vanderbilt sang as well as danced. She was a "name" as a single, so the excitement might have been related to the combination of her and another performer for a two-act, i.e., a two-person act.

71. Page, *Writing for Vaudeville*, 8.

72. "Palace," *Variety*, 26 December 1913, 18.

73. Page, *Writing for Vaudeville*, 9.

74. "Palace," *Variety*, 26 December 1913, 18.

75. Ibid.

76. Page, *Writing for Vaudeville*, 9.

77. Ibid.

78. Charters, *Nobody*, 8, 10.

79. I am indebted to Judith Butler's work on performance and performativity for my discussion of Bert's interventions onstage. See *Bodies that Matter: On the Discursive Limits of "Sex"* (New York and London: Routledge, 1993), 95.

80. Lhamon, *Raising Cain*, 136.

81. Ibid., 142.

82. J. B., "Bert Williams," 22.

83. Ibid.

84. Sigmund Freud, *Jokes and Their Relation to the Unconscious* (New York and London: W. W. Norton, 1960), 118.

85. Ibid., 163.

86. Henry G. Carleton, *The Thompson Street Poker Club from "Life"* (New York: White and Allen, 1899).

87. Boskin, *Sambo*, 79.

88. Ibid., 108.

89. Rush, "New Acts," *Variety*, 26 December 1913, 17

90. Ibid.

91. Elsie A. Williams, *The Humor of Jackie Moms Mabley: An African American Comedic Tradition*, ed. Graham Hodges, *Studies in African American History and Culture* (New York and London: Garland, 1995), 15.

92. Freud, *Jokes and Their Relation to the Unconscious*, 148.

93. Jean Havez, Will Vodery, and Bert Williams, "The Darktown Poker Club" (4 February 1914), *The Complete Bert Williams, Vol. 2, The Middle Years: 1910–1918* (compilation), Archeophone Records CD edition 5003. Transcribed by the author.

94. Emphasis in original. Herbert Blau, *The Audience* (Baltimore and London: Johns Hopkins University Press, 1990), 25.

95. Heywood Broun, "It Seems to Me," *The World,* 7 March 1922, n.p., in Bert Williams File, HTC.

96. Lucas, "How? Fried" (3 January 1913), *The Complete Bert Williams, Vol. 2, The Middle Years: 1910–1918* (compilation), Archeophone Records CD edition 5003. Bert Williams, "You Can't Do Nothing Till Martin Gets Here" (3 January 1913), *The Complete Bert Williams, Vol. 2, The Middle Years: 1910–1918* (compilation), Archeophone Records CD edition 5003. Transcribed by author.

97. Emphasis in original. Kenneth Burke, *Attitudes toward History* (Los Altos, CA: Hermes, 1959), 171.

98. Levine, *Black Culture and Black Consciousness*, 322–5.

99. Freud, *Jokes and Their Relation to the Unconscious*, 216.

100. Henry Louis Gates, Jr., *The Signifying Monkey: A Theory of African-American Literary Criticism* (New York and Oxford: Oxford University Press, 1988), 48, 51.

101. Levine, *Black Culture and Black Consciousness*, 326.

102. Rowland, *Bert Williams*, 98–9.

103. Ibid., 99.

104. Levine, *Black Culture and Black Consciousness*, 361. Levine's use of the term "unmasking" is informed by Anton Zijderveld's work titled "Jokes and Their Relation to Social Reality," *Social Research,* 35 (1968): 286-311.

105. Levine, *Black Culture and Black Consciousness*, 312.

106. Walton, "Bert Williams, Philosopher," 6.

107. Charters, *Nobody*, 8.

108. Douglas, *Terrible Honesty*, 330.

109. Ibid., 330, 331.

110. J. B., "Bert Williams," 22.

111. Ted Shawn, *Every Little Movement: A Book About Delsartre* (New York: Dance Horizons, 1963), 71.

112. Annette Lust, *From the Greek Mimes to Marcel Marceau and Beyond: Mimes, Actors, Pierrots and Clowns; A Chronicle of the Many Visages of Mime in the Theatre* (Lanham, Maryland and London: Scarecrow Press, Inc., 2000), 7.

CHAPTER 10

1. Ziegfeld and Ziegfeld, *The Ziegfeld Touch*, 53.

2. Henderson, *The City and the Theatre*, 220.

3. Higham, *Ziegfeld*, 104-5.

4. Ziegfeld and Ziegfeld, *The Ziegfeld Touch*, 53.

5. Ibid., 241, 83. These figures do not include the cast's weekly salaries and are for the *Ziegfeld Follies of 1918*. They would equal between $1,674,618.75 and $2,131,332.95 in 2006. See S. Morgan Friedman, "The Inflation Calculator," 2006 http:www. westegg.com/inflation (accessed 1 June 2007).

6. Channing Pollack, "Building the Follies," *Green Book*, September 1915, 390.

7. Ibid., 396.

8. Ibid., 397, 394, 398.

9. Ibid.

10. Walton, "Bert Williams, Philosopher," 6.

11. Ibid.

12. "The Ziegfeld Follies," *Green Book*, August 1914, 322.

13. "Bert Williams, World's Greatest Comedian," *Chicago Defender*, in *Tuskegee Institute News Clippings File*, Series 2, Reel 241, Frame 55.

14. *New York Mail*, 21 June 1914, in *Ziegfeld Follies of 1914* File, HTC.

15. *New York World*, 12 June 1914, in *Ziegfeld Follies of 1914* File, HTC.

16. *New York Globe*, 2 June 1914, in *Ziegfeld Follies of 1914* File, HTC.

17. Sime Silverman, "*Ziegfeld Follies*," *Variety*, 5 June 1914, 15.

18. "*Follies* Begin Summer Capers," *New York Times*, 2 June 1914, 11.

19. "Bert Williams, World's Greatest Comedian," *Chicago Defender*, in *Tuskegee Institute News Clippings File*, Series 2, Reel 241, Frame 55; "The Ziegfeld Follies," *Green Book*, August 1914, 323.

20. Ibid.

21. "Excellent Lines of Two Sorts in This Year's *Follies*," *New York Telegram* 2 June 1914, n.p., in *Ziegfeld Follies of 1914* File, HTC; "News of the Theatres," *New York Evening Sun*, 21 June 1914, n.p., in *Ziegfeld Follies of 1914* File, HTC.

22. "News of the Theatres," *New York Evening Sun*, 21 June 1914, n.p. , in *Ziegfeld Follies of 1914* File, HTC. Emphasis in original.

23. Charles Darnton, "Tipsy Tango Chief Novelty of Follies," *New York Evening World*, 2 June 1914, n.p., in *Ziegfeld Follies of 1914* File, HTC.

24. "The Ziegfeld Follies," *Green Book*, August 1914, 323.

25. James Weldon Johnson, *Black Manhattan*, 174.

26. Ibid., 173–4.

27. "Colored Theatre Opens: Old Bijou Shows "*The Dark-town Follies of 1914*," *New York Times*, 16 June 1914, 9.

28. Ziegfeld and Ziegfeld, *The Ziegfeld Touch*, 59.

29. James Weldon Johnson, *Black Manhattan*, 174.

30. Ibid.

31. "Bert Williams, World's Greatest Living Comedian, *Chicago Defender*, in *Tuskegee Institute News Clippings File*, Series 2, Reel 241, Frame 57.

32. "Excellent Lines of Two Sorts in This Year's *Follies*," *New York Telegram*, 2 June 1914, n.p., in *Ziegfeld Follies of 1914* File, HTC.

33. Ibid.

34. "Bert Williams, World's Greatest Living Comedian," *Chicago Defender*, in *Tuskegee Institute News Clippings File*, Series 2, Reel 241, Frame 58.

35. Ibid.

36. "Bert Williams to Be a Citizen," *Boston Herald*, 31 October 1914, n.p., in Bert Williams File, HTC.

37. Ibid.

38. "Bert Williams Home," *New York Age*, 3 September 1914, 6.

39. "Aida Overton Walker Is Dead," *New York Age*, 15 October 1914, 1.

40. Lester A. Walton, "Aida Overton Walker Signs," *New York Age*, 19 January 1911, 6.

41. James Weldon Johnson, *Black Manhattan*, 107.

42. *Variety*, 22 July 1911, in Robinson Locke Collection (Envelope 2461), Williams and Walker, Walker: Aida Overton, BRTC.

43. Lester A. Walton, "Miss Walker's Success," *New York Age*, 2 November 1911, 6.

44. Undated clipping, "B. F. Keith's Theatre Program," in KA.

45. Lester A. Walton, "Miss Walker in 'Salome'," *New York Age*, 8 August 1912, 6.

46. "Salome Was a Dark Secret," in Robinson Locke Collection (Envelope 2461), Williams and Walker, Walker: Aida Overton, BRTC.

47. Krasner, *A Beautiful Pageant*, 67–9.

48. Aida Overton Walker, "Opportunities Stage Offers Intelligent and Talented Women," *New York Age*, 24 December 1908, 1.

49. "Aida Overton Walker Is Dead," 1.

50. Ziegfeld and Ziegfeld, *The Ziegfeld Touch*, 241.

51. "The Changed *Follies*," *Boston Evening Transcript*, 21 September 1915, n.p., in *Ziegfeld Follies of 1915* File, HTC.

52. Lester A. Walton, "Theatrical Comment," *New York Age*, 24 June 1915, 6.

53. "*Ziegfeld Follies of 1915*," *Variety*, 25 June 1915, 15.

54. James Weldon Johnson, *Along This Way*, 176.

55. Louis Chude-Sokei, *The Last "Darky": Bert Williams, Black-on-Black Minstrelsy, and the African Diaspora* (Durham, NC, and London: Duke University Press, 2006), 48–9.

56. For further analysis of the meanings of Bert's choice and its relevance in relation to his own self-representation, see Chude-Sokei, *The Last "Darky."*

57. Tim Brooks, *Lost Sounds*, 130.

58. Ibid., 129.

59. Quoted in Ibid., 130.

60. *Encyclopedia Britannica Online*, "World War I," http:www.britannica.com/eb/article-53114 (accessed 1 June 2007).

61. James Curtis, *W. C. Fields: A Biography* (New York: Alfred A. Knopf, 2003), 120.

62. Pollack, "Building the *Follies*," 394.

63. Will Vodery, "My Years with Ziegfeld," 27, in SC.

64. Ibid., 27, 47.

65. Ibid., 48.

66. Ibid.

67. Ibid., 48–9.

68. "*Ziegfeld Follies of 1916*," *New York Dramatic Mirror*, 17 June 1916, 8.

69. New Amsterdam Theatre Program, 12 June 1916, in HR.

70. "*Follies* Have Beauty Galore," *New York Tribune*, 13 June 1916, 9; "Broadway Gives a Rousing Greeting to the 1916 *Ziegfeld Follies* at the New Amsterdam," *New York American*, 13 June 1916, 9.

71. Sime Silverman, "*Ziegfeld Follies*," *Variety*, 16 June 1916, 13.

72. "Bert Williams," *New York Age*, 16 June 1916, 6.

73. Silverman, "*Ziegfeld Follies*," 13.

74. Nasaw, *Going Out*, 136.

75. Ibid., 139.

76. Ibid., 140.

77. Ibid., 141.

78. Ibid., 141, quoting Terry Ramsaye (term "The Lawless Film Frontier"). Ibid., 142.

79. Ibid., 142, 143.

80. McNamara, *Step Right Up*, 148–9.

81. Nasaw, *Going Out*, 147.

82. Daniel J. Leab, "The Gamut from A to B: The Image of the Black in Pre-1915 Movies," *Political Science Quarterly* 88, no. 1 (1973), 62–3.

83. Anthony Slide, *Early American Cinema*, rev. ed. (Metuchen, NJ and London: Scarecrow, 1994), 101.

84. Ibid., 102.

85. Ibid., 101.

86. Little is known about *Darktown Jubilee*, a lost Bert Williams film that he was said to have made in 1914.

87. Eric Ledell Smith, following Henry Sampson, claims that Williams first appeared in a 1910 all-black film, *The Pullman Porter*, and may have also appeared in a 1912 film, *The Railroad Porter*, produced by the same organization, the Foster Photoplay Company. Smith, *Bert Williams*, 144. It appears, however, that Williams was in neither film. First, *The Pullman Porter*, a 1919 film, does not feature a black cast. Second, *The Railroad Porter*, according to Jacqueline Stewart, "widely regarded as the first film produced by an African American," does not include Bert Williams in the cast list. Unfortunately, there is no extant footage to verify that he appeared. See Jacqueline Stewart, "William Foster: The Dean of the Negro Photoplay," *Oscar Micheaux Society Newsletter* 9 (Spring 2001), 1–2. In addition to the two previously mentioned films, Kemp Niver identifies Williams as appearing in a 1914 Klaw and Erlanger film, *The Indian*, a drama that detailed "a battle between a tribe of Indians and the United States cavalry in which twin sons of an Indian chief become separated." Again, Williams is not on the cast list. If he did appear in it at all, his role is not known. Kemp R. Niver, *Klaw and Erlanger Presents Famous Plays in Pictures* (Los Angeles: Locare Research Group, 1976), 153–8.

88. "Comments on the Films—A Natural Born Gambler," *Moving Picture World*, 12 August 1916, 1103.

89. "Stories of the Films," *Moving Picture World* 30, no. 8 (1916): 1219.

90. "Bert Williams Films Good Drawing Cards," *New York Telegraph* article in Robinson Locke Collection (Envelope 2593), Williams and Walker, BRTC; "Bert Williams in Biograph Comedies," *Motion Picture World*, 1 July 1916, in Robinson Locke Collection (Envelope 2593), Williams and Walker, BRTC.

91. Susan Curtis, *The First Black Actors on the Great White Way* (Columbia and London: University of Missouri Press, 1998), 4, 6, 3.

92. Quoted in Susan Curtis, *The First Black Actors on the Great White Way*, 7.

93. Ibid., 4–6.

94. James Weldon Johnson, *Black Manhattan*, 175; Susan Curtis, *The First Black Actors on the Great White Way*, 8.

95. Susan Curtis, *The First Black Actors on the Great White Way*, 12.

96. *Encyclopedia Britannica Online*, "World War I."

97. W. E. B. Du Bois, quoted in Mark Ellis, *Race, War, and Surveillance: African Americans and the United States Government During World War I* (Bloomington and Indianapolis: Indiana University Press, 2001), 1.

98. Quoted in Ibid., 4–5.

99. Ibid., 5.

100. "New Negro Troops Parade in Fifth Avenue," *New York Times*, 2 October 1916, 22.

101. Ibid.

102. Ibid.

103. Lloyd Lewis, *It Takes All Kinds*, 236.

104. James Weldon Johnson, *Black Manhattan*, 235.

105. Bill Harris, *The Hellfighters of Harlem: African-American Soldiers Who Fought for the Right to Fight for Their Country* (New York: Carroll and Graf, 2002), 70.

106. Eddie Cantor, *As I Remember Them* (New York: Duell, Sloan and Pearce, 1963), 48.

107. Ibid.

108. Ibid., 49.

109. James Curtis, *W. C. Fields*, 122.

110. Lester A. Walton, "The Season's Outlook," *New York Age*, 6 September 1917, 6.

111. "*Ziegfeld Follies* Here Again; Beauty, Fun and Patriotism Meet in Beautiful Production," *New York Herald*, n.p., in *Ziegfeld Follies of 1917* File, HTC.

112. Cantor, *As I Remember Them*, 48.

113. Ibid.

114. "Between Seasons," *New York Times*, 17 June 1917, 5.

115. Ibid.

116. Tim Brooks, *Lost Sounds*, 132.

117. Harris, *The Hellfighters of Harlem*, 23–4.

118. Ellis, *Race, War, and Surveillance*, 31–2.

119. Ibid., 33.

120. Ibid.

121. Walton, "Bert Williams, Philosopher," 6.

122. Ibid.

123. Ibid.

124. Ibid.

125. Ibid.

126. Ibid.

127. Ibid.

128. "Bert Williams? He Was Greatest, Most Imitated Comic in the U.S.," 62.

129. Lester A. Walton, "Bert Williams on Race Problem," *New York Age*, 4 May 1918, 6.

130. Ibid.

CHAPTER II

1. "Bert Williams Now a Full-Fledged Citizen," *New York Age*, 22 June 1918, 6; Naturalization Petition, 29 October 1914, NYMA.

2. Walton, "Bert Williams on Race Problem," 6.

3. Fred L. Boalt, "Bert Williams, Comedian Is a Melancholy Man, *Toledo News Bee*, 4 May 1915, n.p., in Robinson Locke Collection (Envelope 2593), Williams and Walker, BRTC.

4. Walton, "Bert Williams on Race Problem," 6.

5. "Bert Williams Quits the *Follies* in Atlantic City," *New York Age*, 22 June 1918, 1.

6. Ibid.

7. "Bert Williams Quits *Follies*," *Louisville News*, 15 June 1918, in *Tuskegee Institute News Clippings File*, Series 2, Reel 241, Frame 94.

8. Smith, *Bert Williams*, 190.

9. Ziegfeld and Ziegfeld, *The Ziegfeld Touch*, 248.

10. "Bert Williams a Hit in *Midnight Frolic*," *New York Age*, 20 July 1918, 6.

11. Ibid.

12. Williams had somehow managed to develop or acquire a better standard of material than he'd had in recent years.

13. "Bert Williams a Hit in *Midnight Frolic*," 6.

14. Lester A. Walton, "Theatrical Chit-Chat" *New York*, 18 July 1918, 6.

15. Ibid.

16. George W. Walker (music) and Clarke Meyer, Grant (lyrics), "You'll Find Old Dixieland in France," sheet music (New York: Leo Feist, 1918).

17. Tim Brooks, *Lost Sounds*, 132–3.

18. Ibid., 133.

19. Alex Rogers, "Elder Eatmore's Sermon on Generosity" (27 June 1919), *The Complete Bert Williams, Vol. 3, His Final Releases: 1919–1922* (compilation), Archeophone

Records CD edition 5002; Alex Rogers, "Elder Eatmore's Sermon on Throwing Stones" (27 June 1919), *The Complete Bert Williams, Vol. 3, His Final Releases: 1919–1922* (compilation), Archeophone Records CD edition 5002. Transcribed by author.

20. Tim Brooks, *Lost Sounds*, 134.

21. "Bert Williams Leading a Strenuous Existence," *New York Age*, 22 March 1919, 6.

22. Rowland, *Bert Williams*, 192.

23. "Show Reviews," *Variety*, 6 December 1918, 17.

24. "Theatrical Chit-Chat," *New York Age*, 7 December 1918, 6.

25. Walton, "Bert Williams, Philosopher," 6.

26. "Bert Williams: Boy, Gentleman, Comedian," 7.

27. Ibid.

28. "Theatrical Chit-Chat," 6.

29. Bert Williams, "Keeping Up with the New Laughs," *Theatre Magazine*, June 1919, 348.

30. Ibid.

31. Ibid.

32. Ibid.

33. Ibid.

34. Ibid.

35. Ibid.

36. Ibid., 349.

37. Ibid.

38. "Bert Williams a Real Optimist," in Bert Williams File, HTC.

39. Unidentified newspaper clipping, 17 June 1919, in *Ziegfeld Follies of 1919* File, HTC.

40. Robert Hood Bowers and Frances DeWitt, "The Moon Shines on the Moonshine" (1 December 1919), *The Complete Bert Williams, Vol. 3, His Final Releases: 1919–1922* (compilation), Archeophone Records CD edition 5002.

41. Stevens, *Actorviews*, 230.

42. Eddie Cantor, *My Life Is in Your Hands* (New York: Curtis, 1928), 29.

43. Ibid., 29–30.

44. Heywood Broun, "New Edition of the *Follies* Lives Up to Tradition of Beauty," *New York Tribune*, 17 June 1919, 13.

45. James Weldon Johnson, *Black Manhattan*, 246.

46. *PBS Online*, "The Rise and Fall of Jim Crow: Red Summer (1919)," http:www.pb.org/wnet/jimcrow/stories_events_red.html (accessed 1 June 2007).

47. "2 Killed, 50 Hurt in Furious Race Riot in Chicago," *New York Times*, 28 July 1919, 4.

48. "Street Battles at Night," *New York Times*, 29 July 1919, 1.

49. *PBS Online*, "The Rise and Fall of Jim Crow: Red Summer (1919)."

50. Smith, *Bert Williams*, 199.

51. James Curtis, *W. C. Fields*, 131.

52. Smith, *Bert Williams*, 201.

53. Rowland, *Bert Williams*, 129–30.

54. Cantor, *As I Remember Them*, 50.

55. Ibid.

56. "Bert Williams' [*sic*] Tact," *New York Age*, 2 August 1919, 6.

57. Ibid.

58. Rowland, *Bert Williams*, 128.

CHAPTER 12

1. Rowland, *Bert Williams*, 136.

2. "Bert Williams in New Show Now," *Chicago Whip*, 9 October 1920, in *Tuskegee Institute News Clippings File*, Series 1, Reel 12, Frame 720.

3. Rowland, *Bert Williams*, 136.

4. Quoted in Ibid., 137. Emphasis in original.

5. Tim Brooks, *Lost Sounds*, 138.

6. Chris Smith, "I Want to Know Where Tosti Went (When He Said Goodbye)" (28 June 1920), *The Complete Bert Williams, Vol. 3, His Final Releases: 1919–1922* (compilation), Archeophone Records CD edition 5002. Transcribed by the author.

7. Charles Bayha, "Eve Cost Adam Just One Bone" (12 November 1920), *The Complete Bert Williams, Vol. 3, His Final Releases: 1919–1922* (compilation), Archeophone Records CD edition 5002. Transcribed by the author.

8. Rowland, *Bert Williams*, 142.

9. Charters, *Nobody*, 144.

10. Rowland, *Bert Williams*, 144.

11. "'B'way Brevities' Garden's New Hit," *New York Commercial*, 30 September 1920, n.p., in *Broadway Brevities* File, BRTC.

12. "Musical Plays," *New York Evening Post*, 30 September 1920, 9.

13. "*Broadway Brevities, 1920*," *New York Times*, 30 September 1920, 12.

14. "George LeMaire's *Broadway Brevities of 1920*," *New York Evening Post*, 30 September 1920, 9.

15. James Weldon Johnson, *Black Manhattan*, 188; "Chas. Gilpin," *Brooklyn, NY Citizen*, 29 December 1920, in *Tuskegee Institute News Clippings File*, Series 2, Reel 12, Frame 721.

16. Ibid.

17. Ibid.

18. James Weldon Johnson, *Black Manhattan*, 184–5.

19. Maida Castellun, "O' Neill's *The Emperor Jones* Thrills and Fascinates," *New York Call*, 10 November 1920, reprinted in Jordan Y. Miller, *Playwright's Progress: O'Neill and the Critics* (Chicago and Atlanta: Kansas State University, 1965), 22.

20. Rowland, *Bert Williams*, 214.

21. Fletcher, *100 Years of the Negro in Show Business*, 242.

22. Ibid.

23. Alison Smith, "Stage and Screen," *New York Globe*, 12 November 1920, in *Tuskegee Institute News Clippings File,* Series 2, Reel 12, Frame 721.

24. Lester A. Walton, "Charles H. Gilpin," *New York Age*, 10 July 1913, 6.

25. James Weldon Johnson, *Black Manhattan*, 186.

26. Fletcher, *100 Years of the Negro in Show Business*, 201.

27. James Weldon Johnson, *Black Manhattan*, 187–8.

28. Sotiropoulos, *Staging Race*, 233.

CHAPTER 13

1. "Bert Williams to Be Starred," *Afro-American*, 11 February 1921 in *Tuskegee Institute News Clippings File*, Series 2, Reel 241, Frame 97.

2. Henderson, *The City and the Theatre*, 239.

3. Contract between A. H. Woods and Bert Williams, 28 February 1921, 2–5, in SA. Williams's salary of $1,250 would equal roughly $13,642 in 2006. S. Morgan Friedman, "The Inflation Calculator," http:www.westegg.com/inflation/ (accessed 1 June 2007).

4. Ibid., 4.

5. "*Under the Bamboo Tree*, Misc. Ms. Music #343, Pkg. 4," in SA.

6. Emphasis added. Stevens, *Actorviews*, 231.

7. The song "Puppy Dog" is discussed below.

8. "The Pink Slip," *Atlantic City Union*, 22 August 1921, n.p., in *The Pink Slip* Clipping File, BRTC.

9. "*The Pink Slip* Has Opening at Seashore," *New York Morning Telegraph*, 16 August 1921, n.p., in *The Pink Slip* Clipping File, BRTC.

10. Unidentified article in *The Pink Slip* Clipping File, BRTC.

11. "The Pink Slip," *Variety*, 26 August 1921, n.p., in *The Pink Slip* Clipping File, BRTC.

12. 13 October 1921 letter from A. H. Woods to J. J. Shubert, in SA.

13. Unidentified article in *The Pink Slip* Clipping File, BRTC.

14. 24 October 1921 letter from A. H. Woods to J. J. Shubert regarding *The Pink Slip* business agreement, in SA.

15. 4 November 1921 letter from A. H. Woods to J. J. Shubert, concerning theater size, in SA. The sum of $6,000 per week would be roughly equivalent to $65,483 today. S. Morgan Friedman, "The Inflation Calculator," http:www.westegg.com/inflation/ (accessed 1 June 2007).

16. "*Under the Bamboo Tree*," *Cincinnati Enquirer*, 5 December 1921, 13.

17. Rowland, *Bert Williams*, 171. Punctuation added.

18. Ibid., 172. Punctuation added.

19. Amy Leslie, "Bert Williams in *Under the Bamboo Tree*," *The Daily News*, 12 December 1921, 14.

20. Ibid.

21. Ibid.

22. Ibid.

23. Smith, *Bert Williams*, 220.

24. Unidentified article in Bert Williams File, HTC.

25. Unidentified article in Bert Williams File, HTC.

26. Rowland, *Bert Williams*, 167–8.

27. Al Weeks, "Bert Williams; It's His Show," *Detroit News*, 27 February 1922, 16.

28. Ibid.

29. Smith, *Bert Williams*, 223.

30. Ibid.

31. Smith, *Bert Williams*, 223–4.

32. "News of Williams' Death Shock to Theater Men," *Detroit Evening Times*, 6 March 1922, 11.

33. Certificate of Death, NYMA.

34. Unidentified article in Bert Williams File, HTC.

35. "Bert Williams' [*sic*] Stage Career," *New York Age*, 11 March 1922, 6.

36. Lester A. Walton, "Thousands, of All Races, Mourn Bert Williams' [*sic*] Death," *New York Age*, 11 March 1922, 1

37. Ibid.

38. Ibid.

39. *New York Tribune*, "Theater Critics Lament Death of Bert Williams," 6 March 1922, n.p., in Bert Williams File, HTC.

40. Ibid.

41. Ibid.

42. "Bert Williams, Negro Comedian, Dies Here after Collapse on Detroit Stage," *New York Times*, 5 March 1922, 1.

43. "Genius Defeated by Race," *Literary Digest*, 25 March 1922, 28.

44. Ibid.

45. Heywood Broun, "It Seems to Me," *World,* 7 March 1922, n.p., in Bert Williams File, HTC.

46. Ibid.

47. Ibid.

48. Ibid.

49. Ibid.

50. Unidentified 8 March 1922 clipping in Bert Williams File, HTC.

51. Ibid.

52. *New York World*, 9 March 1922, in Bert Williams File, HTC.

53. Ibid.

54. Ibid.

55. Ibid.

56. Ibid.

57. Eddie Cantor, "Bert Williams: An Appreciation," *New York Age*, 22 April 1922, in *Tuskegee Institute News Clippings File*, Series 2, Reel 241, Frame 120.

58. Ibid.

59. Ibid.

60. "Bert Williams," *The Crisis*, April 1922, 284.

61. Ibid.

62. "Who's Who: Bert Williams," *The Messenger* 4.4 (1922), 394.

63. Ibid.

64. Ibid. Emphasis in original.

65. Ibid.

66. Ibid.

67. Ibid. Emphasis in original.

68. Jessie Faucet, "The Symbolism of Bert Williams," *The Crisis*, May 1922, 13.

69. Ibid., 13–4.

70. Ibid.

71. Eric D. Walrond, "Bert Williams Foundation Organized to Perpetuate the Ideals of the Celebrated Actor," *The Negro World*, 21 April 1923, 4.

72. Storm, "All 135th Street Is Missing Bert Williams," 16.

73. Ibid., 16.

74. Lester A. Walton, "Thousands, of All Races, Mourn Bert Williams' [*sic*] Death," 6.

75. "Masons Honor Williams," *New York Times*, 9 March 1922, 17.

EPILOGUE

1. Bert Williams File, 1925–1974, in SC.

2. See Allen Prescott, "Add Bert Williams, Laughter Troubadour of Ziegfeld Days," *New York Post,* 5 March 1940; Charles L. Bowen, "Bert Williams or Stepin Fetchit: Which was the Greater Comedian?" *The Afro-American*, 27 January 1934; Hannibal L. Davis, "Notable Negroes of Other Days," *New York Age*, 25 February 1934; "Egbert Austin Williams," *The Negro History Bulletin,* January (1939): 28.

3. See "Springtime in the 40s," *Newsweek*, 30 May 1949, 76; Lewis Nichols, "Fun Garden of Show Biz," *New York Times*, 6 December 1953, 15+; "Fred Allen's Tribute to Vaudeville," *Life*, 12 November 1956, 72.

4. All material regarding Ben Vereen from personal communication, 4 July 2007, and "Ben Vereen: The Hard Way," *Biography* (A & E Network, 2000).

Bibliography

ARCHIVES AND COLLECTIONS

Academy Film Archive, Academy of Motion Picture Arts and Sciences, Los Angeles
Billy Rose Theatre Collection, New York Public Library for the Performing Arts
Bodleian Library, Oxford University
British Library, Music Collection, London
British Library, Newspaper Library, London
Charles M. Templeton, Sr., Sheet Music Collection, Mississippi State University.
Harry Ransom Humanities Research Center, University of Texas at Austin
Harvard Theatre Collection, Houghton Library, Harvard University
John Hay Library, Brown University
Library of Congress, Music Division
Library of Congress, Recorded Sound Reference Center
Municipal Archives, New York City
Museum of the City of New York
New York Public Library for the Performing Arts
San Francisco Performing Arts Library and Museum
Schomburg Center for Research in Black Culture, New York Public Library
Shubert Archives, New York
Theatre Museum, Covent Garden, London
University of Iowa, Special Collections

BIBLIOGRAPHY

"2 Killed, 50 Hurt in Furious Race Riot in Chicago." *New York Times*, 28 July 1919, 1, 4.
Abbott, Lynn. "'Play That Barber Shop Chord': A Case for the African-American Origins of Barbershop Harmony." *American Music* 10, no. 3 (1992): 289–325.
Abrahams, Roger. *Singing the Master: The Emergence of African American Culture in the Plantation South*. New York: Pantheon, 1992.
"*Abyssinia.*" *New York Evening Post*, 21 February 1906, 7.
"*Abyssinia* at the Park." *Philadelphia Inquirer*, 10 April 1906, 4.
"*Abyssinia:* Williams and Walker Make a Hit with a New Comedy." *New York Age*, 22 February 1906, 1.
"Actors' Field Day Brings Great Crowd," *New York Times*, 20 August 1910, 7.
Adams, Veronica. "The Dramatic Stage as an Upbuilder of the Races." *Chicago Inter Ocean*, 17 January 1909, 2.
"Aida Overton Walker Is Dead." *New York Age*, 15 October 1914, 1.

Aldridge, Benjamin L. "The Victor Talking Machine Company." R.C.A. Victor, 1964.

"The Alexandra, N." *The Stage* (London), 11 February 1904, 15.

Anderson, Ann. *Snake Oil, Hustlers and Hambones: The American Medicine Show.* Jefferson, NC., and London: McFarland, Inc., 2000.

Anonymous. *An Illustrated History of Southern California.* Chicago: Lewis Publishing, 1890.

"Anniversary Celebration of Williams and Walker a Gala Event." *New York Age,* 2 April 1908, 6.

Appelbaum, Stanley. *The Chicago World's Fair of 1893: A Photographic Record.* New York: Dover, 1980.

Aristophanes. *The Frogs.* Edited by Charles Eliot. Translated by B. B. Rogers. Vol. 8, Part 9, of 51, *The Harvard Classics.* New York: P. F. Collier, 1909–14.

"'Art Knows No Color Line,' Says Brooklyn Eagle." *New York Age,* 30 April 1908, 6.

Atkinson, Brooks. *Broadway.* Revised edition. New York: Macmillian, 1974.

"Auditorium." *Philadelphia Inquirer,* 8 October 1901, 16.

B., J. "Bert Williams." *The Soil: A Magazine of Art,* December 1916, 19–23.

"Bandanna Land Pleases." *New York Times,* 4 February 1908, 7.

"Bandanna Land to Stay." *New York Age,* 13 February 1908, 6.

"Bar Fight Pictures to Avoid Race Riots." *New York Times,* 6 July 1910.

Barrymore, Ethel. *Memories: An Autobiography.* New York: Harper and Brothers, 1955.

Beerbohm, Constance. "The 'Cake-Walk' and How to Dance It." *The Tatler* (London), 1 July 1903, 13.

"Behanzin, Deposed King of Dahomey, Probably Perished." *New York Times,* 1 June 1902, 24.

Berlin, Edward A. *Reflections and Research on Ragtime.* Vol. 24, *I.S.A.M. Monographs.* Brooklyn, NY: Institute for Studies in American Music, Conservatory of Music, Brooklyn College, 1987.

"Bert A. Williams & Co. in *Mr. Lode of Koal." Indianapolis Freeman,* 20 November 1909, 6.

"Bert A. Williams Company at Kansas City, Mo." *Indianapolis Freeman,* 2 October 1909, 5.

"Bert Williams." *The Crisis,* April 1922, 284.

"Bert Williams." *New York Age,* 7 March 1912, 6.

"Bert Williams." *New York Age,* 16 June 1916, 6.

"Bert Williams's Funeral." *New York Times,* 6 March 1922, 13.

"Bert Williams' [*sic*] Tact." *New York Age,* 2 August 1919, 6.

"Bert Williams's Will Signed." *New York Times,* 19 March 1922, 21.

"Bert Williams a Hit in *Midnight Frolic." New York Age,* 20 July 1918, 6.

"Bert Williams at Hippodrome." *New York Age,* 20 April 1916, 6.

"Bert Williams at the Shubert." *Kansas City Times,* 20 September 1909, 5.

"Bert Williams: Boy-Gentleman-Comedian." *Chicago Record-Herald,* 25 September 1910, 7.

"Bert Williams Buys Property in New York City." *New York Age,* 7 May 1908, 6.

"Bert Williams Feature of *Follies of 1910." New York Age,* 23 June 1910, 6.

"Bert Williams? He Was Greatest, Most Imitated Comic in the U.S." *Jet,* 12 February 1981, 60–2.

"Bert Williams Home." *New York Age,* 3 September 1914, 6.

"Bert Williams in Demand." *New York Age,* 25 May 1911.

"Bert Williams in Vaudeville." *New York Age,* 20 May 1909, 6.

"Bert Williams in Vaudeville." *New York Age,* 21 April 1910, 6.

"Bert Williams Leading a Strenuous Existence." *New York Age,* 22 March 1919, 6.

"Bert Williams, Negro Comedian, Dies Here after Collapse on Detroit Stage." *New York Times,* 5 March 1922, 1.

"Bert Williams Now a Full-Fledged Citizen." *New York Age,* 22 June 1918, 1.

"Bert Williams Quits the *Follies* in Atlantic City." *New York Age,* 22 June 1918, 1.

"Bert Williams Scores in Chicago." *New York Age,* 7 October 1909, 6.

"Bert Williams' [*sic*] Stage Career." *New York Age,* 11 March 1922, 6.

"Bert Williams' [sic] Team Loses," *Indianapolis Freeman*, 2 October 1909, 4.

"Bert Williams Tells of Walker." *Indianapolis Freeman*, 14 January 1911, 5.

"Bert Williams the World Famous Comedian Now Makes Records Exclusively for the *Columbia*." *Columbia Records Supplement*, November 1910, 6.

"Bert Williams to Star." *New York Times*, 8 November 1913, 13.

"Between Seasons." *New York Times*, 17 June 1917, 5.

Bickford, Charles. *Bulls, Balls, Bicycles and Actors*. New York: Paul S. Eriksson, 1965.

"Bill at Keith's Bijou." *Philadelphia Inquirer*, 23 March 1897, 5.

"Black but Comely." *The Star* (London), 16 May 1903, 3.

Blau, Herbert. *The Audience*. Baltimore and London: Johns Hopkins University Press, 1990.

Blum, Daniel. *Great Stars of the American Stage: A Pictorial Record*. New York: Greenberg, 1952.

———. *A Pictorial History of the American Theatre, 1900–1951*. New York: Greenberg, 1951.

Booker T. Washington, N. B. Wood, and Fannie Barrier Williams. *A New Negro for a New Century*. New York: Arno Press and the *New York Times*, 1969.

Bordman, Gerald. *American Musical Revue: From "The Passing Show" to "Sugar Babies."* New York and Oxford: Oxford University Press, 1985.

———. *American Musical Theatre: A Chronicle*. Expanded edition. Oxford and London: Oxford University Press, 1986.

Boskin, Joseph. *Sambo: The Rise and Demise of an American Jester*. New York and Oxford: Oxford University Press, 1986.

Boston Globe, 13 March 1900, 9.

Braxton, Joanne M., ed. *The Collected Poetry of Paul Laurence Dunbar*. Charlottesville and London: University Press of Virginia, 1993.

"Broadway Belated Night of Follies." *New York World*, 22 October 1912, 5.

"*Broadway Brevities, 1920*." *New York Times*, 30 September 1920, 12.

"Broadway Gives a Rousing Greeting to the 1916 *Ziegfeld Follies* at the New Amsterdam." *New York American*, 13 June 1916, 9.

Brooks, Daphne A. *Bodies in Dissent: Spectacular Performances of Race and Freedom, 1850–1910*. Durham, NC, and London: Duke University Press, 2006.

Brooks, Tim. *Lost Sounds: Blacks and the Birth of the Recording Industry, 1890–1919*. Urbana and Chicago: University of Illinois Press, 2004.

Broun, Heywood. "New Edition of the *Follies* Lives Up to Tradition of Beauty." *New York Tribune*, 17 June 1919, 13.

Bruce, Philip A. *The Plantation Negro as a Freeman*. New York: G. P. Putnam's Sons, 1889.

Burke, Kenneth. *Attitudes Toward History*. Los Altos, CA: Hermes, 1959.

"Burnett to Lose His Fees." *New York Times*, 3 March 1905, 1.

Burns, Ric and James Sanders. *New York: An Illustrated History*. Expanded edition. New York: Alfred A. Knopf, 2003.

Burrows, Edwin G. and Mike Wallace. *Gotham: A History of New York City to 1898*. New York and Oxford: Oxford University Press, 1999.

Burstein, Andrew. *The Original Knickerbocker: The Life of Washington Irving*. New York: Basic, 2007.

"Burt [sic] Williams." *Indianapolis Freeman*, 1 October 1910, 5.

Butler, Judith. *Bodies That Matter: On the Discursive Limits of "Sex."* New York and London: Routledge, 1993.

C., P. "Shaftesbury Theatre. *In Dahomey*." *Daily News* (London), 18 May 1903, 12.

Cantor, Eddie. *As I Remember Them*. New York: Duell, Sloan and Pearce, 1963.

———. *My Life Is in Your Hands*. New York: Curtis, 1928.

———. *The Way I See It*. Edited by Phyllis Rosentaur. Englewood Cliffs, NJ: Prentice Hall, 1959.

Cantor, Eddie and David Freedman. *Ziegfeld, the Great Glorifier*. New York: Alfred H. King, 1934.

Carleton, Henry G. *The Thompson Street Poker Club from "Life."* New York: White and
   Allen, 1899.
Carter, Randolph. *The World of Flo Ziegfeld.* New York: Praeger, 1974.
Charters, Ann. *Nobody: The Story of Bert Williams.* New York: Macmillan, 1970.
Chicago Commission on Race Relations. *The Negro in Chicago: A Study of Race Relations
   and a Race Riot.* Chicago, 1922.
"Chicago Critics on Bert Williams." *New York Age,* 15 September 1910, 6.
Chicago Tribune, 29 May 1906, 6.
Chude-Sokei, Louis. *The Last "Darky": Bert Williams, Black-on-Black Minstrelsy, and the
   African Diaspora.* Durham, NC, and London: Duke University Press, 2006.
City of Riverside, CA. "Frank Miller: Myths, Mission Inn, and the Making of Riverside." http:
   www.riversideca.gov/rlhrc/historydiv/Miller%20Exhibit.htm (accessed 23 April 2007).
Clapp, Sarah L. C. "The Subscription Enterprises of John Ogilby and Richard Blome."
   Modern Philology 30, no. 4 (1933): 365–79.
"Closing of *Mr. Lode of Koal Co.*" *New York Age,* 24 February 1910, 6.
"Clubs Elect Officers." *New York Age,* 26 May 1910, 6.
Cockrell, Dale. *Demons of Disorder: Early Blackface Minstrels and Their World.* Edited by
   Don B. Wilmeth. 10 vols. Vol. 8, *Cambridge Studies in American Theatre and
   Drama.* Cambridge: Cambridge University Press, 1997.
"The Colored Theatre." *New York Age,* 2 September 1915, 6.
"Colored Theatre Opens: Old Bijou Shows '*The Dark-town Follies of 1914*'." *New York
   Times,* 16 June 1914, 9.
"Comments on the Films." *Moving Picture World* 30, no. 10 (1916): 1511.
"Comments on the Films—'A Natural Born Gambler'." *Moving Picture World,* 12 August
   1916, 1103.
"Controversy over W. and W." *New York Age,* 5 March 1908, 6.
Cook, Will Marion. "Clorindy, the Origin of the Cakewalk." *Theatre Arts* 31, no. 9 (1947):
   61–5.
Craton, Michael. *A History of the Bahamas.* London: Collins, 1962.
Craton, Michael and Gail Saunders. *Islanders in the Stream: A History of the Bahamian
   People.* Vol. 2. Athens and London: University of Georgia Press, 1998.
Creamer, Henry S. "Negro Chances." *New York Age,* 11 July 1912, 6.
"Crowd Is Saddened When Johnson Wins." *New York Times,* 5 July 1910, 4.
Crummell, Alexander. *Africa and America: Addresses and Discourses.* Miami:
   Mnemosyne Publishing, 1969.
Curtis, James. *W. C. Fields: A Biography.* New York: Alfred A. Knopf, 2003.
Curtis, Susan. *The First Black Actors on the Great White Way.* Columbia and London:
   University of Missouri Press, 1998.
"Dahomey on Broadway." *New York Times,* 19 February 1903, 9.
Davies, Christie. *Ethnic Humor Around the World.* Bloomington and Indianapolis:
   Indiana University Press, 1990.
DeFrantz, Thomas. "Simmering Passivity: The Black Male Body in Concert Dance." In
   Moving Words: Re-Writing Dance. Edited by Gay Morris. London and New York:
   Routledge, 1996.
Deleuze, Gilles and Félix Guattari. *Kafka: Toward a Minor Literature.* Translated by
   Dana Polan. Vol. 30, *Theory and History of Literature.* Minneapolis: University of
   Minnesota Press, 1986.
DiMeglio, John E. *Vaudeville U.S.A.* Bowling Green, OH: Bowling Green University
   Popular Press, 1973.
Dixon Gottschild, Brenda. *Waltzing in the Dark: African American Vaudeville and Race
   Politics in the Swing Era.* New York: Palgrave, 2000.
Dormon, James H. "Shaping the Popular Image of Post-Reconstruction American
   Blacks: The 'Coon Song' Phenomenon of the Gilded Age." *American Quarterly* 40
   (December 1988): 450–71.

Dorson, Richard M. "The Yankee on the Stage—a Folk Hero of American Drama." *New England Quarterly* 13, no. 3 (1940): 467–93.

Douglas, Ann. *Terrible Honesty: Mongrel Manhattan in the 1920s*. New York: Farrar, Straus and Giroux, 1995.

"Dr. Washington Stops Show." *New York Age*, 13 February 1908, 6.

Drake, St. Clair and Horace R. Cayton. *Black Metropolis: A Study of Negro Life in a Northern City*. Revised and enlarged edition. Chicago: University of Chicago Press, 1993.

Du Bois, W. E. Burghardt. *The Gift of Black Folk: The Negroes in the Making of America*. Boston: Stratford, 1924. Reprint, 1968.

———. *The Souls of Black Folk*. 5th ed. Chicago: A. C. Mc Clurg, 1904.

———. "The Talented Tenth." In *The Negro Problem: A Series of Articles by Representative American Negroes of Today*. New York: AMS Press, 1970.

"Eight Killed in Fight Riots." *New York Times*, 6 July 1910, 1, 4.

Ellis, Mark. *Race, War, and Surveillance: African Americans and the United States Government During World War I*. Bloomington and Indianapolis: Indiana University Press, 2001.

Emery, Lynne Fauley. *Black Dance in the United States from 1619 to 1970*. Palo Alto, CA: National Press Books, 1972.

Ewen, David. *The Life and Death of Tin Pan Alley: The Golden Age of American Popular Music*. New York: Funk and Wagnalls, 1964.

"The Fair's Closing Month." *The Examiner* (San Francisco), 2 June 1894, 8.

Faucet, Jessie. "The Symbolism of Bert Williams," *The Crisis*, May 1922, 13.

Fiddler and Shelton, "A Day with the Bert A. Williams Company," *Indianapolis Freeman*, 9 October 1909, 6.

Fields, Marc, et al. "Episode One: Give My Regards to Broadway (1893–1927)." In *Broadway: The American Musical*, edited by Michael Kantor. Hollywood: Paramount Home Entertainment, 2004.

"Fire in Little Dahomey." *The Examiner* (San Francisco), 20 June 1894, 6.

"First Class Theater." *Virginia Law Register* 13, no. 10 (1908): 819.

Fletcher, Tom. *100 Years of the Negro in Show Business*. New York: Burdge, 1954.

"*Follies* Begin Summer Capers." *New York Times*, 2 June 1914, 11.

"*Follies* Have Beauty Galore." *New York Tribune*, 13 June 1916, 9.

"*Follies of 1910* Arrives." *New York Sun*, 21 June 1910, 9.

"*Follies of 1910* on New York Roof." *New York Times*, 21 June 1910, 9.

"*Follies of 1911*." *New York Evening Post*, 27 June 1911, 9.

"*Follies of 1911*." *New York Herald*, 27 June 1911, 10.

"*Follies of 1911* Here." *New York Tribune*, 27 June 1911, 8.

"*Follies of 1912*." *New York Tribune*, 22 October 1912, 9.

"*Follies of 1912* Is a Beauty Show." *New York Times*, 22 October 1912, 11.

"*Follies of 1917* Is a Fine Spectacle." *New York Times*, 13 June 1917, 11.

Foster, William. "Memoirs of William Foster: Pioneers of the Stage." In *The Official Theatrical World of Colored Artists*, edited by Theophilus Lewis. New York: Theatrical World Publishing, 1928.

"Fred Allen's Tribute to Vaudeville." *Life*, 12 November 1956, 72.

Fredrickson, George M. *The Black Image in the White Mind: The Debate on Afro-American Character and Destiny, 1817–1914*. Hanover, NH: Wesley University Press, 1971.

"The French in Dahomey." *New York Times*, 9 March 1890, 5.

Freud, Sigmund. *Jokes and Their Relation to the Unconscious*. New York and London: W. W. Norton, 1960.

Friedman, S. Morgan. "The Inflation Calculator." http:www.westegg.com/inflation (accessed 23 April 2007).

"The Frogs." *New York Age*, 6 October 1908.

"From 'Dahomey' to Buckingham Palace." *The Era* (London), 27 June 1903, 13.

"From the South." *The Examiner* (San Francisco), 2 January 1894, 10.

Gagey, Edmond. *The San Francisco Stage: A History*. New York: Columbia University Press, 1950. Reprint, 1970.

Gaines, Kevin. *Uplifting the Race: Black Leadership, Politics, and Culture in the Twentieth Century*. Chapel Hill: University of North Carolina Press, 1996.

Gates, Henry Louis, Jr. *The Signifying Monkey: A Theory of African-American Literary Criticism*. New York and Oxford: Oxford University Press, 1988.

———. "The Trope of a New Negro and the Reconstruction of the Image of the Black." *Representations* 24 (Autumn 1988): 129–55.

Gatewood, Willard B. *Aristocrats of Color: The Black Elite, 1880–1920*. Fayetteville: University of Arkansas Press, 1991. Reprint, 2000.

"The Gayety." *Brooklyn Eagle*, 17 January 1898, 5.

"Genius Defeated by Race." *Literary Digest*, 25 March 1922, 28.

Gentz, Will T. "In the Vaudeville Field." (New York) *Dramatic Mirror*, 14 December 1918, 869.

George-Graves, Nadine. *The Royalty of Negro Vaudeville: The Whitman Sisters and the Negotiation of Race, Gender, and Class in African American Theater, 1900–1940*. New York: St. Martin's, 2000.

"George Lederer Interview." *Variety*, 17 March 1922, 14.

"George LeMaire's *Broadway Brevities of 1920*." *New York Evening Post*, 30 September 1920, 9.

"George LeMaire Brings New Production, *Broadway Brevities,* into Winter Garden." *New York Evening Telegram*, 30 September 1920, 20.

"George W. Walker." *New York Age*, 12 January 1911, 4.

"George Walker Dead." *New York Times*, 8 January 1911, 13.

"George Walker's Flashy Clothes." *Toledo Courier*, 20 December 1907.

Gilbert, Douglas. *American Vaudeville: Its Life and Times*. New York: Whittlesey House, 1940.

"Girls and Glitter in *Follies of 1911*." *New York Times*, 27 June 1911, 9.

"Glimpses of the Throng." *The Examiner* (San Francisco), 28 January 1894, 8.

"Globe Theatre." *Boston Post*, 21 March 1905.

"Globe Theatre: *In Dahomey*." *Boston Transcript*, 21 March 1905.

Goldberg, Isaac. *Tin Pan Alley: A Chronicle of American Popular Music*. New York: Frederick Ungar, 1961.

Golden, Eve. *Anna Held and the Birth of Ziegfeld's Broadway*. Lexington: University of Kentucky, 2000.

Gordon, Max with Lewis Funke. *Max Gordon Presents*. New York: Bernard Geis, 1963.

Gottschild, Brenda Dixon. *Digging the Africanist Presence in American Performance: Dance and Other Contexts*. Westport, CT: Praeger, 1998.

Green, Abel and Joe Laurie, Jr. *Show Biz: From Vaude to Video*. New York: Henry Holt, 1951.

Green, Jeffrey. "*In Dahomey* in London in 1903." *The Black Perspective in Music* 11, no. 1 (1983): 22–40.

Guerrero, Ed. *Framing Blackness: The African American Image in Gilm*. Philadelphia: Temple University Press, 1993.

"Hammerstein's." *Variety*, 30 April 1910, 22.

"Hammerstein's." *Variety*, 7 May 1910, 21.

Harlan, Louis R. and Raymond W., eds. *The Booker T. Washington Papers*, vol. 10. Urbana and Chicago: University of Illinois Press, 1977.

Harris, Bill. *The Hellfighters of Harlem: African-American Soldiers Who Fought for the Right to Fight for Their Country*. New York: Carroll and Graf, 2002.

Hartman, Saidiya V. *Scenes of Subjection: Terror, Slavery and Self-Making in Nineteenth-Century America*. New York and Oxford: Oxford University Press, 1997.

Havoc, June. "Old Vaudevillians, Where Are You Now?" *Horizon*, July 1959, 112–20.

Henderson, Mary C. *The City and the Theatre*. Revised and expanded edition. New York: Back Stage, 2004.

———. "*The Voice of the City: Vaudeville and Popular Culture in New York* (Review)." *Theatre Journal* 53, no. 2 (2001): 349–51.

Higginbotham, Evelyn Brooks. *Righteous Discontent: The Women's Movement in the Black Baptist Church.* Cambridge, MA: Harvard University Press, 1993.

Higham, Charles. *Ziegfeld.* Chicago: Henry Regnery, 1972.

Hischak, Thomas S. and Gerald Bordman, eds. *The Oxford Companion to American Theatre*, 3rd ed. New York and Oxford: Oxford University Press, 2004.

Hogan, Ernest. "All Coons Look Alike to Me: A Darkey Misunderstanding." New York: M. Witmark and Sons, 1896.

Howard, J. D. "*Mr. Lode of Koal.*" *Indianapolis Freeman*, 6 November 1909, 5.

Hudson, Nicholas. "From 'Nation' to 'Race': The Origin of Racial Classification in Eighteenth-Century Thought." *Eighteenth-Century Studies* 29, no. 3 (1996): 247–64.

"*In Dahomey.*" *The Era* (London), 23 May 1903, 16.

"*In Dahomey.*" *New York Evening Post*, 29 August 1904, 7.

"*In Dahomey.*" *St. James's Gazette* (London), 18 May 1903, 15.

"*In Dahomey* at the Shaftesbury." *Sphere* (London), 23 May 1903, 162.

"*In Dahomey.* Amusing Production at the Shaftesbury Theatre." *Daily Mail* (London), 18 May 1903, 3.

"*In Dahomey:* At the Shaftesbury Theatre." *The Playgoer* (London), 465+.

Indianapolis Freeman, 2 February 1898, 4.

Indianapolis Freeman, 9 September 1899, 1.

Indianapolis Freeman, 3 July 1909, 5.

Jasen, David A. and Trebor Jay Tichenor. *Rags and Ragtime: A Musical History.* New York: Seabury, 1978.

Johnson, Howard. "Bahamian Labor Migration to Florida in the Late Nineteenth and Early Twentieth Centuries." *International Migration Review* 22, no. 1 (1988): 84–103.

Johnson, James Weldon. *Along This Way: The Autobiography of James Weldon Johnson.* New York: Viking, 1934.

———. *Black Manhattan.* New York: Alfred A. Knopf, 1930.

———. *The Book of American Negro Poetry.* New York: Harcourt, 1931.

———. "The Dilemma of the Negro Author." *The American Mercury* 15.60 (December 1928): 477.

Johnson, Stephen Burge. *The Roof Gardens of Broadway Theatres, 1883–1942.* Edited by Oscar G. Brockett. *Theater and Dramatic Studies*, vol. 31. Ann Arbor: University of Michigan Research Press, 1985.

"Johnson Wins in 15 Rounds; Jeffries Weak." *New York Times*, 6 July 1910, 1.

Keaton, Buster with Charles Samuels. *My Wonderful World of Slapstick.* New York: Doubleday, 1960.

Kees, Uncle Rad. "Williams for Walker, or the Passing of Two of the World's Greatest Entertainers." *Indianapolis Freeman*, 12 March 1910, 5.

Kibler, M. Alison. *Rank Ladies: Gender and Cultural Hierarchy in American Vaudeville.* Chapel Hill: University of North Carolina Press, 1999.

Kingsley, Walter. "Vaudeville Volleys." (New York) *Dramatic Mirror*, 14 December 1918, 867.

Kirkland, Frank M. "Modernity and Intellectual Life in Black." *The Philosophical Forum* 24.1–3 (Fall–Spring 1992): 136–65.

"Klaw and Erlanger's New Productions." *New York Times*, 19 July 1913, 7.

Krasner, David. *A Beautiful Pageant: African American Theatre, Drama, and Performance in the Harlem Renaissance, 1910–1927.* New York: Palgrave Macmillan, 2002.

———. *Resistance, Parody, and Double Consciousness in African American Theatre, 1895–1910.* New York: St. Martin's, 1997.

Laurie, Joe, Jr. *Vaudeville: From the Honky-Tonks to the Palace.* New York: Henry Holt, 1953.

Leab, Daniel J. "The Gamut from A to B: The Image of the Black in Pre–1915 Movies." *Political Science Quarterly* 88, no. 1 (1973): 53–70.

Lemons, Stanley J. "Black Stereotypes as Reflected in Popular Culture, 1880–1920." *American Quarterly* 29 (Spring 1977): 102–16.

Leslie, Amy. "Bert Williams in *Under the Bamboo Tree*." *The Daily News*, 12 December 1921, 14.

Levine, Lawrence W. *Black Culture and Black Consciousness: Afro-American Folk Thought from Slavery to Freedom*. New York and Oxford: Oxford University Press, 1977.

———. *Highbrow/Lowbrow: The Emergence of Cultural Hierarchy in America*. Cambridge, MA, and London: Harvard University Press, 1990.

Levine, Robert S. *Martin Delany, Frederick Douglass, and the Politics of Representative Identity*. Chapel Hill and London: University of North Carolina, 1997.

Lewis, Lloyd. *It Takes All Kinds*. New York: Harcourt, Brace, 1928.

Lewis, Robert M., ed. *From Traveling Show to Vaudeville: Theatrical Spectacle in America, 1830–1910*. Baltimore and London: Johns Hopkins University Press, 2003.

Lhamon, W. T., Jr., *Raising Cain: Blackface Performance from Jim Crow to Hip Hop*. Cambridge, MA, and London: Harvard University Press, 1998.

Litwack, Leon F. *Been in the Storm So Long: The Aftermath of Slavery*. New York: Vintage, 1979.

Logan, Rayford W. *The Betrayal of the Negro: From Rutherford B. Hayes to Woodrow Wilson*. New and enlarged edition. London: Collier, 1965. Reprint, 1969.

Logan, Tom. "The Coon's Trade-Mark." New York: Jos. W. Stern, 1898.

Lott, Eric. *Love and Theft: Blackface Minstrelsy and the American Working Class*. New York and Oxford: Oxford University Press, 1993.

Lust, Annette. *From the Greek Mimes to Marcel Marceau and Beyond: Mimes, Actors, Pierrots and Clowns; A Chronicle of the Many Visages of Mime in the Theatre*. Lanham, MD, and London: Scarecrow, 2000.

"Lyceum." *Cleveland Plain Dealer*, 18 January 1910, 4.

Mahar, William J. *Behind the Burnt Cork Mask: Early Blackface Minstrelsy and Antebellum American Popular Culture*. Urbana and Chicago: University of Illinois Press, 1999.

"Majestic—*Bandanna Land*." (New York) *Dramatic Mirror*, 15 February 1908, 3.

Mander, Raymond and Joe Mitchenson. *The Lost Theatres of London*. London: Rupert Hart-Davis, 1968.

Mark. "Palace." *Variety*, 2 January 1914, 20.

"The Marlborough." *The Stage* (London), 25 February 1904, 17.

Marston, Williams M. and John H. Feller. *F. F. Proctor: Vaudeville Pioneer*. New York: Richard R. Smith, 1943.

Martin, C. T. "Deac." "The Evolution of Barbership Harmony." *Music Journal Annual* 34 (1965): 106–7.

"Masons Honor Williams." *New York Times*, 9 March 1922, 17.

Mawer, Irene. *The Art of Mime: Its History and Technique in Education and the Theatre*. London: Methuen, 1932.

McArthur, Benjamin. *Actors and American Culture, 1880–1920*. Philadelphia, PA: Temple University Press, 1984.

McLean, Albert F., Jr. *American Vaudeville as Ritual*. Louisville: University of Kentucky Press, 1965.

———. "Genesis of Vaudeville: Two Letters from B. F. Keith." *Theatre Survey* 1 (1960): 82–95.

McNamara, Brooks. *Step Right Up*. Revised edition. Jackson: University Press of Mississippi. 1995.

McNeal, Violet. *Four White Horses and a Brass Band*. Garden City, NY: Doubleday, 1947.

Meier, August. *Negro Thought in America, 1880–1915: Racial Ideologies in the Age of Booker T. Washington*. Ann Arbor: University of Michigan Press, 1969.

Meyer, George W. (music) and Clarke, Grant (lyrics). "You'll Find Old Dixieland in France." New York: Leo Feist, 1918.

Miller, Jordan Y. *Playwright's Progress: O'Neill and the Critics*. Chicago and Atlanta: Kansas State University, 1965.

Mitchell, Loften. *Black Drama: The Story of the American Negro in the Theatre.* New York: Hawthorn, 1967.

Mizejewski, Linda. *Ziegfeld Girl: Image and Icon in Culture and Cinema.* Durham, NC, and London: Duke University Press, 1999.

Monfried, Walter. "Bert Williams: The Modern Pagliaccio." *Negro Digest,* November 1961, 28–32.

"*Mr. Lode of Koal* an Amusing Play." *New York Herald,* 2 November 1909, 8.

"*Mr. Lode of Koal* on the Road." *New York Age,* 9 December 1909, 6.

"*Mr. Lode of Koal* Wins Favor Uptown." *Philadelphia Inquirer,* 14 December 1909, 6.

"Mrs. Lottie Williams Convalesces." *New York Age,* 7 May 1908, 6.

Murray, R. C. "Williams and Walker." *Colored American Magazine,* September 1905, 496–502.

"Music and the Stage." *New York Age,* 16 July 1914, 6.

"Musical Plays." *New York Evening Post,* 30 September 1920, 9.

"The *N.Y. Globe* on W. and W. Anniversary." *New York Age,* 9 April 1908, 6.

Nadis, Fred. *Wonder Shows: Performing Science, Magic and Religion in America.* New Brunswick, NJ, and London: Rutgers University Press, 2005.

Nasaw, David. *Going Out: The Rise and Fall of Public Amusements.* Cambridge, MA: Harvard University Press, 1999.

"Negro Actors to Have a Society." *New York Telegraph,* 25 January 1906.

"Negro Company Has Season at Majestic: In a Musical Play, 'His Honor the Barber,' Begins an Indefinite Engagement." *New York Times,* 9 May 1911, 11.

"Negro on the Stage." *New York Age,* 24 November 1910, 6.

"New Negro Troops Parade in Fifth Avenue." *New York Times,* 2 October 1916, 22.

"New Plays and Old This Week." *Philadelphia Inquirer,* 12 September 1920, 8.

Newman, Richard. "*The Brightest Star:* Aida Overton Walker in the Age of Ragtime and Cakewalk." In *Prospects: An Annual of American Culture,* edited by Jack Salzman, 465–81. Cambridge: Cambridge University Press, 1993.

"News of Williams' [*sic*] Death Shock to Theater Men." *Detroit Evening Times,* 6 March 1922, 11.

New York Age, 13 May 1909, 6.

New York Age, 21 October 1909, 7.

New York Age, 5 January 1911, 2.

New York Dramatic Mirror, 19 June 1895, 11.

New York World, 19 February 1903, 3.

"The 1916 *Follies* Full of Splendor." *New York Times,* 13 June 1916, 9.

Niver, Kemp R. *Klaw and Erlanger Presents Famous Plays in Pictures.* Los Angeles: Locare Research Group, 1976.

"Nobility Learns the Cakewalk." *London Notes,* 4 July 1903.

"Now Playing in First Class Theatres." *New York Age,* 24 December 1908, 6.

Ogilby, John. *Africa: Being an Accurate Description of the Regions of Egypt, Barbary, Lybia, and Billedulgerid, the Land of Negroes, Guinee, Æthiopia and the Abyssines.* London: Printed by Tho. Johnson for the author, 1670.

"Only Afro-American Theatre in World." *New York Age,* 18 October 1906, 5.

Osofsky, Gilbert. *Harlem: The Making of a Ghetto, New York, 1890–1930.* 2nd ed. New York: Harper and Row, 1963. Reprint, 1971.

Page, Brett. *Writing for Vaudeville.* Springfield, MA: Home Correspondence School, 1915.

"Palace." *Variety,* 26 December 1913, 18.

Palmer, Greg. "Vaudeville: An American Masters Special." In *American Masters.* Seattle: Thirteen/WNET, KCTS/Seattle, 1997.

"Pekin Stock Co." *New York Age,* 1 December 1910, 6.

Phelan, Peggy. *Unmarked: The Politics of Performance.* London and New York: Routledge, 1993.

Pickett, Williams P. *The Negro Problem.* New York: G. P. Putnam's Sons, 1909.

"Plays and Players." *New York Evening Telegram,* 17 June 1919, 10.

"Plays and Players." *Weekly Dispatch*, 24 May 1903, 8.

Pollack, Channing. "Building the Follies." *Green Book*, September 1915, 388–403.

Prill, Arthur. "The 'Small-Time' King." *Theatre Magazine* 19 (March 1914): 139–40+.

"Prince Edward's Birthday Party." *St. James's Gazette* (London), 24 June 1903, 7.

"Prisoners in Dahomey: A Number of Europeans in the Hands of King Behanzin." *New York Times*, 15 April 1892, 6.

The Public Health Museum. "Patent Medicine." http:www.publichealthmuseum.org/exhibits-patentmed.html (accessed 10 April 2007).

"Queer People at the Fair." *The Examiner* (San Francisco), 8 May 1894, 14.

Ramsaye, Terry. *A Million and One Nights: A History of the Motion Picture*. New York: Simon and Schuster, 1964.

"Rebellion in Dahomey Feared." *New York Times*, 17 January 1901, 7.

Renaud, Ralph E. "Ziegfeld Offers Big Attraction." *San Francisco Chronicle*, 17 April 1911, 2.

"Retirement of Lottie Williams." *New York Age*, 24 December 1908, 6.

Riis, Jacob A. *How the Other Half Lives: Studies among the Tenements of New York*. Edited by David Leviatin. Boston and New York: Bedford of St. Martin's, 1996.

Riis, Thomas L. *Just before Jazz: Black Musical Theater in New York, 1890–1915*. Washington, DC, and London: Smithsonian Institution Press, 1989.

———. *More Than Just Minstrel Shows: The Rise of Black Musical Theatre at the Turn of the Century*. Vol. 33, *I.S.A.M Monographs*. Brooklyn, NY: Institute for Studies in American Music, Conservatory of Music, Brooklyn College, 1992.

———, ed. *The Music and Scripts of* "In Dahomey." Madison, WI: A-R Editions for the American Musicological Society, 1996.

Roach, Joseph. *Cities of the Dead: Circum-Atlantic Performance*. New York: Columbia University Press, 1996.

Robinson, W. W. *The Story of Riverside County*. Los Angeles: Pioneer Title Insurance Company, 1957.

Rogers, Alex, and Will Marion Cook. "Bon Bon Buddy." Providence: Gotham-Attucks Music Publishing, 1907.

Rolfe, Bari. *Behind the Mask*. Oakland, CA: Personabooks, 1977.

Rose, Julie. *The World's Columbian Exposition: Idea, Experience, Aftermath*. http:xroads.virginia.edu/~MA96/WCE/title.html 1996 (accessed 23 April 2007).

Rourke, Constance. *American Humor: A Study of the National Character*. Reprint edition. Tallahassee: Florida State University Press, 1986.

Rowland, Mabel, ed. *Bert Williams: Son of Laughter*. New York: English Crafters, 1923.

Royle, Edwin Milton. "The Vaudeville Theatre." *Scribner's Monthly* 26 (October 1899): 487.

Rush. "New Acts." *Variety*, 26 December 1913, 17.

———. "New Acts of the Week." *Variety*, 23 April 1910, 12.

Russell, Sylvester. "Bert A. Williams in *Mr. Lode of Koal*." *Indianapolis Freeman*, 16 October 1909, 5.

———. "Bert Williams in a White Show Makes a Big Hit at the Colonial." *Indianapolis Freeman*, 10 September 1910, 7.

———. "The Bert Williams Interview and Its Value and Importance." *Indianapolis Freeman*, 8 October 1910, 2.

———. "George Williams [*sic*] Walker of Williams and Walker." *Indianapolis Freeman*, 14 January 1911, 5.

Sacks, Marcy S. *Before Harlem: The Black Experience in New York City before World War I*. Philadelphia: University of Pennsylvania Press, 2006.

Sampson, Henry. *The Ghost Walks: A Chronological History of Blacks in Show Business, 1865–1910*. Metuchen, NJ, and London: Scarecrow Press, 1988.

Samuels, Charles and Louise. *Once Upon a Stage: The Merry World of Vaudeville*. New York: Dodd, Mead, 1974.

Saxton, Alexander. "Blackface Minstrelsy." In *Inside the Minstrel Mask: Readings in Nineteenth-Century Blackface Minstrelsy*, edited by Annemarie Bean, James V. Hatch, and Brooks McNamara, 67–85, Hanover and London: Wesleyan University Press, 1996.

Scheiner, Seth M. *Negro Mecca: A History of the Negro in New York City, 1865–1920*.
New York: New York University Press, 1965.

Scholes, Percy A., ed. *The Oxford Companion to Music*. London: Oxford University
Press, 1938.

Scott, Emmett J. *Scott's Official History of the American Negro in the World War*. New
York: Arno Press and the New York Times, 1969.

"The Secret of Williams and Walker's Success." *New York Age*, 27 February 1908, 6.

"*Senegambian Carnival*." *Boston Globe*, 2 September 1898, 2.

Shackford, James Atkins. *David Crockett: The Man and the Legend*. Lincoln: University
of Nebraska Press, 1956. Reprint, 1994.

"The Shaftesbury." *The (London) Stage*, 21 May 1903, 14.

"Shaftesbury Theatre. *In Dahomey*." *Daily News* (London), 18 May 1903, 12.

Shawn, Ted. *Every Little Movement: A Book About Delsartre*. New York: Dance Horizons,
1963.

Shirley, Wayne D. "The House of Melody: A List of Publications of the Gotham-Attucks
Music Company at the Library of Congress." *The Black Perspective in Music* 15, no.
1 (1987): 79–112.

"Show Reviews." *Variety*, 6 December 1918, 17.

———. "*Ziegfeld Follies*." *Variety*, 25 October 1912, 22.

———. "*Ziegfeld Follies*." *Variety*, 5 June 1914, 15.

———. "*Ziegfeld Follies*." *Variety*, 16 June 1916, 13.

Slide, Anthony. *Early American Cinema*. Revised edition. Metuchen, NJ, and London:
Scarecrow, 1994.

———, ed. *Selected Vaudeville Criticism*. Metuchen, NJ: Scarecrow Press, 1988.

Slout, William Lawrence. *Theatre in a Tent: The Development of a Provincial
Entertainment*. Bowling Green, OH: Bowling Green University Popular Press,
1972.

Smith, Eric Ledell. *Bert Williams: A Biography of the Pioneer Black Comedian*. Jefferson,
NC: McFarland, 1992.

Snyder, Robert W. *The Voice of the City: Vaudeville and Popular Culture in New York*.
New York: Oxford University Press, 1989. Reprint, 2000.

"The Sons of Ham." *Denver Post*, 25 May 1901, 1.

Sotiropoulos, Karen. *Staging Race: Black Performers in Turn of the Century America*.
Cambridge, MA, and London: Harvard University Press, 2006.

*Southern California, Comprising the Counties of Imperial, Los Angeles, Orange, Riverside,
San Bernardino, San Diego, Ventura*. Southern California Panama Expositions
Commission, 1914.

Spear, Allan H. *Black Chicago: The Making of a Negro Ghetto*. Chicago and London:
University of Chicago Press, 1967.

"The Stage Negro." *Variety*, 14 December 1907, 30.

"Star—Sons of Ham." (New York) *Dramatic Mirror*, 20 October 1900, 17.

Stearns, Marshall and Jean. *Jazz Dance: The Story of American Vernacular Dance*. New
York: Schirmer, 1979.

Stein, Charles W., ed. *American Vaudeville as Seen by Its Contemporaries*. New York:
Alfred A. Knopf, 1984.

Stevens, Ashton. "Bert Williams's Last Interview." In *Actorviews*, 227–31. Chicago:
Covici-McGee, 1923.

Stewart, Jacqueline. "William Foster: The Dean of the Negro Photoplay." *Oscar
Micheaux Society Newsletter* 9 (Spring 2001): 1–2.

"Stories of the Films." *Moving Picture World* 30, no. 8 (1916): 1219.

Storm, Marian. "All 135th Street Is Missing Bert Williams." *New York Evening Post*, 7
April 1922, 16.

"Strange Sports of Strange People."*The Examiner* (San Francisco), 9 June 1894, 10.

"Street Battles at Night." *New York Times*, 29 July 1919, 1.

"Sunday at the Exposition." *The Examiner* (San Francisco), 15 January 1894, 5.

"Sunset City's Dedication." *The Examiner* (San Francisco), 27 January 1894, 8.

Swann, Thomas Wallace. "Bert Williams Wins West." *Indianapolis Freeman*, 9 November 1909, 6.

"Tells About Larkins' [*sic*] Company." *New York Age*, 6 July 1911, 6.

"The Theaters." *Cincinnati Enquirer*, 20 September 1898, 3.

"Theatrical Chit-Chat." *New York Age*, 7 December 1918, 6.

"Theatrical Comment." *New York Age*, 1 June 1911, 6.

Thompson, R. W. "Theatrical Chit-Chat of Washington." *Indianapolis Freeman*, 14 January 1911, 5.

"Thousands at the Fair." *San Francisco Examiner*, 2 January 1894, 10.

"Throng at Bert Williams Funeral." *New York Times*, 8 March 1922, 15.

Toll, Robert C. *Blacking Up: The Minstrel Show in Nineteenth-Century America*. London and New York: Oxford University Press, 1974.

"Tonguesters of the Midway." *The Examiner* (San Francisco), 11 March 1894, 1.

"To Pension President." *New York Times*, 7 January 1905, 1.

Torgovnick, Marianna. *Gone Primitive: Savage Intellects, Modern Lives*. Chicago: University of Chicago Press, 1990.

Traub, James. *The Devil's Playground: A Century of Pleasure and Profit in Times Square*. New York: Random House, 2004.

Tuskegee Institute, Division of Behavioral Science Research, Carver Research Foundation. *Tuskegee Institute News Clippings File*. Sanford, NC: Microfilming Corp. of America, 1981.

"Two Noted Negroes Meet." *Kansas City Times*, 21 September 1909, 5.

"Two Parades at the Fair." *The Examiner* (San Francisco), 30 May 1894, 4.

"A Unique Situation." *New York Age*, 5 January 1911, 6.

U.S. Bureau of the Census. *Statistics of the Population of the United States, 1880*. Prepared by the Department of the Interior, Bureau of the Census. Washington, DC, 1880.

Van Aken, Kellee Rene. "Race and Gender in the Broadway Chorus." Ph.D. diss., University of Pittsburgh, 2006.

Van Vechten, Carl. *In the Garrett*. New York: Alfred Knopf, 1920.

"Vaudeville Correspondence—Chicago, Ill." (New York) *Dramatic Mirror*, 18 June 1898, 18.

"Vaudeville Correspondence—San Francisco, Cal." (New York) *Dramatic Mirror*, 30 April 1898, 18.

"Vaudeville Correspondences." (New York) *Dramatic Mirror*, 27 March 1897, 20.

"Vaudeville Stage—Koster and Bial's." (New York) *Dramatic Mirror*, 31 October 1896, 19.

"Vaudeville Stage—Koster and Bial's." (New York) *Dramatic Mirror*, 16 January 1897, 19.

"Vaudeville Stage—Koster and Bial's." (New York) *Dramatic Mirror*, 20 February 1897, 17.

"Vaudeville Stage—Last Week's Bills: Keith's Union Square." (New York) *Dramatic Mirror*, 17 April 1897, 17.

"Vaudeville Stage—Last Week's Bills: Koster and Bial's." (New York) *Dramatic Mirror*, 9 January 1897, 17.

"Vaudeville Stage—Last Week's Bills: Koster and Bial's." (New York) *Dramatic Mirror*, 27 February 1897, 17.

"Vaudeville Stage—Last Week's Bills: Koster and Bial's." (New York) *Dramatic Mirror*, 13 March 1897, 18.

"Vaudeville Stage: Proctor's." (New York) *Dramatic Mirror*, 1 January 1898, 16.

Waldo, Terry. *This Is Ragtime*. New York: Hawthorn, 1976.

Walker, Aida Overton. "Opportunities Stage Offers Intelligent and Talented Women." *New York Age*, 24 December 1908, 1.

———. "Respect Memory of the Dead." *New York Age*, 1 August 1912.

Walker, George W. "Bert and Me and Them." *New York Age*, 24 December 1908, 4.

———. "The Negro on the American Stage." *The Colored American Magazine*, October 1906, 243–8.

———. "The Real 'Coon' on the American Stage." *Theatre Magazine*, August 1906, 224+.

Walrond, Eric D. "Bert Williams Foundation Organized to Perpetuate the Ideals of the Celebrated Actor." *The Negro World*, 21 April 1923, 4.

Walsh, Jim. "Favorite Pioneer Recording Artists: Bert Williams, a Thwarted Genius." *Hobbies*, September 1950, 25.

Walton, Lester A. "Aida Overton Walker Signs." *New York Age*, 19 January 1911, 6.

———. *"Bandanna Land." New York Age*, 6 February 1908, 6.

———. "Bert Williams on Race Problem." *New York Age*, 4 May 1918, 6.

———. "Bert Williams Turns Philosopher." *New York Age*, 1 December 1910, 6.

———. "Bert Williams, Philosopher." *New York Age*, 29 December 1917, 6.

———. "A Big Undertaking." *New York Age*, 21 August 1913, 6.

———. "Broadway Individual Success." *New York Age*, 31 August 1911, 6.

———. "Charles H. Gilpin." *New York Age*, 10 July 1913, 6.

———. "The Coming Season." *New York Age*, 30 July 1908, 6.

———. "Death of George W. Walker." *New York Age*, 12 January 1911, 6.

———. "The *Follies of 1912." New York Age*, 24 October 1912, 6.

———. "The Future of the Negro on the Stage." *Colored American Magazine*, May and June 1903, 439–42.

———. "Have Williams and Walker Separated?" *New York Age*, 27 January 1910, 6.

———. "Hill's Follies Repeat." *New York Age*, 23 July 1914, 6.

———. "Historic Pilgrimage." *New York Age*, 7 August 1913, 6.

———. "In First-Class Theatres." *New York Age*, 26 November 1908, 6.

———. "A Memorable Event," *New York Age*, 5 March 1908, 6.

———. "Miss Walker's Success." *New York Age*, 2 November 1911, 6.

———. "Miss Walker in 'Salome.'" *New York Age*, 8 August 1912, 6.

———. "Monster Show Planned." *New York Age*, 24 July 1913, 6.

———. "More Praise for Comedian." *New York Age*, 14 September 1911, 6.

———. *"Mr. Lode of Koal,* a Broadway Show." *New York Age*, 16 September 1909, 6.

———. "Music and the Stage." *New York Age*, 22 October 1914, 6.

———. "Music and the Stage." *New York Age*, 23 February 1911, 6.

———. "Responsibility of Theatre-Goers." *New York Age*, 26 August 1909, 6.

———. "The Season's Outlook." *New York Age*, 6 September 1917, 6.

———. "The Star among Stars." *New York Age*, 6 July 1911, 6.

———. "Theatrical Chit-Chat." *New York Age*, 18 July 1918, 6.

———. "Theatrical Comment." *New York Age*, 9 September 1909, 6.

———. "Theatrical Comment." *New York Age*, 30 September 1909, 6.

———. "Theatrical Comment." *New York Age*, 10 March 1910, 6.

———. "Theatrical Comment." *New York Age*, 18 December 1913, 6.

———. "Theatrical Comment." *New York Age*, 15 January 1914, 6.

———. "Theatrical Comment." *New York Age*, 24 June 1915, 6.

———. "Third Week of *Bandanna Land." New York Age*, 20 February 1908, 6.

———. "Thousands, of All Races, Mourn Bert Williams' Death." *New York Age*, 11 March 1922, 1.

———. "A Time for Action." *New York Age*, 16 October 1913, 6.

———. "An Unusual Bill." *New York Age*, 14 August 1913, 6.

———. "W. and W. In Vaudeville." *New York Age*, 4 June 1908, 6.

———. "Williams as 'Friday.'" *New York Age*, 24 July 1913, 6.

———. "Williams without Walker." *New York Age*, 18 March 1909, 6.

———. "A Word of Warning." *New York Age*, 16 March 1911, 6.

Washington, Booker T. "Interesting People: Bert Williams." *American Magazine*, May–October 1910, 600–4.

———. *The Story of the Negro: The Rise of the Race from Slavery*, vol. 2. New York: Doubleday, Page, 1909.

———. *Up from Slavery*. New York: Doubleday, 1998.

"Washington, Williams and Walker." *New York Age*, 3 August 1905, 7.

Watkins, Mel. *On the Real Side: Laughing, Lying and Signifying—The Underground Tradition of African-American Humor*. New York: Simon and Schuster, 1994.

Webb, Barbara L. "Authentic Possibilities: Plantation Performance of the 1890s." *Theatre Journal* 56 (2004): 63–82.

Weeks, Al. "Bert Williams; It's His Show." *Detroit News*, 27 February 1922, 16.

"White Is as White Does." *New York Age*, 25 July 1912, 6.

"White Rats Answer the Age." *New York Age*, 19 May 1910, 6.

"The White Rats of America." *New York Dramatic Mirror*, 21 July 1900, 7.

White, Shane and Graham White. *Stylin': African American Expressive Culture from Its Beginnings to the Zoot Suit*. Ithaca and London: Cornell University Press, 1998.

Whitten, David. "Depression of 1893." *EH.Net Encyclopedia*, edited by Robert Whaples, 15 August 2001, http:eh.net/encyclopedia/article/whitten.panic.1893.

"Who's Who: Bert Williams." *The Messenger* 4.4 (1922): 394.

"Williams Alone Next Year." *Variety*, 22 May 1909, 5.

"Williams and Walker's Fine Show." *Toledo Blade*, 28 January 1907.

"Williams and Walker's *Senegambian Carnival* at the Academy." *Washington Post*, 11 October 1898, 7.

"Williams and Walker Again." *New York Times*, 21 February 1906, 9.

"Williams and Walker in *A Lucky Coon* at the Academy." *Washington Post*, 9 May 1898, 7.

Williams, Bert. "Bert Williams Tells of Walker." *Indianapolis Freeman*, 14 January 1911, 5.

———. "The Comic Side of Trouble." *American Magazine* 85 (January 1918): 33–4, 58, 60–1.

———. *The Complete Bert Williams* (compilation). *Volume 1*, Archeophone Records CD Edition 5001.

———. *The Complete Bert Williams* (compilation). *Volume 2*, Archeophone Records CD Edition 5003.

———. *The Complete Bert Williams* (compilation). *Volume 3*, Archeophone Records CD Edition 5002.

———. "Fun in the Land of J. Bull." *The Green Book Album*, July 1909.

———. "Keeping Up with the New Laughs." *Theatre Magazine*, June 1919, 348–9.

———. "Oh! I Don't Know, You're Not So Warm!" London: Charles Sheard, 1896.

Williams, Elsie A. *The Humor of Jackie Moms Mabley: An African American Comedic Tradition*. Edited by Graham Hodges. Studies in African American History and Culture. New York and London: Garland, 1995.

"Williams in 'Philly.'" *New York Age*, 8 January 1914, 6.

Wintz, Cary D. *Black Culture and the Harlem Renaissance*. Houston, TX: Rice University Press, 1988.

Wolf, Rennold. "The Greatest Comedian on the American Stage." *Green Book*, June 1912, 1173–84.

Woll, Allen. *Black Musical Theatre: From Coontown to Dreamgirls*. Baton Rouge and London: Louisiana State University Press, 1989.

———. *Dictionary of Black Theatre*. Westport, CT: Greenwood Press, 1983.

Woodward, C. Vann. *The Strange Career of Jim Crow*. 2nd. revised edition. New York and London: Oxford University Press, 1955. Reprint 1966.

"Work for French Armies." *New York Times*, 10 October 1892, 6.

"Would Enjoin Bert Williams." *New York Times*, 13 May 1910, 9.

"The Ziegfeld Follies." *Green Book*, August 1914, 322–5.

"Ziegfeld Follies Here Resplendent." *New York Times*, 22 June 1915, 15.

"Ziegfeld Follies of 1915." *Variety*, 25 June 1915, 15.

"Ziegfeld Follies of 1916." (New York) *Dramatic Mirror*, 17 June 1916, 8.

Ziegfeld, Richard and Paulette Ziegfeld. *The Ziegfeld Touch: The Life and Times of Florenz Ziegfield, Jr.* New York: Harry N Abrams, 1993.

Zijderveld, Anton. "Jokes and Their Relation to Social Reality." *Social Research,* 35 (1968): 286–311.

Index